教育部人文社会科学研究青年基金项目（19YJC740097）成果

数据新闻多模态语类研究

——系统功能符号学视角

幸君珺　著

A Multimodal Genre Analysis of Data News:

A Systemic Functional Approach

WUHAN UNIVERSITY PRESS
武汉大学出版社

图书在版编目(CIP)数据

数据新闻多模态语类研究：系统功能符号学视角：英文/幸君珺著. —武汉：武汉大学出版社,2023.9
ISBN 978-7-307-23847-3

Ⅰ.数…　Ⅱ.幸…　Ⅲ.数据处理—应用—新闻学—符号语言(语言学)—研究—英文　Ⅳ.①G210.7　②H087

中国国家版本馆 CIP 数据核字(2023)第 118232 号

责任编辑:罗晓华　　责任校对:汪欣怡　　版式设计:韩闻锦

出版发行：**武汉大学出版社**　(430072　武昌　珞珈山)
(电子邮箱：cbs22@ whu.edu.cn　网址：www.wdp. com.cn)
印刷：武汉邮科印务有限公司
开本:720×1000　1/16　印张:25.25　字数:374 千字　插页:1
版次:2023 年 9 月第 1 版　2023 年 9 月第 1 次印刷
ISBN 978-7-307-23847-3　定价:78. 00 元

Contents

List of Figures

List of Tables

Introduction

Data journalism or data-driven journalism (DDJ) is journalism based on data analysis and the presentation of such analysis (Coddington 2015: 334). In the news industry, data journalism is an umbrella term that encompasses an ever-growing set of tools, techniques and approaches to storytelling.

Data journalism offers new approaches to news storytelling—it can help a journalist tell a complex story through engaging infographics or help explain how a story relates to an individual. Data can be the source of data journalism, or it can be the tool with which the story is told—or it can be both. Data journalism is very prominent today and it has been changing the ways journalists tell news stories.

Data journalism is now a key term in the news industry, yet there is no term to refer to the discourse presenting the analysis in various modalities. In the present study, we use the term "data news" to refer to the news reports based on data analysis and presented in visualized texts (verbal texts, interactive and/or static images) and/or videos. Data news organizes large amounts of random and sometimes meaningless data into structured and meaningful information, and often comes to new findings or ideas countering common sense understandings.

It is of social and semiotic significance to conduct a genre analysis of data news and to describe and analyze genre relations in data news. As a result of the open data movement and the advancement of computer science, data news has become a major form of reporting in journalism (Coddington 2015, Roger 2013). Many data reports have exposed corruption in government agencies (e. g., *The Guardian*'s 2009 report "Investigate your MP's expenses") or crimes (e. g., 2013 Data Journalism Award Winner "America Under the Gun" by *Mother Jones*, a reader-supported investigative news organization in the United States). Journalists work together with data analysts, researchers and possibly many other professionals relevant to the news topics to push for accountability in other institutions in the era of big data. By looking at how data is analyzed and visualized to reveal meaning and less visible or invisible reality, the research can offer insights into how reporters can force accountability in other institutions while enhancing their own leverage in the era of big data.

Semiotically, data news is a new genre to cope with the datafication trend (Appelgren & Nygren 2014; Loosen et al. 2017) and can be instantiated as multimodal mixed genres or "genre complexes" or "macrogenres" (Martin & Rose 2008: 218), worthy of exploration from a semiotic perspective. Previous studies show that data news has demonstrated salient changes in its generic features. There are multiple text segments in a piece of data news which are organized as a single discourse. In this sense, a piece of data news is often composed of multiple elemental genres or contains embedded genres. More precisely, a piece of data news is a hypertext of mixed genres. Moreover, the narrative or storytelling style of data news is influenced by a "quantitative turn" as noted by Coddington (2015). The main purpose of data news has thus shifted from telling stories to deducing factual conclusions, which is more similar to social investigation (Wu 2017; Zeng et al 2017). Scholars in the field of journalism have noted such generic changes, but scholars in linguistics and semiotics have not yet conducted a systematic study of these features. However, the existing research from the field of journalism centers on data journalism as an industry, not on data news as discourse or artefact.

Data news is thus multimodal in nature, with data visualizations and verbal texts as its key components. Acknowledging the fundamental multimodality of data news has two implications. First, it means subscribing to the view that data news is more than simple combinations of pie charts, scatter plots and other graphs with decorative illustrations and typographically-emphasized text. The meaning-making process and meaning potential of data news should be described. Then, it means that we need to take a multimodal approach, describing the meaning potentials of each semiotic mode involved and the interaction between the semiotic modes involved so as to reveal the meaning-making processes in data news. To our knowledge, multimodality and generic shifts in data news have not been explored sufficiently. However, in linguistic and semiotic studies, especially in Systemic Functional Linguistics that has evolved into Systemic Functional Semiotics, there are well-developed theories on genre and multimodality which can provide a theoretical basis for the multimodal genre study of data news.

Against such background, the present study selects 15 data works from the Data Journalism Awards winners from 2016 to 2019. These works or projects represent the "gold-standard of DDJ" (Loosen et al. 2017: 2). A study of the multimodal meaning-making processes in the projects can reflect the discursive features of data news. Our objective is first to describe the discourse semantic patterns or configurations of the semiotic modes instantiated in the data. Such instantiated semiotic modes include verbal texts, data visualizations, photographs, drawings, and videos. Then, based on the configurations, we aim to discern the elemental genres in the sample and describe their generic stages by following Martin and Rose's genre model (Martin & Rose 2008). Finally, we hope to describe the genre relations between these elemental genres. We hope the study can shed lights on how big data and the quantitative turn in journalistic practice transform and shape the news genres.

To achieve these objectives, we focus on the following questions:

(1) What meaning patterns or configurations can be found in each semiotic mode in our data?

(2) What patterns of intermodal interaction can be identified in the data?

(3) How do the meaning patterns identified relate to register and what generic configurations can be revealed by the register patterns and discourse semantic configurations?

(4) What are the relations between the elemental genres in the data and how are they modeled as genre complexes or macro-genres?

We propose a multimodal genre model for data news analysis (See Figure 3-10 in Chapter 3). In the model, analysis can be conducted from the dimensions of metafunction, stratification and instantiation. In terms of stratification, genre is a pattern of register patterns, register a pattern of discourse semantic patterns, discourse semantics a pattern of grammatical patterns which is in turn a pattern of patterns of expression forms like phonology/graphology and graphical elements. In terms of metafunction, the axes of choice (system) and chain (structure) are also considered when we describe the meaning patterns at each stratum, though we may focus more on presenting the possible choices in systems. Following the model, we conduct a qualitative research based on detailed descriptions of each project which is seen as an instance of multimodal discourse. The descriptions include: the major semiotic modes instantiated in the data; the discourse semantic patterns of these major modes and their realizations at the strata of grammar and expression form; the intermodal interaction patterns of the semiotic modes in each project; and finally, the meaning configurations at the stratum of register and at the stratum of genre.

When analyzing the meaning patterns in the data, we will follow the trinocular descriptive principle in SFL. The highly abstract strata of genre and register are connotative semiotics which have another semiotic system as their expression plane (Martin & Rose 2008: 16). Therefore, a systematic description of the meaning patterns at the strata within each semiotic mode can serve as the basis for capturing the generic features (Martin & Rose 2008). The SFL description of meaning patterns in language is characterized from a trinocular perspective—looking "from above", "from below" and "from around". This means that a meaning pattern at a certain stratum is described and interpreted by relating to the patterns from a stratum above, its realizations from a stratum below and other patterns at the same stratum.

With these in view, the research can make a theoretical contribution to the current studies on news genres. It can contribute specifically to

(1) the description of discourse semantic systems and the way they relate to register and genre;

(2) the description and interpretation of the generic features of data news, which can be a good start for capturing genre evolution in news discourse;

(3) the description and interpretation of the meaning patterns in data visualizations, the intermodal interaction and the multimodal genre in data news.

The study can also contribute to the existing rich yet still fragmentary research on multimodality in communication.

No single book can be the final word for genre (Martin & Rose 2008: 47). This is even more true for the study of multimodal genre. In the present study, as our ultimate goal is genre analysis, we focus on the patterns which can differentiate genre or reveal genre relations. This means that some more local meaning patterns are not analyzed and that our treatment of semiotic realizations is necessarily sketchy and exemplary. Nor can we give full justice to genre as a configuration of field, tenor, and mode variables for reasons of space and clarity, leaving ample room for future research.

Chapter 1 Journalism and Data Journalism: The Production Side

Data journalism is an emerging reporting style in response to the datafication of society (e.g., Hans-Bredow-Institut for Media Research 2017; Loosen et al. 2017; Wu 2017). Its emergence and development are inseparable from technological advancements. Every time a new medium or technology (printing, radio, television, and the Internet together with the popularity of computer or mobile devices like smartphones) was introduced, there appeared new forms of discourse and new ways for representing news or messages. Therefore, a brief review of journalism's development, particularly its relations with technological advancements, allows us first to locate exactly the position of data journalism in the long history of journalistic development, then to see its continuities with other forms of journalism as well as its unique features, and finally better to understand how to approach and interpret the multimodal artefacts or discourses represented to readers or consumers.

As this book aims to analyze data news written in English, the brief survey in this chapter will be mainly about the history of journalism and technology in Britain and the US. In addition to technological innovations, economic, political and cultural factors also have had great impact on the development of journalism. However, technology has been regarded as a primary cause of organizational and professional changes in the newsroom, and studies have suggested that journalists frequently view "technology and technological development as inevitable, impersonal forces, that directly cause many of the changes taking place within journalism forces, that directly cause many of the changes taking place within journalism" (Örnebring 2010: 58). Besides, in the studies on news discourses from linguistic and multimodal perspectives, the role of technology in producing discourses has not been studied systematically. In view of these two factors, this survey of journalism history will focus on the interplay of technology and journalism in different periods of time.

1.1 An Overview of Journalism Development

Many scholars (e.g., Stephens 1988, Li 2009, Li 2009, Xie 2015) have approached the development of journalism from a broad perspective. They regarded journalism as information communication, viewed news as an important category of information and took into consideration the cultural, social, political, economic and technological influences on the development of news. Generally, they traced the origin of news or journalism to the oral or spoken messages before the invention of writing and ended their journalism history with electronic news.

Mitchell Stephens, in his seminal monograph *A History of News: From the Drum to the Satellite* (1988), examined four major stages or forms of news: spoken news, written news, printed news and electronic news broadcast by radio and television. It is estimated that people started to talk and master the spoken language approximately 35,000-40,000 years ago (Tong, 2020) and oral news systems must have arrived some tens or even hundreds of thousands of years ago, together with the development of oral language. Though oral language is fluid, the oral news systems are "neither incredible nor incomprehensible; they feature a series of logical and effective methods for gathering and disseminating information, methods that testify to the importance these societies placed on the circulation of news" (Stephens 1988: 23). Then humans entered the age of written language about five thousand years ago (Tong 2020). The written word, through its ability to last, can preserve the past and predict the future. In this sense, writing was the "medium of choice for related news over distance" (ibid: 62), and hence the emergence of hand-written news. However, the speed of handwriting was slow and the size and number of news audiences were limited. Therefore, only with the invention and application of printing technology was news enabled to be transported to a larger public and at faster speeds. "Before the arrival of the newspaper, print had proved itself a remarkably powerful news medium" (ibid: 86). With the development of the printed newspaper in the 17th century, masses of news were produced and disseminated to the masses at a remarkable speed. In 1844, newspapers began taking advantage of Samuel Morse's telegraph, which allowed publishers to publish "*today* news of the major events *yesterday* in any city to which they were connected by a reliable wire" (ibid: 227). The 19th century also witnessed the emergence and growth of new agencies. Then, the development of "wireless telephony" by Lee De Forest and Reginald Fessenden of the United States early in the early 20th century gave birth to radio journalism. Television journalism started in 1930s after BBC presented the first piece of television news in 1929. In the next two decades, radio journalism and television journalism developed in parallel. However, in the 1950s, radio's stars, including many of its star newscasters, left for television, and "radio surrendered its position as the nation's central gathering place" (ibid: 279). The great power of television was realized in the 1960s, with satellites for broadcasting and twenty-four-hour cable news services available. Electronic journalism was brought forth first by radio and then television, and there would be new forms of electronic journalism with the wide application of computers, as Stephens predicted in the final chapter of his book.

Li (2009) and Xie (2015) proposed similar demarcations as Stephens (1988), and yet elaborated more on the electronic journalism brought by the application of computers and the Internet. Both proposed that electronic communication extended from radio and television news to web or online news and mobile news. Generally speaking, web or online news started in the 1990s after *San Jose Mercury News* first released news online.

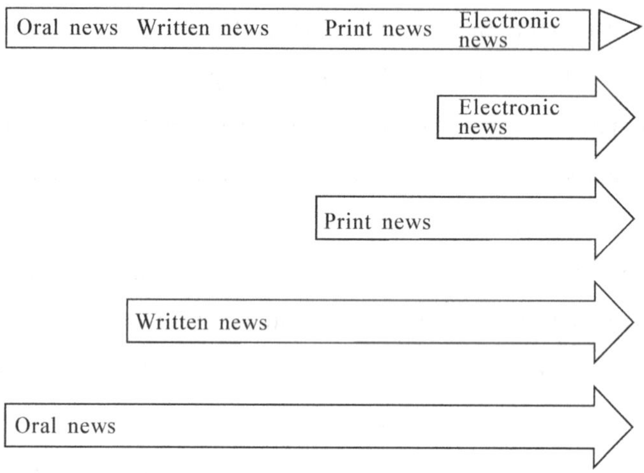

Figure 1-1 Development of Journalism as Human Communication
(Adapted from Li 2009)

Li (2009) categorized five stages. 1) The early period which lasted from ancient times to the Renaissance. This era was characterized by oral information communication and then by handwritten newssheets. 2) The first rapid development of print news in the 17th century. The news industry began to develop quickly in Europe, particularly in Britain, for two reasons. The first was the invention and popularity of the printing technology and the second was the necessity of spreading political ideas and the assertion of freedom for press. 3) The development of the news industry in the 18th century. This centenary was characterized by rationalism and various social revolutions such as the French revolution and the American War of Independence. In such a social context, the print news played an increasingly important role in spreading new, particularly political ideas and influencing public opinions. 4) The prosperity of the news industry in the 19th century. Generally speaking, three great leaps in news industry can be found in this century: the shift from political newspapers to commercial newspapers, the emergence of news agencies and the status of newspaper enhanced as a mass media. Newspapers had a wide circulation and a large readership. 5) The era of electronic media. This era features the wide application of electronic technologies. The first was the application of radio to news reporting in the first 10 year of the 20th century, with the maturation of broadcasting in the 1920s and the golden age of broadcasting in the 1930s and 1940s. This was followed by the popularity of television since the 1960s. In the the 21st century, the dominant role of television as a news medium has been replaced by the Internet.

The above divisions of developmental stages are not made purely from the perspective of technological advancement, yet all emphasize the great impact of technology on the development of news or journalism. "When a new news medium arrives, journalists do have to develop applications and techniques appropriate to that medium", wrote Stephens (1988: 167). Therefore, it can be said that every time a new medium or technology (printing, radio, television, and the Internet together with the popularity of computer or mobile devices like smartphones) was applied, new forms of discourse and new ways for representing news or messages emerged.

The above studies tend to group radio news, television news and online news into the broader category of electronic news, as all three are disseminated through electronic channels. However, if we delve into, particularly, the technologies involved, the ways of news production and the styles of presenting news, we can find that these three media display salient differences. Therefore, in the present study, we take them as separate forms of news so as to capture their differences in more detail.

1.2 Technological Innovations and Journalism Development

As is reviewed in the above section, the divisions of developmental stages are made by considering political, economic and technological factors, but the impact of technology on journalism is undeniably great. "Journalism has always been shaped by technology", commented Pavlik (Pavlik 2000: 229). Technology not only makes possible the rapid production of news, but also brings innovation in news design, representation and dissemination. Historically, the incorporation of new systems such as printing, radio or television has shaped communicative processes, creating a balance between the adaptation of the known and the experimentation of the possibilities that are opened (Vázquez-Herrero et al. 2020). In recent decades, narratives have mutated, constantly influenced by technologies that surround the birth and evolution of the Internet and "a mobile and convergent scenario of multiple platforms" (ibid: 37).

In terms of the application of technology in human communication, we identify four stages that are most relevant and significant, namely, the print news era, the radio or wireless news era, the cabled or television news era and the digital or online news era. The contents and styles of news reporting at these stages are greatly impacted by the technologies applied to collect and produce news and the medium to transmit and spread news, but the basic principles are the same for all these stages of journalism. Therefore, we will concentrate on aspects specific to each era.

1.2.1 News and Technologies in the Print Era

Of the four stages, the print news has, so far, been the dominant news source for the longest time. Its emergence and development should be first attributed to the invention of mechanical printing. Later, the invention of telegraphs in 1837 and telephones in 1876 has promoted the massification of newspapers, changed the ways of news collection and transmission, and also enriched the news forms in the print era. The photographing technologies also changed the form of news discourses from monomodal to multimodal ones with photographs.

1.2.1.1 Written and Handwritten News

Written news had transmitted information long before the printed news. A brief introduction of written news would be conducive for us to have a diachronic view of printed news. Writing was "medium of choice for related news over distance" (Stephens 1988: 62). Not surprisingly, China and Rome, two of the empires with the earliest writing systems and cultures, employed an advanced system of written news (ibid). The earliest form of written news in China can be traced back to Western Han Empire. It was called *tipao* (邸报). *Ti* is the residence of provincial prefects for purpose of communicating official reports, and *pao* is report. Written news in ancient Rome was called the *acta*, written on papyrus. The *acta* includes the transactions of the Senate (the *acta senatus*) and the daily transactions of the Roman people (the *acta diurnal populi Romani*) (ibid). The main contents were government announcements, news of the law courts, births, deaths, marriages, official ceremonies and building projects, and human-interest stories. In the 15th century, handwritten "newsletters" began trickling across some of the same paths as the *acta* had followed more than a dozen centuries earlier. Handwritten news, as it had demonstrated in ancient

China and Rome, "could orient a limited but important audience toward the monarch" (ibid: 72). But written news, being time-consuming, could not access a mass of readers at a fast speed.

1.2.1.2 Printing, Telegraph, Telephone and News Structure

(1) Printing and News

The invention of printing offered an easier and faster way to give and receive information. The Chinese had been experimenting with movable type in earlier centuries, though not on a press. The oldest known printed text originated in China during the first millennium A. D. *The Diamond Sutra* (*Jin Gang Jing*), a Buddhist book from Dunhuang, China from around 868 A. D. during the Tang Dynasty, is said to be the oldest known printed book. *The Diamond Sutra* was created with block printing. Then the first movable type machine, and therefore, the first printing press was created Bi Sheng (毕昇), an engineer and inventor in the Northern Song Dynasty (960-1127). Bi Sheng's movable type was carved into clay and baked into hard blocks that were then arranged onto an iron frame that was pressed against an iron plate. His method was recorded in the book *Dream Pool Essays* (*Meng Xi Bi Tan*) written by Shen Kuo (沈括), a scientist in the Song Dynasty.

Gutenberg, who was born four full centuries after Bi Sheng, further developed Bi Sheng's movable printing in 1440s. By his "reinvention" based on Bi Sheng's movable printing (Stephens 1988: 84), Gutenberg did make a mighty difference to the history of the printing press by making it accessible to the public. He was able to streamline the technology to require only capital letters, lowercase letters, and punctuation. In addition, his machine, which still had to be operated by a person, was much easier to use, making it accessible to many people and businesses. As a result, the printing press made the printed word easier to create and less expensive for those who wanted to purchase books and other printed materials. As Xie commented, "Block printing was used to publish newssheets in the fifteenth century, particularly in Germany. However, Gutenberg's letter press, in which each letter could be removed and reused after a page was printed, offered huge advantages of speed, convenience and quality of impression... The birth of printers is a revolution in communication technology: it is this revolution that gave birth to journalism" (Xie 2013: 7).

Printing led to a procession of journalistic advances. The development and wide circulation of newspapers can be said the most important advance brought by the printing press. The newspaper was a new media in the 17th century. The earliest printed newspaper can be dated to 17th century Europe when printed periodicals began rapidly to replace the practice of handwriting newssheets. According to Stephens (1988), newspapers were being printed in Europe in 1609 and the first English-language newspaper, *Corrant*, was published in Amsterdam in 1620. A year and a half later, *Corante* (weekly news from Italy, Germany, Hungary, Poland, Bohemia, France and the Low Countries), was published in England (Stephens 1988). The first newspapers circulating in Britain in the 1620s carried mainly foreign news because of the domestic censorship (ibid). Newspaper publishing took off through the 18th century and in the 19th century it became a mass medium (Xie 2013). The printing press not only enlarged the production and circulation of books, but also ushered in the era of mass communication. In other words, the rapidity of typographical text production by the printing press, as well as the sharp fall in unit costs, led to the emergence of the first newspapers which opened up an entirely new field for conveying up-to-date information to the public. From then on, the newspaper developed its unique features which distinguished itself from the one-shot news publications that preceded it. According to Stephens (1988: 149-150), in addition to the availability to a signification portion of the public, the newspaper had three additional attributes: it was published regularly and frequently (at least weekly), included a variety of different stories in each issue and displayed a consistent and recognizable title or format. In other words, it gained an identity independent of whatever particular news items it happened to be carrying. Gradually, the newspaper established its status as the main media for spreading printed news text in the print age.

Later, the invention of the telegraph in 1837 brought the massification of newspapers and further enriched the news forms in the print era. They gave new technical support to news dissemination and changed the style of news reporting.

Some scholars (e. g. Czitrom 1982; Stephens 1988; Xie 2013) argued that the success of the first electric telegraph line in 1844 opened the era of modern communication in America. In Britain, it was also in 1844 that the first story written from news printed in *The Times* was transmitted by telegraph (Stephens 1988; Xie 2013). Telegraph allowed reports to be transmitted with minimal delay from almost anywhere in the world. In Stephens' words (1988: 227), the telegraph would allow publishers "to publish *today* news of the major events *yesterday* in any city to which they were connected by a reliable wire". The application of telegraph transformed the business of gathering news and facilitated the emergence of reporting which embarked into the field in search of news. Through their investigations, newspaper reporters were able to expose new areas of the world to public view. Telegraphy made possible, indeed demanded, systematic cooperative news gathering (Rudin & Ibbotson 2002).

(2) Telegraph and News

The telegraph annihilated time and space and accelerated the transmission of news in newspapers. As Walter Fox, an American journalist, pointed out in his book *Writing the News*, "Telegrams are married to newspapers within hours of birth" (quoted from Lí 2009: 50).

Rudin and Ibbotson (2002) further clarified the significant role of telegraph in massifying newspapers and shaping modern journalism:

> "Insofar as the invention and spread of the telegraph provided the crucial catalyst and means for regular, cooperative news gathering, it supplied the technological underpinning of the modern press; that is, it transformed the newspaper from a personal journal and party organ into primarily a disseminator of news.
>
> Other technological developments helped reshape the nineteenth century press too. Steam presses in the 1830s and later rotary presses of the 1890s allowed faster and larger press runs; linotypes developed in the 1880s introduced automatic typesetting; photoengraving, beginning with halftones in 1877, played an important part in the pictorial journalism and sensationalism of the 1880s and 1890s. But the telegraph led the way not only to large-scale news gathering and modern news concepts, but also to standardization, perhaps the most remarkable characteristic of modern journalism." (p. 18)

Besides, as telegrams were charged according to the number of words, such reports needed to be kept as brief and succinct as possible, leading to a more objective, factual style (Rudin & Ibbotson 2002). Hard news changed from "news without structure" to the "inverted pyramid structure", and news editors put forward the concept of the "news lead" (Fox 1977; Stephens 1988; Li 2009). During the American Civil War in particular, journalists rushing to transmit their most newsworthy information over often unreliable telegraph lines had begun to develop the habit of compressing the most crucial facts into short, paragraph-long dispatches, often destined for the top of a column of news (Stephens 1988: 253). The inverted pyramid organizes stories not around ideas or chronologies but around facts. It weighs and shuffles the various pieces of information, focusing with remarkable single-mindedness on their relative news value (ibid: 254). This style of newswriting took decades to establish its dominance in modern news writing. Another change—preference for point of view in news writing being gradually replaced by emphasis on facts—is also worth mentioning, though it was probably not a direct result of the application of telegrams and telephones in news collection and production. The eighteenth-century journalists like Joseph Addison, Richard Steele and Daniel Defoe placed emphasis on point of view, but along with the social, political, economic, and technological developments, this narrative style "began to seem too subjective" and the views of the writers "were simply distractions" (Stephens 1988: 253). With the arrival of the "inverted pyramid structure" for reporting hard news in the second half of the 19th century, facts found their true voice.

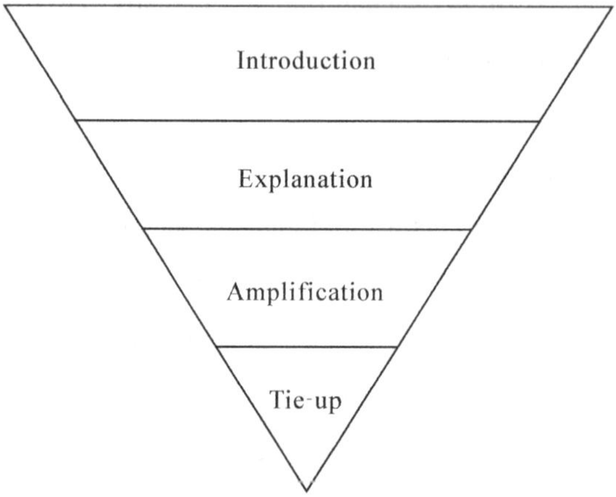

Figure 1-2 Inverted Pyramid Structure (Rudin & Ibbotson 2002: 53)

Later on, telephones, enjoying unique technological affordances in news collection and transmission, also brought changes in newspaper news reporting. Alexander Graham Bell won the first US patent for the device in 1876. In 1877-1878, the first telephone line was constructed. Three years later, almost 49,000 telephones were in use. This led to additional advances in networked communications, making the world smaller and increasing contact between peoples of all nations. A valuable tool for journalists, the telephone had been in the newsroom since the late 1800s. For instance, in 1901, the *New York Evening Post* reported a boat race via telephone reports from its correspondents some 87 miles north of New York City, and other newspapers in Ohio and Missouri were also experimenting with the use of phones for news gathering (Mari 2017). Yet, their adoption took some time because of the high cost in the first decades of its application. Besides, the news staff needed to master the skills to operate phones. Generally speaking, telephone was widely used in the 1930s and by the end of World War II, "'telephone reporting' was ingrained in journalistic culture" (ibid: 12). Moreover, telephones could transmit news stories or parts of stories in whole words, rather than in code that required decrypting, and increased the flexibility of news gathering and the numbers of potential correspondents (ibid). As a result, telephones were used as an important tool for news collection because telephone calls enlarged reporters' access to news sources and telephone interviews were very efficient (Rudin & Ibbotson 2002). As a *New York Times* reporter said, "A telephone interview makes it easier to confine a man to the subject you want him to talk on" (quoted form Mari 2017: 9). The pace of reporting was accelerated. More importantly, thanks to the application of telephones in news reporting, breaking news could be related from the scene of a story by a reporter to a rewrite man. As a result, the style of reporting in newspapers changed: the "wretched telephone... the biggest detriment and the greatest help the newspaper world has ever known" had changed stories into "fragmentary bulletins and scrap-ends" (Philip Schuyler, 1925, quoted from Mari 2017: 10).

1.2.1.3 Camera, News Photos and Multimodality

Photographs, drawings, pictures, and other forms of images are also important means of visual communication and expression. Graphic works were used in early new texts in newspapers. Line drawings, scraperboard, charcoal and wash, even woodcuts were among early forms of newspaper graphics. However, they were not seen to be as important as language at the beginning. They were just "illustrations". Social changes and technological innovations made images as important as language in realizing meanings. The development of technology that allowed photographs to be published in newspapers and to be sent over long distance transformed the look, scope and contents of newspapers and other media coming in later eras as well.

The camera has been a vital means of communication and the most important technology that made possible the publication and dissemination of news photos. It was invented, or rather developed, by multiple people, over the course of history. But the camera, as we know it today, was invented by French inventor Joseph Nicéphore Niépce in around 1816 (Newhall 1949). He technically took the first photo on a homemade camera, with silver chloride covered paper. He described his camera as "a kind of artificial eye, simply a little box, each side six inches square, which will be fitted with a tube that can be lengthened carrying a lenticular glass" (quoted from Newhall 1949: 12).

Before him, other forerunners had made various experiments and invented devices that led to the camera we know today. According to Britannica, the forerunner of the camera was the invention of the *camera obscura*, a dark chamber or room with a hole (later a lens) in one wall, through which images of objects outside the room were projected on the opposite wall. The principle was probably known to the Chinese and to ancient Greeks more than 2, 000 years ago. In 1727 the German professor of anatomy Johann Heinrich Schulze proved that the darkening of silver salts, a phenomenon known since the 16th century and possibly earlier, was caused by light and not heat. His discovery, in combination with the *camera obscura*, provided the basic technology necessary for photography.

The photograph by Mr. Niépce's camera was of poor quality and required about eight hours' exposure time. After his invention, other inventors went further. Louis Daguerre, a professional scene painter for theatre, also attempted to retain the duplication of nature, which led in 1829 to a partnership with Niépce. However, Daguerre's interest was in shortening the exposure time necessary to obtain an image of the real world, while Niépce remained interested in producing reproducible plates. By 1835, three years after Niépce's death, Daguerre had discovered that a latent image forms on a plate of iodized silver and that it can be "developed" and made visible by exposure to mercury vapour, which settles on the exposed parts of the image. Exposure times could thus be reduced from 8 hours to 30 minutes. Therefore, he was credited with the invention of the first practical process of photography, known as the daguerreotype.

Roughly at the same time, the British scientist William Henry Fox Talbot was experimenting with a photographic process to record by chemical means the images he observed, and by 1835 he had a workable technique. When news of Daguerre's process reached England in January 1839, Talbot rushed publication of his "photogenic drawing" process and subsequently explained his technique in complete detail to the members of the Royal Society. Already, in 1833 the French-born photographer Hercules Florence had worked with paper sensitized with silver salts to produce prints of drawings, calling this process "photography". However, since he conducted his experiments in Brazil, apart from the major scientific centres of the time, his contributions were lost to history until 1973, when they were rediscovered.

Like the printer and the printing press, "[T]he camera and the printing press were linked from the very birth of photography" (Newhall 1949: 219). News photos were taken as early as 1842, but at that time they were reproduced in weeklies like the *Illustrated London News* by wood engravings. The engraved images lost their tonal subtleties during the engraving process required by publication. Daguerreotypes were made into printing plates, but their exposure time allowed the reproducer only to catch the silhouettes of the original photos. Experiments were also made with lithographic process, but the reproduction of photographic images in this way was not efficient enough. Due to these deficiencies, photography aroused no great enthusiasm on the part of the early 19th century publishers.

Technological experiments were carried on so that photos could be printed faithfully, efficiently and with high quality. In the 1880s the invention of the halftone plate "enabled photographs to be reproduced economically and in limitless quantity in books, magazines and newspapers" (ibid: 221). It also enabled publishers to reproduce photographs faithfully. Thus, by the turn of the 20th century, the public began to expect to see the news in photographs and photographers began to specialize in covering events by photos. As a result, photographs became increasingly important in transmitting news in newspapers, and "there is greater reliance on visual devices to tell stories and provide insight" (Horton 2001: 5). The birth of press of photography in 1900s was a watershed. It was not only important to the newspaper design, but also functioned as important information carrier. Certain news stories gained in actuality if the words could be accompanied by a picture. Certain features were more intelligible if a point could be made visually. A picture on a page created a focal point for the eye. Good pictures and series of pictures were given special spreads. Nowadays, we find that newspaper texts are more often than not presented in both image and written language.

With the invention of the first 35mm camera, the Leica, came in the 1920s the modern photojournalism, a new reporting style of using photos to tell news stories. Before the invention, a photo of professional quality required bulky equipment. Afterwards, photographers could go anywhere and take photos without bulky lights or tripods. The 1930s through the 1950s are often considered as the golden age of photojournalism.

The technologies to shoot, transmit and reproduce photos enabled photos to become a main conduit for news and served as important meaning-making resources in journalism. News photos are empowered to tell stories together with verbal news texts or independently in photojournalism. In either case, they engage readers in ways different from verbal news because they have specific compositional rules, are able to capture and present the participants' emotions directly, and so can tell stories on their own. They are also different from paintings in that "while the painter *interprets* events and happenings, the photographer is able to *reflect* them in a precise and accurate form" (Gidal 1973). Some take photography as the faithful reflection of reality (Gidal 1973; Frued 1974) while others point up "the tension between the mechanical objectivity of the camera and the subjectivity of choice of the photographer" (Newhall 1982; Frizot 1998; Gervais 2017). Photos can also be shot in studios, but news photos are able to capture "the spontaneity of a moment in time in all of its natural beauty" (Horton 2001: 9). Whatever the differences, photographs have become ubiquitous in journalism. The commonality of news photos and other forms of images in newspaper reporting leads to the commonality of multimodal news discourses. It is no exaggeration to say the photography, photojournalism in particular, shaped the 20th century news. Therefore, it is of vital importance to analyze the multimodality of news discourses.

When analyzing the multimodal news texts with images, issues like the information value and "seduction potential" (Gervais 2017) of photos, the text/image balance and interaction should be taken into full consideration. Various types of images play such an important part that Ludwig and Gilemore argue "[N]o news presentation is complete without photographs or other artwork" (2005: 187). Thanks to these developments, the image has been recognized as an important means of communication in news texts, and multimodality has been a key feature of news discourses.

Giles and Hodgson (1990) find that thanks to the technological innovations, great advances were also made in the words, the headline writing and ultimately in the typography in the newspapers of the 1930s. As design techniques were moving forward, font types were used more consistently and in a set pattern of sizes so that many dailies were assuming a distinctive appearance of their own. A watershed newspaper design was the innovative use of typography in the 1960s when *The Sunday Times* was revolutionized with a new type dress employing mainly lowercase light and bold serif faces in a horizontal format with multicolumn single line headlines crossing the pages below the fold, and with the pages tabbed and segmented by horizontal thick and thin rules. Such new approach gave genuine strength below the fold to text size pages. The pages that resulted were characterized by more daring and artistic cropping of pictures as design elements, creative use of white space around the headlines and pictures as well as the liberal placing of logos on regular items.

Technology also influenced the newspaper industry in other ways. It improved the quality and diversity of newspapers. Newspapers used to be printed on cheap, off-white paper known as newsprint. Since the 1980s, the newspaper industry has largely moved away from lower-quality letterpress printing to higher-quality, four-color process, offset printing. In addition, with television becoming the dominant news source in the 1960s, newspapers not driven out by changing patterns of consumption "began to specialize in more background and lifestyle material, away from a concentration on a hard news agenda" (Conboy 2004: 201). Also, under the influence of more intrusive television reporting of politics, the 1960s became the great decade for investigative newspaper journalism (ibid: 179). In addition, desktop computers, word processing software, graphics software, digital cameras and digital prepress and typesetting technologies have revolutionized the newspaper production process. These technologies have enabled newspapers to publish color photographs and graphics, as well as innovative layouts and better design. In one of the more recent developments, the British Tabloid *The Sun* published a 3D edition on June 5, 2010 complete with 3D glasses, 3D editorial images, 3D adverts and a 3D Soccer World Cup schedule wall chart. There was "a convergence with agendas of popular and in particular television culture" (ibid: 181) and the 1980s saw the popular press retreat from political journalism towards an increasing "symbiosis with television's brand of mass popular culture" (ibid: 183). In spite of enormous challenges from radio, television and the Internet, the popular press has not been replaced by the new media; instead, thanks to technological and cultural convergence, it has evolved along a more digital path. Traditional print news organizations also offer web-based content that can be accessed through the Internet or smartphones.

It should be pointed out that not all the technological inventions succeeded in bringing new media and changes to the newspaper industry. The radio facsimile, a system for "sending written and printed matter with high speed by radio" (Facsimile and multiplex, 1934) was one of the failures. During the 1930s and 1940s, dozens of newspapers and broadcasters experimented with the technology of radio facsimile. This form of broadcasting transmitted condensed, tabloid-like newspapers over the airwaves to specially designed facsimile printers (Arceneaux 2011) and aimed to deliver "radio editions" of newspapers into the homes of consumers (Arceneaux 2011; Simmons 2016). An October 1934 article described how the technology could be used to "send photographs or flash messages in their entirety exactly as written by the sender, from city to city" (quoted from Simmons 2016: 413). Though seen at the beginning as a technology that could revolutionize how news was distributed to the reading public, the broadcast radio facsimile ended up being little more than a footnote in history.

1.2.2 News and Technologies in the Radio Era

The 1920s saw the emergence of radio broadcasting as a viable form of mass communication (Simmons 2016). The birth of radio news was undoubtedly the result of the invention of radio, which itself was "the product of a series of breakthroughs: the discovery of electromagnetic waves in 'the ether' by James Clerk Maxwell of Scotland and Heinrich Hertz of Germany in the second half of the nineteenth century; the innovation of methods for freighting those waves with coded messages—'wireless telegraphy'—by Guglielmo Marconi of Italy at the end of the century; the development of techniques for transforming human speech into and out of such codes—'wireless telephony'—by Lee De Forest and Reginald Fessenden of the United States early in the twentieth century" (Stephens 1988: 276).

1.2.2.1 AM Radio, FM Radio, and Golden Age of Radio

As was mentioned, radio started with the discovery of radio waves—electromagnetic waves that have the capacity to transmit music, speech, pictures, and other data invisibly through the air. Television also uses electromagnetic waves. It is perhaps in this sense that radio journalism and television journalism are also called broadcasting journalism.

Scottish physicist James Clerk Maxwell first predicted the existence of radio waves in the 1860s. In 1886, German physicist Heinrich Rudolph Hertz demonstrated that rapid variations of electric current could be projected into space in the form of radio waves, similar to light waves and heat waves. Serious experimentation with radio waves were conducted as early as the 1890s. But it was Guglielmo Marconi, an Italian inventor, who proved the feasibility of radio communication. He sent and received his first radio signal in Italy in 1895. In addition to Marconi, two of his contemporaries, Nikola Tesla and Nathan Stubblefield, took out patents for wireless radio transmitters. Nikola Tesla is now credited with being the first person to patent radio technology. Their inventions constituted the early radio communication which used spark-gap transmitters for long-distance wireless communication. A spark-gap transmitter is a device for generating radio frequency electromagnetic waves using a spark gap. Uncomplicated in design, it was widely used in early radio communication.

In the early 1900s, the development of radio was hampered by the lack of an efficient detector of electromagnetic radiation. Lee de Forest, an American inventor and an early pioneer in electronics, provided that detector. His invention made it possible to amplify the radio frequency signal picked up by antennae. This allowed for the use of much weaker signals than had previously been possible. De Forest was also the first person to use the word "radio". The result of Lee de Forest's work was the invention of amplitude-modulated or AM radio, which allowed for a multitude of radio stations. It was a huge improvement over the earlier spark-gap transmitters. His invention of the Audion vacuum tube also made possible live radio broadcasting and became the key component of all radio, telephone, radar, television, and computer systems before the invention of the transistor in 1947 (Britannica).

Then, true radio journalism began. In 1915, spoken words were first transmitted by radio across the continent from New York City to San Francisco and across the Atlantic Ocean. On November 2, 1920, Westinghouse launched the first commercial radio station—KDKA in Pittsburgh and began regular broadcasts. In the same year Westinghouse also aired the results of the 1920 presidential election before they could be read in the newspapers. Across the United States 576 such radio stations were in operation by the end of 1922 (Stephens 1988: 276). The Second World War gave radio news what the Civil War had given newspapers: the medium's power to bring news home was fully recognized. In Britain, the first live radio broadcast was heard on 14 November 1922 by a station called 2LO in London, which became the precursor for the British Broadcasting Corporation (Crook 2002; Conboy 2004). "The introduction of radio journalism, particularly in its British variant, was designed to produce a strong normative influence on society as a whole." (Stephens 1988: 189)

Meanwhile, technological improvements did not stop. In 1933, the American inventor Edwin Howard Armstrong invented frequency-modulated or FM radio. FM improved the audio signal of radio by controlling the noise caused by electrical equipment and the earth's atmosphere. FM radio attracted new listeners for its high-fidelity sound effects. The year 1937 witnessed the construction of the first FM broadcasting tower. By the late 1930s, the popularity of radio news broadcasts had surpassed that of newspapers. By 1941 there were 50 FM stations in the United States. Radio news became even more important in the Second World War because reporters could record events in the field and bring more sober news stories to be broadcast over the airwaves. For instance, the attack on Pearl Harbor was first broadcast through radio news outlets. As a result, the period between the 1930s and the mid-1950s is always regarded as the golden age of radio, which was characterized by radio's overwhelming popularity and a wide range of programs.

1. 2. 2. 2 Digital Convergence of Radio and Radio Journalism

Since the 1950s, radio journalism has been facing increasingly fierce challenges from the newer medium, television. In the 1950s, radio's stars, including many of its star newscasters, left for television, and radio began to surrender its position as the central gathering place in the US (Stephens 1988: 279). But it was never entirely replaced. Instead, thanks to technological advancements and the convergence culture (Jenkins 2006), radio journalism, though with a smaller group of listeners, has been enabled to survive and even revive by the profusion of transistor radios, car radios, digital radios and Internet radios.

The mobile, short-range radio, later resulting in a "radio car" and subsequently the handled radios, changed the news production in news outlets, which permited editors to keep in constant touch with reporters. The radio car became a reality after WWII when it became more affordable and commercially available (Mari 2008; Salaverria & de-Lima-Santos 2020). The development of the transistor in the 1960s meant a complete reconsideration of the reach and content of radio (Conboy 2004). Radio journalism also developed an experiment in audience participation using the phone-in in the late 1960s. Digital radio broadcasting has emerged, first in the UK in 1995 and later in the United States and many other countries worldwide. In 2012 the International Telecommunication Union recognized four digital wireless radio systems: the Digital Audio Broadcasting (DAB), Digital Radio Mondiale (DRM), the HD Radio and the ISDB-T.

Thanks to these digital technologies, broadcasters have achieved continued success, taking advantage of new ways to reach listeners. For instance, the UK general election of May 1997 became the first multimedia Internet election with the main broadcast services, BBC and ITN. The two broadcast services offered substantial World Wide Web sites that contained lateral structures of text, pictures, audio and video information. The websites were promoted by terrestrial TV and radio channels. This can be regarded as the earliest attempt in technological and media convergence. In the USA, WXYC was the first radio station to announce its broadcasting on the Internet. Its broadcasting is referred to as webcasting since it is not even transmitting through wireless means (Kuyucu 2019). Jianjie et al. (2016) also stated that radio stations are leading the media convergence phenomena. Radio stations are compelled to create audiovisual content where users need to browse visually instead of the text. This encourages stations to generate websites with large graphics and icons. In the view of Nielson and Kreutzfeldt (2016), radio convergence makes it clear that smartphones are emerging as the new radio and not only as the new laptop computer. According to Kuyucu (2019), in 2018 over 51% of the radio listening was by means of a digital platform such as online or through digital TV and DAB. Radio listening is done mainly through the digital means rather than through analogue on FM.

In short, radio's future must be both digital, convergent and multiplatform. In today's world of technological and cultural convergence, radio, television, mobile phones, web and social media can no longer be treated as separate media. They are interconnected through diverse pathways that might lead to the pooling of information.

1.2.2.3 Spoken Style of Radio News

The use of radio for broadcasting (as opposed to one-to-one communications) allowed the spoken word to again become prominent in the communication. Most radio journalism is written before it is broadcast, but radio gave newsmongers back their voices (Stephens 1988: 280). It can be argued that radio became the first major technological shaper of a new national public in the 20th century and allowed the once inscribed and virtual voice of the journalist to become an aural and immediate reality. This has helped to shape the style of radio news—spoken, or written for speaking, rather than purely written news.

Radio journalism borrowed and imitated the techniques of newspaper journalism: "The modern newswriting style—short sentences, simple, clear, concise wordings—was honed on the radio" (Stephens 1988: 277), but it has its own principles. Rudin and Ibbotson (2002: 110-111) summarized the main principles of good radio news writing:

> "Be concise—the number of words available to tell a story is far fewer than that generally used in the print media so every word must convey maximum impact.
>
> Play on the listener's imagination—to paint pictures so that the listener can 'see' what is being talked about...
>
> Be simple, clear and unambiguous. Radio listener has only one chance to understand what is being said, so it's better to avoid using unnecessarily complicated sentences.
>
> Use a personal, one-to-one approach. Listeners should not be addressed as an anonymous group. Always try to write as if you are addressing a single person—'you' is much better than 'listeners' or 'people'.
>
> Be written to be read out loud. We tend to use less formal language when speaking compared with when we write, so radio writing needs to reflect the difference in styles."

In short, radio news is different from written English. Radio English is spoken English: even though the script is written, the style should be kept "in the way that people talk rather than the way people write" (Crook 2002: 122). The language used in radio news can be more informal and personal than that for the print media. Text-based information has to be converted into writing for the listener's ears, into a style suitable for radio.

1. 2. 3 News and Technologies in the Television Era

No one would doubt about the role of television as a mass media and its dramatic impact on people's life in the 20th century. Innovations in televised programming encouraged gathering around television sets, informed people of key events around the world, altered public understanding of the world, and perhaps also killed people's imagination and creation to some extent (Postman 2005). Technological innovations in television also brought great changes in news production and presentation.

1. 2. 3. 1 Televisions: Mechanical, Electronic, Digital and Smart

As early as 1884, the Russian engineer Paul Gottlieb Nipkow came up with a system of transforming moving pictures into and out of electronic signals through wires via spinning discs. This method used a rotating disk with spiral perforations and was the earliest form of mechanical television. The first commercially produced television sets in the US were based on the mechanical television system and were shown off to the public in September 1928.

In 1897 the German scientist Karl Ferdinand Braun invented the cathode ray tube scanning device to scan and transmit images. Later, in the early 1900s, the Scottish engineer Alan Campbell-Swinton worked to improve on Nipkow's system by replacing the spinning discs with cathode ray tubes. He placed cathode ray tubes both inside the receiver and the camera that sent a picture. His system was regarded as the earliest electronic television system. In 1923 Russian-born engineer Vladimir Zwaorykin applied for this first television patent, for the "iconoscope" in the United States. In the following year he again brought kinescope to the world. In

1929, Zworykin demonstrated his all-electronic television system at a convention of radio engineers. Also in the US, Philo Farnsworth had been working on his own television system and in 1927 he completed the prototype of the first fully electronic TV system based on his image dissector. Meanwhile in the UK, Scottish engineer John Logie Baird also worked on the development of electronic television. In the same year, he made the world's first public demonstration of electronic television in his London laboratory before 50 scientists. So far, experimenters in Britain and the United States had succeeded in sending such signals through the air to receivers, and the earlier rotating disk was replaced by the electronic scanning system of cathode ray tube. TV had become electronic. In 1938 electronic television sets were produced and released commercially.

Color television had been experimented with almost as soon as black-and-white televisions. In 1897 Polish inventor Jan Szczepanik patented a color television system and in 1928 Baird demonstrated the world's first color transmission. However, color television was only converted into reality in the 1940s when CBS created the first color TV sets based on Baird's mechanical television system. Another communication giant RCA continued to develop their own color TV system, which was acknowledged in 1953 to be better than the CBS system. Starting in 1954 color RCA TV systems were sold across America. But due to the lack of color TV content provided by broadcasters, it was not until 1966 when color TV programming was broadcast across America that color TV sets became popular.

After the 1950s, television burgeoned from a niche technology into an important and powerful form of communication. And technological innovations continued. The use of satellite technology in the 1970s enabled television to become a best provider of overseas news as well. "Satellite and video technology have combined to give us truly live reporting from overseas in areas where traditional cameras are unsuitable" (Conboy 2004:

207). Digital television (DTV) that transmits audio and video by digitally processed signals was made into reality in the 1990s. According to Kinsey (2009), by 2007 nearly nine million homes had satellite television and the same again had DTT (digital terrestrial television). Flat screen TVs and HDTVs were introduced in 2005 and in the following year they became affordable to the public. In 2010 3D televisions started hitting the market. And finally, with the convergence trend, television has been merged with other broadcasting technologies, particularly the Internet and smartphones, giving the birth to smart television sets. Also called hybrid TV, smart television is integrated with the Internet and has Web 2.0 features and is thus a typical case of technological convergence of computers and television sets. Besides offering traditional television entertainment and news programs, smart television can also provide Internet TV, online interactive service and home networking access, etc. Old media are never completely replaced by new ones, not was television. It keeps its vitality by converging with other media, particularly the Internet.

1.2.3.2 Television Journalism: Immediacy and Entertainment

The first television station in America started broadcasting in 1928 and was commercially free for the first 13 years of its existence. In Britain, television broadcasting was formally inaugurated by the BBC on November 2, 1936 (Barnett 2011: 21).

Early television was quite primitive and television journalism was seen initially as an amalgam of radio news and movie newsreels. Coverage of events was severely limited by the scarcity of film crews, by the bulkiness of their 16mm or 35mm cameras, by the time-consuming process of developing the film and transporting it to newsrooms, and by the limitations of the genre—the newsreel had emphasized on-scene photography, not on-scene reporting (Stephens 1988: 281). Since filmed reports might not be aired for days after they were shot, film tended to be reserved for planned events and timeless features. Nonetheless, viewers were captivated simply by the opportunity to witness, from their living rooms, live reports of diverse events.

The "age of television" took off in the 1950s, using by and large the same technology worldwide. By the early 1960s television had succeeded in attracting a new audience to the news. Once television sets become affordable, news became available to audiences of many millions, including even those lacking the energy, skill or maturity to read a newspaper or concentrate on a radio narrative (Stephens 1988: 284-285).

In 1957, 30 percent of people in Britain chose newspapers as their main news, 46 percent radio and 24 percent television. By 1962, 52 percent were treating television as their main news source with only 31 percent opting for newspapers and 17 percent for radio (Crisell 1997). Since then, television journalism has become the dominant popular medium and the news/features balance in the press as a whole has shifted to accommodate television's demonstrable superiority in dealing with the news of the moment (Conboy 2004).

Television has undoubtedly brought a wealth of news into our homes with astounding speed and immediacy, but it is "predominantly an entertainment genre" (Conboy 2004: 209). According to the *Many Voices One World Report* issued in 1980 by the International Commission for the Study of Communication Problems, television secured and held its audience largely by offering entertainment in a cheap and convenient form. Media researchers (Postman1986; Conboy 2004; Barnett 2011) also argue that the inherent qualities of television as a communication medium made it incompatible with intelligent journalism, that the medium could speak only with "the voice of entertainment". Television has "extended" dramatically our access to news but, as cars weaken the legs they have "extended", reliance on television news may have weakened our ability to hear and tell our *own* news (Stephens 1988: 288). The nature and appeal of television is for relaxation and entertainment. It is perhaps in this sense that Postman criticized television as a culprit who kills human creativity and amuses humans to death.

1.2.3.3 Television News: Spoken, Multimodal and Less Serious

Television is a medium of impression and mood as much as news. Television news demonstrates unique features as compared with print news and radio news.

Television news writers have room for fewer words than their newspaper counterparts—their stories are measured in seconds, not column inches. They work in time—minutes and seconds, with a rough formula that three words of English (or any European language) take on average one second to read aloud on the air. Besides, since their words are intended for a less acute, less painstaking sense—hearing—television news writers must forswear the more complex formulations a newspaper reporter might hazard (Stephens 1988). As a result, the wordings of television news need to sound conversational. This informal tone in reporting news and current affairs had been established by the end of 1960s (Chapman 2009). Also, to let the information sink in, the focus of the television news story has to be as concise as possible, which is quite different from print and online new stories packed with as much detail as possible. Just enough should be said and shown to leave the viewer with a strong general impression of the story. "Too much detail swamps the images and saturates the senses" (Stewart & Alexander 2022: 305).

Moving pictures certainly contribute information of their own in television news (Stephens 1988: 286). Sometimes they even tell stories of their own. They are powerful meaning-making resources. In television news, a moving picture can contain just enough information to get its message across in a few seconds, and the language of television scripting also cherishes the pictures and sound and embellishes them with the words. In this sense, television news is visual and multimodal in nature, with sound, images, spoken language and captions as the main semiotic modes to convey meaning and messages. There is nothing quite as dramatic as a breaking story, preferably with sensational pictures and even better if accompanied by a live, breathless commentary from a journalist on location to offer their own vivid description and interpretation of events (Barnett 2011). In addition, almost from the beginning, television's on-screen presenters and journalists became household names whose fashion choices, hairstyles, accents and appearance were matters of daily conversation. These features add to the multimodal nature of television journalism.

The third feature, also a weak point of television news, is its inability to do scrious journalism (Postman 1986; Barnet 2011). According to Barnett (2011), many correspondents who made the transition from print to screen were struck by the need to be simple and concise, and by the volume of material that needs to be omitted. To retain this brevity and simplicity and also to "retain more of an audience which is fragmenting because of the variety of options open to it" (Convoy 2004: 208), television stories are undeniably shallower than most newspaper stories in terms of the depth of coverage (Stephens 1988: 286).

1.2.4 News and Technologies in the Digital or Online Era

The digital era ushered in the technological systems and digitalization that surrounded the birth and evolution of the Internet. Today we are living in a digital world created by the Internet. The Internet has become embedded in every aspect of our day-to-day lives, changing the way we interact with others, including the way news is produced and consumed. At present, digitalization covers everything and places us facing a digitalized world in a data society (Hintz et al. 2019).

Generally speaking, journalism in this era is characterized by the computerization of news production, the introduction of electronic newsrooms, and the digitization of the product (Díaz Noci 2013). In this era, the Internet, together with computers, mobile phones and other mobile platforms, has become the dominant medium of news communication, and "the Internet media has also made mobile phones the real fifth media" (Xie 2015: 5). Meanwhile, the more traditional media of newspapers, radio, and television remain a part of news media, but the trend, of course, is more for their digitalization or the convergence with the digital media. Accordingly, the media of news reports have become rich and news comes "in ever more diverse forms and stories are told in innovative ways to cater to the reading habits and catch the eye of digital natives" (Tong 2017: 2).

1.2.4.1 Computers, the Internet and Digital Technologies Today

Digital journalism started in the 1990s, but the technologies enabling its birth should be traced back to the experiments with computers that began in the 1940s because computers are the core in the digital world.

According to Li (2009), back in 1941 Germany produced the world's first working electromechanical programmable, fully automatic digital computer—the Z-3. It was designed by Konrad Zuse in 1938. The computer had a monitor, keyboard and a 21-inch flat screen and was used to solve flutter problems. While Zuse was busy in Germany, Alan Turing was designing the Colossus computer in England. It was also a fully programmable, digital computer and was developed to aid British codebreakers in decrypting German radio telegraphic signals. The ENIAC (Electronic Numerical Integrator and Computer), the electronic general-purpose digital computer, was launched at Pennsylvania University,

Philadelphia, the USA. It was very large, filling an entire room, and electricity-consuming, but it was able to solve a complex number of problems. It took only 20 seconds to complete its first calculation. In 1948, the first electronic stored-program computer, the Manchester Baby, was completed in Manchester, the UK. This was the first computer to store its programs digitally, rather than via wires and switches. It was also the first computer to use random-access memory and paved the way for the Farrenti Mark 1, one of the world's first commercially available computers. These were the first generation of computers.

The 1950s witnessed the emergence and development of the second-generation computers, the transistor computers. The first transistor computer was developed by Manchester University in 1953, but it did not run exclusively on transistors and contained several tubes in its clock. Two years after this, two fully transistorized computers were designed and produced: one was the Harwell CADET (Transistor Electronic Digital Automatic Computer—backward acronym) announced in February by the electronics division of the Atomic Energy Research Establishment at Harwell, the UK, and the other was the IBM 608 calculator announced in April. IBM claims its calculator to be "the first completely transistorized computer available for commercial installation".

Thanks to further advances in computer hardware, the late 1960s and the 1970s witnessed the development of the third-generation computers. One type of the computers in this period used the integrated circuit, a solid-state device containing hundreds of transistors, diodes and resistors on a tiny silicon chip. It offered computers higher operating speech, capacity and reliability at significantly lower cost. The 1970s also saw the development and commercial success of personal computers. Francois Gernelle invented the Micral N., the world's first personal computer in 1973, but it was not a commercial success. The MITS Altair 8800 launched in 1974 was the first

PC that was of great commercial success. It was sold at $439, roughly around $2,100 in 2020. The IBM 5100 launched in 1975 was the first, commercially successful portable computer. Although it was labelled "portable", it weighed 23 kilograms!

The digital computers of the 1980s and 1990s employing LSI (large-scale integration) and VLSI (very large-scale integration) are often seen as the fourth-generation computers. Laptops also emerged in the 1980s. The first laptop was the Epon HX-20 launched in Japan in 1981 and released internationally in 1982. It weighed just 1.6kg and was about the size of an A4 sheet of paper.

Compared with today's supercomputers, the first computers were much more primitive, but without these earlier attempts and successes, today there would be no supercomputers that are endowered with great computing and learning powers and are able to perform multiple complex tasks.

Another core technology for digital journalism is the Internet which revolutionized the computer and communications world like never before. The pioneering attempts to establish social interactions through networking include the Centralized Networks, the Distributed Networks and the ARPANet developed in the 1960s. In 1970 the Network Control Protocol, the NCP, was completed and later evolved into the Internet. The leading information retrieval service of the Internet, the World Wide Web, was begun in 1989 by Tim Berners-Lee and his colleagues at CERN (European Laboratory Particle Physics) in Switzerland (Li 2009; Britannica). They created the HyperText Transfer Protocol, the HTTP which standardized communication between servers and clients and gives web users access to a sea of files and documents connected to each other by hypertexts or hyperlinks. Their text-based Web browser was made available for public use in 1992, but it could only be used by professionals and was not suited to the general public. The creation and application of Web browsers solved the problem. In September 1993 the first Web browser, Mosaic, was released and in 1994 the Netscape Navigator was released. The Netscape Navigator became the dominating browser soon after its release. The year 1994 also witnessed the release of the first browser with tabs, in which a user could visit another Website without opening an entirely new window. By the mid-1990s, the World Wide Web had millions of active users. Just as Wu (1998) summarized, the creation of the World Wide Web injected great vitality into the Internet and made the computer, an information processing tool, a real and powerful mass medium.

Then, the development of WiFi, the wireless fidelity, gives wireless Internet access to computers, smartphones, and other devices. The wireless fidelity was developed by Vic Hayes in 1997. As WiFi was accessible to the general public and smartphones became computer-like, web usage on smartphones steadily increased. In 2016 web usage on smartphones accounted for more than half of web browsing. Communication became much more mobile and less unrestricted by time and space. The popularization of smartphones and app-based communication systems also gave rise to the development of a new discipline: mobile journalism or mojo (Westlund 2013; Wolf & Schnauber 2015; Salaverría 2019).

Digital technologies also play an important role in the digital communication. Followings are some of the digital technologies that contribute greatly to the development of journalism in the digital era.

The latest technologies applied in journalism are automation technologies. The past decade has seen an increasing use of automation to influence the production and dissemination of journalism. Generally speaking, automation takes the forms of algorithm and artificial intelligence. In computer science, algorithms are specifications for performing tasks like calculations, data processing, automated reasoning and even decision making. They are used in all areas of computing because it is a fantastic way of automating computer decisions. The development and analysis of algorithms is fundamental to all aspects of computer science, including artificial intelligence. Artificial intelligence is about intelligence demonstrated by machines like computers. *The Oxford English Dictionary* defines artificial intelligence as "the theory and development of computer systems able to perform tasks that normally require human intelligence, such as visual perception, speech recognition, decision-making, and translation between languages". The most advanced example of AI is perhaps Natural Language Processing (NLP). NLP strives to build machines that can understand and respond to text or voice data with text or speech of their own and in much the same way as humans do. NPL draws on many disciplines, including computer science and linguistics to enhance human-machine communications. It is rapidly advancing thanks to the availability of big data, powerful computing and enhanced algorithm. Now NLP has been applied to translation, natural language generation, sentiment analysis and many other fields.

Algorithm and artificial intelligence began with changing the routines of the journalist by automating some of the functions of search, classification or processing of information and has begun to install itself already in its functions by also covering the tasks of news writing (Túñez-López et al. 2020). In other words, the application of automation technologies has resulted in leaps in data mining and processing, in automated content production, and content optimization. Thanks to their power in automatic data processing and decision making, these technologies, algorithms and NLP in particular, "are the origin of applications for automatic writing of texts, known as robots for news writing" (Veglis & Maniou 2019). These applications in journalism have given rise to a new discipline called "automated journalism" (Carlson 2014; Graefe 2016; Túñez-López et al. 2020), or "algorithmic journalism" (Dorr 2016; Salaverría & de-Lima-

Santos 2020; Kotenidis & Veglis 2021) or "robot journalism" (Oremus 2015; Túñez-López, et al. 2020).

These technologies also make possible the micro-targeting of content. As users continuously use certain digital devices and platforms, algorithm and artificial intelligence allow the content providers to know every detail about the preferences and consumption patterns of each user (Salaverría & de-Lima-Santos 2020: 2). In fact, the audience or viewers "are subject to automated decision-making by algorithmic systems" (ibid).

Another new area in the media industry is exploring is IoT(Internet of Things) technologies; they also affect the three main phases of journalistic work: information gathering, processing, and especially, news content production and distribution (Salaverría & de-Lima-Santos 2020; Wang 2022). IoT makes our world extremely interconnected and ushered "the news business into a new paradigm: ubiquitous journalism" (Wang 2022). Real-time analytical systems of big data, self-improving algorithmic systems (machine learning), interaction systems between sensors for data capture, monitoring tools and remote control of electronic objects are some of the IoT technologies (Greengard 2015; Salaverría & de-Lima-Santos 2020).

Tools to gather news and information and big data analytics also contribute greatly to the development of digital journalism in the 21st century. Since the 1990s, reporters can effectively use online tools to gather news and information, check facts and even find sources off the web (Pavlik 2000). Journalism has been enriched by the enormous volume of information coming from the automatic sensors, present in almost any digital device. These sensors capture data in an uninterrupted way and can transform it into quantitative measures of all kinds. Practically any activity of nature and human beings begin to be monitored and quantified. All this immense volume of information, known as big data, is becoming raw material for the preparation of journalistic information, which is added to the traditional sources of the journalists: personal observation, documents checking and interviews (Salaverría & de-Lima-Santos 2020: 3). Unmanned aerial vehicles (UAV) or unmanned aircraft systems (UAS), more commonly known as drones are also commonly utilized to take photos particularly in places beyond human reach and have thus enriched the graphic database.

Big data analytics is the use of advanced analytic techniques for very large, diverse big data sets that include structured, semi-structured and unstructured data (IBM, big data analytics). Big data promises to make news possess greater depth than even before. With the right tools, big data can reveal stories that cannot be discovered by pure observations or interviews. As a result, news making today is increasingly relying on data. With big data analytics, data journalism, or data-driven data journalism, has become a new trend in journalism.

As Pavlik (2010) summarized, from the first steps of digital journalism, the impact of technology influenced how journalists do their work, the content of the news, the structure and organization of the newsrooms, and the relationships among journalism organizations, professionals, and the users. Therefore, it is of great value to analyze and discover the evolving and complex interplay between digital technologies and journalism.

It should be pointed out that the rapid and accelerating changes in computer and digital technologies are so breathtaking that those written about here are far from being complete and could easily be out of date between completion of the book's manuscript and publication. However, a glimpse of them does offer insights into the question of the interplay between technologies on the one hand and news production and consumption on the other. It is also hoped that the present study will prompt researchers worldwide to contribute to a more comprehensive study of the role

technologies in promoting the development of digital journalism.

1.2.4.2 Digital Journalism: Adapted and Native Outlets

Digital journalism is also referred to as online journalism (Deuze 2001, Steensen 2011), cyber journalism (Díaz Noci & Salaverría 2003, quoted from Salaverría 2019), or multimedia journalism (Deuze 2004). However, according to Salaverría (2019), the most widespread expression among professionals in most countries is "digital journalism", and in the last 10 years "digital journalism" has been gradually taking over and is now the most popular expression in the research community. Therefore, we adopt the term "digital journalism". We prefer the term also because it can cover both journalism on the web and on mobile digital devices.

Basically, there are two major types of outlets for digital journalism: outlets adapted from traditional journalism brands and native media outlets (Díaz Noci 2013; Salaverría 2019). In the 1990s, journalists already envisioned the Internet's potential; but in this decade, the more prevalent practice was to adapt the printed (or even audiovisual, in the case of radio and television-based websites) material for online websites. Some newspapers are considered to be the pioneers in this adaptation practice. In the United States, *Chicago Tribune* was distributed by America Online (now called AOL) since May 1992 and in 1993 the Californian *San Jose Mercury News* had its advanced digital edition called *San Jose Mercury Center* (Li 2009). Scholars like David Carlson (2003) and Javier Díaz Noci (2013) point to January 1994 as the time when the first news publication appeared on the World Wide Web. According to them, the honor of inaugurating the history of Web-based journalism belongs to the *Palo Alto Weekly*. In spite of the differences, it is widely accepted that the year 1995 was a key year as there were already 150 newspapers on the WWW (Díaz Noci 2013; Salaverría 2019). Some larger media outlets such as *The New York Times* and BBC placed their print contents on the website later. *The New York Times On The Web* (not just *The New York Times*) debuted in January 1996 and *BBC News* did not go online until November 1997 when the Web audience was growing 10% every month (Thorsen et al. 2010; Díaz Noci 2013). These earlier digital publications mainly used the shovelware approach (Bardoel & Deuze 2001), a publishing model that consists of simply reproducing on the Internet the content originally created for another platform.

After these earlier practices, practitioners are more concerned and critical about the question how should journalism be presented on the Internet. It is definitely not simply transferring material from print copies or broadcast material to the new medium. Instead, being regarded as a completely new medium, it demands new conventions and approaches from its older brethren, hence the birth of native digital outlets or websites. Actually, as early as 1996 there were attempts to differentiate online practices from the print and broadcasting formats and practitioners were consciously taking some steps toward a proper online or digital journalistic model (Díaz Noci 2013). For instance, *San Jose Mercury Center* gave birth to an interactive strategy with readers which is now a common practice in the online world (ibid). The *Drudge Report* and the *HuffPost* are two typical examples of native digital outlets. The *Drudge Report*, debuted in 1997, is a US-based news website founded by Matt Drudge. It was the first news source to break the Clinton-Lewinsky scandal. Its website consists mainly of selected hyperlinks to news websites all over the world, with each link carrying a headline written by *Drudge* or its editors (see Figure 1-3). The news site is conservative in its political stance. *HuffPost*, formerly called *The Huffington Post*, was founded in May 2005 as a liberal counterpart to the *Drudge Report*. Besides news updates, it features blogs from unpaid bloggers drawn from the worlds of politics, entertainment, and academia; the site also has content-sharing partnerships with various other content providers (www.britannica.com/topic/The-Huffington-Post). *The Huffington Post* also launched Huffpost Live in 2012. This online network rejected typical television programming formats and encouraged viewer participation. The contents on these native digital platforms are also characterized by a rich and organic blending of graphic, audio, video and textual elements. In other words, most of their news stories are presented multimodally.

Figure 1-3 A Screenshot of Hyperlink Contents at the *Drudge Report* Website (https://www.drudgereport.com/)

Radio and TV media also moved their contents to online platforms. According to Li (2009), there are two major online broadcasting forms—live web broadcasting (or webcasting) and video/audio on demand. Live webcasting includes streaming television and online radio. Streaming television is the digital distribution of television content as streaming media delivered via the Internet. Online radio, also called web radio, net radio, streaming radio, e-radio or IP radio, is a digital audio service provided and consumed via the Internet. Internet radio services offer news, sports, talk and various genres of music—every format that is available on traditional broadcast. Television video on demand (VOD) systems can stream content both through television and devices like computers, tablets and smartphones. VOD users can also download the contents for continued viewing. An increasingly popular medium of VOD is streaming media, the multimedia that is delivered and consumed in a continuous manner from a source, with little or no intermediate storage in the network. Netflix, Amazon Prime Video, YouTube and Hulu are some of the main providers or platforms of online broadcasting. Online broadcasting enjoys two advantages over the traditional broadcasting journalism (Li 2009). First, it is accessible to more audience, particularly oversea audience. Second, it allows the viewers or listeners to customize what they watch or listen to. The content is always available and accessible. It offers total freedom regarding time and program selection. Viewers or listeners can enjoy the programs they like at any time and any place, if they have access to the Internet. These practices also demonstrated once more that confluence of technologies further promotes media convergence.

From these media practices, it can be seen that over time, digital media have become increasingly independent in both form and content (Salaverría 2019). Convergence, hyperlink, viewer participation or interactivity, multimedia and multimodality are the major features that differentiate digital journalism from more traditional ones. The next section will explain these features in more detail.

1.2.4.3 Digital Journalism and Media Convergence

In the previous sections, we mentioned that convergence was a maneuver of the traditional media—the print newspapers, radio and TV—to cope with their decline and the challenges from the online or digital media. In the digital age, the old or traditional media have not been replaced by the new digital media. Rather, as Nile Finneman (2006) pointed out, what we have is a process of co-evolution of old and new media. The Internet and digital media provide new features and facilities and digital media contribute to a general change in the overall media matrix. But while old media are refunctionalized/repurposed, they are also influential actors in the development of Internet forms (Dwyer 2010: 32).

The term "convergence" has been widely applied to account for the development of digital technology, the integration of text, numbers, images and sound since the 1990s (Dwyer 2010). Over the years, media convergence has surged from "a trickle" by the early years of the new millennium into "a roaring torrent" now (Infotendencias Group① 2012: 23). It becomes a key factor of today's media industry and journalism studies and also a core concept to understand the journalistic practices today. However, interpretations about convergence are somewhat heterogeneous (Infotendencias Group 2012).

Most practitioners see it as "the process by which editorial teams are merged together" to adapt to the challenges of the digital environment (Infotendencias Group 2012). For instance, *The Daily Telegraph* and BBC established their new working dynamic in 2007, by which the television, radio and Internet editorial departments were reorganized in accordance with the production flow. In 2008, the integration schemes proliferated and were implemented in different forms in a large number of main media groups, including *The New York Times*, and the British Guardian Media Group, *Financial Times* and *The Times*. According to Infotendencias Group (2012)

① Infotendencias Group is a research team working on online journalism, made up of researchers from various Spanish universities.

and Salaverría & Negredo (2009), the first significant international example of editorial teams was carried out in 2000 by the US Media General in Tampa, Florida. They put into practice a model of *three-way convergence*—newspaper, Internet and television. The benefits of such coordination in the production process are obvious to media companies or groups. First, "an integrated editorial team would be able to meet the demands of readers who were increasingly operating on a variety of platforms" (Infotendencias Group 2012: 23). Second, it can increase the productivity of journalists. Finally, it would be more economical to run the news business.

There are also interpretations of the concept from other perspectives. According to the article by the Infotendencias Group (2012), earlier research on media convergence (e.g., De Sola Pool 1984; Pavlik 1996) laid emphasis on the "generation of new communicative messages through the combination of different linguistic codes" (Infotendencias Group 2012: 25). De Sola Pool (1984) pointed out that "a single physical means—be it wires, cables or airwaves—may carry services that in the past were provided in separate ways", and Pavlik (1996: 132) saw convergence as the "coming together of all forms of mediated communications in an electronic, digital form, driven by computers". To sum up, these earlier scholars regarded media convergence as a journalistic product (ibid) and highlighted the multimodal and multimedia features of today's news discourses.

Some other scholars on media convergence focus on the way it affects the whole journalism system, but they have different interpretations about the areas that are affected. For instance, Gordon (2003) proposed five forms of convergence: convergence of ownership, tactical convergence, structural convergence, convergence of information gathering and narrative convergence; Jenkins (2006) summarized five areas of convergence, technological, economic, social or organic, cultural and global; and Dennis

(2006) analyzed the following five areas of media convergence: technology, regulatory issues, business matters, contents, and human resources.

Despite the discrepancies, it is generally acknowledged that media convergence is about the process that affects both the way in which contents are produced and the way in which they are consumed (Jenkins 2006; Infotendencias Group 2012). Based on the profound implications convergence has for the technological, business, professional areas and the contents presented, the Infotendencias Group (2012) identified four types of media convergence: technological convergence, business convergence, professional convergence and convergence of contents. We will follow their categorizations and analyze how these types affect the production and consumption of data news stories in the following section and so we will give only a brief introduction of these types here.

Technological convergence is the core area of media convergence because the concept of convergence had been formulated as the result of a confluence of technologies. The rapid expansion of the Internet in the mid-1990s "acted as a catalyst for initiatives that led to greater coordination between people working in different media" and gradually news business has come to be organized typically as multimedia (Infotendencias Group 2012: 22). The multiplication of mobile devices in the last two decades is also giving way to a multimedia system where all devices, mobile and desktop, large and small, interact with each other. As a result, the media are related to each other, constantly exchanging data and presenting to the users the messages that best fit their profile (Pavlik 2021; Salaverría & de-Lima-Santos 2020).

Business convergence has been triggered by the process of technological convergence, which means that news organizations "have to reconfigure their production structures and processes" (Infotendencias

Group 2012: 31) to generate more flexible and diverse ways of news production that can respond to the requirements of the new digital platforms brought by the Internet. News production now requires greater coordination between people working in different departments or platforms. This naturally leads to the merger of editorial staff and to the concentration of the production process.

Professional convergence is a logical consequence of technological convergence and business convergence. Today's journalists are expected to be capable of taking on different types of work within the merged editorial departments, writing on different topics, and even working for different media. It is common to see that "multi-skilled journalists are filing copy first for the online site to be followed by a video report and then a more in-depth article for the traditional newspaper product" (Dwyer 2010: 12). In short, journalists are increasingly involved in "a process of polyvalence" (ibid: 32).

Convergence of contents results from all the above modes of convergence. Based on Infotendencias Group (2012: 31), we sum up three effects on contents. First, the contents are usually offered in multiple platforms, and thus multimedia products are produced. Second, the contents presented to readers combine different communicative or semiotic modes, which means that the contents presented are multimodal. The third effect is the trend toward coordinated news coverage in different media and hybridization of contents offered to the public via different platforms. The trend has resulted in the wide use of hypertexts or hyperlinks on digital platforms.

The features—multimedia, multimodality, hypertext and interactivity—are important for us to analyze the contents of data news and so will be discussed in more detail in the next section.

1.2.4.4 Multimediality, Multimodality, Hypertextuality, and Interactivity

Multimediality, hypertextuality and interactivity are regarded as three assets or defining features of digital journalism (Deuze 2001, 2004; Paulussen 2016; Steensen 2011; Domingo 2006). To have a more delicate differentiation between the use of different semiotic or communicative modes in a single news discourse and the adoption of multiple platforms to represent similar contents, we add a fourth dimension—multimodality.

Thanks to digital technologies and media convergence, news businesses came to be organized typically as multimedia (Infotendencias Group 2012). Dwyer (2010) also noted that the new media reality is a multimedia one. Deuze (2004) pointed out that the concept of multimedia in digital journalism is generally understood in either of two ways: 1) as a distribution of a news story packaged through different media like newspaper, radio, television, website, and mobile terminal, or 2) as a presentation of a news story package where two or more media formats, like text, audio, video, and graphics, are utilized. In the present study, we use multimedia to refer to the former definition, namely the distribution of a new story through different media, and we use multimodality to refer to the latter interpretation.

So, when news is packaged for delivery via media as different as domestic television sets, laptop computers and the personal mobile phone screen, it is multimedia. Today's world is flooded with new stories which are shared between platforms and devices 24 hours a day. When a single new story is presented with two or more semiotic codes or media formats, it is a multimodal discourse. Figure 1-4 is a screenshot of an online multimodal news discourse with verbal text and images (including photos, graphics and data visualization).

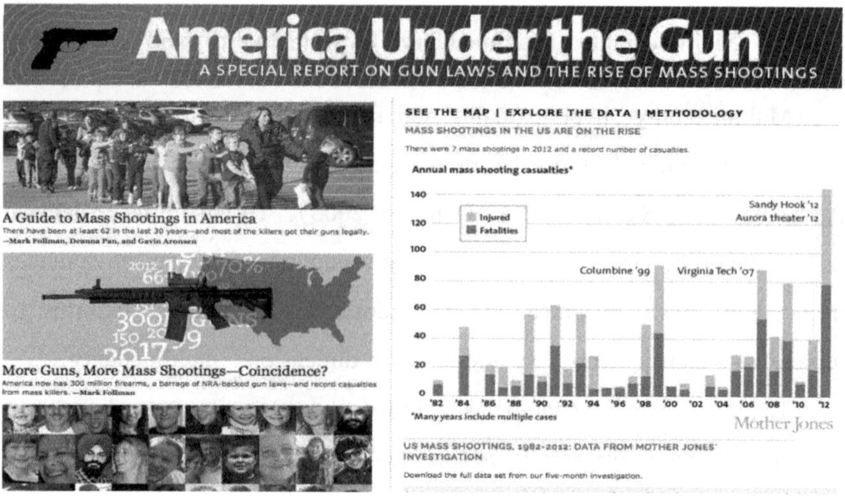

Figure 1-4 An Examples of Multimodal News Discourse

(http://www.motherjones.com/special-reports/2012/12/

guns-in-america-mass-shootings①)

The evolution of technology is allowing publishers to have new ways to create multimodal forms of multimedia news storytelling. For instance, autonomous video production systems can automatically combine and edit texts, pictures, and short videos through out-of-the-box solutions (Lassila-Merisalo 2014). Multimedia journalism has demonstrated a tendency for the reports with visual prominence and *scrollytelling* (Lassila-Merisalo 2014; Vázquez-Herrero, et al. 2020), which leads to semiotic or linguistic changes in the news discourse. Research on multimedia is rich and diverse, yet not much attention has been paid to the multimodality of news discourses in journalism studies.

It should be noted that although publications for multiple platforms are

① The report has been updated all the time after its first coverage in December 2012 and now it is redirected as part of the report titled "Guns" (https://www.motherjones.com/topics/guns/). The story was accessed in July 2017.

the norm, there continue to be publications designed solely for viewing on personal computers, while publications designed exclusively for tablets or smartphones are also emerging.

Hypertextuality, realized as hyperlinks, has also become "an established feature of digital news" (Dimitrova & Neznanski 2006: 256). It refers to the property of connecting "one story to other stories, archives, resources and so on through hyperlinks" (Deuze 2001: 3). Shipley and Fish (1996) identified three types of hyperlinks: target links (links within documents), relative links (links to other pages within a site), and external links (links from one site to another). According to Steensen (2011), relative hyperlinks are the most common form found in digital journalism, while target links and external links are used to a lesser degree.

The series of texts connected by links is a hypertext, which offers the readers different pathways to the online contents and so is non-linear in its textual organization. The hypertext provides a range of advantages both for the news producers and viewers. It can facilitate greater depth in reporting, allow stories to be told from multiple perspective (Doherty 2014), provide more comprehensive coverage of an issue or event of interest, and allow viewers to choose whatever they have interest in. There is also no limitation of space. It is no wonder that hypertext has been used as a narrative tool and opened new spaces for the development and research of news stories.

Interactivity is a big topic in journalism, and as with multimediality and hypertextuality, there are different definitions, explications and ways of operationalizing the concept of interactivity (McMillan 2005). Generally speaking, the term can be defined and explained from two perspectives: the general perspective of seeing interactivity as describing the processes related to communication in general and the specific one of viewing it as explaining practices like digital journalism in particular (Steensen 2010).

From the general perspective, interactivity in communication can be defined "in terms of the extent to which the communicator and the audience respond to, or are willing to facilitate, each other's communications needs" (Ha & James 1998: 461). From this perspective, three types of interactivity can be identified in the literature: human-to-human, human-to-computer, and human-to-content (McMillan 2003, 2005). Common conceptions or features of interactivity were noted by scholars as early as 1980s. For instance, Rafaeli (1988: 461) argued, "interactivity is generally assumed to be a natural attribute of face-to-face conversation, but it has been proposed to occur in mediated communication settings as well".

Researchers have been actively exploring the interactivity in mediated settings and interactivity has been explained more specifically as a central characteristic in digital journalism. It refers to the extent to which the users/viewers can interact with the news contents and their creator, and even the possibility of customizing certain stories (Deuze 2001; Dimitrova & Neznanski 2006; among others). Topics explored include: the way people interact through media, the nature of interactive contents, greater user choice and control, the way users interact with the producers and the contents they create, the user-generated content in the age of We-media, and the user-user interaction, etc. (Deuze 2001; Steensen 2011; Jonsson & Ornebring 2011; Weber 2014; O Dowling 2022; Sundar et al. 2022; among others). From the literature, we can see that interactivity in digital journalism highlights the user or viewer participation in news consumption and even in news production (e. g. user-generated videos and images). In traditional media, letters to the editor, radio programs with audience participation and phone-in, and talk show programs on TV are regarded as being interactive. But as Pavlik (2000) summarized, "For at least 500 years, since Gutenberg invented the printing press, the basic relationship between publishers and their publics has been defined by a 'broadcast' model of communication. The broadcast model emphasizes a one (or few)-to-many communications flow, with little feedback between source and receiver (or journalist and audience) and a relatively anonymous, heterogeneous audience. The intent of this communication is a combination of persuasion and information." (p. 234) In the age of digital journalism, the process is becoming much more of a dialog between the press and the public, with comments and thumb-ups from the readers/viewers. Interactivity also occurs when a user performs an action in one platform that causes an action to occur in another platform, as when a video-game player controls an on-screen character's action (Kalogeras 2014: 21). In short, we are experiencing what Grunig calls a "two-way symmetric model of communication in 21st century news operations" (Grunig 1976; Pavlik 2000). In the present study, interactivity highlights the user or viewer participation in news consumption, and refers specifically to the interaction and dialogue between the producer/site creator and the viewer/audience, or the interaction between the media and the consumer.

With technologies to realize interactivity between the producer and the viewer, digital news presented online or on mobile devices is becoming more engaging. In this sense, digital technology is transforming the nature of storytelling and the presentation of digital news. In Pavlik's words, "The once basic inverted pyramid news-writing style is becoming obsolete in the online news world. It is being supplanted increasingly by immersive and interactive multimedia news reports that can give readers/viewers a feeling of presence at news events like never before" (Pavlik 2000: 232).

In a nutshell, news in the digital era comes "in ever more diverse forms and stories are told in innovative ways to cater to the reading habits and catch the eye of digital natives" (Tong 2017: 2). A news discourse is usually presented with multimodal modes on multimedia and linked with other discourses through hyperlinks. In this way, the user-producer interactivity is also broadened and enhanced.

1.3 Data Journalism

Data journalism, also called data-driven journalism (DDJ), is a news practice in the era of big data. We do not assume that the term refers to a unified set of practices or theories. Rather it is a prominent label which refers to a diverse set of practices which can be empirically studied, specified and experimented with from different perspectives. In this section, we intend to clarify what data journalism is, what it does, what it does with, and how it evolves.

1.3.1 Understanding Data Journalism

1.3.1.1 Definition

Data journalism evolved at the start of this century. It seems to be a fast-growing trend in the way to future journalism, thanks to the Internet with various online search engines and to the easier access to big databases (Salaverría & de-Lima-Santos 2020). Scholars and practitioners in the journalistic circle have carried numerous studies from diverse perspectives. The most basic question is how to define the new journalistic practice or concept. They have offered definitions of data journalism from the perspectives of news production, news transmission, narrative styles, and its development as an industry.

Let's first review the definitions framed by journalistic practitioners. *Data Journalism Handbook*, the world's first data journalism book that was completed by a group of practitioners in the industry, describes data journalism as "journalism done with data" (Bradshaw 2012), covering a set of evolving storytelling tools, techniques, and methods. The handbook lists several merits of data journalism: it can help a journalist tell a complex story through engaging infographics, or help explain how a story relates to an individual, as the BBC and the *Financial Times* now routinely do with their budget interactives (where you can find out how the budget affects you, rather than 'Joe Public'), or open up the news gathering process itself, as *The Guardian* does so successfully in sharing data, context, and questions with its Datablog.

Simon Rogers① (2011), one of the most famous and quoted data journalists, said that data journalism is "about telling the story in the best way. Sometimes that will be a visualization or a map. But sometimes it's a news story. Sometimes, just publishing the number is enough". He emphasized that data journalism, whatever techniques are used or whatever forms are adopted to present the content, is "still about stories" (ibid). Then in an online article on his website (Rogers 2014), he further strengthened the idea of "story coming first". He said, "Data journalism is about using numbers to tell the best story possible... It is about telling stories first and foremost—the math and the charts and the code in service to that." He also noted the importance of big and open data for the evolution of data journalism, as he pointed out that data journalism is all about diverse sources and is a result of open data (Rogers 2011). Heravi and Lorenz (2020) regarded data journalism as a practice which uses datasets, computation tools and algorithms to create news stories.

---

① Simon Rogers is an award-winning data journalist, data journalism initiator and advocate. He worked as a news and data editor on *The Guardian*, working with graphics team to visualize and interpret huge database. He edited and created guardian. co. uk/data, an online data resource which publishes hundreds of raw datasets and encourages its users to visualize and analyze them. He won several awards and was the director of the Data Journalism Awards. He was also the author of *Facts Are Sacred*. He moved to Twitter as its first data editor in 2013 and then moved to Google. He is now the data editor on the News Lab team at Google and teaches data journalism at Medill-Northwestern University.

From the above definitions and explanations, we can see that in the news industry, data journalism is an umbrella term that encompasses an ever-growing set of tools, techniques and approaches to storytelling. Practitioners focus more on the production process and highlight the importance of technological innovations in producing and presenting data journalism. For them, data can be the source of data journalism, or it can be the tool with which the story is told—or it can be both①. But the core is still storytelling. What are the kinds of stories that can be found in data? This question is a big concern for practitioners and also scholars in the field (Rosenbaum 2012). Data journalism practitioners also think that data journalism is the future and it has been changing the ways journalists tell news stories. Its impacts on the ways journalists tell new stories will be explored further when we summarize its evolution.

The extensive attention that practitioners pay to data journalism has also fueled "an explosion in data journalism-oriented scholarship" (Fink & Anderson 2015: 476). Their first concern was to define what data journalism involves and implies (Loosen et al. 2017). The scholars have different understandings and definitions of the concept, but most of them consider data journalism as journalism's response to the datafication of society, focus more on the presentation or form of data journalism, and see data journalism as a news form presented with visualizations based on data analysis and computer technology (e.g., Fang & Yan 2013; Chang & Yang 2014; Coddington 2015; Ausserhofer et al. 2017; Loosen et al. 2017; Loosen 2018).

The articles in CNKI show that data journalism has become a hot field in China since 2013. One of the big concerns is the definition and connotation of the concept "data journalism". For instance, Wen and Li

① See *The Data Journalism Handbook*. https://datajournalismhandbook.org/handbook/one/introduction/what-is-data-journalism.

(2013) regarded it as an interdisciplinary news production mode emerging in the era of big data; Fang and Yan (2013) defined it as a new way of reporting that is based on data mining, data analysis and visualization and highlighted the core status of data in data journalism; Chang and Yang (2014) interviewed four scholars, who agreed that data journalism organizes stories based on data, and data processing methods and techniques (such as statistics, data analysis, and data mining) are in the center of the data news production, thus bringing about a certain paradigm shift in news production. Most of the scholars and practitioners take data journalism as a form of news storytelling. A few years later, scholars offered definitions from more diversified perspectives. For instance, Wu (2017) argued that it is not purely narrative, but more similar to a research report in social science. He further explained that it may have some narrative elements, but its main purpose is not to tell stories but to deduce factual conclusions, so it is an argumentative genre. Wu (2017) noticed the change of the narrative structure of data journalism.

Research in the West has also been extensive and scholars have offered definitions from different perspectives. The definitions may focus on the change in the process of newswork, including the impact of big data and technologies employed for data processing (e.g., Appelgren & Nygren 2014), or the news items based on data analysis that include various visualizations. However, a large corpus of works highlights that data journalism is both a process and a product (e.g., Coddington 2015; Knight 2015; Ausserhofer et al. 2017). Coddington (2015) noted the "quantitative turn" in journalism and defined data journalism as journalism based on data analysis and the presentation of such analysis. Ausserhofer et al. (2017) gave equal emphasis to the process and product. Research like Loosen et al. (2017) and Loosen (2018) took data journalism as a young and fast evolving genre and a new reporting style, focusing more on the narrative features. Loosen (2021), after exploring the relationship between the datafication of society and a datafied journalism, highlighted the societal role data journalism can be played in contemporary society. According to him, all social domains rely increasingly on an ever more diverse range and greater amount of data; "journalism's function is an observer of society, and so the more the fields and social domains that journalism is supposed to cover are themselves datafied, the more journalism itself needs to be able to make sense and produce data to fulfil its societal role".

To sum up, data journalism is regarded as a trend for the future news industry and is commonly carried out by cross-disciplinary teams characterized by a division of labor into data analysis, visualization, and writing (Loosen et al. 2017: 3). The definitions have different focuses, but "there are common elements which essentially outline a journalistic process [developing 'data news' by analyzing large sets of data with (mostly) quantitative, computational methods and a special form of presentation (interactive visualizations)]" (Ausserhofer et al. 2017: 4). The definitions also highlight the significance of the technological aspects and the processes of storytelling in data journalism. It can be viewed from different perspectives: in term of how data news is produced (through collecting, analyzing, visualizing, and narrating data), how it organizes relations, who and what these stories bring together (including audiences, sources, methods, institutions and social media platforms), etc. But as the literature indicates, practitioners and researchers in this field are more concerned with the productional and technological aspects, namely what stories can be found in data, what tools and techniques are suitable, and what presentations are more appropriate to represent the stories. Less attention has been paid to the narrative structure and meaning generation process from the perspective of readers or consumers, namely how the different modalities or semiotic modes work interactively to make a coherent and complete (perhaps also appealing) story and how the data news as the outputs of data journalism appeals to the readers or consumers.

In our view, data journalism combines data analysis, graphics, data visualization and news storytelling, and by this combination, it offers news approaches to news storytelling—it can help a journalist tell a complex story through engaging infographics or help explain how a story relates to an individual. The outputs of data—such as visualizations which quickly and powerfully convey an understanding of an aspect of the figures, or interactive searchable databases—can be very valuable for good storytelling. But how are these semiotic modes or resources combined and how do the readers or consumers interpret the data news presented in these resources? These questions have not been explored systematically. In the present study, we would try to answer these questions by taking data news as the outputs of data journalism. In other words, we will focus on the outputs, rather than reflecting on the different kinds of processes and collectives involved in doing journalism with data. We also intend to explore the narrative structure and meaning generation process of data news and establish a framework for its genre analysis. In section 1.3.2, we will elucidate the term "data news".

1.3.1.2 Data Journalism, Precision Journalism and Computer-assisted Reporting (CAR)

New journalism practices come together with continuity with the past (Hammond 2017). Data journalism can be said to be closely related to CAR and precision journalism, two previous journalistic practices which also employ computational techniques to analyze datasets. The comparison of the three is one of the most common historical comparisons. Anyway, there are both continuity and differences between data journalism and the two previous practices.

Coddington (2015) argued that precision journalism (Meyer 1973) was later renamed as computer-assisted reporting, whose wave finally transformed into what is known today as data journalism or data-driven journalism. He took Philip Meyer as "the *de facto* godfather of CAR" (Coddington 2015: 333) and regarded CAR as a "recast" of precision journalism. Scholars like Bournegru (2012), Uskail and Kuutti (2015) as well as Wien (2017) attributed the inventions of precision journalism and CAR to Philip Meyer and thought that both practices emphasize the importance of statistics and processing of great amounts of quantitative data in journalism. The National Institute for Computer-Assisted Reporting argued that the only thing to have changed between CAR and data journalism is the name (Hammond 2017). Though not everyone agrees with these views, many commentators have suggested that there is an underlying continuity between data journalism, CAR and precision journalism (Bournegru 2012; Hammond 2017).

The term "precision journalism" is from Philip Meyer's 1973 book *Precision Journalism* which "announced and advocated the arrival of data analysis as a significant part of the journalistic repertoire" (Hammond 2017: 410). It was "modeled after social science, using empirical methods (particularly surveys and content analysis) and statistical analysis to achieve more definitive answers to journalistic questions" (Coddington 2015: 333). In the book, Meyer promoted a "scientific approach": "The new precision journalism is scientific journalism... adopting the scientific method, scientific objectivity and scientific ideals." (Meyer 1973: 5) For Meyer, precision journalism introduces a reporter to social science methods. In the late 1980s and early 1990s precision journalism was recast as CAR and began to make significant inroads into newsrooms (Houston 1996; Coddington 2015). CAR first emerged in the United States in the late 1960s and early 1970s and is regarded as being closely tied to investigative reporting, often being seen as an auxiliary tool to aid in long-term, public-affairs journalism projects (Coddington 2015). It has also been used as "a label for stories revealing injustice in society by pointing out the existence and the causes of social issue, identifying solutions to it" (Parasie & Dagiral 2012). Since the turn of the century, CAR has fallen out of favor as its technology has broadly diffused throughout the newsroom and data journalism has taken up its mantle (Coddington 2015). Data journalism has inherited its scientific and data-based approach, scientific objectivity, the emphasis on statistics and quantitative analysis, the cause-analysis and problem-solution pattern in reporting. Perhaps it is due to these features that Wu (2017) argued that data journalism is not purely narrative, but more similar to a research report in social science.

There are also differences between data journalism and the two previous practices. In Coddington's view, "data journalism's decoupling with investigative journalism and integration into broader journalistic practices makes a significant break between CAR and data journalism" (2015: 335). Bournegru (2012) summarized two differences between CAR and data journalism. First, CAR is a technique for gathering and analyzing data as a way of enhancing (usually investigative) reportage, whereas data journalism pays attention to the role that data plays within the whole journalistic workflow; data journalism pays more attention to data. Second, in the past investigative reporters suffered from a poverty of information relating to a question they were trying to answer or an issue that they were trying to address, but now due to an overwhelming abundance of information, the biggest difficulty for data journalists is that they may not know what to do with the big data or how to get value out of it. Philip Meyer's words in his letter to Bournegru are another way to put this difference. He wrote, "When information was scarce, most of our efforts were devoted to hunting and gathering. Now that information is abundant, processing is more important" (quoted from Bournegru 2012).

The big volume of data that is freely available online combined with sophisticated user-centric tools, self-publishing and crowdsourcing tools enable data journalism to thrive in the 21st century. It carries on the legacies of precision journalism and computer-assisted reporting while demonstrating its own unique features. All these are worthy to be explored so as to reveal how data journalism appeals to the readers in the digital age.

1.3.1.3 Categories of Data Journalism Practices

As was mentioned, data journalism is a label which refers to a diverse set of practices. Categorization of the common practices can help us understand what data journalism does and what it does with. The two awards, the Data Journalism Awards and the Sigma Awards, can be a good start. Both awards select best works by data journalists or groups and so can represent the trends and models in doing data journalism.

The Data Journalism Awards was started in 2012 by the Global Editors Network (GEN) and is the first international award recognizing outstanding work in data journalism. It was sad that 2019 was the final year for the Awards, which means that the Awards folded after 8 years due to a lack of sustainable funding. Still, all the finalists, namely the projects nominated for the Awards, can represent the "gold-standard of DDJ" (Loosen et al. 2017: 2)

The Awards categories show some changes over the years. In 2012 there were three categories: "data-driven investigative journalism", "data-driven mobile or web applications", and "interactive data visualization and storytelling", and four categories in 2014, with the new category "data journalism website or section". In 2014 the categories increased to 8, in 2015 and 2016 there were 10 categories each year, and in the following three years, namely 2017, 2018, 2019, there were 12 categories. Table 1-1 lists the categories shared throughout the years from 2014 to 2019, Table

1-2 lists the categories shared from the year 2015 to 2019, and Table 1-3 lists the categories that were shared by less than four years or specific to a certain year①.

Table 1-1 Categories Shared Throughout the Years from 2014 to 2019

Number	Same categories (2014-2019)	Description
1	Investigation of the year(2014 had two categories: best data-driven investigation and best story or group of stories on a single topic)	The best data-driven investigation, which uses data collection and analysis to disclose or bring light on a significant abuse of power or failure to uphold the public interest.
2	Data visualization of the year (Best journalistic data visualization on a single theme in 2014)	Best interactive or static visualization based on one or several datasets. It may be self-contained or combined with a story, but must accomplish a journalistic purpose and use data significantly.
3	Website of the year(Best data journalism application or website in 2014)	Best data-driven journalism website, based on the quality of content, frequency and variety of subjects covered.
4	News data App of the year (Best data journalism application or website in 2014)	Best data journalism application. Interactivity is important and the project should provide both explanations of the topic and user engagement.

① The categories are originally from the official website of the Awards www.datajouranlismawards.org/, but now the website is inaccessible due to the shutdown of GEN. GEN was an association of editors-in-chief and senior news executives, established in 2011 as independent NGO to help news media navigate the disruption brought on by technology, to facilitate collaboration, promote innovation and support sustainable business models. It was shut down in November 2019 due to a lack of funds.

Continued

Number	Same categories (2014-2019)	Description
5	Best individual portfolio	Based on the quality of content, frequency and variety of subjects covered. A maximum of ten examples per entry.
6	Best team portfolio (only small newsroom in 2015, no this category in 2016; two categories in 2017, 2018 and 2019: large team and small team/newroom)	Best portfolio of work by a data journalism team, based on quality and innovation of data use and analysis, content, frequency of updates, range of coverage and variety of approaches. Teams from organizations with 30 or fewer editorial staff compete for the small newsroom category.

Table 1-2 Categories Shared from the Year 2015 to 2019

Number	Same categories (2015-2019)	Description
1	Best use of data in a breaking news story, within first 36 hours	Best data-driven journalism project around a breaking news story within the first 36 hours of the story breaking. It is judged on the quality of content, frequency and variety of subjects covered.
2	Open data award	Using freedom of information and/or other levers to make crucial datasets open and accessible for re-use and for creating data-driven journalism projects and stories. Publishing the data behind your project is a plus.
3	Public choice	An entry of high excellence selected by the public from the year's Shortlist.

Table 1-3 Other Categories

Number	Other categories	Description
1	Student and young journalist of the year (2017, 2018 and 2019)	Awarded to the best portfolio of data-driven work by a new and young talent, a student or an individual early in the professional career aged 27 or younger at the time the work was created.
2	Innovation in data journalism (2018 and 2019)	Awarded to the entry that demonstrates the most innovative approach to collecting, analyzing or examining data or to the most innovative approach to presenting data-driven journalism, to shed light on a topic of public interest.
3	General choice award (Jury's choice) (2014, 2015 and 2016)	An entry of high excellence not otherwise honored in this competition.

Luckily, the Sigma Awards, a new international competition which has simpler categories, helps fill the void left behind by the Data Journalism Awards①. It was created in 2019 by Aron Pilhofer (the James B. Steele Chair in Journalism Innovation at Temple University) and Gian Chua (formerly Reginald Chua, Reuters), with support from Simon Rogers (Google), Merianne Bouchart (HEI-DA), and Kuek Ser Kuang Keng (HEI-DA). It is supported by the Google News Initiative. In 2022 the Sigma Awards received 603 entries from 379 countries and organizations in

① See the article "The Sigma Awards are a new successor to the Data Journalism Awards" by Hanaa' Tameez posted at https://www.niemanlab.org/2020/01/the-sigma-awards-will-replace-the-data-journalism-awards-this-year/.

76 countries/areas①. The Awards have six categories and nine awards②:

- Best Data-Driven Reporting (small and large newsrooms), awarded to the entry that best utilizes data as part of a substantial piece of investigative or explanatory reporting. The winning entry will be a story or series that stands on a foundation of data and analysis... Narrative, graphics, interactives and presentation will be considered, but the primary focus of this category is on the use of data acquisition and analysis to tell a story that could be told any other way. Two awards will be given in this category: one to a small newsroom, and one to a large newsroom.
- Best Visualization (small and large newsrooms), awarded to the entry that best utilizes data in visual form to tell a story around an important topic of public interest. Key considerations will be how well the visualization conveys key journalistic findings, and whether it does so in a clear, concise, engaging and methodologically sound fashion... the primary focus will on the visual narrative itself. Two awards will be given in this category: one to a small newsroom, and one to a large newsroom.
- Innovation (small and large newsrooms), awarded to entries that push the boundaries of what's possible. This award will recognize innovation in any part of the data journalism process, form data acquisition, cleaning and analysis to

① See the website of the Awards: https://sigmaawards.org/about/.

② See the "Categories" section at the website http://datajournalism.com/awards.

design presentation or anything in between. This award could be given to a published piece of data journalism or for the tool, technique or process used to develop it. Two awards will be given in this category: one to a small newsroom, and one to a large newsroom.

- Young Journalist, which honors outstanding work done by a student or early-career professional aged 27 or younger at the time the work was created. Judges will consider the quality and innovation of data use, analysis, reporting and/or presentation. The work should have been solely or principally created by the entrant.
- Open Data, awarded to the entry that best reflects a commitment to making data open, accessible and relevant to other journalists, researchers and/or the general public.... Impact is key...
- Best News Application, awarded to the entry that empowers users to find their own narrative within a larger dataset. The winning entry should stand on its own as a piece of journalism, not requiring additional reporting or explainers for context.... This is a stand-alone site that might provide users with the tools they need to sift through a dataset or datasets in order to discover what's most relevant to them. Or it may be a site that covers a single themes or topic in dept—but, again, providing users the ability to interrogate the data and find their own stories.

From the categories in the two Awards, we can see that they aim to push forward the development of data journalism by encouraging innovations in content (including in-depth investigation, narrative or storytelling style and visualization), innovative applications of big data technology (open data, applications and websites) and the future development of data journalism (awards for individuals and teams). The present study focuses on the product or discourse of data journalism, so we will focus on the innovations in news contents as embodied in award winners of the above two awards.

Scholars also have tried to generalize models or main streams of data journalism practices. Uskail and Kuutti (2015) generalized two mainstreams, investigative data journalism (IDJ) and general data journalism (GDJ), and a third, still rather weak one, real-time data journalism based on algorithms that automatically create news from data sources. They summarized six points of differences between IDJ and GDJ (pls. see Table 1-4 for details).

Table 1-4 A Comparison of IDJ and GDJ

(Based on Uskail & Heikki 2015: 84-85)

	IDJ	GDJ
Time	Plenty	Hours or a few days
Data skills	Advanced level: coding, etc.	Basic level: Excel, some data visualization and analyzing tools
Way of story writing	Topic and point of view define the data to be gathered	Datasets define the story's topic and point of view
Data source	Unofficial and confidential information and data leaks have great significance in starting and directing investigations	Massive public and open access datasets decide the direction of the investigation

Continued

	IDJ	GDJ
Role of journalists	Confirm, cross-check and verify all the gathered information because they cannot trust only a single source.	Datasets are often uncritically accepted as trustworthy sources.
Stories	Based on gathered facts and journalists' own interpretations.	Based almost solely on computer assisted analysis.

The real-time data journalism is based on algorithms that automatically create news from data source, and so is actually algorithm or automated journalism termed by some other practitioners and scholars. Automated journalism, also known as robot journalism (Carlson 2015; Hammond 2017), is another emergent news practices in the view of other scholars. It has been defined as "algorithmic processes that convert data into informative narrative texts with limited or no human intervention beyond the initial program" (Carlson 2014: 417) or as the "process of using software or algorithms to automatically generate news without human intervention, after the initial programming of the algorithm" (Graefe 2016). In March 2014 the *Los Angeles Times* reported a 4.7 magnitude earthquake in the city three minutes after the rumbling stopped; the news was written by a robot (Salaverría 2019). Narrative Sciences, one of the leading companies in automated writing technologies, also offers to transform data into stories and insight and promises to "Let your data tell its story"①. The slogan indicates that data need to be analyzed and transformed into a story before they can offer insight, but now the story is not written by human journalists but by algorithms (Hammond 2017). The company started with sports events like

① Slogan from the company's website www.narrativescience.com.

baseball and is now heading towards financial news (Uskail & Kuutti 2015: 84). The technology behind is the natural language generation (NLG), which involves automatic creation of text from digital structured data (Carlson 2015; Salaverria & de-Lima-Santos 2020).

Despite the high volume of automated stories, algorithmic reporting still remains only a minor aspect of journalism (Hammond 2015) and is most widely applied to the creation of routine sports and financial news. It has not been a mainstream practice yet, but there is an increasing tendency towards it. This category or new practice of data journalism is not included in the present study. In the present study we take as research object the data journalism award winners done by human journalists.

Though there are some discrepancies in categorizing data journalism practices in the professional and academic circles, these categorizations by practitioners and scholars offer insights into what data journalism does and what it does with. Story or storytelling is still the focus though it tells, always in-depth, stories based on big data analyses and visualizations with the assistance of new technologies.

1.3.2 Data News

Data journalism is now a key term in the news industry. It usually has a broad reference, referring to both the journalistic process, namely analyzing large datasets and telling stories with data, and the product, including data visualization and textual outputs (Weber et al. 2018). The present study focuses on the product or discourse based on data analysis and presented in visualized texts (verbal texts, interactive and/or static images) and/or videos, so we use the term "data news" to refer to this multimodal artifact or discourse. In studies like Kennedy et al. (2016), Cairo (2016), Weber (2017), Engebretsen and Weber (2017), as well as Weber et al. (2018), the scholars used the term "data story". Some scholars also referred the product of data journalism as data journalism stories (e. g. Appelgren & Nygren 2014). But the data visualizations and textual outputs may serve for purposes other than narration, like explanation and persuasion. Previous studies show that data news has demonstrated salient changes in its generic features. The narrative or storytelling style of data news is influenced by the "quantitative turn" as noted by Coddington (2015). The main purpose of data news has shifted from telling stories to deducing factual conclusions, which is more similar to a social investigation report (Wu 2017; Zeng et al 2017). Data news organizes large amounts of random and sometimes meaningless data into structured and meaningful information and always comes to some new findings or some ideas countering common sense understandings. It is a new genre to cope with the datafication trend (Appelgren & Nygren 2014; Loosen et al. 2017) and has become a major form of reporting in journalism (Coddington 2015, Roger 2013) as a result of the open data movement and the advancement of computer science. Besides, studies in newsrooms have shown that when journalists use the term "story" they often mean "news", because both story and news refer to events (Weber 2020). When journalism practitioners talk about storytelling, they mean not only the text-linguistic practice of narrating but also describing, explaining, or arguing (Weber 2020). Therefore, to cover all the communicative goals of data journalism, we prefer the term "data news" in the present study.

As the product of data journalism, a piece of data news can be instantiated as multimodal discourses or artifacts, worth exploring by linguists and semioticians. There are more than one text segments in a piece of data news and these text segments can be regarded respectively as a single discourse, or as part of the whole data story. In this sense, data news as a hypertext is often composed of multiple elemental genres or contains embedded genres. To be more accurate, a piece of data news is a hypertext of mixed genres. Socially, quite many projects of data news have exposed corruption in government agencies (e.g., *The Guardian*'s 2009 report "Investigate your MP's expenses") or crimes (e.g., 2013 Data Journalism Award finalist "America Under the Gun" by Mother Jones, a reader-supported investigative news organization in the United States). Journalists work together with data analysts, researchers and possibly many other professionals relevant to the news topics to force accountability in other institutions in the era of big data. Therefore, it is of linguistic and social significance to describe and analyze genre relations in data news.

Scholars in the field of journalism have noticed such generic changes, but scholars in linguistics and semiotics have not yet conducted a systematic study of these features. It is of theoretical and practical significance to explore data news from a social semiotic perspective.

1.3.3 Data Visualization and Its Categorization

1.3.3.1 Data Visualizations, Infographics, Graphics and Images

As is mentioned, data visualization is a key element in presenting the contents of data journalism. It is one of the core outputs of data journalism (Heravi et al. 2021) and many practitioners take it as the driving force of their story (Kennedy et al. 2012). What is it? How do practitioners and scholars conceptualize it? How has it been embedded into newsroom practice? And what are the common types of images employed in journalism? The questions need to be clarified.

Data visualization is widely studied in the fields of statistics, computing science and journalism, and there are different interpretations for this term. For Friendly (2008a, 2008b), it is a relatively modern development in statistics and refers to "the graphic representation of quantitative information". He also argued that it connects with the rise of statistical thinking and a variety of advancements including technologies for making and reproducing images, advances in mathematics and statistics, and new developments in data collection, analysis and representation, particularly since the 1950s when data could be processed and graphs be generated by computers. For scholars like Unwin et al. (2008), data visualization is related to the new field of information visualization and includes visualization of all kinds of information, not just of data or quantitative information. They further pointed out that data visualizations "expresses the idea that it involves more than just representing data in a graphical form (instead of using a table). The information behind the data should also be revealed in a good display; the graphic should aid readers or viewers in seeing the structure in the data" (ibid: 6).

According to Post et al. (2003), in computing science, data visualization has evolved from "Visualization in Scientific Computing" (or "Scientific Visualization") that refers to visualization as a part of a process of scientific computing. More recently, as visualization is increasingly concerned with data from other sources, including large and heterogeneous data collections found in business and finance, administration, digital media, and data visualization is gaining acceptance to include both the scientific and information visualization fields and has become a very active and vital area of research in computing science.

In journalism, data visualizations are also called data-driven graphics (Touriño 2017). Scholars generally follow the definitions made in the fields of statistics and computing science. For instance, Weber and Rall (2012) followed the definition proposed by Friendly; Engebresten et al. (2018) defined data visualizations as "the visual representation of (most often numeric) data, created to amplify the cognitive processing and social application of data represented". The visualizations can be in the form of static graphics, but they can also be dynamically generated at the time of viewing, by computer code (e.g., JavaScript), and hosted online. These are interactive data visualizations or interactive graphics more generally. According to Weber and Rall (2012), an interactive graphic is "a visual representation of information or knowledge with the following elements: Verbal elements (text, audio, typography) and visual elements (photo, illustration, diagram, map, symbol, icon, pictogram, video, moving image) are combined in such a way that they create a new hybrid form" (p. 349). In many cases, a data story presents the original dataset and consists of tools that readers can use to explore the information to see how it relates to them (Touriño 2017: 23). These are also regarded as interactive data visualizations.

In journalism, data visualizations are used with a broad range of communicative intentions, including: "to offer insight (UK)", "to explain more easily (SE)", "to communicate clearly, more clearly than words can (UK)", "to tell several facets in detail, which in text is only possible in an aggregated form (DE)", to make stories "more accessible (DK)", "to reveal deplorable states of affairs (CH)", "to help people understand the world (UK)" (Kennedy et al. 2019). Data visualizations can "facilitate understanding", to use Kirk's term (2016: 19), and they can also facilitate other things, such as persuasion (Kennedy& Engebretsen 2020). However, as is emphasized in section 1. 2. 1, the core of data journalism is still storytelling. This means that data visualizations should also serve for this essential goal. When doing data journalism, journalists are concerned with meaningful relations and patterns that can be found in data and the ways that can best organize and visualize them into engaging news stories. And looked at from the consumers' perspective, data visualizations work together with verbal texts to create multimodal data news. Consequently, we follow the definition proposed by Kennedy and Engebretsen and see "data visualizations as cultural artefacts with distinct semiotic, aesthetic, and social affordances" (2020: 22). To put it simply, we take data visualizations as multimodal discourses to be understood, interpreted and consumed by readers or viewers in the digital era.

Infographics, as indicated from the compounding of "information" and "graphic", are "visual representations of data, information or concepts" (Chandler & Munday 2011: 208), or "a visual representation of information or data" (Lexico 2019). Their primary function "is to consolidate and display information graphically in an organized way so a viewer can readily retrieve the information and make specific and/or overall observations from it" (Harris 1999: 198). The term "infographic" has now been co-opted by the marketing industry to refer to combinations of words and visuals intended mainly to bring traffic to websites or to advertise products, not to inform the public (Velasco 2015; Touriño 2017). The definitions imply that some infographics are about non-statistical information or relation. This distinguishes infographics from data visualizations, which are based on data analysis and demonstrate quantitative information. But in much of the literature, infographics is used interchangeably with data visualization (e.g., Weber & Rall 2012; Dick 2015). In the present study, we will follow the tradition and use the term "data visualization" when the graphics present or visualize information or knowledge based on data analysis.

Graphics generally means any non-photographic illustrations, whether they be maps, diagrams, cartoons, comic strips or drawing symbols submitted or ordered, or provided in-house, used to illustrate the contents of a page (Giles & Hodgson 1990). They can represent patterns of complex systems and visualize relationships and are also capable of capturing the structure of data commonly encountered in statistics. Let's take charts as an example. A chart can represent both statistical and non-statistical information. Figure 1-5 is a data visualization as the bar chart represents quantitative information based on data analysis, while Figure 1-6 is termed graphics because it deals with non-statistical knowledge about the relations of the items involved in human communication.

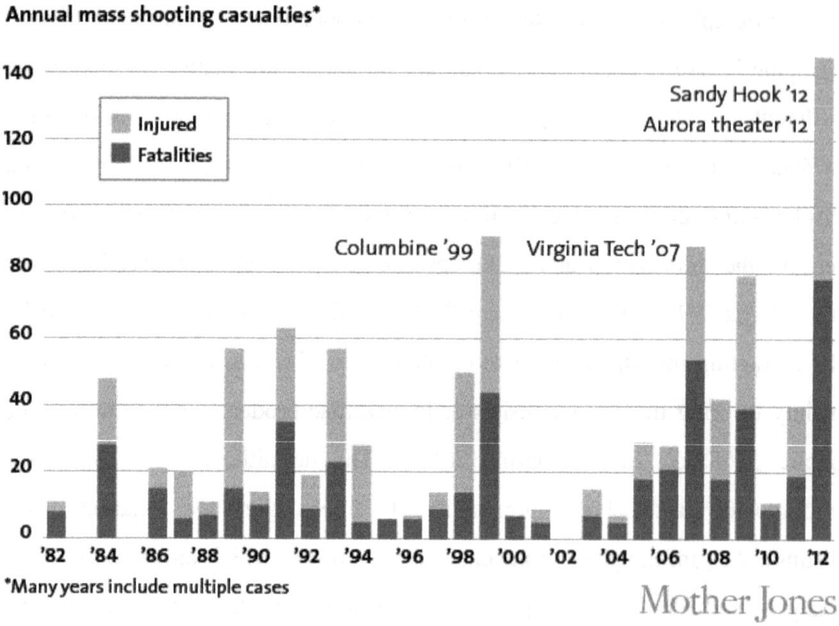

Figure 1-5 Data Visualization: Annual Mass Shooting Causalities Done by Mother Jones

(http://www.motherjones.com/special-reports/2012/12/guns-in-america-mass-shootings)

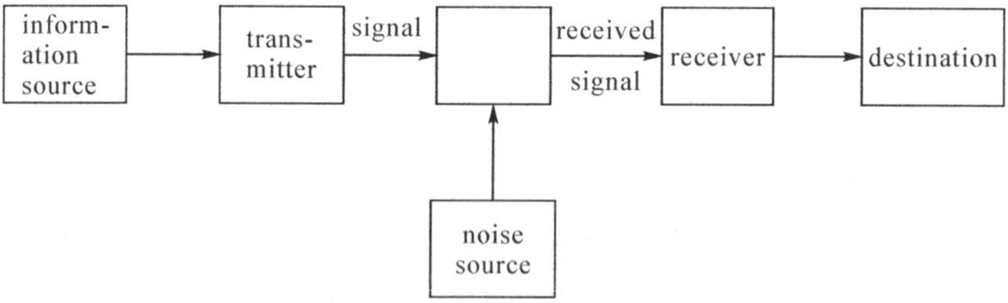

Figure 1-6 Graphics: Shannon and Weaver's "Communication Model"

(Copied from Kress & van Leeuwen 2006: 22)

In our understanding, graphics is a broader term which includes data visualization and infographics. In the present study, we will use the term "graphics" to refer to all the non-photographic visualizations, including the statistical and non-statistical.

Drawings, paintings, pictures and photographs are also common in various types of discourses. They are more concrete, less coded and more naturalistic compared with the abstract graphics which are usually coded in conventional symbols. In the present study, we will use the term "image" to cover paintings, pictures, photographs and the non-photographic graphics.

Data visualizations are a core element in data news, but other types of images like cartoons and photographs are also common ways to visualize the story or part of the story. According to semioticians Kress and van Leeuwen (2006) diagrams or graphics are different from photographs but their grammar does not differ from the grammar of the naturalistic photographs. They said, diagrams "are abstract and schematic where the photograph is concrete and detailed; conventionalized and coded where the photograph presents itself as a naturalistic, unmediated, uncoded representation of reality" (pp. 14-15). The two may often make different choices from the resources offered by the grammar, but one grammar underlies both. In Chapter 4, we will explore how these different types of image work together to create coherent and engaging data news.

1.3.3.2 Categorization of Data Visualizations

The craft of news graphics encompasses different kinds of products, from simple statistical graphs, charts, and maps, to large, standalone interactive animations, data visualizations, and explanation schemes. From the literature, we can see that some types of graphics can represent both statistical and non-statistical information, like charts and maps. In this section, we just focus on the major categories of data visualizations, namely graphics representing statistical information.

In statistics and computing science, data visualizations are often categorized based on the number of variables to be presented or visualized (e.g., Unwin 2008; Friendly 2008b; Myatt & Johnson 2009; Mirkin 2011).

Unwin (2008) pointed out that there are bar charts, pie charts, histograms, dot plots, boxplots, scatterplots, rose plots, mosaic plots and many other kinds of data display. The choice depends on the type of data to be displayed (e.g., univariate continuous data cannot be displayed in a pie chart and bivariate categorical data cannot be displayed in a boxplot) and on what is to be shown (e.g., pie charts are good for displaying shares for a small number of categories and boxplots are good for emphasizing outliers). Myatt and Johnson (2009) grouped data visualizations more systematically into five types:

- **tables**, which include simple tables, summary tables, two-way contingency tables, supertables;
- **univariate data visualization**, including bar chart, pie chart, histogram, frequency polygram, box plot, dot plot, and stem-and-leaf plot;
- **bivariate data visualization**, scatter plot belongs to this type;
- **multivariate data visualization**, histogram matrix, scatterplot matrix, multiple box plot, and trellis plot are the common subcategories;
- **visualizing groups**, including dendrograms, decision trees and cluster image maps.

Scholars in statistics, computing science and journalism have also pointed out that data visualizations are widely applied in scientific articles, business reports and news stories. In journalism, news professionals and teams are creating many more data visualizations based on abstract charts, graphs, and maps, and pictorial schemes and explanations (Touriño 2017: 17). Data visualizations in journalism may be less complicated than those used in academic articles and they are first categorized more generally into static and dynamic ones based on the interactivity with viewers or readers, rather than the number of variables involved (e.g., Weber & Rall 2012; Touriño 2017; Engebresten et al. 2018).

Undoubtedly, there is a growing use of data visualization within journalism, which means that there is a shift from writing as the main semiotic mode to data and visualization as central elements in journalistic storytelling (Weber et al. 2018; Kennedy et al. 2019). Besides, thanks to the datafication of society and the development of related technology, "data visualizations have innovative semiotic forms and result in novel types of communication and interactivity" and "their meaning potentials for meaning-making, for evoking emotions, democratic participation, and other forms of engagement is also in a state of transformation" (Kennedy & Engebretsen 2020: 20). As a type of discourse, what are the meaning potentials of data visualizations, or what meanings can different data visualizations create or convey? How do they work as semiotic resources? What are the ways they interact with verbal texts to generate data news? And how do they contribute to coherent and engaging data news? These questions are worthy to be explored.

1.4 Studies on Data Journalism: The Production Side

In section 1.2, we took data journalism as a label which refers to a diverse set of practices which can be empirically studied, specified and experimented with from different perspectives. In this section, we will focus on the theoretical studies on data journalism.

Research on data journalism has increased exponentially in the past years, so it is impossible for us to cover them all. Instead, we will just focus on those that are most relevant. Generally speaking, the existing research, mainly from the field of journalism, centers on data journalism as an industry, not on data news as discourse or artefact. The existing research involves many aspects, but it is still in "granularity and fragmentation" (Ausserhofer et al. 2017), and there is plenty of room for further exploration. The literature shows that the current research mainly focuses on the following aspects: 1) the definition of data journalism, 2) production and practices of data journalism, 3) content analysis, and 4) its evolution. The definition of data journalism has been discussed in section 1.2, so here we focus on the latter three aspects.

1.4.1 Data Journalism Production

Data journalism stems from the practice in newsrooms, so it is no wonder that its production practices have become a heated theme. Studies started from practices in Western societies, including the United States (Parasie & Dagiral 2012; Fink & Anderson 2015; Boyles & Meyer 2016), Sweden (Appelgren & Nygren 2014), Norway (Karlsen & Stavelin 2014), the United Kingdom (Hannaford 2015; Tandoc & Oh 2017), Belgium (De Maeyer & Libert 2015), and Canada (Tabary et al. 2016). Now studies have covered practices in non-Western developing countries like China (Zhang & Feng 2018) and Zambia and Tanzania (Gondwe & White 2021). There are also studies generalizing or comparing data journalism practices globally (Heravi & Lorenz 2020; Mutsvairo 2022).

The literature shows that the practice and development of data journalism vary across countries, but the focuses, principles and working methods are similar. For instance, data journalism has become a global trend and it enjoys clear advantages as an innovative form of journalism; technology-driven innovations and big data are highlighted; access to open data and the involvement of activists are crucial factors for the development of data journalism in many countries; crowdsourcing is a common method or strategy for practitioners to collect and analyze big data and even to collect and find stories from the data; the roles and functions of actors in the production, namely journalists or news producers, and production and perception of data visualizations are among the focuses in research on the production of data journalism.

The roles or functions of news producers are also dealt with in other studies. For instance, Loosen et al. (2017) found that among actors producing projects nominated for Data Journalism Awards (DJA for short) from 2013 to 2016, newspapers represent the largest group among all nominees as well as the award-winners (total: 43.1%; DAJ-awarded: 37.8%). Another important group comprises organizations involved in investigative journalism such as ProPublica and the International Consortium of Investigative Journalists.

These practice-centered and actor-centered studies provide valuable insights into the production of data journalism, in particular, that it is commonly carried out by cross-disciplinary teams characterized by a division of labor into data analysis, visualization and writing (Loosen et al. 2017: 3). They also reveal "the need to promote empirical studies involving this largely unresearched journalism genre" (Mutsvairo 2019).

1.4.2 Content Analysis

Another strand of research analyzes the content that is produced. Most of the studies are empirical analysis, adopting the research methods of case study, short-term observation or survey (Ausserhofer et al. 2017).

Loosen (2021) found that while the first studies in journalism research tended to focus more on the actors involved in its production and were mainly based on interviews, more and more studies have recently been using content analysis to better understand data journalism on the basis of its products. For instance, Young et al. (2017) and conducted quantitative analyses of the finalists of the Data Journalism Awards from 2012 to 2015. Loosen et al. (2017) investigated projects that were nominated for Data Journalism Awards from 2013 to 2016. Using content analysis, they examined the data sources and types, visualization types, interactive features, news topics and producers.

Specifically, the content includes visualization, interactivity, news topics, visual narration and so on. Visualization is a heated theme in data journalism. Knight (2015) concluded that data journalism "is practiced as much for its visual appeal as for its investigative qualities" (p. 55). Appelgren (2017) observed that images, though not data-related, are a prevalent type of visualization in data journalism and also common for any other kind of news content. Studies like Appelgren and Nygren (2014), Knight (2015) as well as Young et al. (2017) conclude that charts and maps are the most common form of data visualization. Loosen et al. (2017) found that the projects nominated for DJA from 2013 to 2016 mainly include images (which do not depict the data of the story), simple static charts and maps, while tables, static diagrams that combine information of at least three variables and animated visualizations are less common. Young et al. (2017) also suggested that these visualizations are popular because they can be easily produced, often using free software that many practitioners turn to due to financial and time constraints. Touriño (2017) explored how news graphics has changed as a practice, as a professional endeavor, and as a set of products (information graphics, data visualizations, etc.). He found that news graphics professionals and teams are creating many more data-driven graphics, based on abstract charts, graphs, and maps, and fewer pictorial schemes and explanations (p. 236). Hermida and Young (2019) looked at data journalism through the lens of materiality and attempted to unpack how technology and journalistic methods are shaped by the nature of the data and tools available. Indah and Hasanah (2022) carried out a content analysis of Covid-19 vaccine issues of data journalism-based media. Their analysis shows that vaccine and vaccination issues are presented with statistical-based writing elements, graphics, photos, icons, and diagram elements.

Chinese scholars have also done much research on visualization. Huang and Qiu (2018) conducted a comparative analysis of data news in major data journalistic platforms in China, Britain and the United States, and found that the main visualizations are static charts and information charts. Zhang (2018) pointed out that visualizations enable data news to present complex narration. From these studies, we can see that visualization is one of the most characteristic elements of data journalism and has drawn wide attention in the academic circles and there has been multidisciplinary and multifaceted academic conversation concerning the forms, uses, and roles of data visualization in society.

The interactive feature of data journalism is another theme. The analyses of Data-Journalism Award projects conducted by Loosen et al. (2017) and Young et al. (2017) indicate that the most frequent interactive features are 'the functionality of zooming inside an interactive map', features that let the audience 'inspect one data point in more detail by clicking on it and accessing more information', as well as filters through which users can refine the provided data with respect to different variables" (Loosen et al. 2017: 4-5). According to Young et al. (2017) and Loosen et al. (2017), the simplest interactive techniques are most prevalent, while more sophisticated features are rarely offered, partly because that the former are "the most commonly available (or default) functions of the free software tools and platforms" (Young et al. 2017: 9), while the latter require expertise and hand coding (Loosen et al. 2017).

In terms of the topics covered in data stories, the DJA projects are characterized by an invariable focus on the "serious" hard news topics, namely, political, societal and economic issues, and that the share of stories about education, culture and sports is small (Loosen et al. 2017).

Some practitioners and scholars have also investigated the visual narrative characteristics of data news from perspective of visual rhetoric. For example, Bradshaw proposed a "double pyramid structure" in the *Data Journalism Handbook*. Liu (2016) conducted a comparative analysis of the data news on China in some key Western media, and proposed a visual rhetoric analysis framework based on data rhetoric, relational rhetoric, temporal rhetoric, spatial rhetoric and interactive rhetoric. Li (2017) used the visual rhetoric framework to analyze the data news works on environmental issues in some Chinese media. Loosen et al. (2017: 14) found that the data journalistic reporting style is flexible but also with frequently occurring patterns: "Different types of data, analyses, visualizations and interactive functions are combined in various ways, but our analysis also suggests that some compositions have already stabilized into typical combinations as they reoccurred frequently over the years." Vǘzquez-Herrero et al. (2020) pointed out that data journalists have experimented with narrative models based on hypertextuality, multimedia and interactivity, and those techniques linked to temporalization and spatialization, and the narrative voice are among the most used resources for storytelling in data journalism. These studies highlight the meaning-creating significance of hypertextuality, multimedia, interactivity and graphics, but pay little attention to genre shifts manifested or realized in data news.

1.4.3 Evolution of Data Journalism

Many studies argued that data journalism is a further development of computer-assisted reporting and precision journalism (e.g., Rogers 2011; Uskail & Kuutti 2015; Hammond 2015; Túñez-López et al. 2020) and that the origin of robotic journalism, the automated generation of news, is linked to data journalism (Túñez-López et al. 2020).

Simon Rogers (2011) argued that *The Guardian* has been doing data journalism since May 1821, when its first edition (then the *Manchester Guardian*) carried a table of data about Manchester School and Florence Nightingale's famous graphics and report into the conditions faced by British soldiers of 1858 was among the earliest practices of using data graphics for storytelling. She developed the visual representation of information, including the pie chart, first developed by William Playfair in 1801. She also used statistical graphics in reports to Parliament, realizing this was the most effective way of bringing data to life. Data analysis and visualization has a long history. As Hammond (2015) noted, "the 'big difference' (between data visualization in traditional print media and that in data journalism) is that data used to come in the form of very expensive books, whereas now there are 'spreadsheets and files formatted for computers'... The change is understood to be basically technical, a matter of old analogue formats being superseded by new digital technologies" (p. 410).

Data journalism has become more established. In 2011 data journalism as such was very much a field "in the making", with only a handful of people using the term. It has subsequently become socialized and institutionalized through dedicated organizations, training courses, job posts, professional teams, awards, anthologies, journal articles, reports, tools, online communities, hashtags, conferences, networks, meetups, mailing lists and more.

Some scholars also proposed ways to study the evolution of data journalism. Loosen et al. (2017) argued that one way of tracing the evolution of data journalism as a reporting style is to look at its output. Loosen (2021), after exploring the relationship between the datafication of society and a datafied journalism, introduced awards as a means to study the evolution of data journalism. According to him, all social domains rely increasingly on an ever more diverse range and greater amount of data; "journalism's function is an observer of society, and so the more the fields and social domains that journalism is supposed to cover are themselves datafied, the more journalism itself needs to be able to make sense and produce data to fulfil its societal role".

Studies on its evolution make clear the continuity and change of data journalism. Such a diachronic perspective sheds light on what legacies data journalism carries on and what its unique features are.

1.5 Summary

In this chapter, we first had a brief review of the development of journalism, particularly by looking at its relations with technological advancements. In terms of the application of technology in human communication, we identified four stages: the print news era, the radio or wireless news era, the cabled or television news era and the digital or online news era. The contents and styles of news reporting at these stages are greatly impacted by the technologies applied to collect and produce news and the medium to transmit and spread news. We then gave a working definition to data journalism and data news respectively. Data journalism is a prominent label which refers to a diverse set of practices which can be empirically studied, specified and experimented with from different perspectives, and data news is the product of data journalism that is instantiated as multimodal discourses or artifacts. Data visualizations and verbal texts are the key components of data news. Finally, we reviewed the relevant existing research on data journalism from the production side.

The reviews reveal three points which are important and inspiring for the present study.

1.5.1 The Role of Technology in Meaning-making Processes

All methods or technologies for moving information over distances more effectively—from the use of writing and the printing press to the telegraph and railroad—have contributed to the expansion of human societies and to the extension of bonds of identity and interests (Stephens 1988: 279). This holds true for the computer and the Internet which have brought the online media. They have brought at least two salient changes in the production and representation of discourse.

First, interactivity. Today's new technologies promise a more real-time, multi-platform news consumption, accessible to almost everyone and anywhere via Internet livestreaming (Salaverria & de-Lima-Santos, 2020; Uskali 2018). Then, technologies have brought increasing adaptability and advanced personalization of content. The increasing interactivity may influence the enactment of the relationship between data news/its producer and the viewers.

Second, hypertextuality. A news discourse is usually presented with multimodal modes on multimedia and linked with other discourses through hyperlinks. The series of texts that are connected by links is a hypertext, which offers the readers different pathways to the online contents and so is non-linear in its textual organization. The changes in reading path and textual organization may have impact on the organization of contents.

From the semiotic perspective, the technologies involved have expanded the meaning potentials of semiotic modes. Then what role does technology play in the meaning-making process of data journalism? How can its contributions to meaning making be conceptualized from the consumption perspective? In other words, from which perspective can we approach the role of technology in the interpretations of news discourses, particularly multimodal data news which include dynamic and interactive visualizations?

1.5.2 Multimodal Nature of Data News

Human beings communicate or exchange information in many ways or modes: verbal language, body language, music or pictures. Though they primarily communicate through speech and written discourses, other semiotic modes also play and are playing an increasingly important role. Data news with verbal texts and images like photographs and data visualizations, are multimodal in nature. They are discourses made into meaningful story or argumentation in the same way as speech or verbal text is used. Various images including data visualizations, drawings, pictures and photos perform are important meaning-making resources in data news. They perform a design function as well as an informative one (Giles & Hodgson 1990: 75).

Acknowledging the fundamental feature of multimodality has two implications. First, it means "subscribing to the view that data visualizations are more than simple combinations of pie charts, scatter plots and other graphs with decorative illustrations and typographically-emphasised text" (Hiippala 2020). The meaning making process and meaning potential of data visualizations should be described. This means that we need to take a multimodal approach, describing the meaning potentials of each semiotic mode involved and the interaction between the semiotic modes involved so as to reveal the meaning-making processes in data visualizations. In other words, two questions are to be addressed: What meanings can be conveyed by data visualizations? And how do different semiotic modes in multimodal data news interact to create coherent data news?

1.5.3 Genre Shift in Data Journalism

Data journalism has inherited the scientific and data-based approach, the scientific objectivity, the emphasis on statistics and quantitative analysis, and the cause-analysis and problem-solution pattern in reporting. The storytelling style of data news is influenced by the "quantitative turn" as noted by Coddington (2015) and it has shifted from telling stories to deducing factual conclusions, which is more similar to a social investigation report (Wu 2017; Zeng et al. 2017). Perhaps it is due to these features that Wu (2017) argued that data journalism is not purely narrative, but more similar to a research report in social science. But how is such a genre shift reflected or realized in multimodal data news? How can we conceptualize a model to describe and interpret such a shift from a semiotic perspective? These are other new questions to be explored.

The linguistic and multimodal studies on news discourse have put forward more systematic theoretical frameworks to the description and interpretation. In linguistics and semiotics studies, especially in Systemic Functional Linguistics, there are well-developed theories on genre which can provide a theoretical basis for the genre study of data news. To answer all these questions and to build up a theoretical framework for analyzing multimodal data news, we will have a review of studies on multimodality and on news discourse in the next chapter.

Chapter 2 Data News as Multimodal Discourse: The Consumption Side

The present chapter will focus on the interpretation of data news as multimodal news discourses, which we refer to as the consumption side in opposition to the production of data journalism as outlined in Chapter 1. Data news is the output or product of data journalism and consists mainly of verbal texts and data visualizations. In this chapter, we will first review the studies on data news and data visualizations from the consumption side, then those on multimodality and news discourses as the two fields can offer insights for questions raised in Chapter 1 and lay the foundations for building up a theoretical framework for analyzing multimodal data news.

2.1 Discourse Analysis of Data News

There has not been much research exploring the discursive features of data news. Weber et al. (2018), Xing (2019) and Hannaford (2022) are what we can find in the literature. Weber et al. (2018) took data news as a new form of storytelling and identified seven key discursive features of journalistic data stories: data, the communicative function, the textual-visual relationship, structure and design of a story, interactivity, and the meta-story. These findings contribute to the narrative or discourse approach to data journalism, yet as the findings are based on interviews with editorial leaders, data journalists, developers, and designers in 26 major news organizations in Europe, the study is, in effect, from the practitioners' perspective or the production side.

Xing (2019), with *America Under the Gun* (one of the 72 Data Journalism Award finalists in 2013) as the data, analyzed the differences of participants and their realizations in semantic density and semantic gravity by integrating SFL's discourse semantic systems and LCT's dimension of semantics. The analysis shows that the discursive pattern of participants and the realizations is quite different from those in non-data news reports, which reveals different semantic features of the participants in data journalistic reports. According to the study, semiotic entities and thing entities are selected more frequently in the data, and generic reference resources are selected quite frequently. Such a discursive pattern is closely related to the semantic gravity and semantic density of the text: symbolic entities and thing entities realizing specialized fields are of relatively high semantic density and low semantic gravity; generic references can lower the participants' semantic gravity. These semiotic resources enhance the generality and abstractness of the data news discourse. This study focuses specifically on the discourse semantic patterns of data news, but the meaning configurations at the level of context have not been discussed.

Hannaford (2022) applied Foucault's distinctive conceptualization of discourse to investigate how data journalism knowledge is produced, the practices that reinforce it and the strategic power relations it conceals. She highlighted the inbuilt material injustices of the established power structures data journalism appeals to and then called for more attention to power relations in journalism education. Her research focuses on the social practices or "non-language 'stuff'" (Gee 2000: 7) rather than language or semiotics in use, namely the verbal text and data visualizations in data news.

2.2 Social Semiotic Studies on Data Visualization

In contrast to the lack of studies on data news as a new genre and as multimodal artefacts, research on data visualization from a social semiotic approach abounds.

2.2.1 Visualization of Culture

Different kinds of data visualization have become privileged signs to mark the rationality of particular processes and promote specific attitudes towards various aspects of everyday life (Aiello 2020). They have become so popular and prevalent that Beer and Burrows (2013) argued that we have witnessed the rise of a "culture of visualization" across spheres of social activities and cultural productions: "There are not many things that have yet to be visualized and archived." (Beer & Burrows 2013: 62) People generate, create and consume data both actively and passively through their engagements with popular culture, and consequently various forms of data are lending themselves to various forms of vernacular social research, particularly in the sphere of visualization. Ledin and Machin (2018) held a similar view, though they did not use the term "a culture of visualization". They argued that diagrams, charts, and other types of visualization are often used not only to illustrate how things are but also, above all, "how things should be done" (p. 335). Precisely because of the increasing social significance of visualizations, there is a growing body of academic literature centered on critical, practical, and combined approaches to their formal and overall qualities (Aiello 2020). The following section will focus on studies from the social semiotic perspective as the present study is mainly concerned with the discursive features of data news as a multimodal discourse or artifact.

2. 2. 2 Data Visualizations as Social Semiotic Resources

Among the abundant studies on data visualization from a social semiotic approach, the book *Data Visualization in Society* edited by Martin Engebretsen and Helen Kennedy (2020) is perhaps the latest seminal work. The articles in the collection draw on a range of conceptual and theoretical resources and have carried out "multidisciplinary and multifaceted academic conversation concerning the forms, uses, and roles of data visualization in society" (Kennedy & Engebretsen 2020: 25). The first three chapters sketch out three significant issues or theoretical perspectives that concern the study of data visualizations: epistemology, semiotics, and politics, respectively. The chapters in the second section deal with data visualizations in private and professional settings, e.g., in weather reports, social media analytics companies, and for people with disabilities, not specifically dealing with data news. The chapters in the third section focus on the skills needed to engage with and make sense of data visualizations. The fourth section of the book, called "Data Visualization Semiotics and Aesthetics", includes contributions which focus on the semiotic, aesthetic, visual, and stylistic dimensions of data visualizations and the ways these intersect with social and cultural considerations. The contributions to the final section, entitled "Data Visualization and Inequalities", focus on the political dimensions of the social and cultural embedding of data visualization. In spite of different topics and theoretical focuses in the chapters, the authors take "a discourse studies approach which combines the micro level with the macro level" (ibid: 26). They regard data visualization as an important instance of text-in-society and focus on the relations between the specific structures and forms of the semiotic artefact on the one hand, and the social, technological, and cultural contexts which form it and are formed by it, on the other. However, not much research has tackled the interactions between verbal texts and data visualizations, nor the evolution of data news as a new genre.

Among the articles in the collection, some are worth special mention. First, Aiello's article "Inventorizing, situating, transforming: Social semiotics and data visualization" offers an overview of social semiotics as a productive framework for research on data visualization. It provides conceptual instruments that can be used to explore the relationship between the formal properties of data visualization and the meanings and practices that these may promote or hinder among users. Social semioticians are concerned not only with the politics but also with the potentials of semiosis. Aiello argued that social semiotics, with its ability to link texts with contexts, semiotic production with social action, and meaning with power, is an especially congenial framework for research on data visualization. She also proposed a three-step framework for doing social semiotic analysis of data visualizations. The first step in our social semiotic approach is to "inventorize" the semiotic resources that are typical of data visualization across media and contexts, namely, to identify and catalogue resources that are representative of data visualization as a whole. In her opinion, "this first step of the social semiotic approach may be interpreted as an attempt to outline a 'grammar' of data visualization design, or what Machin (2007) defines as a 'lexicon of elements that can be chosen to create meaning in combinations' and 'a finite system of rules' for their combination" (p. 56). The next step entails an attempt to situate data visualization resources in their social and cultural contexts, to find out what the major resources are and how these resources are mobilized in particular contexts and for specific purposes. The third and final stage in her social semiotic framework focuses both on the politics and potentials of data visualization to capture the ways major semiotic resources and their combinations can be transformed to promote particular forms of social action and social change. The study highlighted the necessity to describe exhaustively the "grammar" of data visualizations and to relate the meanings of data visualizations to context of culture and context of situation.

Another article worth mentioning is Tuomo Hiippala's "A multimodal perspective on data visualization", which discusses the multimodality of data visualizations, that is, how they combine multiple modes of expression, such as written language, photographs, diagrammatic elements, and illustrations, in various printed and digital media. He applied the idea of ergodic work proposed by Bateman et al. (2017) to analyze the different kinds of engagement between data visualizations and viewers. Ergodic work "emphasizes how participants co-construct the communicative situation they are interacting with/in and to what extent the participants may manipulate the situation" (p. 281) and draws attention to how data visualizations set up different types of communicative situations or registers. The study contributed to the theoretical conceptualization of the relations between register and semiotic modes as its realizations, though it did not venture into an in-depth description of the meaning potentials of data visualizations.

There are also other important studies. In the collaborative study on visualization conventions by a group of researchers led by Helen Kennedy (Kennedy et al. 2016), the researchers laid the foundations for a social semiotic approach to research on data visualization, with the explicit aim to understand how power works through some of the key semiotic resources found across visualization. They also identified four conventions which imbue visualizations with a sense of objectivity, transparency and facticity. The conventions are two-dimensional viewpoints, clean layouts, geometric shapes and lines, and the inclusion of data sources. Engebretsen and Weber (2017) have defined data visualization as a 'super-genre' that is used to accomplish a wide variety of communicative tasks across an increasing number of professional and institutional communities of users. They highlight that data visualization is multimodal, as it usually deploys multiple graphic modes including, for example, "typography, layout, maps, diagrams, and drawings" (p. 279) together with color as "an integrated component in all the other ones" (p. 279). Ledin and Machin (2018) examined different types of "data presentation" through a social semiotic lens, including lists, bullet points, line graphs, bar charts, and flow charts and proposed a general framework for the study of 'data presentation' as a semiotic material, or a particular form of communication set apart by unique affordances and canons of use. In the analysis, they identified a set of semiotic resources, namely paradigms, spatialization, vertical and horizontal orientation, graphic shapes and icons, temporality, and causality. Other studies focus on specific types of data visualizations such as diagrams (Ledin & Machin 2016a, 2016b; Bateman et al. 2017) and infographics (Bateman et al., 2017; Amit-Danhi & Shifman 2018). They argued for the existence of a diagrammatic mode (Ledin & Machin 2016a; Bateman et al. 2017; Aiello 2020), which can manifest itself both independently (e.g., through charts, graphs, and schematic drawings, or "self-standing" diagrams) but also in combination with other semiotic modes. Bateman et al. (2017) further explained that the diagrammatic mode can work together with other modes to "form composite units" that are often set apart by the "stacking" of elements such as labels and connecting lines over illustrations, maps, or photographs (p. 279).

A social semiotic approach takes data visualizations as discourse and as part and parcel of much broader semiotic practices. It highlights the bidirectional interaction or relationship between semiotic systems and context. On the one hand, social semioticians relate the semiotic systems to contexts of culture and situation to reflect on the social and cultural implications and constraints of meaning-making. On the other hand, they also stress the role which semiotic systems play in changing and shaping contexts, the "semiotic innovation which can contribute to engendering social change" in Aiello's wordings (2020: 51). Therefore, data visualizations as well as the data news that employs them should be and have already been interpreted within the larger and more abstract level of context. A social semiotic framework also contributes to a systematic investigation of semiotic resources like color and layout, for example, together with visualization elements like graphs and charts. The existing research has offered insights into and invites more research on the following questions:

- What are the meaning potentials of data visualizations?
- How may data visualizations be used in different social and cultural contexts?
- How do the broader power structures and work practices shape data visualization design?
- How are key semiotic resources used and interpreted by specific groups of people?

2.2.3 Data Visualizations in Journalism

Some semiotic studies also focus specifically on data visualizations in journalism, though the literature is not rich. Engebretsen and Weber (2017) explained that, in digital media, data visualizations "can be static and monologic, but they can also be dynamic and dialogic", be more or less explorative or open to interpretation, be pictorial or non-pictorial, with building blocks like photographs, illustrations, geometric shapes, and abstract motifs being equally available to visualization designers. Weber (2017) pointed out that with the emergence of "data journalism", new hybrid forms and patterns of interactive information graphics have arisen.

The study presents a theoretical framework that spans the basic characteristics and different types of interactive information graphics (see Table 2-1 for details). Weber (2020) analyzed various forms of narrativity in data visualization and, based on a corpus analysis of 73 data visualizations, described the basic visual elements that constitute narrativity: the instance of a narrator, sequentiality, temporal dimension, and tellability. Her study shed light on how data are transformed into visual stories, yet did not cover the multimodal meaning-making mechanisms in data visualizations.

Table 2-1 A Framework for Classifying Interactive Data Visualizations (Weber 2017: 252)

Category	*Criterion*	*Types*	*Patterns/hybrid forms*
Image	Types of imagcs	Diagram, map photo, video, drawing...	Pie chart, bar chart, table, timeline, cartogram...
Text	Five Ws: who what, when, where, why +one H: how	*How-type* *Who-type* *When-type*	What/when→timeline What/how→process diagram How much/where → choropleth map, cartogram
Structure	Linearity	Linear, nonlinear, linear-nonlinear	Step-by-step dramaturgy, explorative...
Feature	Interactivity	Low, medium, high	Linear interactivity, object interactivity, immersive interactivity
Producer/user	Communicative function	Narrative, explicative, descriptive	Hyper comic (narrative), how-to diagrams (descriptive-explicative)

To sum up, data visualization and data news have drawn an increasing attention, but the current research has not yet fully benefited from the interdisciplinary perspective that defines most of the current research on multimodality (Hiippala 2020). Similarly, research on data news has not fully benefited from the various perspectives on news discourses. Studies on the multimodality in human communication in general and in news discourses in specific can shed lights on how meanings are realized multimodally in data visualizations and become interpretable across a wide range of different media. They can also offer insights into how meaningful combinations of written language, illustrations, photographs, diagrams, maps, layout, and other modes of expression work interactively to create data news and contribute to the evolution of genres. There remains a wide and open research space for these questions. Therefore, in the next two sections, we will review the major studies on multimodality and news discourses to benefit the present study on data news as multimodal discourses or artcfacts.

2. 3 Studies on Multimodality

Studies on multimodality are extremely rich and diverse. There have been various attempts to find analytical methods or frameworks for investigating multimodal discourse interpretation. Since our final goal is to interpret the meanings communicated in data news as a genre of multimodal discourse, we need to elaborate the approaches to understanding what a multimodal discourse is communicating and how it does so. The analytical perspectives that we review in this section are accordingly drawn from different approaches to multimodal discourse analysis, but mainly from the Systemic Functional approach. Then, as the present study will focus on data news with verbal texts and images, the review of multimodal studies in this section concentrates on the relevant aspects, namely studies on images, intermodal interaction between image and text, and multimodal genre.

2.3.1 Approaches to Multimodality

Jewitt (2014) pointed out that multimodality has been taken up within four main disciplines: Systemic Functional Linguistics (SFL hereafter), social semiotics, anthropology, and conversation analysis, and combinations of these.

SFL takes language as a social semiotic (Halliday 1976) and is primary concerned with "what language does, and how it does it, with a focus on the linguistic choices present in a communicative utterance" (Jewitt 2014: 129). One of the focuses is to describe the meaning potentials of different semiotic modes at the strata of discourse semantics, lexicogrammar and graphology. Just as Jewitt (2014: 130) commented, "SFL development of multimodality aims to produce a meta-theory capable of theorizing semiotic resources, their functionality and meaning potential, and their integration in multimodal phenomena that are interpreted in the context of situation and culture."

Halliday's idea of social semiotic and his metafunctional theorization of language have been extended by scholars like Gunther Kress and Theo van Leeuwen to the study of images (Kress & van Leeuwen 1988, 2006). According to Jewitt (2014), (the) social semiotic approach to multimodality uses a flexible notion of grammar, with a focus on people's situated use of resources rather than emphasizing the system of available resources. But this approach also focuses on the relations between context and the instantiated multimodal discourses created by the users. Moreover, the approach mainly takes SFL as its theoretical foundation.

In our understanding, both the SFL and social semiotic approaches are concerned with the meaning potential of semiotic resources distributed across strata (i.e., context, discourse semantics, lexicogrammar and phonology, and typography/graphology) and the theory/analysis of the integrative meaning of semiotic choices in multimodal discourse. Besides, SFL serves as the main theoretical basis for current multimodal discourse analysis (Zhu 2007; Painter et al. 2012). Therefore, we borrow O'Halloran's (2008a) label "Systemic functional-multimodal discourse analysis" (SF-MDA) to cover the two approaches in Jewitt's categorization.

Anthropology, according to Jewitt (2014), has been developed into a diverse interdisciplinary field combining cultural studies, linguistics and sociology. Its analytical focus is on the bi-directional relations between communicative practices and the social context, namely how communicative practices come to have meanings and how the use of communicative resources presupposes and creates social relations in cultural contexts. This bi-directionality is inherited and further developed by SFL scholars and social semioticians as well.

Conversation Analysis, developed by sociologists in the USA in the 1960s, is "known for its detailed, moment-by-moment transcription and analyses of speech" (Jewitt 2014: 127); but now, there is an increasing amount of research on the multimodal features of people's communication which includes speech, gesture, and facial expressions. "Conversation analysts define their work in terms of interaction and action rather than communication or multimodality" (ibid: 128), but undoubtedly talk and oral communication are multimodal and "have been reconfigured or adapted by technology-remediated environments that re-orientate face-to-face communication (e.g., video conferencing)" (ibid).

Besides these approaches, there have been studies following the cognitive approach, which focuses on the interpretation of multimodal metaphor and metonymy in multimodal discourse like cartoons and advertisements from the perspective of conceptual metaphor and metonymy (See section 2. 3. 2. 2 for more detail).

Based on the above review, we argue that there are mainly three approaches: the SF-MDA approach, cognitive approach, and conversation analysis (CA approach). As the present study focuses on data news with images and written texts, we will not go into detail about the CA approach and will focus more on the achievements made by systemic functional or social semioticians, whose analytical models or perspectives are the major contribution to developing the present model.

SF-MDA, drawing on and complementing the model of language provided by SFL, has provided rich and extensive research on various semiotic modes or modalities: 1) 'grammars' of image (Kress & van Leeuwen, 1996, 2006), displayed arts (O'Toole, 1994), sound (van Leeuwen, 1999), movement (Martinec 2000, 2001), three-dimensional space (Stenglin 2004, 2008) and film (Bateman, 2007, 2009); 2) "discourse semantics" of picture books (Painter 2013), images (Economou 2006, 2008; Caple 2009a, 2013), film (van Leeuwen 1991; Tseng 2009; Tseng & Bateman 2011), TV news (Feng 2015) and advertisements (Tan 2009); 3) "expression form" of language and images, namely graphology and graphic elements (Kress & van Leeuwen 1996; van Leeuwen & Jewitt 2001; Lim 2004; van Leeuwen 2006); 4) intermodal interaction or text-image relations (Lemke 1998; Royce 1998; Lim 2004; Martinec & Andrew 2005; Kong 2006; Royce 2007; Bateman 2008; Painter et al. 2013; Zhang & Wang 2016 etc.); and 5) multimodal genre (Delin et al. 2003; Bateman 2008, 2014; Hiippala 2012; Xing 2012; Bateman et al. 2017; Hu & Li 2018). We will have a more detailed review in sections 2.3.2, 2.3.3 and 2.3.4.

2.3.2 Meanings in Images

As images contribute to the multiplication of meanings in multimodal discourse, it is of great necessity to have a systematic analysis of their meanings. There have been various attempts to decode the meanings in different types of images: Barthes' penetrating study of the meanings in news photographs and the text-image relations in them, Forceville's (1998) cognitive study of pictorial metaphor in advertising and then multimodal metaphor in various genres of multimodal discourses, and various studies of multimodal discourses drawing on notions from SFL—studies of various semiotic modes, studies on image-text relations, and studies on multimodal genre. The semiotic modes described include images (Kress & van Leeuwen 2006; Painter et al. 2013, et al.), display arts (O'Toole 1994), films (Bateman & Schmidt 2012; Tseng 2013), and video games (Bateman et al. 2017). We will focus more on the achievements made by systemic functional semioticians, whose analytical models or perspectives are the major contribution to developing the present model.

2.3.2.1 Barthes' Two-ordered Photographic Message

In talking about meanings in images, we need first to mention Barthes' idea of the two-ordered photographic message. Barthes (1977) conducted a foundational study of the meanings in press photographs, which are seen to be a mechanical analogue of reality rather than an "artistic" product. He decodes their meanings through two orders: the first-order denotative meaning and the second-order connotative meaning. The denotative meaning is the "*analogon*" of reality of a photograph, and the connotative meaning is "the manner in which the society to a certain extent communicates what it thinks of it" (p. 17). He argues that the description of a photograph consists precisely in joining to the denoted message the connoted message.

Barthes' denotative meaning roughly corresponds to the Kress and van Leeuwen's (2006) representational meaning, whereas his connotative meaning is the communicative value above the representational content, which is decoded by referring to context and ideology. His analysis does not interpret the pictorial meanings comprehensively, for it does not consider the layout arrangement as meaning potential in image. In addition, his analysis is confined to photographs only, and does not consider the meanings in other types of images, such as cartoons, diagrams and data visualizations.

2.3.2.2 Cognitive Approach

There have been cognitive studies of metaphors and metonymy in multimodal discourses with image and verbal text as well as their persuasive effect. Forceville (1996) argued that metaphors can occur in pictures, more specifically in printed advertisements and billboards. He defines a visual metaphor in terms of the replacement of an expected visual element by an unexpected one. He adapts the Jakobsonian model of the communication with its six components—message, channel, code, context, communicator, and addressee—and examines how these elements are combined and interacted in an advertising situation. He makes a distinction between text-internal and text-external elements of context to show the role context plays in the interpretation of advertisements generally, and of pictorial metaphors occurring in them specifically. With these components, he then proposes a theoretical framework for decoding these pictorial metaphors by combining Black's interaction theory of verbal metaphor with the insights of Sperber and Wilson's relevance theory. He also proposes a subdivision of pictorial metaphors with one pictorially present term (MP1), pictorial metaphors with two pictorially present terms (MP2), verbo-pictorial metaphors (VPMs), and pictorial similes. Jeong (2008) tested the persuasive effects of visual metaphors in advertising and finds that visual metaphors may be more persuasive due to both visual argumentation and metaphorical rhetoric. Sobrino (2017) proposed a framework to "incorporate the investigation of multimodal metonymy and the patterns of interaction between metaphor and metonymy arising in advertising" (p. 12) and thus to complement the existent research on multimodal metaphor.

These studies are mostly concerned only with the images or pictures in printed advertisements. There are also studies on decoding the metaphors and metonymy in newspaper cartoons and other genres of images. Refaie (2003) explored the ways in which metaphors are expressed in the visual mode, more specifically in newspaper cartoons. He suggested that visual metaphors are best described in terms of their underlying metaphorical concepts, rather than in terms of their surface realization as defined by Forceville (1996). He also suggested that metaphors must always be studied within their socio-political context for "the differentiation of 'literal' image and a visual metaphor is never absolute but it will always depend on the discourse context and on the degree to which particular metaphors have become accepted as the 'natural', commonsensical way of representing certain meanings" (Refaie 2003: 90). He concluded by suggesting that the specific form in which a metaphor is expressed may have an important influence on its meaning and impact. Bounegru and Forceville (2011) studied how metaphors systematically structure concepts in multimodal discourses. They analyzed 25 metaphors that structure a sample of 30 political cartoons pertaining to the global financial crisis. They found that political cartoons pertaining to the global crisis rely heavily on pictorial and multimodal metaphors, and that these are rooted in conceptual metaphors. Forceville and Urios-Aparis (2009), the first book-length study to investigate multimodal occurrence of metaphors, offered case studies in a variety of discourse genres (advertising, cartoons, films, comics, and music, etc.) and provided ideas and methodological angles enabling further theorizing and testing in the rapidly expanding field of multimodality. Zhao (2019), drawing on theories such as conceptual metaphor, metonymy and blending in cognitive linguistics, analyzed the construction, mechanism and representation patterns of verbal-pictorial irony. Zhao (2022), by integrating cognitive analysis of multimodality and ecological discourse analysis, investigated the representation of ecological stance in some English political cartoons on bioenergy and proposed an analytical framework of multimodal metaphor scenario-based ecological discourse analysis.

These studies capture the metaphorical meanings in various discourses with images. However, they are not applicable to capture "literal" or "congruent" meanings in images, on which metaphorical meanings are based.

2.3.2.3 SF-MDA Approach

There have been studies of pictorial meanings at three strata: grammar, discourse semantics and expression form. These serve as the bases for the analytical model for analyzing data news, particularly the various types of images in data news, so we will give a more detailed introduction of the studies at the three strata.

(1) The Stratum of "Grammar"

① Visual Grammar or Grammar of Visual Design

The most widely applied framework for systematic analysis of pictorial meaning potentials is perhaps that of visual grammar developed by Kress and van Leewen (2006). This framework is applicable to analyze the meanings of different types of images in different multimodal genres. The two authors applied the theoretical idea of metafunction from the work of Michael Halliday (Halliday 1994/2000) and built a system for the description of the ideational, interpersonal and textual resources in visuals/images ("visuals" refer to images in their study).

A. The Ideational/Representational Meaning

The visual mode offers a set of choices of different ways in which participants and their relations to other participants can be represented—this is the representational or ideational meaning. Generally speaking, the representational metafunction in visuals is realized by two kinds of structures, *narrative* structures which present "unfolding actions and events, processes of change, transitory spatial arrangements (Kress & van Leeuwen 2006: 79), and *conceptual* structures which represent "participants in terms of their more generalized and more or less stable and timeless essence, in terms of class, or structure or meaning" (ibid).

Each of the two structures has a set of choices of processes and participants. In narrative processes, the participants are "represented as doing something to or for each other" (2006: 59), and the relation of two participants could be visually realized by vectors, visual realizations of the "action verbs" in language and usually formed by depicted elements that form an oblique line, often a quite strong diagonal line. Thus, different kinds of narrative process can be distinguished on the basis of "the kinds of vector and the number and kind of participants involved" (2006: 63). When images or diagrams have only one participant, the resulting process is *non-transactional*, as the action "has no 'Goal', is not 'done to' or 'aimed at' anyone or anything" (ibid). When the action is done to some participant in the image or diagram and it has a Goal, a *transactional* process is presented. When the two participants in a transactional process each now play the role of Actor, now the role of Goal, it is a *bidirectional* process and the participants are called Interactors. When "the vector is formed by an eyeline, by the direction of the glance of one or more of the represented participants, the process is *reactional*" (67), and the participant who is the source of the eyeline is termed Reacter, and the participant who the eyeline is directed at Phenomenon. When transactional processes are presented in a chain and a participant is the Goal with respect of one participant and the Actor with respect to another, they are *conversion* processes and the participants Relay. When the content of thought or speech is not represented directly, but mediated through a Reacter, a Senser (in the case of a thought balloon), or a Sayer (in the case of the dialogue balloon), then they are *mental* processes and *verbal* processes respectively.

As in language, narrative processes in visuals may contain secondary participants which are related to the main participants. Kress and van Leeuven (2006) refer to these participants as Circumstances, following Halliday (1994). The Setting, or Locative Circumstance, is recognizable because of contrasts in color saturation overall darkness or lightness between foreground and background, even though it is often drawn or painted in less detail, or has a softer focus. The Means of a process is formed by the tool with which the action is executed. An Accompaniment is a participant in a narrative structure which has no vectorial relation with other participants and cannot be interpreted as a Symbolic Attribute.

Conceptual structures contain *Classificational* Processes, *Analytical* Processes and *Symbolic* Processes. Classificational processes "relate participants to each other in terms of a 'kind of' relations, a taxonomy: at least a set of participants will play the role of Subordinate with respect to at least one other participant, the Suprordinate" (2006: 79). Analytical processes "relate participants in terms of a part-whole structure" (2006: 87). They involve two kinds of participants: Carrier (the whole) and any number of Possessive Attributes (the parts). Symbolic processes are "about what a participant means or is" (2006: 105). When there are two participants, the Carrier and the Symbolic Attribute, and the symbolic meaning is established by the relation between the two participants, we call the process Symbolic Attributive. When there is only one participant, the Carrier, and the symbolic meaning is established as "being conferred to the Carrier", we call it Symbolic Suggestive.

B. The Interpersonal/Interactive Meaning

The interpersonal or interactive metafuntion is about the relations and interaction between the interactive participants, i. e., the producer and the viewer, and the relation between the interactive participants and the represented participants (the people and objects represented in the images). As in the case of the ideational meaning, there is a set of choices for representing different interpersonal relations. The relations are realized by the systems of CONTACT, SOCIAL DISTANCE and ATTITUDE.

If the represented participants look directly into the viewer's eyes, then vectors are formed by participants' eyelines, and *contact* is established and it results in a "demand", the participant's gaze demanding something from the viewer. If there is no eye contact, then it results in an "offer", the picture offering the represented participants to the viewer as items of information.

The choice of *distance* between the interactive participants and represented participants is related to the "size of frame", the choices between close-up, medium shot and long shot. Generally speaking, intimate or personal social distance is realized by the close-up, social distance by medium shot and impersonal by long shot.

The selection of an *angle* provides the potential to express the viewer's attitudes towards represented participants. The frontal angle invites the viewer's involvement, while the oblique angle implies detachment. High angle can realize the viewer's power, low angle the power of the represented participant and eye level equality between them. There are also pictures which encode an objective attitude. The usual way of these pictures is a directly frontal or perpendicular top-down angle. These angles "neutralize the distortions that usually come with perspective, because they neutralize perspective itself" (Kress & van Leeuwen 2006: 144).

Other interpersonal choices are the system of *modality*, which contains means of expressing "meanings of truth and falsehood, fact and fiction, certainty and doubt, credibility and unreliability" (2006: 154). Modality is interpersonal rather than ideational because it "produces shared truths aligning readers or listeners with some statements and distancing them from others" (2006: 155). Modality is a cline running from the high modality to the low. We have to note that modality "rests on culturally and historically determined standards of what is real and what is not and not on the objective correspondence of the visual image to a reality in some ways independently of it" (2006: 163). Therefore, when we analyze the modality of an image, we have to take into consideration the coding orientation, the different reality principles. Kress and van Leeuwen list four code orientations: technological, sensory, abstract, and the common-sense naturalistic. For the time being, common sense naturalistic coding remains the dominant in our society.

Modality in naturalistic coding is generally realized by *modality markers* or cues: 1) Color saturation, 2) Color differentiation, 3) Color modulation, 4) Contextuali-zation, 5) Representation, 6) Depth, 7) Illumination, and 8) Brightness. Naturalistic modality increases as articulation of these markers increases, but for color saturation, modulation and differentiation, the articulation reaches its highest value at a certain point and thereafter it decreases again.

C. The Textual/Compositional Meaning

According to Kress and van Leeuwen, the textual or compositional meaning relates the representational and interactive meanings of the image to each other through three interrelated systems: INFORMATION VALUE, SALIENCE and FRAMING. One thing to be noted is that the choices in the systems of SALIENCE and FRAMING are in graded contrasts, in "more-or-less" rather than "either-or" relation.

1) **Information value**. The information of an image can be presented as centred or polarized. The centered value is usually realized by circular or triptych arrangement, and by center-margin or mediator-polarized arrangement. The polarized information is usually realized by a horizontal

polarization or vertical polarization. The horizontal polarization realizes the Given/New information structure, i. e., the element on the left is the Given information and that on the right the New information. The vertical polarization realizes the Ideal/Real information structure, with the element on the top being the Ideal and the one at the bottom the Real.

2) **Salience**. Attentive use of foreground/background placement, different sizes, contrasts in tonal value, and differences in sharpness can make the elements attract the viewer's attention to different degrees.

3) **Framing**. "The presence or absence of framing devices disconnects or connects elements of the image, signifying they belong or do not belong together in some sense" (p. 177).

Kress and van Leeuwen construct a system network to describe the metafunctional meanings and their realizations in images, but they stay at the grammar level and do not take into consideration the levels above, i. e., the register and genre, and the level below, the "word" level (to borrow the term from linguistic description) or the level of expression form. Furthermore, they do not discuss the differences in different types of images. They focus on the images and do not elaborate much the interaction between images and verbal texts. Their framework can be applied to the analysis of images but has to be improved if multimodal texts with writing and images are to be analyzed. However, their pioneering work has inspired scholars and linguists to enhance systemic functional theory and models for the analysis of multimodal discourses.

② Grammar of Press Photographs

Caple (2013) drew on the grammar of visual design and conducted a detailed analysis of press photographs from with a dataset of 100 press photographs published in *The Sydney Morning Herald*. Caple took press photos as a new genre in journalism, photojournalism in the terms of media practitioners. Drawing on the visual grammar framework, the systems of meaning-making for press photographs are described around the three metafunctions (Halliday 1994; Kress & van Leeuwen 2006).

As visual structures in the press photography data are narrative structures "presenting unfolding actions and events, processes of change, transitory spatial arrangements" (Kress & van Leeuwen 2006: 79), Caple(2013)'s analyses focused on narrative structures and adapted the ideational systems of visual grammar to describe the phenomenon that representational structures in press photography almost invariably involve participants/ processes and circumstances. The author changed the square "or" bracket to a curly "and" bracket to allow for simultaneous choices of both Processes and Circumstances, and altered the brackets around Settings, Means and Accompaniment to allow more detailed description of news photos.

When analyzing the interpersonal meaning in press photographs, Caple not only gave a detailed description around the three simultaneous systems of CONTACT, SOCIAL DISCTANCE and ATTITUDE, but also highlighted "the combination of the configurations of meanings simultaneously occurring across these systems" (Caple 2013: 73). For instance, when the gaze of the represented participant enters into a demand relationship with the viewer, such images also tend to enact intimate to social relations of Social Distance as well as involvement through being photographed from a frontal angle. This means that along the dimension of instantiation, choices from these systems form certain kinds of inter-system coupling (See "A coupling perspective" in section 2. 3. 4 for more detailed explanation of coupling).

When analyzing the compositional meanings in press photographs, the author argued that the systems of INFORMATION VALUE, SALIENCE and FRAMING "apply not only to individual pictures but also to multisemiotic texts, where images combine with other texts and images on a page" (ibid: 80) and layout can be viewed as "the glue that holds the other two metafunctions together to make a complete and cohesive whole" (ibid: 80). Her framework for compositional metafunction is quite different from Kress and van Leeuwen's.

Salience can be realized in a photograph "through variations in the size of the represented participants (in relation to other elements in the image), colour, sharpness/depth of field, foregrounding/backgrounding and overlap with other elements" (ibid: 81). Framing, like Salience, is a matter of degree of connection and can relate both internally (between elements in the image frame) and externally (between images/stories on the page). Internally, framing can be achieved through the use of vectors, or lines, to separate or connect elements, or by grouping elements together to create a single unit of information. Externally, framing can be used to relate the image/story to other parts of the page through the use of strong or weak framing devices. Caple pointed out that applying the meanings of Given/New, Ideal/Real becomes more problematic when we examine the compositional configurations of types of texts other than advertisements. It is hard or improper to understand participants in polarized images as being Given/New or Ideal/Real. So, Caple, drawing also on ideas from the visual arts, proposed an alternative system, the Balance network, which also takes aesthetic value into consideration. Studies in visual arts highlight the clarity of visual information and how this is achieved through the use of principles like the Golden Mean, the Rule of Thirds and Dynamic Asymmetry. By taking these into consideration, Caple established the Balance Network (see Figure 2-1). The system is made up of two simultaneous systems. There are two basic patterns of organizing elements within the image frame to create a visual unit of information. The option [isolating] captures the first pattern, namely someone or something is singled out and made the focus of our attention while the [iterating] option the second, the regular, repeated pattern between several elements and their

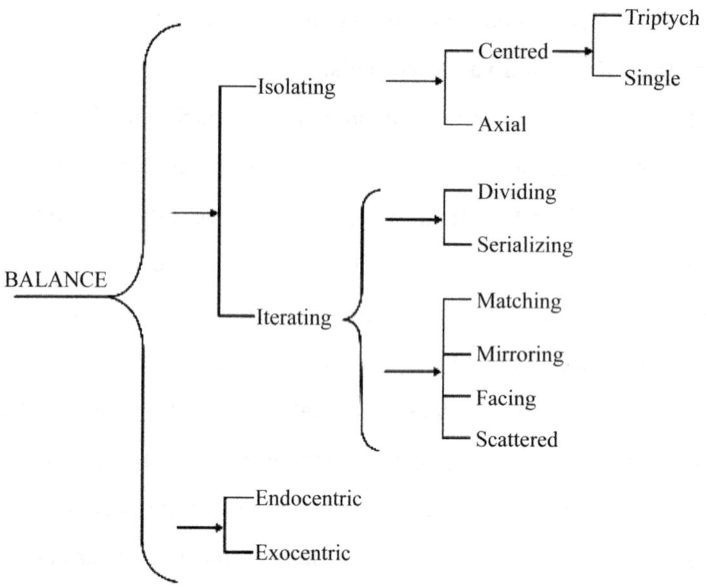

Figure 2-1 The Balance Network (Caple 2013: 97)

position in relation to each other. The iterating pattern can be a relationship between just two elements in the frame, (the option of [dividing]), or many (the option of [serializing]). When two elements in the image frame are captured doing the same thing, this can be taken as a matching relationship. When two elements are turned towards each other, this can be taken as a facing relationship. When elements are reflected in a surface, be it a mirror, water, glass or any other reflecting surface, this is a mirroring relationship. When elements, usually more than two, are more randomly configured, this can be a scattered relationship. A scattered option only occurs in the serializing relationship; this is indicated by the If/Then (I/T) labels next to [scattered] and [serializing]. The subsystem of ISOLATING has two options. When an image has a single element in the center and the viewer is expected to focus on/engage with the single element, this forms an isolating single configuration. When "the main focus of attention may remain on the centrally located element (thus it is isolating) but this central element is also shown in relation to two separate elements either side of it" (ibid: 106), this can be seen as a triptych relation. As can be seen, Caple's choices in the system network emphasize the relationships between the elements in the image, rather than relationships between the image and the viewer. Caple's Balance network generalizes the meaning patterns of attention focus when viewers view and interpret an image.

Like those in the visual grammar, the systems are applied to the analysis of a single image, not a composite visual text consisting of a series of images.

(2) The Stratum of Discourse Semantics

① Visual Narrative in Picture Books

Painter et al (2012) analyzed picture books with a sequence of images, rather than a single image. They built on Kress and van Leeuwen's visual grammar for analyzing the "grammar" of single images, but more importantly, they also moved to the discourse level by looking at the affectual and ambient dimensions of interpersonal meaning, character relations and action relations construing representations/ideational meaning, as well as framings and focus groups composing textual meaning. Their framework, though based on visual grammar, is established by extending the discourse semantic systems of language to the analysis of meanings in images. The framework can be applied to describing the meaning potential of news photographs and adapted to describing data visualizations, which in many cases consist of several single images. So, we will give a detailed review of their analysis.

A. Enacting Interpersonal Meaning

Like language, images can also enact social relations. The relations enacted include those between viewers and characters depicted in the image and between depicted characters themselves. In pictures books, these relations can be enacted through systems of PROXIMITY, ORIENTATION, FOCALIZATION, PATHOS/AFFECT, AMBIENCE, and GRADUATION.

The degree of closeness between depicted characters and between characters and viewers is very relevant to the way readers or viewers read the social relationships between the depicted characters. The system of SOCIAL DISTANCE in visual grammar captures the social relations between viewers and depicted characters (or represented participants in Kress and van Leeuwen's term). According to Kress and van Leeuwen (2006: 124-129), choices in SOCIAL DISTANCE are realised by the "size of frame"—in other words by the presentation of the character in "close up" as against "mid shot" or "long shot". In picture books, characters can also be presented in full-length depictions, mid shot, long shot, or a combination of them in depicting the same character to push forward the narrative. But besides the viewer-character relations, the depicted characters are also "involved in social relations with one another" (Painter et al. 2012: 16). Therefore, Painter et al. proposed the system of **PROXIMITY** to describe "the closeness or otherwise of the characters to each other in the image at any moment in the narrative" (p. 16). Characters depicted in picture books can be separated from one another by space, placed in close proximity or even touching/hugging. If two characters are separated from one another, readers can infer the distant or cold relations between them; if they very often have body touch or hug, an intimate or close relationship is realized. In this sense, the system of **PROXIMITY** is an extension of that of SOCIAL DISTANCE.

The system of **ORIENTATION**, parallel to that of INVOLVEMENT in visual grammar, takes into account the bodily orientations of the depicted characters to describe the social relations. According to Kress and van Leeuwen (2006), depicted characters or represented participants can be approached by viewers from a horizontal, oblique, horizontal oblique, or vertical angle, which creates a certain viewing position and involve viewers to different degrees. For instance, a horizonal front angle achieves a maximum sense of viewer involvement in the depicted world, whereas an oblique angle suggests a more detached relationship between viewers and depicted characters. Besides the viewer-character interaction, there are also different degrees of involvement and power between depicted characters: "Whatever their orientation to the viewer, two characters may face each other directly in the depiction, be placed side by side (suggesting solidarity if close), or angled away from each other, perhaps even in a back-to-back orientation." (Painter et al.: 17) And just as a vertical angle of viewing realizes the power relation between viewer and depiction, so two characters may enact a comparable relation if one is depicted looking up to or down on another character.

The system of **FOCALIZATION** is a reinterpretation and elaboration of Kress and van Leeuwen's system of CONTACT and is very much concerned with the viewing perspectives on the depicted world, or the "viewing personas" (Painter et al. 2012: 18) of the viewer. The viewer can be positioned as an outside observer or a viewer "'participating' fleetingly in that world through a relationship with, or identification as, one of the characters" (ibid). Different from the "demand" and "offer" choices in visual grammar, the opposition between the presence and absence of gaze in picture books can be construed as indicating whether the viewer has been positioned to engage with the character via eye contact, or just to observe the depicted participant. This becomes the primary opposition within the system of focalization, between the two features [contact] and [observe]. The choice of [contact] may be more delicately classified as either [direct] or [invited], because it may be used to introduce the reader to the characters in the opening image without any verbal use of second person address or overt melding of story world and viewer's world. Then, the viewer can be positioned to see through the character's eyes, simply through visual choices. The visual option of viewing through the eyes of a character is termed [mediated], as opposed to the [unmediated] option when the reader observes or makes contact without being positioned as a character.

The system of **PATHOS / AFFECT** is realized by the styles of character drawing that are interpreted as realizing a system of reader alignment (pathos) and as affording particular ways of presenting a character's emotions or affect. Painter and his co-authors identified three major styles in picture books—minimalist, generic and naturalistic, and the caricature style with "hyper-real" quality or "eerie unreality" (ibid: 34). The caricature or hyper-real style realizes an alienating reader alignment in which viewers "feel the otherness of the characters without the sympathy conjured by others who are like us" (ibid: 35). By contrast, the minimalist, generic and naturalistic styles are more engaging, though to different degrees because of their different degrees of detail and realism of drawing. In broad terms, the minimalist style for a human character does not need to maintain accurate facial or body proportions and—in its extreme form—has minimal depth, so the depiction of emotion in this style is highly schematic. The generic style is more detailed, with the brush or pencil strokes based on the musculature of the human face, and the emotional repertoire is therefore extended with more "behavioral" emotions enabled. It creates characters of the "everyman" type. Many picture books using this style are likely to be more injunctive in nature, implicitly expecting the child readers to see themselves in the protagonist role and to "be/do like this". The naturalistic is the most subtle, restrained and nuanced of all and the expressions are to be read much as are those of real people. The emotional repertoire that can be suggested therefore extends to the nuanced, impressionistic, ambiguous and indefinable. In picture books presented in the naturalistic style, the reader engages with the characters as individuals rather than as types, and through that sympathetic engagement with the other/s in the story the reader is led towards ethical discernment. Depicted gestures and bodily stance are also key in the representation of affect.

The system of **AMBIENCE** is "a visual meaning system for creating an emotional mood or atmosphere, principally through the use of colour" (ibid: 35). It creates "the most instant bonding effect" (ibid: 35) on the viewer. There is a continuum between bare line drawings with no ambience, drawings that include shading, hatching or dotting to create some texture and solidity with minimal ambience, and finally those that emphasise lighting effects to create a greater sense of atmosphere. Accordingly, in the system of **AMBIENCE**, first is the choice of [ambient] or [non-ambient]. Outline drawings are interpreted as non-ambient choices. When ambience is "activated", there are three core systems: VIBRANCY, WARMTH and FAMILARITY, all of which are available simultaneously and are realized by dimensions of color. The system of VIBRANCY depends on the depth of saturation to the colors used. Full or high saturation—the choice of [vibrant] from the network—creates a maximal vibrant effect, while a [muted] choice within vibrancy creates a gentler more restrained feeling. In the system of WARMTH, the warmer colors, such as red and yellow hues are in contrast with cooler blues and greens. Choices here may depict hot and cool physical environments but are also used to reflect emotional shades. The system of FAMILARITY is realized by the amount of color differentiation in the image. The basic principle is that the more different colors are present in the image, the greater the sense of the familiar, since we usually experience the world day to day in all its variety of color. If, by contrast, an image is restricted to one or two hues, or to modulations of a single color, the effect of meaning of being "removed" from the normal, everyday world is realized. If the images, excluding outline drawing, are entirely in black and white, the ambience is downplayed rather than entirely absent.

The system of **GRADUATION** is the way to scale up or play down attitudinal meanings in images. The term "graduation" is borrowed from SFL work on appraisal and is about grading evaluation in language. Economou (2009) extended the linguistic graduation to work on the evaluative meaning of news photographs and proposed corresponding systems of VISUAL GRADUATION. In picture books, graduation can be realized by three choices of quantification: [quantification: number], [quantification: mass/amount] and [quantification: extent]. For instance, a crowd of people can be a choice of upscaled quantification [quantification: number] which can invoke viewer's emotional response more strongly than the case of a single character; an unrealistic large or small size of a character in comparison with other elements [quantification: mass/amount] can realize the power of the character; and eating a dinner of sausages may not trigger negative evaluation from the viewer, but if the sausages and/or the eating activity (ideational meaning) occupy an excessively large or small amount of space, a case of [quantification: extent], negative evaluation about the eater can be triggered. Quantification choices often work together with other interpersonal choices and can play an important role in ensuring an attitudinal response in the viewer. The system of **GRADUATION** is comparatively underexplored and there is much room for further research.

Photographs in data news realize interpersonal meanings in ways similar to those in picture books. For data visualizations, the ways may be different. We will elaborate on them in the following chapters.

B. Construing Ideational Meaning

The systems construing ideational meaning include those depicting characters (participants in visual grammar) and their relations, those depicting actions and their relations, as well as circumstances and their relations.

a. Depicting Characters

In picture books, **the identity of the character** can be construed in images mainly through the participant's physical features or attributes both in a single image and in relation to the story sequence. Even conceptual images which lack vectors can invite interpretation of the participant's attributes, including symbolic attributes. These attributes can help readers infer the participant's identity categories, such as age, class, ethnicity, social roles and social status. **Character attribution** is typically realized by analytical and symbolic processes in the "clause" rank of images. In picture books, this type of images can occur at the beginning of the story to introduce the character(s), or at moments when the rhythm of the story calls for a pause or a reflective moment rather than a depiction or evocation of action and movement. They can also be used to guide the child in reading for significance rather than simply recognition of the character in action.

Then characters can be recognized and tracked in the stories through choices in the two simultaneous systems of **CHARACTER MANIFESTATION** and **CHARACTER APPEARANCE**. In a purely visual story, a character is inferred to have the same identity when salient features of his/her appearance are repeated in subsequent images. Usually this means that at least the head is depicted again so that facial features and hair can aid recognition; this is the realization for the choice of [complete] in the system of CHARACTER MANIFESTATION. More experienced readers can also recognize a character simply from a depiction of a body part and/or shadow/silhouette, the [metonymic] representation in the system of CHARACTER MANIFESTATION. A character can reappear in the very next image or at some later point in the story. A reappearance that occurs immediately strengthens the inference of "same identity" compared with a later reappearance that may rely much more strongly on mediation by the verbal text, hence the choices of [immediate] and [later] in the system of CHARACTER APPEARANCE. The place of reappearance may be significant for the theme of the story. Character reappearance can also demonstrate a character's status variation in picture books. The option of [unchanged] means that the character is depicted recognizably the same in appearance and status as previous depiction. The option of [varied: status] can be used to symbolize a character's changing status as a protagonist by depicting the character by means of differrent circumstantiation. Character reappearance can also involve variations in a character's attribution which may have different descriptive details and symbolic significance.

(Re)appearance of each character serves for recognizing and tracking them with the same function as the IDENTIFICATION system which Martin and Rose (2003/2007; 2007/2014) proposed for analyzing linguistic texts. But "... the principal means of 'tracking' a character within a visual picture book narrative is by inferring identity from the reappearance of the face or salient features of the depicted participant. In other words, it is necessary to construe character identity from the ideational representation rather than from a system of deixis: it is through ideation rather than phoricity that we recognize the characters" (ibid: 60). Therefore, explicit and implicit reappearance realizes ideational meaning rather than textual meaning as interpreted in Tseng (2009). Such observations also bespeak the different affordances of images and verbal texts.

Relations between characters include co-classification and comparison. Being spatial and compositional in nature, the visual semiotic is especially well adapted to enabling comparison and contrast (ibid: 66). A symmetrical presentation of comparable images on the page is a way of "covertly" constructing them as members of the same class (Kress and van

Leeuwen 2006). Such co-classificational relation is found not just between/among different images, but also within a single image where, for example, characters are lined up in a row. Characters in images can also be compared and contrasted by attributes/accessories of different characters (the option of [attributive]) or similar shape and contours of different characters (the option of [configurational]). Comparison and contrast can ALSO occur in single or adjacent images (the option of [concurrent]) or be done with characters from previous appearances in image (the option of [retrospective]).

Many picture books aim at telling stories, so it is expected that the majority of their images to constitute what Kress and van Leeuwen (2006) refer to as narrative processes; or in other words to depict some kind of event or activity and thus to contain oblique lines or vectors. The types of activity include: non-transactional action realized by vectors such as body movement, transactional action between two characters realized with vectors pointing at one character, verbal activity realized with speech bubbles as vectors, and mental activity. There are two options realizing mental activities: cognition realized by thought bubbles and perception with vectors like gaze.

Besides the activities depicted in a single image, the way one activity relates to another in successive images is another key aspect. Choices of different activity sequences constitute the INTER-EVENT system network. The expansion and projection relations in language are also found in images of picture books, though with far fewer subcategories available than for language and fewer resources. The expansion relation is renamed as "unfolding" in the visual activity sequence. "Activity sequence can be of different sizes, whether construed verbally or visually." (ibid: 73) That is to say, an activity sequence can be construed as a series of successive images, each depicting of moment of this activity sequence, or as a single image. Hence the options of [succession] and [simultaneity]. A picture narrative book also involves the relation of counter-expectancy and a relation of causality to be inferred between the actions of different characters in the image. However, in images, "reading a causal relation between two depicted events will always be a matter of inference, dependent on our understandings of how actions relate to one another and on our ability to interpret the reactions of depicted characters" (ibid: 74). Projection relations appear in mental and verbal activities. Where the projection of speech is concerned, a visual image can only form part of a multimodal (visual-verbal) figure, since speech itself can only be construed explicitly by language. The situation is a little different with the representation of thoughts and perception because they can be represented as image.

b. Depicting Circumstances or Settings

Images in picture books may include a setting which functions ideationally to provide details of the physical environment in which the characters act or an activity occurs. Circumstantial meaning in an image is predominately concerned with specifying the details of spatial location, although the depiction of clocks, lighting, the moon, and so on, may also be used to show location in time. It is necessary to consider not only the individual image and what, if any, circumstantiation is depicted, but what relations there are between successive images. The system generalizing the options for these relations is called INTER-CIRCUMSTANCE. When we consider them from the point of view of the circumstances depicted, the settings of successive images can be in consistency (the choice of [sustain degree] or changed (the choice of [vary degree]. The consistency or changes can be in the degree of circumstantial detail and consistency or change in the location itself that is important. In the subsystem of VARY DEGREE, there are the choices of [decontextualize] and [recontextualize]. "In the case of variation, a shift to decontextualize by removing any background setting brings any depicted participant into focus, highlighting and provoking appraisal, while a shift to recontextualize returns our attention from the depicted participant to the story as a distinct imagined world and affords tone-setting ambience." (ibid: 80) In the subsystem of SUSTAIN DEGREE, there is the option to maintain the same context [maintain context] or to change and depict a new location [change context].

c. Composing Textual Meaning

Let's begin with the arrangement or layout of the verbal text and the image in a single or double-page spread. Painter and his colleagues name it the system of **INTERMODAL INTEGRATION**. The single or double-page spread is regarded as a kind of "macro" frame, within which other frames may be present. Within the macro frame, the verbal text or verbiage is a visual unit and so is the image. The verbiage can be overlaid onto the image or separated out into its own identifiable space in the layout. These basic alternative forms of intermodal integration are identified as [integrated] and [complementary], respectively.

Within the subsystem of **COMPLEMENTARY**, three aspects of arrangement can be identified: the type of polarized layout, the "weight" and the adjacency of either visual unit. The choices from the three aspects are in both-and relation, so there are three simultaneous systems named AXIS, WEIGHT and PLACEMENT, respectively. In the system of AXIS, the visual and verbal components can be facing each other horizontally (the choice of [facing]) or adjacent to one another vertically in descending "layers" (the choice of [descending]). In the system of WEIGHT, three possible forms of arrangement are identified: verbal text and image are given the same amount of visual space([equal]), the verbal text occupies more space ([verbiage privileged]), or the image occupies more space ([image privileged]). In the system of PLACEMENT, there is the possibility of side-by-side, or "interpolation" of text by image or image by text. An interpolating layout can serve to punctuate the story, staging the visual and verbal material to provide the desired rhythm for the telling.

Within the subsystem of **INTEGRATION**, verbiage and image can be integrated to form a visual unity in two distinct ways: either by utilizing the choice of [projected] or that of [expanded]. "Where the verbiage is presented in a speech or thought 'bubble'... a multimodal figure is created, which in terms of ideational meaning comprises a depicted projector and a verbal projection. This form of integration is therefore referred to as [integrated: projected]." (ibid: 98) The second major type of integrated layout, the [expanded] choice, has two subtypes ([instated] and [reinstated]), with [instated] being easily the most common in picture books. The choices of [integrated: instated] can create fusion between text and image, guiding the reader to view the two as an integral whole. The [reinstated] option means that the verbiage is presented on the picture but instead of being subsumed into the image, it appears on its own distinct background strip or panel.

We now move to the layout of the image. There are two aspects to be considered: how and whether the image is framed (the system of **FRAMING**) and what information focus is formed by the different forms of layout (the system of **FOCUS**).

In the system of **FRAMING**, "the basic choice is whether the image extends right to the page edge as an 'unbound' image or whether there is a margin of space fully or partly enclosing it, rendering it 'bound'". Where an image is unbound, there is in effect no boundary (other than the page edge). There are two choices within the subsystem of UNBOUND: [contextualized] and [decontextualized]. In unbound contextualized image, the setting fills a page while unbound decontextualized images are framed by the white background of the page. In decontextualized images, the character(s) rather than the imaginative story world become(s) the focus of attention throughout. Bound images are those set within a page margin or border. They can "demarcate the story world as more distinctly separated from the reader's world than unbound ones and may also serve to 'contain' or confine the character" (ibid: 105). Within the subsystem of BOUND, five simultaneous systems of choices are identified by the authors. The authors did not name each system, but only listed the options they had identified in the picture book. We can see that there is much room for further exploration. The options identified are: [refocalized], [ambient], [limited] vs. [surrounded], [contained] vs. [breaching], and [framed]. If a character is outside the image, this "allows for a past and present representation of a character simultaneously and signals a refocalization, reinforcing the fact that the depicted 'flashback' in the main image constitutes the memory of the character shown in the margin" (ibid: 105), thus the choice of [bound: refocalized]. The margin of a bound image may also afford interpersonal meaning: it can create ambience through the choice of color, thus the choice of [ambient]. In terms of the extent of the margin, the margin may extend only from a single picture edge, thus limiting the area contained by the main picture (the choice of [limited]) or enclose the main picture (the choice of [surrounded]). The margin may be intruded upon by part of the image (the choice of [breaching]), or it may totally hold the image in "confinement" (the choice of [confined]). A bound image can also be distinctly framed within that margin, usually by a defined black or colored line, thus the option of [framed].

Boundaries formed by spreads, pages, margins and frames can function to "enclose and delimit focus group—visual elements placed in a compositional relation so as to be apprehended at a glance, with each such 'eyeful' constituting a pulse of information" (ibid: 109). The **FOCUS** network describes the principal choices found in relation to spatial organization and pictorial information structure in images from picture books. "[T]here are two basic and contrasting focus options. Either a focus group can be placed in or balanced around a center in various ways—the [centrifocal] option, or else it may consist of same/ similar ideational elements repeated in a series across the image—the choice of [iterating]." (ibid: 111) There are two options within the subsystem of ITERATING, namely [aligned] and [scattered]. In the former case, the elements are nearly always organized in fairly regular "lines", whether vertical, slanted or horizontal, while in the latter, the elements scatter on the page without regularity. A centrifocal focus group "can take a number of forms, with the principal contrast being between the features [centered] and [polarized]". An image can center on a single character, drawing the viewer's gaze to that participant in an unambiguous way (the option of [simple]), or on a central element or space with additional elements (the option of [extended]). A simple centered image can also serve as an effective way to introduce a character. The polarized compositions can be realized by balancing or opposing different depicted elements on a diagonal, vertical (top/down) or horizontal (left/right) axis, which are the features of [diagonal] and [orthogonal]. In some cases, there are vectors (e.g., character gaze) strongly guiding the reader to "'take in' the focus group at a single glance as a cohering unity" (ibid: 116), thus the option of [deictic vector]. A polarized focus group has one further option, where the depicted elements in a polarized relation "mirror" one another. This is most likely "when a character looks at their reflection, a choice which signals that issues of identity and self-worth are at stake in one way or another" (ibid: 118). Along the hierarchy of stratal realization, the Center/ Margin, Given/New, and Ideal/Real information structure in visual grammar (Kress & van Leeuwen 2006) are the main realizations of the

FOCUS system.

One thing to be noted is that in the visual systems, the options are often in a continuum or "cline" rather than categorical opposition. Therefore, when drawing the systems with features in non-categorical opposition, scholars usually follow the tradition of tilting the square brackets.

Feng (2015) introduced the visual narrative framework to Chinese readers. He thought that the detailed system networks are significant for the more systematic analysis of complex multimodal discourses.

To sum up, the description of visual meanings and their realizations in picture books is detailed, systematic and applicable to other types of images with characters, like photographs, paintings and caricatures. The theorization process and the systems described also demonstrated that meanings in images are also organized with different levels of abstraction. But the framework may have one limitation: when building up the systems and realizations, they mainly focus on images with "narrative representations", disregarding images with "conceptual representations" (Kress & van Leeuwen 2006). These deserve further research as images with conceptual representations, like diagrams, maps, and data visualizations, are also widely applied in various genres for different generic goals.

(3) Discourse Semantic Analysis of News Photos

Bednareck and Caple (2012) offered a quite detailed description of the meanings in news photos, though their focus was news values in images. The authors outlined the following aspects of news images that construe news values. These aspects present mainly the resources for evaluation, conjunction, and reference in news photos and so are better interpreted from a discourse semantic perspective.

1) Evaluative elements. The central place and size of a depicted

personality, the angle of photographing, attributes like uniforms and official regalia indicating status can construe the news value of Prominence. If the character(s) in the central place is/are surrounded or flanked by lawyers, the ideational meanings can also invoke the news value of Negativity. This may also indicate that evaluation meanings in images can be invoked by ideational meanings. From the explanation, we can see that central place and size of a depicted personality are based on the layout choices in the compositional system network of visual grammar (Kress & van Leeuwen 2006) and can be interpreted as the realizations of the FOCUS system in visual narrative proposed by Painter et al (2012). The angle of photographing is based on the choices of viewer power, equality and represented power in the interactive system network and is also related to the ORIENTATION system realizing interpersonal meaning in picture books. Certain attributes can symbolize the social status of a character; this symbolization is realized by symbolic processes in visual grammar and can be regarded as a choice in the system of CHARACTER ATTRIBUTION in visual narrative.

2) Intensification. "An image that serializes/repeats information in the image frame (e.g., a line of soldiers bearing arms, rather than focusing on one solider) is a device for intensification and as such can construe Superlativeness. Similarly, photographs depicting the aftermath of natural disasters can be intensified by including many, repeated participants." (Bednareck & Caple 2012: 59) These are the realizations or choices in the QUANTIFICATION systems of GRADUATION in visual narrative.

3) Comparison. This can be depicted by "placing elements of differing sizes next to each other" and so construe the news values of Superlativeness and possibly Novelty. The effect of such comparisons can be further intensified and even exaggerated by manipulating technical elements in the camera. Reinterpreting this from a discourse semantic perspective, we can

take comparison as a relation connecting activities in one image or between two images. And the choices of both comparison realizing logical ideational meaning and intensification realizing interpersonal meaning is a case of inter-metafunctional coupling (see Section 3.3.6 "Coupling and Commitment" in Chapter 3 for a more detailed explanation of coupling).

4) Reference to emotion. The authors relate news characters' emotional response to the news values ranging from Negativity (depicting negative emotions) to Personalization (an individual's emotional response especially when combined with the use of a close-up shot), Novelty (depictions of surprise/shock), Impact (in terms of caused emotions), to Superlativeness (depicting strong emotional responses). The authors' interpretation of characters' emotions from the perspective of news values opens up more space for the interpretation of the interpersonal meanings in photographs realized by the characters' facial expressions.

5) Negative elements. The depiction of negative events is the most common one and construes the news value of Negativity. Reinterpreted from a discourse semantic perspective, such depiction can invoke negative appreciation or judgement.

6) Reference to time and place. Easily recognizable geographical landmarks and architecture included in a shot may be used to construe Proximity (as may be cultural symbols like national flags). Seasons can be depicted through the inclusion of certain typical weather conditions as well as cultural artefacts (Christmas trees) and may thus construe Timeliness, Proximity and even Consonance. These aspects can be reinterpreted within the system network of ideational meanings in images.

7) Role labels. The mere depiction of well-known (and easily recognizable) celebrities and politicians construes Prominence. For less-recognizable figures like academics the recognizability of their roles can be enhanced by placing them in a particular context. This aspect can be

reinterpreted as the choices for exophoric reference for introducing and tracking characters.

8) References to individuals. A picture of an individual construes Personalization by rendering an abstract issue more personal, especially when that individual comes to represent an entire event; but a photo of celebrity construes Prominence [see point (7)] rather than Personalization.

9) Aesthetic elements. How participants are arranged in the image frame can impact on the balance and aesthetic quality of the image. This aspect can be reinterpreted as a factor constraining the choices of layout and design which realize textual metafunction. As it relates to norms or conventions shaped in the long history of aesthetics in specific cultures, it is better described and interpreted at the more abstract strata of context.

The study of news images has adopted a discursive approach and applied SFL theoretical ideas and terms to the description of news photos. A discursive approach means that the focus is "not on the 'nature' of news events, but rather on how such events are mediated through language and image—how news discourse makes them newsworthy" (Bednareck & Caple 2012: 52). These aspects are also applicable to describing meanings in other images in news discourses.

Other scholars have also conducted analysis of news discourses from the perspective of discourse semantics. The system of APPRAISAL has also been applied to the analysis of news photos or verbal-visual journalistic texts (Martin 2000; Economou 2006, 2008; Caple 2009a, 2013) and advertising campaigns (Tan 2009). Martin (2000) pointed out that prominent images in news discourses can function as a Macrotheme for the whole text, like a kind of topic sentence in verbal text. More than that, they also function as higher-order Interpersonal Themes. He likens this to the Comment Adjunct in language; both can thematize interpersonal meanings as well as topical (or representational) meanings. Economou (2006) compared two verbal-visual journalistic texts—one from a high circulation Greek newspaper and one from an Australian newspaper. The author argued that "the role played by prominent images in print media feature stories is a critical and primary one in positioning or orienting readers attitudinally towards the text that follows or accompanies the image" (Economou 2006: 211). In analyzing the evaluative role played by these prominent macro-thematic verbal-visual media texts, "Martin's suggestion of the higher-order interpersonal orientation of prominent images has proved a very fruitful approach" (ibid: 232), as have the appraisal systems. Economou (2008) applied the system of ATTITUDE to investigating naturalistic photos which introduce long, front-page feature stories in a weekend "news review" section of a Greek broadsheet and an Australian one. He concluded that, while photos introducing weekly news review feature stories clearly have a more evaluative aim than those accompanying daily news stories, they are selected and presented more attitudinally to pull readers into the ensuing long written feature story, and also, together with headlines, to position them on the issue explored in the following written story. Caple (2009a) focused on the evaluative effect of press photographs that are deployed in another type of news story genre, the image-nuclear news story. Tan (2009) applied the APPRAISAL system, or more specifically its subsystem ENGAGEMENT, to the analysis of an internet-based advertising campaign, though such applications are in their relative infancy compared to the extensive work on appraisal in language.

(4) Discourse Semantic Studies in Other Semiotic Modes

In addition to the application to picture books, some of the discourse semantic systems proposed for describing language have been applied to the study of other semiotic modes.

The IDENTIFICATION system has been applied to the analysis of textual meanings in other semiotic modes. Tseng (2009) proposed filmic identification and defined it as a multimodally extended version of Jim Martin's IDENTIFICATION discourse semantic system for verbal language. Tseng sees these techniques as being deictic in nature, pointing the viewer elsewhere for identity retrieval. In the view of Painter and his collaborators (Painter et al. 2012), by interpreting explicit and implicit reappearance as a deictic means for participant identification, Tseng locates these choices within the textual rather than ideational metafunction. Tseng and Bateman (2010) introduced the endophoric reference into film studies and considered audiovisual reference as a "reappearance" of filmic elements. Such reappearance is realized by presenting and presuming those elements across shots or scenes (Tseng & Bateman 2010: 222). Feng (2015) presents a generalized model of reference relations in the discourse of television news. The study analyzes reference patterns from the verbal track (verbal reference), the visual track (visual reference) and across the two tracks (visual-verbal reference) and classifies visual reference as personals (such as visual appearance), demonstratives (such as proximity and direction) and comparatives (such as similarity and difference). Their studies focus on how reference works in achieving cohesion. The present study concerns how the discourse semantic systems are realized semiotically in verbal texts and images and how the systems work interactively to realize the more abstract strata of register and genre.

These studies prove again the applicability of discourse semantics stemming from language to describe meanings in other semiotic modes.

2.3.2.4 The Stratum of "Expression Form": Graphology and Graphic Elements

Graphology and graphic elements are also meaning potentials in multimodal discourses. Writing (verbal text in data news in the present study) has typographic systems to make meanings and image has graphic elements—color, shape, line, angle, distance, etc. —to make meaning. Comparatively speaking, there is more literature on graphology, while less research is needed to describe the systems of the expression form of images.

Graphology is a linguistic level of analysis that comprises the study of graphic aspects of written language. In his article "Graphology and meaning", McIntosh (1961) introduced the term into linguistic studies on written language and took it a counterpart of phonology in the realm of spoken language. Later, Halliday et al. (1964) broadened the concept and connected it to spelling, punctuation and other resources for writing or printing texts. They said, "Graphology, however, is an essential part of the description of any written language... It has been chosen to parallel 'phonology', and the term includes orthography, punctuation, and anything else that is concerned with showing how a language uses its graphic resources to carry its grammatical and lexical patterns" (Halliday et al. 1964: 50).

According to Gómez-Jiménez (2015), the importance and status of graphology as a linguistic level of analysis is particularly prominent in stylistics and multimodality. Within stylistics, some scholars (e.g., van Peer 1993; Nänny 2001) have studied how graphological deviation may affect meaning and produce aesthetic effects. Within multimodality, there is currently an attempt to integrate some graphological elements into the study of modes of communication (Gómez-Jiménez 2015). Kress and van Leeuwen (2006), van Leeuwen and Jewitt (2001), and van Leeuwen (2006) have highlighted the semiotic potential of typography, and Nørgaard (2009, 2010) has delved into the creation of meaning through certain graphological elements such as typography and color.

Graphology and graphical elements contribute to the meanings and functions in a text and are "organized metafucntionally" (Lim 2004). Kress and van Leeuwen (2006) also note that graphical choices in the system of graphics (e.g., shape, line, angle, distance) are part of compositional/textual meaning which relates the representational and interactive meanings of the image to each other. Language (speech and writing/printed text) and images each have their functions and strengths which cannot be transcribed into the other. Therefore, the grammar and discourse systems of each need to be considered in relation to how they are organized to interact with each other to accomplish particular functions within a single multimodal text.

Typography is the most important and explored graphological system. It is the art and technique of arranging type in order to make language visible. The arrangement of type involves the selection of typefaces, font size, line length, leading (line spacing), adjusting the spaces between groups of letters (tracking) and adjusting the space between pairs of letters (kerning). In the field of design, graphics are visual presentations on some surface, such as a wall, canvas, screen, paper, or stone, to brand, inform, illustrate, or entertain. Examples are photographs, drawings, Line Art, graphs, diagrams, geometric designs, maps, data visualizations or other images. In the present study, graphic elements refer to the realizations of these types of graphics. The realizing systems of writing/printing and image materialize the meanings of the linguistic and pictorial resources into concrete visual entities presented on a page.

Lim (2004) presents two system networks of the common selections of Typography and Graphics (as graphics is also a type of image, we use the term "graphical elements") (See Figure 2-2 and Figure 2-3). Meaning can be created through the selections of the system of FONT or the system LAYOUT in typography. The term *font*, more traditionally referring to all the characters of a given typeface's style and size—for example, 9-point Times Roman italic would be a font of the Times Roman typeface family—

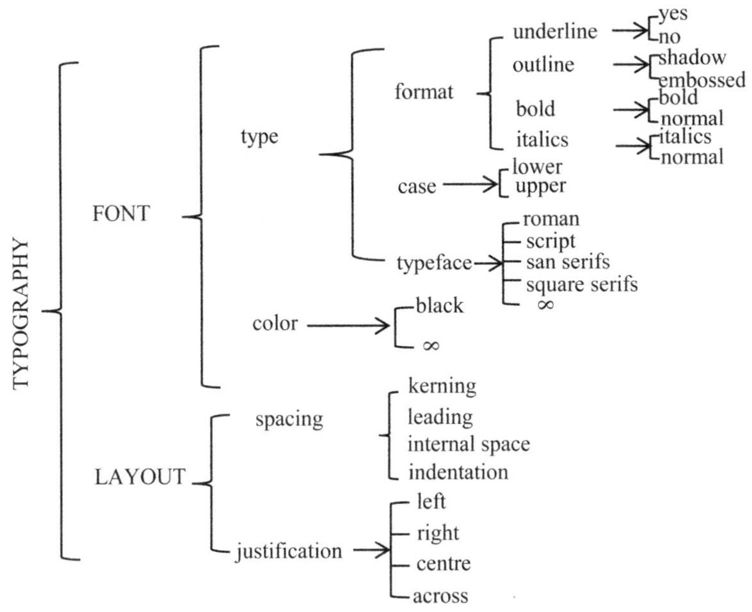

Figure 2-2 System Network for Typography①(Adapted from Lim 2004: 235)

has now become synonymous with typefaces. The system of FONT has three sub-systems, TYPE, SIZE and COLOR, each with its own sub-systems, as is presented in Figure 2-3. In the system of TYPE, there is a wide variety of choices ranging from serif types to sans serif types, and other novelty faces (Giles & Hodgson 1990). Of them, serif and sans serif types are the two major type families that are widely used. According to Giles and Hodgson (1990), Old English is referred to as Fraktur in Europe. It is commonly seen in newspaper mast-heads to achieve aesthetic effect. These are the alphabets derived from the hand-produced quill pen letters of the scriptoriums. Serif is an important range of old and new typefaces used

① We follow the conventions of drawing system networks in SFL: a brace symbolizing a both-and system of choices and a bracket [ ] an either-or system. See Chapter 3 for more conventions in SFL's system drawing.

in all manner of printing, which are characterized by letters that do not finish square on their strokes but carry a horizontal line or tail. Roman, Times New Roman and Century are among the widely used categories of serif type. Sans serif describes alphabets in which the letter strokes are without serifs and the characters have generally a uniform thickness and weight throughout. Helvetica, Univers, Grotesque, Franklin, Tempo, Futura and Metro are examples. Type families contain various weights and styles, such as lights, boldfaces, ultrabolds, italics and so forth.

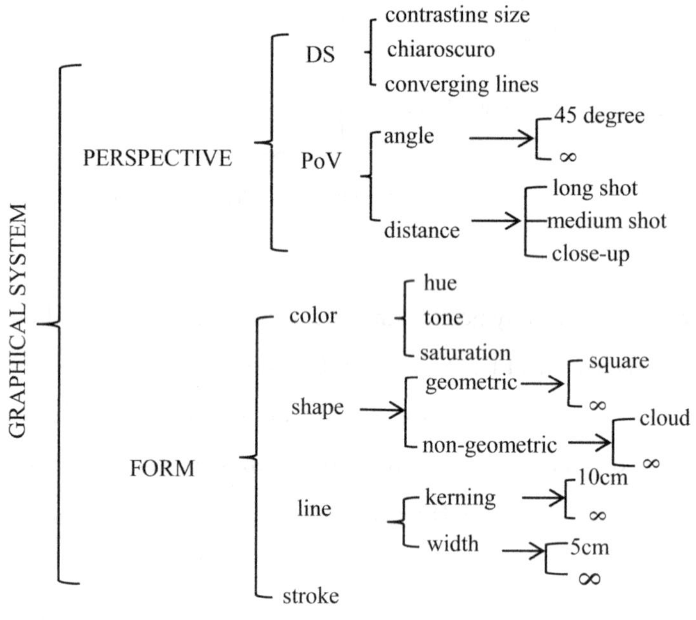

Figure 2-3 System Network for Graphics (ibid: 236)

The system of SIZE contains many options from 5 point to 72 point. The LAYOUT system has two sub-systems, SPACING and JUSTIFICATION. SPACING is about the choices of spaces between letters, words, lines, etc. Kerning is the space between letters; the internal space refers to the space between words; and leading is the spacing between lines, which include options for double or single space. Indentation, also indent, is a space left at the beginning of a line of print or writing. It " allows a clearer demarcation between paragraphs and functions primarily to signal a shift in direction or text-type from the preceding lines" (Lim 2004: 234). "The system of JUSTIFICATION is the alignment of the sentences." (ibid)

" As the meaning potential of particular systems is theoretically infinite, it is not possible to list all the possible options." (Lim 2004: 234) The two networks represented in Figure 2-2 and Figure 2-3 confine themselves to a few common selections for the purposes of exemplification.

Typography has long been used to impart meanings in writing/printing. For instance, capitalized initials are a convention to label a word or phrase as a technical term, instead of a common word. For instance, in SFL, typographic means are used systematically to differentiate functional labels from grammatical terms in representing systems in writing/printing. A term with capitalized initial is a functional label, while a term in lower case is a grammatical one (e.g., Process, Carrie, Attribute are functional terms, and nominal group, verbal group, determiner are grammatical labels). The different types of letters printed can also achieve different meanings. In newspaper design, according to Giles and Hodgson (1990), the Old English type is commonly seen in newspaper mast-heads to achieve aesthetic effect. (e.g., **The New York Times**); serif type, which are characterized by letters that do not finish square on their strokes but carry a horizontal line or tail, sometimes at a slight angle, may have the effect of adding dignity or authority to the letters. Much of the austerity of *The New York Times* stems from typography, for the type and layout indicate tradition and formality (Ludwig & Gilemore 2005: 127).

In addition to these studies, Bezemer and Kress (2009) provide an empirically based, social semiotic account of changes in textbook design between 1930 and the present day. They look at the multimodal design rather that at image or written language in isolation. They find that profound changes have taken place not just in the use of image but equally in writing, typography and layout. They explore how typography is used to represent an excerpt from a literary work and explore the layout of pages, including the page form and grid. Their research finds that, from the late 1980s, type face has begun to serve to separate out different curricular and pedagogic entities on the page and suggest that what these different entities are about: the "literary" effect of serif is used to represent poems. Handwritten font may be used to represent annotations, suggesting they are "notes", that is, provisional, unpolished. Instructions or exercises may be set in sans serif, suggesting they are transparent, straightforward, and unambiguous. Their research also finds that, with the increasing use of images in textbooks, there has been a clear shift from predominantly written, single-or two-column grid to a composition of (typo) graphically irregular writing and image-based elements placed fluidly on a two-page spread. They also argue that the layout suggests "assemblage", the bringing together of different materials and representations.

In images, as Kress and van Leeuwen note, graphic elements also realize metafuncitons. For instance, color saturation and tone are modality markers indicating different scales of modality or truthfulness of an image. But the expression forms of images are not systematically described.

To conclude, the studies from the above three perspectives demonstrated that there are also levels of abstraction of meanings in images, and hence there is necessity to describe images along the hierarchy of realization in language.

It should also be noted that color is repeatedly mentioned in the descriptions of images at all three strata. This is because that color itself is a visual resource that can serve all three metafunctions (Kress & van Leeuwen 2002; van Leeuwen 2011; Painter et al. 2012). Ideationally, color can be used to represent the appearance of things in the world, with green for grass, yellow for gold sovereigns, white for snow or purity, red for blood or passion, and so on. Interpersonally, different choices of color can arouse different emotional responses from the viewer, as is reflected in the system of AMBIENCE, which describes the different bonding effects on the viewer created in picture books. Textually, color may be used to frame different parts in an image or on a page or used contrastively to highlight or foreground some element within a composition to make it especially salient to the viewer. Repetitions of a color may be also used cohesively as a kind of visual rhyme to link different parts of a text.

2. 3. 3 Intermodal Interaction

There have been various accounts of the interaction between semiotic modes in a multimodal discourse. Some studies describe the relations based on precise observation (Barthes 1977), some draw on traditional rhetoric (Bateman 2008), others draw on linguistic accounts of inter-clausal relations in SFL (e. g. Lemke 1998; Royce 1998; Lim 2004; Martinec & Salway 2005; Kong 2006; Royce 2007), some approach the interaction from the perspective of coupling (Caple 2008b; Painter et al. 2013), and still others from perspectives other than the above mentioned (e.g., Norris 2004; Lim 2004; Royce 2007; Zhang & Wang 2016).

2. 3. 3. 1 Barthes' Study of Image-text Relations

The earliest linguistic study on photographic meanings and image-text relation should perhaps trace back to Barthes (1977). Barthes argues that the meaning of images and other semiotic modes is always related to and, in a sense, dependent on the verbal text. Images are too polysemous and floating by themselves and language is one way to fix the floating meanings of the image. He distinguishes two image-text relations: 1) extension, in which the verbal text adds new meanings to the meaning of the image, or vice versa; 2) elaboration, in which the same meanings are restated in a different way. According to him, there are two types of elaboration: 1) the verbal text comes first and so the image forms an illustration of it, and 2) the image comes first and so the text anchors or fixes the meaning of it, the anchorage relation.

His study can be said to be a foundational study of image-text relations. However, his view on images (news photographs) is what Kress and Van Leeuwen call "the old visual literacy" (2006: 23), in which visual communication is regarded as being subservient to language though he thinks that images have structures. In addition, his study of image-text relations is "based on a simple logic of three possibilities of how images and text relate to one another and relies on penetrating observation rather than on any specific realizations" (Martinec & Salway 2005: 341) and he fails to reveal the nature of intersemiotic semantic relations to explain "what features make multimodal text visually-verbally coherent" (Royce 2007: 63).

2.3.3.2 Rhetoric Structure

Bateman (2008), when building his GeM model, extends *Rhetorical Structure Theory* (commonly referred to as RST) to account for the meaning relations that can hold between and within document elements. He holds that just as segments of a text contribute to the text's coherence in systematic and specifiable ways, so can segments of a multimodal document, involving pictures, diagrams, and texts be related in an analogous manner. Bateman's description is fruitful to describe the hierarchical rhetorical structure behind the elements or parts in a multimodal document, which makes it different from studies from other perspectives. His description of asymmetrical and symmetrical relations is quite similar to the logico-semantic account of image-text relation we shall review in the next section. However, the relations he describes, especially the asymmetric relations, are not systematically distinguished and lack of generalization. In addition, the description does not capture the means or devices through which such rhetorical relations are built. Coherence is also achieved by use of cohesive devices. Standard examples are reference, lexical repetition and other lexical semantic relationships, such as hyponymy.

Caple (2008a) investigated the complementarity between the image along with its heading and the ensuing verbiage in image nuclear news stories in the *The Sydney Morning Herald*. The author described how nuclearity is established in these news stories before moving on to explain how the interpersonal metafunction within the systemic functional framework can be put to work in the analysis of this intersemiotic complementarity between the image, heading and verbiage. She also argued that the heading and image work together to provide the evaluative stance from which the story is to be read and it is through this interplay that the voice of the newspaper can be identified. The study applied RST to the analysis of image-text relations, but it actually focused more on the interpersonal meanings realized in image nuclear news stories.

2. 3. 3. 3 Logico-semantic Perspective

Lemke (1998) gave a detailed explanation of a scientific article with a diagram and text. In his analysis, he made no attempt to specify a system of intersemiotic relations between the diagram and text. However, thematic systems are adopted to model semantic patterns in language which could be used to integrated meaning realized by both verbal and visual representations. Following Halliday's metafunctional theory, he presented "various ways of intersemiotically relating the ideational, interpersonal and textual aspects of the image and text in the advertisement" (Martinec &

Andrew 2005: 339).

Combining Halliday's (1994) logico-semantic relations in clause complexes and Barthes' (1977) text-photograph relations, Martinec and Andrew (2005) presented networks of the image-text relations and their realizations. Just like the parataxis and hypotaxis relationships between clauses in a clause complex, images and texts have two statuses, equal and unequal. When one of them modifies the other, the modifying element is considered to be dependent on the modified one. Dependent or subordinate status has two subcategories: image subordination (image modifying the text) and text subordination (text modifying the image). Equal status can be further divided into independent and complementary. "An image and a text are independent and their status equal when they are joined on an equal footing and there are no signs of one modifying the other" and when an image and a linguistic text are "joined equally and modify one another, their status in considered complementary" (Martinec & Andrew 2005: 343).

As they observe, independent and complementary status are realized by the whole image being related to the whole text. Generally speaking, "the units related by status relations are the whole image and the whole text, or the whole image and a part of the text" (Martinec & Andrew 2005: 348). When an image and a text are independent, they do not combine to form part of a larger syntagm, but rather the information they provide exists in parallel—they each form their own processes. When the relative status of an image and a text is complementary, this is realized by them combining to form part of a larger syntagm. In most cases, this means that they play the role of participants in a type of process. Image subordination is realized by the image relating to a part of the text and text subordination realized by "deixis from text to image, either by reference items or present tense combined with material or behavioral processes" (ibid).

In language, there is a wide range of different logico-sementic relations, but they can be grouped into a small number of general types, based on the two fundamental relationships of 1) EXPANSION and 2) PROJECTION (Halliday, 1994). Halliday (1994) identified three main types of expansion—elaboration, extension and enhancement, and two main kind of projection—locution and idea. Likewise, the two main types of logico-semantic relations and their subcategories can be used to model image-text relations.

Kong (2006) identified the potential image-text relations by arguing for a multilevel description of their logico-semantic relationships. The relations he identified are largely the same as those identified by Martinec and Salway (2005). However, he identified a decoration relation in addition to the expansion and project relations. Furthermore, he identifies in more detail the sub-relations within the expansion system, but he does not explain the realizations of these relations. In his network, there are four sub-categories under elaboration: explanation (exposition in Halliday's SFL) which is equivalent to "in other words"; exemplification which is equivalent to "for example"; specification (clarification) which is equivalent to "to be precise"; and identification which is equivalent to "namely". Under extension, there are subcategories of collection, variation, sequence, response, and alteration. Collection is the addition of information by one unit adjoining to the other, just like the use of "and" in language. In the case of variation, one unit is regarded as being a total or partial replacement of another, similar to the function of "comparing and contrasting". Sequence is the chronological way that pictures and words convey ideas, without one subordinated to another. Alternation is different from variation in that one of the entities can completely replace another without losing any meaning. Response is embedded in the mode of question and answer. The enhancement relation is basically about the enhancement unit qualifying another unit by specifying time, purpose, condition, goal, etc. The subcategories of enhancement in Kong's network are different from Martinec and Salway's in that Kong's identification is based on the idea of symmetry of relations. The multiple, evaluative and metaphorical functions of the relations are also discussed.

The studies of image-text relations from the logico-semantic perspective regard verbal text and image as components in a unified multimodal text, just like clauses composing a verbal text. The image-text relations in a multimodal text are like the inter-clausal relations in a verbal text. Understanding image-text relations is an important step in analyzing the meaning of multimodal texts, and image-text relations are integrated into the present model. There is "just one very general reoccurring problem common to all current discussions. This problem consists in the fact that the organizational structures proposed are typically single relations between elements: for example, between a picture and the text functioning as its caption, or between a map and its legend" (Bateman 2008: 145). As a consequence, analyses collapse to a listing of text-image relations drawing together any elements, and any collections of elements, on a page that "appear" connected. Another problem with these studies is that lacking structure, they cannot go beyond surface descriptions.

2.3.3.4 A Coupling Perspective

Some studies (Caple 2008b; Martin et al. 2012; Painter et al. 2012; Martin 2017) applied the idea of coupling① proposed by Martin (2012/

① See section 3.3.6 in Chapter 3 for the definition and evolution of coupling and its application in the analysis of language.

2000①; 2008) to analyze intermodal interaction in multimodal discourses. Caple (2008b), based on a corpus of 900 image-nuclear news stories, examined the ways in which the words and images combine to make meaning from the perspective of instantiation and commitment. She found that the co-construal of meaning in image nuclear news stories occurs across two semiotic modes, that of verbal language in the heading and that of the visual representation of an event in the photographic image. In the article "The coupling of gesture and phonology" (Martin et al. 2012), Martin and his co-authors extended the idea of coupling to uncover the multimodal interactions of gesture and phonology in spoken discourse, but their focus was more on taking phonological structure as a useful starting point for analyzing gesture, not on theorizing coupling. In *Reading Visual Narratives* (Painter et al. 2012), coupling was further developed as a perspective to analyze the binding patterns of two or more meanings in two or more semiotic modes. In this foundational manuscript on intermodal interaction in picture books from a SFL perspective, coupling is clearly defined and more systematically elaborated. The authors defined coupling as the "repeated co-patterning within a text of realizations from two or more systems" (ibid: 143). They argued that, in principle, coupling can bc within or across metafunctions, as "the realization hierarchy radically underspecifies the ways in which systems from different strata, metafunctions and ranks combine with one another; it is the responsibility of instantiation to account for the way in which cultures enact patterns of interacting meaning" (ibid). In addition, coupling can happen within one semiotic mode or across semiotic modes. For instance, intramodally there can be a consistent

① In this quotation format, the time before the slash is the year when the book was republished in Chinese mainland, and also the edition quoted in this book. The time after the slash is the year when the book was published in countries other than China.

coupling of linguistic choices from two interpersonal systems such as graduation: force and attitude: affect/negative; multimodally, there might be a consistent co-patterning of particular ambience choices in the visual with complementary choices of positive attitude in the verbal (ibid). Be it convergent or divergent, coupling can make each semiotic amplify one another and thus multiply corresponding kinds of meaning.

Converging ideational couplings create concurrence, converging interpersonal couplings create resonance, and converging textual couplings create synchrony across all or part of the text. More recently, Martin (2017) applied the idea of coupling to analyze secondary school science and humanities discourse. He emphasized that couplings draw on meanings from different ranks, strata, metafuntions or different modalities and occur along the cline of instantiation as being complementary to analysis alongside the realization hierarchy.

Coupling occurs along the cline of instantiation and can be identified at each stratum along the hierarchy of realization, and thus multimodal discourses can be approached from both dimensions of realization and instantiation. As a result, the realization between context and different semiotic modes in a multimodal discourse can also be modelled. The coupling perspective on intermodal interaction offers a path for modelling multimodal genre.

2.3.3.5 Other Perspectives

Norris (2004) offered a methodological framework for multimodal interaction analysis. The framework aims to incorporate numerous communicative or semiotic modes in an analysis and links interaction to cognition. According to the author, multimodal interactional analysis grew out of interactional sociolinguistics, mediated discourse and nexus analysis.

Zhang and Wang (2016) reviewed the theories and methods of multimodal interaction analysis to Chinese readers. After discussing the characteristics and drawbacks of the framework, the authors proposed their own. Their framework involves five levels: context of culture, context of situation, interaction discourse, modality and media. These levels are of different abstraction and, like in language, a level of higher abstraction is realized by a lower level. The framework takes into consideration the hierarchy of realization, but the levels are not accurately named and it is not very clear what should be described at the levels of interaction discourse, modality and media.

Lim (2004) proposed the Integrative Multi-semiotic Model (IMM) as a "meta-model" for the analysis of a page or a printed text which involves the use of both language and pictures. The model demonstrates topologically the complex multifaceted nature of meaning made in a multi-semiotic text. As shown in Figure 2-4, the rectangular blocks are used metaphorically to represent the strata, planes and dimensions of meaning within and across language and visual images. The top view of the model displays the Expression plane referred to as "Typography" for language and "Graphics" for images. Below the Expression plane is the Content plane which consists of the lexicogrammatical and discourse semantics strata for language and the visual grammar and discourse semantics strata for images. The medium and materiality mediates the other planes and the interface between the text and the reader (the Expression plane). The Content, register and genre of the text are related to the materiality option of the medium (such as the type of paper and print used in a wedding invitation). Together these choices carry ideological implications. In-between the two semiotic modes is the Space of Integration (SoI), the elevated platform in the model, which incorporates the language and visual images. It is the "theoretical platform where intersemiosis occurs through contextualizing relations" (Lim 2004: 223). It is elevated above the language system and pictorial system, signifying the semantic expansions or "multiplications of meaning" (Lemke, 1999) that result from the interaction and negotiation between semiotic resources.

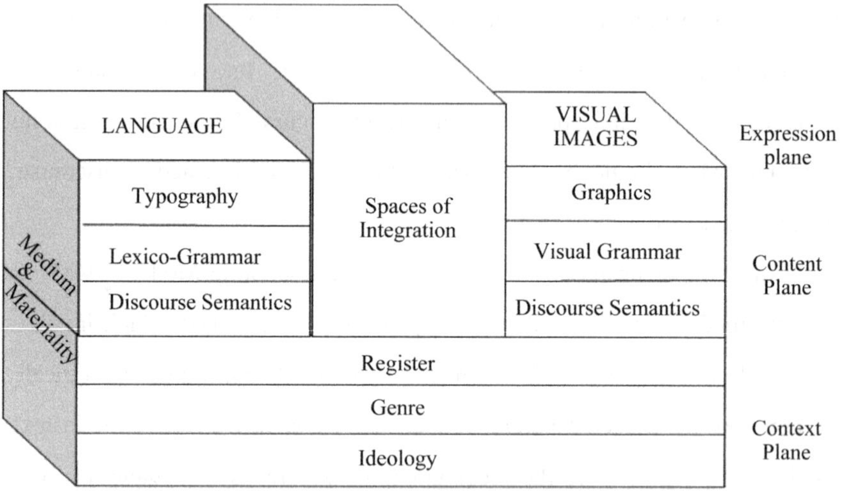

Figure 2-4 IMM Model (Lim, 2004: 222)

Lim's IMM model is "a tentative attempt undertaken with the aim of unifying the contributions from the various matrixes on the different planes and dimensions at a meta-level" (Lim 2007: 197). Mechanisms are also proposed to account for the semantic expansion of different semiotic modes in a single multimodal text. In addition, the model draws attention to the functions of the Expression plane in realizing metafunctional meanings. However, in his study (2004) he investigated only two issues raised by the IMM. The first is concerned with the systems such as Color which operates on the Expression plane. The second is about the interaction and negotiation between the two semiotic modes on the SoI which lead to semantic expansion or "multiplication of meaning" (Lemke 1998) in visual multimodal texts. As he himself comments, "Further research is needed to understand the conditions under which certain metafuncional orientations are realized through choices from the systems operating on the Expression strata". Besides, Lim's model does not regard the multimodal text as a whole visual entity; and the integrating mechanism is not clearly shown in the model. In our view, though language and images belong to different semiotics, they integrate into a complete whole when they make a multimodal text.

Royce (2007) studied of *intersemiotic complementarity* with respect to the three metafuntions. He presented the framework of the intersemiotic complemetarity of image and verbal text in page-based multimodal texts and applied the framework to a multimodal text extracted from the Finance section of *The Economists* magazine. The intersemiotic complementarity study is conducted with respect to the three metafuntions, namely ideational, interpersonal, and textual/compositional functions. The examination of the ways that the visual and verbal modes interact intersemiotically in ideational terms involves deriving "Visual Message Elements" (VME or VMEs) (ibid: 70), the represented participants, processes, circumstances, and attributes in the two semiotic modes. This ideational intersemiotic complementarity is realized by various intersemiotic sense relations of Repetition, Synonymy, Antonymy, Meronymy, Hyponymy and Collocation. The examination of the intersemiotic interpersonal features of a multimodal text involves a look at the ways that relations between the visual and the viewer/reader are represented (Kress & van Leeuwen 2006). The interpersonal complementarity is realized though MOOD and MODALITY. An examination of compositional features of a multimodal text involves an examination of those features of its layout which allow the elements on the page to cohere as part of the one multimodal text. Its layout can convey to readers a sense of unity or cooperation, and of consistency in terms of the total message. The ways to realize a coherent layout include Information Valuation, Salience, Degree of framing of elements, Inter-Visual synonymy and Reading path.

2.3.4 Studies on Multimodal Genre

Recent years have seen a steady increase in genre research which deals with genres which are realized by language and other semiotic modes and transmitted through both the print and electronic media—the Internet, mobile phones and other mobile devices. In other words, the scope of genre analysis has extended from linear, monomodal genres transmitted through speech or print to non-linear, multimodal genres transmitted through both print and electronic media.

2.3.4.1 Genre in Document Layout

Delin et al. (2002/2003) presented a framework for describing the genres of illustrated documents, based on analysis at five levels: content structure, rhetorical structure, layout structure, navigation structure, and linguistic structure. Document genres are conceptualized as complex specifications composed of descriptions at each of the five levels. They also include three sources of constraints under which a document might be produced and interpreted: canvas constraints, production constraints, and consumption constraints.

2.3.4.2 Bateman's GeM Model and Its Applications

Bateman (2008) made further improvements and proposed GeM (genre and multimodality) Model for describing genre and multimodal documents. He suggested that document genre is constituted both in terms of levels of description, and in terms of the constraints that operate on the information at each level in the generation of a document. The constraints are canvas constraint, production and consumption constraints. *Canvas constraints* are those "arising out of the physical nature of the object being produced: paper or screen size; fold geometry such as for a leaflet" (Bateman 2008: 18). *Production constraints* are "constraints arising out of the production technology: limit on pages, color, size of included graphics, availability of photographs; ... arising from the micro-and macro-economy of time or materials, e.g., deadlines; expense of using color; necessity of incorporating advertising" (ibid). Finally, *consumption constraints* are those "arising out of the time, place, and manner of acquiring and consuming the document, such as method of selection at purchase point, or web browser sophistication and the changes it will make on downloading; also, constraints arising out of the degree to which the document must be easy to read, understand, or otherwise use; fitness in relation to ask; assumptions of expertise of readers" (ibid). Each source of constraint may bring restrictions for the concrete forms that may appear in the artifact itself.

The principal layers of structure can also be characterized by the types of elements that they identify as follows:

- "the GeM base: the basic elements physically present on a page;
- layout base: the layout properties and structure;
- rhetorical base: a detailed account of the rhetorical relationships between the content expressed by elements on a page and their communicative purpose
- navigation base: the elements that contribute explicitly to navigation and access in the page, supporting 'movement' around the document in various ways;
- genre base: a representation of the grouping of elements from

> other layers into generically recognizable configurations distinctive for particular genres or document types." (p. 108)

In his model, Bateman takes as his study object the "multimodal written documents", i. e., pages of spatially orchestrated static content in a combination of modes. He regards "the page as a visual entity that is acting as a unit of communication in its own right" (Bateman 2008: 100). By introducing the foundational notion of genre into his model, Bateman not only extends the study of multimodal discourses to the higher level of genre, but also explores new potentials realizing the metafunctions. For instance, there are other information structures besides Given/New, Ideal/Real, and Margin/Centre structures. In some genres, *access* and *navigation* are the strongest functional motivations for the compositional arrangements. However, his GeM model studies multimodal genre in the broad sense. It is not quite plausible to apply it to the genre analysis of multimodal texts with the same canvas, production and consumption constraints. In addition, some of the layers in the model do not function in all multimodal texts, such as the Navigation structure. Finally, the GeM model does not capture the meaning potential of typography, which is important contribution to meaning-making in multimodal texts.

Hiippala (2012) applied the GeM model to the study of multimodal meaning-making in five tourist brochures published between 1967 and 1988 for the purpose of advertising the city of Helsinki. The findings concern mainly the representational and compositional meanings: the semiotic resources of language and image convey ideational meaning for the purpose of construing a persuasive image of the locations and to guide the reader to and around the location, and consistent patterns in layout and typographical and graphical features are used to make the document accessible to the reader. There has been no analysis and discussion of the interpersonal meaning and the realizational relations of the strata are not discussed either. Bateman et al. (2017) provided the first introduction to the practice, methodology and theoretical frameworks for analyzing various multimodal artifacts or discourses which range from performances and the performing arts to diagrams and infographics, to comic and graphic novels, to webpages and dynamic visualizations, and to computer and video games, etc.

There have been a few studies by Chinese researchers. Xing (2012) analyzed multimodal news discourses in print newspapers. Based on Bateman's GeM model, the dissertation attempted to build a genre-based model which not only presents a systematic way to decompose a multimodal newspaper text into analyzable parts and makes it possible to analyze the pictorial and verbal elements separately, but also captures the mechanisms that make the different parts of the multimodal text into a coherent whole. Hu and Li (2018) pointed out that the predictive capability of current monomodal genre theory is under question. Theoretically, scholars don't hold a consistent view on the roles and functions of modes other than languge in the multimodal genre definition and understanding of the compatibility between linguistic genre space and multimodal genre space has been insufficient. Empirically, automatic data collection and machine analysis of those diversified modes such as picture and music are urgently needed. Zhang (2018) proposed a systemic functional synthetic framework for multimodal discourse analysis. The framework is developed along the dimensions of realization and instantiation. It integrates the affordances of the semiotic systems involved, the unity of system and function, the systems of choice at every stratum (including the stratum or level of substance which highlights the materiality of media and the technologies involved in text generation), and the relations between modes are important.

To sum up, from Bateman's elaboration of the GeM model and its applications to various multimodal discourses, we can find that the relations among the five bases are not clear. As a result, it may fail to explain how the meaning patterns of different semiotic modes and their interactions are related to the more abstract meaning patterns at the stratum of context. Zhang's framework proves that realization and stratification developed for the description of language are conducive to the study of multimodal genres as well, yet more empirical studies on different types of multimodal discourses are necessary.

2.4 Studies on News Discourse

2.4.1 Major Approaches to News Discourse

News discourse has a long history of being explored in a variety of disciplines, including journalism, sociology, linguistics and semiotics (Bednareck & Caple 2012), because its study "has much to offer to the different disciplines on whose territory it touches" (Bell 1991: 5). So, it is no wonder that there have been a variety of approaches. Bednarek and Caple (2012) summarized eight key approaches①:

1) The systemic functional linguistic approach. This research, following the theories in Systemic Functional Linguistics, "approaches news discourse from the perspective of register and genre and describes and discusses the different purposes, linguistic features and structures of various types of news discourse as well as the notion of authorial voice and the expression of subjectivity in news discourse" (ibid: 8). In our

① The order of listing the approaches is rearranged based on the relevance to the present study.

understanding, this approach to news discourse has a systematic theory relating context and language (now also various semiotic modes or modalities) as the theoretical foundation and so can describe and discuss the different linguistic features and structures of various types at different strata around the three metafunctions, and the interaction between context and semiotic modes. Social semiotic research inspired by SFL (e.g., Economou 2006, 2010; Knox 2007; Caple 2008a, b, 2013) is also included in this approach.

2) The pragmatic/stylistic approach. The two authors take the approach as one that is not located within a specific linguistic school but draws on various linguistic concepts to investigate the language of news discourse. Crystal's analysis of newspaper reporting (Crystal 1969) is one of the key studies from the stylistic perspective. He first pointed out that the underlying aims of the two extracts in his analysis are identical: "They are both concerned to present a certain number of facts in as interesting a manner as possible to audiences." (Crystal 1969: 174) Then he identified the linguistic characteristics, and "graphetic and graphological" (ibid, means "visual") features in the two extracts of news reporting.

3) The critical approach, or the critical discourse analysis (CDA). Studies from this approach (e.g., Fowler 1991; Fairclough 1995) focus on working out how ideology influences production of news reporting text and how news reporting counteracts ideology and power. Being problem-oriented, the approach has gained the most popularity in news discourse analysis (Wang et al. 2021). It adopts Systemic Functional Linguistic as its theoretical framework and as its analytical tool as well. It aims at de-mystify inequality and power implicit in discourses and "reveal ideology imbedded consciously by institutions and unconsciously by long-standing conceptions, beliefs, and values" (ibid: 116) in a given society and culture.

4) The sociolinguistic approach. The main concerns "tend to center on

correlation between style and social factors" (Bednarek & Caple 2012: 7). In other words, the correlation between features of news discourse and the presumed social status of the audience has been the focus of most studies.

5) The conversation analytical approach. Following the tradition of Conversation Analysis, this approach to news discourse explores "spoken interaction in the context of news interviews" (Bednarek & Caple 2012: 8).

6) The practice-focused approach. This approach focuses on journalistic practices and the social processes that lead to the construction of news. This approach is often pursued by researchers who also worked as journalists themselves and focuses more on the production side of journalism.

7) The corpus linguistic approach. The approach differs from others in its use of large datasets or corpora and computer software to analyze news discourse. In our understanding, corpus is more a tool than a theoretical framework.

8) The diachronic approach. As is indicated by "diachronic", the approach "concerns change in news discourses over time or studies of early news discourse".

Bednarek and Caple (2012) pointed out that not all linguistic research on news discourse fits neatly into one of the above-listed categories. Many studies may combine two or more approaches in their analyses. And some studies were not included, for instance, van Dijk's (1988) social-cognitive approach, which analyzes practices of news production and emphasizes the processes of social cognition—how cognitive models and schemata shape news production and comprehension.

The articles in Part I of *The Routledge Handbook of Language and Media* (Cotter & Perrin 2018) also offered a summary of key research frameworks and methods for the analysis of media discourses. The approaches are: medialinguistic approaches summarized by Daniel Perrin (the second editor), sociolinguistic approaches by Jane Stuart-Smith, discourse approaches by Collen Cotter (the first editor), critical approaches by Michal Krzyzanowski and David Machin, cognitive approaches by Anna Pleshakova, and corpus approaches by Silvia Jaworska. The approaches are quite diverse and not all focus on the news discourses as a multimodal product, so we will not go into details.

SFL has been one of the linguistic theories widely used in news discourse analysis, particularly since 2001 (Wang et al. 2021). And as has been mentioned, the systemic functional approach to news discourse has a systematic theory relating context and language (now also various semiotic modes or modalities) as the theoretical foundation and so can describe and discuss the different linguistic features and structures of various types at different strata around the three metafunctions, and the interaction between context and semiotic modes. Therefore, the SFL approach will be adopted in the present study and studies on multimodal news discourse following this approach will be reviewed in detail.

2. 4. 2 SFL Studies on Multimodal News Discourse

As has been noted in Chapter 1, the use of web-mediated or mobile phone-mediated communication has skyrocketed during the past ten years. This has led to a steady increase in research which deals with genres of news discourses transmitted through the electronic media—the Internet, mobile phones and other mobile devices. In other words, the scope of discourse analysis has extended from linear, monomodal genres transmitted through speech or print to non-linear, multimodal genres transmitted through various electronic media. SFL scholars have carried out research on multimodal news discourses both in the traditional print newspapers and the newer online or electronic news platforms, but with an increasing attention on the online news. Among the wide range of themes covered in the studies, the main themes include: the image-text relation, the meaning potential of images, particularly news photographs, the layout or design of print newspapers and online news platforms, and multimodal genre of news discourse. Helen Caple, Monica Bednareck and John Knox are among the most active and productive SFL scholars in the study of multimodal news discourses.

1) The image-text relation. Knox (2007) conducted a study of visual-verbal communication on the home pages of three English-language online newspapers from different national cultures. His article shows how digital, discursive and ideological convergences are contributing to the development of a grammar of visual design in the English-language online newspapers. Newsbite, a new sub-genre of online news reporting, has emerged as part of the interaction between the emerging grammar of visual design and existing verbal practices in English-language newspaper reporting. The study further makes clear the interactional, representational and compositional meanings in newsbite. His study can be seen as an initial contribution to a critical description of the developments of online newspapers, the evolution of verbal news genres and the development of conventions of visual design. But it does not focus on the meanings in individual instantiations of news texts. Caple (2008a, 2008b)① investigated the complementarity between the photograph and the verbiage in image nuclear news stories. Caple and Bednarek (2010) unpacked the play in the image-nuclear news stories, news stories with a heading, a dominant photograph and a caption. They found that in these stories, the heading and image enter into a verbal-visual play that relies on the manipulation of common (often idiomatic) expressions, while the caption elements elaborate on the story's news value. Their study identifies a new genre of news texts and unpacks the image-text play in this genre. However, their study focuses more on reader's linguistic

① The two studies have been reviewed with more details in section 2.3.3.

experience in the unpacking of the image-text play and on the "bonding" function of the image-nuclear news stories to build community and reader loyalty through shared understanding of puns and allusions. Moreover, their study does not analyze image-embedded news stories. Caple and Knox (2012) investigated the online news gallery as a site for new genres of multimodal news reporting and explored the relation between online news galleries, and genres such as photo essays, picture stories, portfolios, verbal news stories, and other verbal texts. They analyzed the realizations of online news galleries as storytelling devices, focusing particularly on the realizations of interpersonal meanings. They concluded that online news galleries offer new possibilities for storytelling and allow for the development of new genres.

2) The meaning potential of news photographs. The meaning potential of photographs in news reporting, or news photos in photojournalism, has attracted much attention from SFL scholars. Badnareck and Caple (2012) and Caple (2013) have given systematic descriptions of the meaning potential of news photos in and of themselves as well as in combination with other semiotic resources. As has been reviewed in section 2.3.2.3, Caple (2013) drew on the grammar of visual design and focuses on single images. Her description is interpreted as being done at the stratum of grammar. For more details, please read "Grammar of Press Photographs" in section 2.3.2.3. Badnareck and Caple (2012) identified nine aspects of news images that construe news values. These aspects present mainly the resources for evaluation, conjunction, and reference in news photos and so are better interpreted from a discourse semantic perspective. The part titled "Discourse Semantic Analysis of News Photos" in section 2.3.2.3 offered a more detailed review of their work. Other articles which apply the discourse semantic systems proposed by Jim Martin for language to the analysis of multimodal news discourse include Martin (2000), Economou

(2006, 2008), Caple (2009a), Chen (2010a, 2010b). The part titled "Discourse Semantic Analysis of News Photos" in section 2. 3. 2. 3 offered a more detailed review of their studies.

3) The layout or design. Kress and van Leeuwen (1998) apply functional grammar to developing an analytical framework for the analysis of newspaper front pages. They regard all the elements on the front page, such as headlines, photographs and text blocks, as meaningful entities. Their study finds that the layout of front page has three signification systems simultaneously: information value, salience, and framing devices.

4) Multimodal genre of news discourse. Yang (2001) analyzed the generic features, including lexico-grammatical features and typographic features of editorials from the SFL perspective. The lexico-grammatical features are mainly about the features at the clause level, covering the choices of transitivity, mood structure and thematic structures. The typographic features include the length of the text, the numbers of paragraphs and their length, and the length of sentences. Yang's study identifies the role typographical features play in editorials, yet it does not give detailed description and interpretation of features of the layout, type format, case, type face and size, etc. Bateman et al. (2007) mapped the multimodal genres of traditional and electronic newspapers and aim to capture the spatial information implicit in the visual design of traditional and electronic newspaper front pages. They found that "within web documents, a sizeable proportion of the layout elements of a page are devoted to navigational elements that assist their readers to access the document", and that "with newspapers the layout structure and the typographical realization of its elements are predominantly devoted to functions specific to the genre of news delivery" (p. 171). They also commented that news genres are now forming very rapidly as news forms of expression are attempted with electronic documents. Old genres are changing under the influence of these

news genres, while new genres also revise existing forms. The studies by Kress and van Leeuwen (2006) and by Bateman et al (2007) take into account different semiotic modes on the newspaper front page and are valuable to examine the layout of newspaper front pages, but they do not analyze the other inherent features and do not study single news texts. Bateman (2008) proposed a GeM model for analyzing multimodal documents. There have been a few studies by Chinese researchers. Xing (2012), based on Bateman's GeM model, attempted to build a genre-based model which not only presents a systematic way to decompose a multimodal newspaper text into analyzable parts and make it possible to analyze the pictorial and verbal elements separately, but also captures the mechanisms that make the different parts of the multimodal text into a coherent whole.

More recent contributions to multimodal news analysis from the SFL perspective include the monograph *Multimodal News Analysis Across Cultures* written by Helen Caple, Changpeng Huan and Monika Bednareck (2020) and the articles collected in *Discourse, Modes, Media and Meaning in an Era of Pandemic: A Multimodal Discourse Analysis Approach* edited by Sabine Tan and Marissa K. L. E. (2023). The book *Multimodal News Analysis Across Cultures* combined corpus linguistic techniques for language analysis with multimodal discourse analysis of news language and news photography. The book also presented a cross-linguistic comparison of multimodal news discourses from China and Australia and so moves beyond analysis of a single language. The articles in the collection "examine various discourses, modes and media in circulation during the early period of the COVID-19 pandemic" (Tan & Marrissa 2023: 3), which range from news discourses spreading information of the virus created by national and international news organizations, and social media discourses created by health organizations, government organs and individuals, to education and classroom discourses on the virus. The authors also tried to figure out "how these have significantly impacted our daily lives in terms of the various meanings they express that have come to form the (new) realities we experience and interact with daily" (ibid).

There have been fruitful attempts to study multimodal news reporting from other perspectives. Barthes (1977) decoded the messages in press photographs and the image-text interplay in news stories. His study can be said to be a foundational study of news photographs and image-text relations. However, it is "based on a simple logic of three possibilities of how images and text relate to one another and relies on penetrating observation rather than on any specific realizations" (Martinec & Salway 2005: 341). Hartley (1982) studied the semiotic modes and conventions underlying both linguistic and visual aspects of news reporting, but he focuses on the analysis of visual codes to different ways of presentation on television, such as the use of graphics and pictures, various types of factuality, and camera movements and the sequencing of shots. Hartley's study offers in-depth investigation on news photographs, but does not bring the coexistent news text into his analyses. Askehave and Nielsen (2005) applied the Swalesian genre theory used in academic settings to the analysis of non-linear, multimodal, web-mediated documents. Digital genres act not only as text but also as medium and the media constraints have a significant effect on the production and reception of digital genres. They proposed a revised two-dimensional genre model incorporating media elements into the concept of genre, but the observation is restricted to a limited number of commercial websites, as the authors wrote in their article.

2.4.3 SFL Studies on Monomodal Verbal News

There has also been a rich literature on verbal news discourses conducted by SFL scholars, for instance, White (1997, 2004, 2006), Wang (2004), Martin and White (2005), Wang and Wang (2012), Huan

(2016) as well as Xing and Zhu (2018). As these studies also offer inspiration and foundation for the analysis of verbal texts in data news, we will review the key studies.

Most studies apply the system of APPRAISAL and focus on the stance and evaluative meanings realized in verbal news texts. White (1997) analyzed English hard news metafunctionally to describe the narrative impulse and the communicative function of the news story's generic structure. He identified the "Event Story" and "Issues Report" and argued that "the 'canonical' 'hard news' circumscribe a key set of interpersonal values" (p. 25). He highlighted the interpersonal orientation of English hard news, including the voice of the reporter, the profuse use of intensification resources, the interpersonal role of headlines and leads. White (2004) focused on the issue of evaluation, particularly on how news reports might influence or position readers/viewers to take a negative or positive view of the people, events and states of affairs being depicted in the reports. White (2006) also focused on the evaluation in news stories. The article offered a framework for the analysis of the evaluative aspect of news reporting and how individual news items may vary in the evaluative mechanism and hence in their ultimate ideological effect. Wang (2004) applied the sub-system of ATTITUDE to the analysis of both Chinese hard news and English hard news. The analysis finds that the linguistic realizations of judgment are employed more than those of affect and appreciation. Martin and White (2005) established the highly quoted system network of Appraisal based on their detailed analyses of verbal news discourses. Wang and Wang (2012), adopting the APPRAISAL system, contrasted two new discourses and explored the use of attitudinal inscriptions and tokens and their functions in setting up particular linguistic contexts in news discourses. Huan (2016), based on the analysis of comparable corpus of Chinese and Australian hard news reporting on risk events, investigated the cultural variability of engagement patterns and how such patterns point to distinctions in the ways the power relations are reproduced in news production processes.

Unlike the above studies, Xing and Zhu (2018) focused on the interplay or coupling between ideational and identification resources. The study analyzed how experiential meaning, together with textual meaning, constrains the choice of identification resources in news reports. It is found that in news reports, noun phrases and proper names are the most commonly used introducing and tracking resources because they expand the experiential meaning of participants by adding qualifiers or elaborating elements. It is demonstrated that identification resources realize textual meaning, but the choice of these resources partly depends on how much experiential meaning needs to be made explicit.

2.5 Summary

In conclusion, news texts today are dominantly presented multimodally with language, images and other semiotic modes. Data news, as a new genre in journalism, is one of such multimodal discourse, whose meaning-making processes have not yet been sufficiently explored from the viewers' or consumption perspective. Data visualizations, benefitting from technological innovations, become important information carriers and also a core component in data news. Their meaning potentials and interaction with verbal texts in a unified data story have also been underexplored compared with their wide application in journalism. Studies have to be conducted to describe and interpret those changes and the meaning multiplication by the combination of language and various types of images in data news. The review in this chapter covers mainly the SFL approach to multimodal discourse analysis: the strata of expression form, grammar and discourse semantics of images (including news photographs), intermodal interaction mostly between image and text, and multimodal genres. These studies have investigated the relationships between context (genre and register) and features at different levels of different semiotic modes and the interplay between different semiotic modes. However, an integrated model is needed to give a sufficient description and interpretation of the features in data news. In the next chapter, we will build up a framework which can describe the generic features of data news and reveal how images and verbal texts work together to create coherent and engaging data news discourses.

Chapter 3 Towards a Multimodal Genre Model for Data News

3.1 Genre Studies

3.1.1 Three Genre Traditions

The concept of genre has been a matter of considerable discussion in research communities throughout the world (Askehave & Nielsen 2005). Traditionally a term in literary and rhetorical studies, genre has become a popular framework for analyzing the structure and function of nonliterary discourse in linguistic studies since Bakhtin's (1999) application of the term to nonliterary discourse. Hyon (1996) provided a map of current genre theories in three research areas where genre scholarship has taken significantly different paths: 1) English for specific purposes (ESP) (Swales 1986, 1990), 2) North American New Rhetoric studies (Freeman & Medway 1994a, 1994b), and 3) Australian Systemic Functional Linguistics (SFL) (Martin & Rose 2008).

The three approaches lay equal emphasis on the purposive nature of genre, on the relationship between discourse and social context/practice as well as on the application of genre to language teaching, although they differ in their conceptualizations of genre and the methods adopted for text analysis. The genre studies following these traditions have contributed to in-depth understanding of the concept of genre by "defining the concept, introducing models suitable for performing genre analysis and capturing the complexities of genre systems and genre development" (Askehave & Nielsen 2005: 120).

3. 1. 1. 1 ESP Approach

Scholars in this field have framed genres as "oral and written text types defined by their formal properties as well as by their communicative purposes within social contexts" (Hyon 1996: 695). The representative scholar in this model is John Swales, whose ideas are most clearly elaborated in his manuscript *Genre Analysis: English in Academic and Research Settings* (Swales 1990). In his genre model, Swales, though focusing on the linguistic forms of different genres, takes an ethnographical view of genre. To him, social purposes of texts as "recognized by the expert members of the parent discourse community... constitute the rationale for the genre" (Swales 1990: 58). Besides, his ESP model takes a correlational view of genre and language. In other words, when doing genre analysis, an expert or a scholar first intuitively recognizes the structural patterns in texts, arrives at a model, and then applies the model to other texts, looking for correlating language patterns in other texts. The lack of a consistent theoretical model to identify genre and its moves problematizes its application in empirical research.

There have been analyses describing global organizational patterns in genres, such as experimental research articles (Swales 1990), Master of Science dissertations (Hopkins & Dudley-Evans 1988), medical abstracts (Salager-Meyer 1990), popularized medical research reports (Nwogu 1991), business letters (Bhatia 1993), and university lectures (Thompson

1994; Hyon 1996). These studies focus more on the forms of different genres of texts. From an SFL perspective, they lack a consistent theory to relate linguistic forms with context, and the concept genre in ESP (e.g., email, letter, essay, discussion, presentation, interview) conflates genre, mode, tenor and field. Besides, there can also be mixed genres or macro-genres which ESP model fails to identify.

3.1.1.2 New Rhetoric Genre Approach

North America and New Rhetoric traditions of genre characterize genre as actions (Swales 1990). This perspective is more concerned with the socio-cultural rather than linguistic characteristics of texts. "Here, language events were most readily seen as instantiating particular social activity types." (Bateman 2008: 188) Studies from this perspective tie genre to situation. "Genre in this way ... becomes pragmatic, fully rhetorical, a point of connection between intention and effect, an aspect of social action." (Miller 1984: 153)

Studies from this perspective make two contributions to the study of genre. First, they notice the dynamic change of genres with time. They take more interest in "explaining certain aspects of the way social reality evolves than just providing a taxonomic system" (Miller 1984: 153). Campbell and Jamieson commented: "The critic who classifies a rhetorical artifact as generically akin to a class of similar artifacts has identified an undercurrent of history rather than comprehend it as an act isolated in time." (ibid: 26) Thus, the set of genres becomes "an open class, with news members evolving, old ones decaying" (ibid: 153). Second, some studies (e.g., Yates & Orlikowski 1992) propose genre as a powerful means of investigating changes in organizational practice over time. Yates and Orlikowski (1992) provided a detailed illustration of their approach to genre change over time drawing on the business memo. Though we focus on the synchronic aspect of multimodal genre in our perspective, a sketch of the evolution of a certain genre, especially the aspect resulting from the change of technology, can offer more insights into it. In addition, changes as those reported for the business memo can be tracked more effectively when we have a model which can sufficiently characterize the features at different layers.

Genre scholars in these areas have "focused more on the situational contexts in which genres occur than on their forms and have placed special emphases on the social purposes, or actions, that these genres fulfill within these situations" (Hyon 1996: 696). They regard genre as "social action" (Miller 1984). Their definition of genre centers "not on the substance or the form of discourse but on the action it is used to accomplish" (Hyon 1996: 696). Scholars in New Rhetoric fields, similar to ESP scholars, have used ethnographic methods for analyzing texts, such as participant observation, interviews, and document collection, etc. They, in line with their theoretical focus on socio-contextual aspects of genres, have been more concerned with the role of genres in "helping university students and novice professionals understand the social functions or actions of genres and the contexts in which these genres are used" (Hyon 1996: 698).

The New Rhetoric genre model has described the role of social contexts in analyzing genres of texts, but from an SFL perspective, the studies under this model have not explored systematically the link between language and context.

3.1.1.3 SFL Genre Approach

SFL regards language as a social semiotic (Halliday 1978). Its views on genre are also termed as "genre as social semiotic" (Martin & Rose 2008). SFL perspective on genre lays emphasis on the mutual predictability and bi-directionality between text and genre. These two points are best presented in Hasan's comments: "the speaker's perception of the context *activates* her choices of meaning" and "the meanings meant in speaking *construes* contexts" (original emphasis) (Hasan 1999: 223). To put it more simply, context constrains the individual's instantiated text or discourse while the instantiated text or discourse constructs context. This link between text or discourse and genre along the clines of realization and instantiation is one factor that distinguishes it from the study of genre as social action.

Among the three traditions, the SFL tradition highlights the bi-directional interaction between social practice/context and the discourse, or the mutual predictability between discourse and genre, and the dynamism and flexibility of the discourse structure in the clines of both instantiation and realization. Most researchers now agree that there is conventionalized structure of a genre, but instances of a genre do not necessarily contain a fixed set of obligatory moves. Instances of a genre elect their structural elements from a common move repertoire (Martin & Rose 2008); they may share stages but differ in their moves realizing each stage. This offers a consistent model for integrating the patterns identified at different strata to come to a more systematic study of genre.

Therefore, to capture the dynamic interaction of how different stratifications of language and other semiotic modes realize genre and to contribute to the exploration of multimodal repertoire, we will follow the SFL tradition of genre studies in the present research.

3.1.2 SFL Models on Linguistic Genres

SFL has an extensive theoretical framework associated with the study of genre (e.g., Halliday & Hasan 1985, Halliday 1999; Hasan 2009, 2014; Martin 1985, 2004/1992, 1999, 2001; Martin & Rose 2008).

Hasan and Martin follow the SFL traditions set up by Halliday to model the relation between language and context. They all use the three abstract categories of register, namely field, tenor, and mode to describe the relationship between language and context. They share the view that register can capture the variation in linguistic choices with respect to context. The three categories are realized by three systems of metafunctional resources in language or other modalities. Ideational resources point to the topic/content (field); interpersonal resources enact relationships and convey attitudes (tenor); and textual resources indicate the role language plays in the context (mode), for example, whether the language constitutes or accompanies activity. The authors also describe the choices available to speakers/writers in systems or axial relations. Drawing on different systems of language in different combinations realizes different registers, because the particular language choices and the meanings made, vary according to situational and cultural context. For them, language is a reservoir for meaning-making, and speakers/ writers draw on this reservoir in different ways, depending on what is going on, whom we are interacting with, and the role language is playing. Therefore, a systematic analysis of linguistic choices can reveal important differences in how content, role relationships, and information flow are constructed in different contexts, as these differences realize and reveal different registers (see Halliday & Hasan 1985; Halliday 1994, 1999; Hasan 2009; Martin 1999 et al.).

But the three authors do differ slightly, particularly in their conceptualizations of the relationship between genre and register. We will review their studies on context, genre, register and their relationships with language in more detail. As Halliday and Hasan have similar views on these points, we term their perspective as Halliday and Hasan's model and term Martin's perspective as Martin's model.

3.1.2.1 Halliday and Hasan's Model

Talking about their model, we need to begin with their definition and interpretation of the term "context". We know that Halliday inherited and further developed the ideas of "context of situation" and "context of culture" developed by Malinowski, Firth, Sapir and Whorf. "Malinowski and Firth stressed 'the situation as the context for language as text', —context of situation, while Sapir and Whorf stressed 'the culture as the context for the language as system'—context of culture." (Ghadessy 1999: xi) But as Halliday emphasizes the complementarity between the two, he uses context to refer to "context of culture" and "context of situation".

Before Malinowski, context meant mostly "'co(n)-text', the words and the sentences before and after the particular sentence that one was looking at" (Halliday & Hasan 1985: 6). Malinowski, who carried out research about people in the Trobrian Islands, a group of islands in the South Pacific Ocean, encountered the problem of how to interpret and expound his ideas on the culture to English-speaking readers. To solve this, besides giving a free translation and a literal translation, he provided a rather extended commentary, which was "the kind of commentary that placed text in its living environment" (ibid). So, he coined the term "context of situation" to refer to "the total environment, including the verbal environment, but also the situation of in which the text was uttered" (ibid). He also saw that it was necessary to give more than the immediate environment—"information not only about what was happening at the time but also about the total cultural background... the whole cultural history behind the participants, and behind the kind of practices that they were engaging in..." (ibid). This is what he meant by context of culture.

In the model presented by Halliday and Hasan (1985), "genre" is not a specifically systemic term but rather the traditional term for what is now construed as functional variation—register—or an aspect of the mode variable of context (see Halliday, 1978: 145). Genre is close to situation type in Halliday(1991)'s model of context based on the intersection of the hierarchy of stratification and the cline of instantiation. To be more exact,

Halliday associates genre with relation to mode (Matthiessen et al. 2010).

In her canonic study, Hasan (1985) defined genre as "text types". Looked at "from below", from the vantage point of language, genre corresponds to text type (seen from the instance pole of the cline of instantiation) or register (see from the potential pole of the cline of instantiation) (Matthiessen et al. 2010: 107). For her, genre is determined by context and expressed by the *Generic Structure Potential*, or GSP. Three terms are important—obligatory elements, optional elements and sequence. Elements that must occur are termed obligatory, while elements that can occur are termed optional; the order in which elements appear is called sequence. Genres can only be considered "complete" if all obligatory elements of structure are realized. Her GSP theory (Hasan 1978) is one of the key representations of genre within systemic functional models. But Hasan identifies the GSP of different genres or text types by relating more to the variable of field, not considering much about the tenor and mode variables.

3.1.2.2 Martin's Model

In the model of context developed by Martin (Martin 1992; Martin & Rose 2008), genre is one of the connotative semiotic planes constituting the context; it maps culture and is realized by register, the contextual variables of field, tenor and mode. In other words, Martin sees genre realized by the configurations of the three register variables, which is different from Halliday who associates genre with relation to mode, and also from Hasan who associates genre with field (Matthiessen et al. 2010). More specifically, Martin's genre model lays emphasis on the following four points:

(1) Stratification of Genre and Register

Though reflecting Halliday's concern for linking language and social context, Martin takes a stratified view of language, register and genre (Figure 3-2 is Martin's stratification of context and language). Halliday and Hasan take context as one stratum (see Figure 3-1), though they distinguish context of culture and context of situation. The two terms of register and genre are regarded as the same in Halliday and Hasan's model and some other SFL scholars (Ventola 1984; Hasan 1985; Halliday 1999, 2008) and the relationship between genre and the longer established concept of register is not always very clear in early systemic functional studies. But Martin distinguishes genre from register. According to him (Martin 2004/1992), genre and register are said to be on different "semiotic or communicative planes". Genre is the context of culture, while register is the context of situation. Genre and register are different, working at different levels to create texts. Genre is a social process in which participants within a culture uses language in predictable sequential structures to fulfill certain communicative purposes. Genres are realized through registers and constrain the ways in which register variables of field, tenor and mode can be combined in a particular society. So, for Martin, genre and register are the two strata of context.

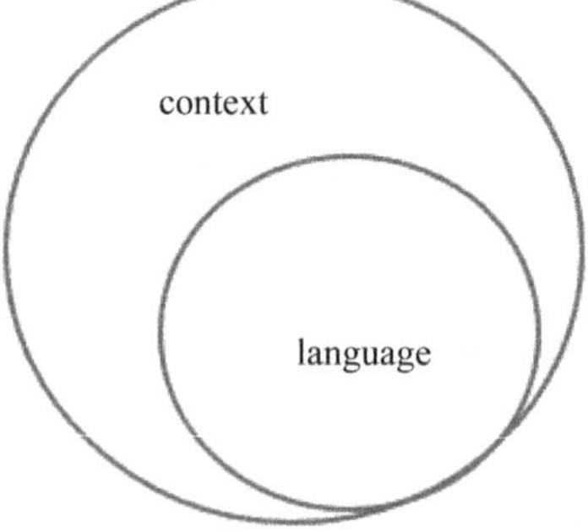

Figure 3-1 Halliday and Hasan's Stratification of Genre and Language

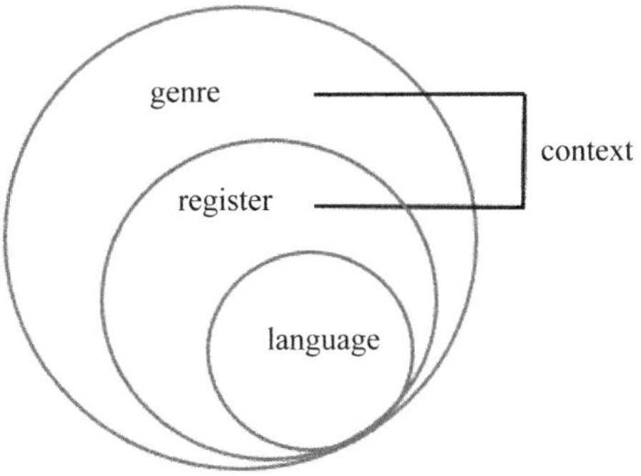

Figure 3-2 Martin's Stratification of Genre and Language

Seven advantages of the stratified model of context as register and genre have been summarized by Martin himself (Martin 1999).

"(i) *the need for a multi-functional characterization of genre* (original emphasis)...

(ii) *the desire to strengthen field, mode, tenor and metafunction solidarity...*

(iii) *the importance of accounting for the combinations of field, tenor and mode variables a culture recurrently exploits...*

(iv) the question of handling variation in field, tenor and mode from one stage to another within a genre...

(v) a concern with the distinction between activity sequence (field time) and generic structure (text time) ...

(vi) the formalization of trans-metafunctional valeur—as part of our ambition to map a culture as a system of genres, we were concerned to show how the combinations of field, mode and tenor variables a culture regularly phased into social processes were related to each other...

(vii) the problem of contextual metaphor—by which I mean the use of one text type to stand for another..." (Martin 1999: 31-34)

Martin has positioned genre as an abstract level of analysis coordinating field, mode and tenor (known collectively as register), and register is realized in turn through language (discourse semantics, lexicogrammar and phonology/graphology). His model "does privilege genre as its ultimate level of abstraction, thereby giving genre responsibility for coordinating the recurrent configurations of meaning in a culture. In such terms, genre mediates the limits of our world—at the same time as offering systemic linguists a wholistic perspective on their metafunctionally and stratally diversified analyses" (Martin & Rose 2008: 230).

In Martin's genre model, the relation between context (genre and register) and language is also a realization relation. In other words, genre is realized by configurations of register, which is realized by configurations of meaning in language. Genre and register serve as part of the semiotic environment for understanding language, and the use of language is constrained by context. Language system and the context are described at several distinct levels or *strata*, with realization relationship between the more abstract and higher stratum and the stratum one level down. All of these strata carry meanings to a complete language event. Any of these strata may take up the role of constructing and carrying meaning patterns. What should be noted is that it is the meaning patterns or configurations that realize meanings at a higher and more abstract stratum. In this sense, Martin's genre model takes a configurational view of genre. In his model, genre is theoretically defined as "a configuration of meanings, realized through language and attendant modalities of communication" (Martin & Rose 2008: 20). Martin also focuses on the development of genre-based pedagogy, therefore, genre in his model has a working definition, defined as "a staged, goal-oriented social processes" (Martin & Rose 2014/2007: 7).

(2) Genre Agnation

Martin has not just analyzed structures of individual genres, but also tried to map culture as a system of genres—as a set of agnate social processes (Martin 1999; Martin & Rose 2008). For him, GSP was "limited to accounting for variation among text types which shared obligatory elements of structure" (Martin 1999: 40) and failed to describe and interpret the relationships among genres with distinctive obligatory elements, so he deployed system networks to model genre relations (Martin 1992, 1999; Martin & Rose 2008). By comparing and contrasting genres, he moved "from a conception of genre as a kind of text (with stages) to a conception of genre as a system of texts" (Martin 1999: 43). In other words, he focused on genre agnation and genre families categorized according to the inter-generic relations. This view is highly compatible with his assertion of analyzing genre both typologically and topologically.

Genre agnation deals with relations among separate genres known as elemental genres. Rose and Martin (2012) provided a taxonomy categorizing four broader genre families based on their social purpose. These families include the functions of engaging, informing, directing procedures and evaluating and their more delicate typologies. Elemental genre members in the engaging story family include recount, narrative, anecdote and exemplum that are sequenced in field time, and news story that is sequenced in text time. The informing genre family include history, explanation, and report. The history genre can be further categorized into autobiographic recount that recounts one's own significant life events, biographical recount that narrates stages in an individual's life, historical recount that recount stages in history, and historical account which explains history. Explanations can be sequential, factorial, consequential, and conditional, while reports can be descriptive, classifying, and compositional. The procedural directing genre family include procedure, protocol, and procedural recounting. Exposition, discussion, personal response, review, and interpretation texts are member of the evaluating genre family.

(3) The Idea of Genre Rank

Martin (2012/1994) began to think about how texts get bigger than a page, namely how elemental genres are combined into longer and more complex texts. He proposed the concepts of macrogenre① and embedded genre to theorize the ways elemental genres are combined. Macrogenre deals with relations between short elemental genres. By applying Halliday's logico-semantic relations, Martin modelled macrogenres as serial structures, i. e., the combination of several elemental genres into a univariate serial structure (Szenes 2017). In other words, the elemental genres instantiated in a complex text represent the parts in the univariate sequence which are linked together by logico-semantic relationships, i. e., expansion and projection (Halliday 1994; Halliday, 2008). Macrogenre is like a clause complex, and so it is also called genre complex. With embedding, "a genre is made to function as one multivariate stage in the development of another" (Martin 2012/1994: 102). In other words, apart from combining genres into a serial univariate structure, longer and more complex texts can also grow bigger through embedded genres (Martin & Rose 2008; Szenes 2017). It also means that elemental genres can function as stages of another genre in a multivariate structure. Embedded genre is like a rankshifted clause in this sense. If macrogenres are proportional to clause complexes, then elemental genres are proportional to clauses and embedded genres to rankshifted clauses. Thus, it can be said that there is also a rank within genre.

The concepts of elemental genre, embedded genre and macrogenre are

① When the term first appeared in Martin (1994), it was hyphenated and spelt as "macro-genre", but later uses of the term are inconsistent (i. e., macro-genre versus macrogenre). Since the term has become a technical term in SFL, in the present study we follow Szene's practice and spell the term as one word, i. e., macrogenre, unless it appears in a quote in which the hyphenated usage occurs.

further developed in later works by Martin and his colleagues. Martin (1997: 16) illustrated that longer texts and complex multimodal texts may be created by combining familiar elemental genres such as recount, report, explanation, exposition and so on" into macrogenres, which are genre complexes. Having canvassed the extensive work on elemental genres, Martin and Rose (2008) found that in fact, many of the shorter genres were found inside longer texts. Later, they discovered that longer texts such as websites, novels or textbooks have complex social purposes, within an overall goal that takes multiple genres to accomplish (Rose & Martin 2012). The ideas of elemental genre, embedded genre and macrogenre (or genre complex) are important for us to capture the genre relations in data news, which is often instantiated as complex multimodal discourses.

(4) Discourse Semantics as Tools for Genre Description

Martin and Rose (2008) pointed out that defining genre as a configuration of meanings imples that these meanings need to be analyzed. Then how can they be analyzed? For language, the systems of phonology (Halliday 1970), the systems of lexicogrammar (Halliday 1994; Halliday 2008) and the systems of discourse semantics (Martin 2004/1992; Martin & Rose 2007/2003, 2014/2007) can all be relied on. However, in Martin's view, the discourse semantic systems are good toolkits for genre description because these are "the resources which interface most directly with register and genre" (Martin & Rose 2008: 30) and they focus on "text-size rather than clause-size meanings (Martin 2004/1992: 1). Section 3.4.1 below includes more details of the discourse semantic systems.

In summary, Halliday associates genre with relation to mode, Hasan with field, while Martin sees it realized by the configurations of the three register variables. In spite of the differences, their contributions on genre lie in 1) genres as types of goal-directed communicative processes; 2) genres as realized by meaning patterns of language; 3) genre provides a theoretical mechanism that is both predictive and explanatory. "Membership of some text in a genre allows firm predictions to be made concerning the linguistic details of that text and conversely, the occurrence of particular combinations of linguistic features can in turn be a strong indicator of genre membership" (Bateman et al 2007: 147). The SFL perspective on genre offers an operable framework of multimodal genre study. Genre gives rise to stable structural forms by imposing constraints on the use of lexico-grammatical as well as discoursal resources. Studies of genre can capture how writers achieve their communicative purposes by using various resources.

Besides the theoretical conceptualization outlined above, SFL analyses have also described features of the genres of different disciplines, e.g., Halliday and Martin (1993) on science; O'Halloran (2008b) on mathematics; Coffin (2003) on history; Christie (1999) on subject English; Wignell (1997) on social science; Christie (2002) for analysis of the role of disciplinary differences in the recontextualization of knowledge for education. Martin's conceptualization of genre has also been widely used in empirical studies of practices within and across fields. It provides a consistent correlate in research. For example, Martin, Maton and Matruglio (2010) described how configurations of meaning are presented differently in science compared to history; Hood (2010) analyzed what kinds of story genres appear in research writing and why they appear; Zappavigna et al. (2012/2008) explored how the practice of Youth Justice Conferencing as a genre has evolved over time with changes to the composition of the member of the conference.

The present study will follow the SFL genre tradition, particularly Martin's model because his stratification of context renders genre, register and language as different meaning-making strata and he expounded how to explore the bidirectional interaction between genre, register and language (and other semiotic modes) with discourse semantics systems as a powerful toolkit.

3. 2 Moving to Multimodal Genre

As has been reviewed in section 2. 3. 4 of Chapter 2, the use of web-mediated or mobile phone-mediated communication has skyrocketed during the past ten years. Therefore, recent years have seen a steady increase in genre research which deals with genres transmitted through the electronic media—the Internet, mobile phones and other mobile devices. In other words, the scope of genre analysis has extended from linear, monomodal genres transmitted through speech or print to non-linear, multimodal genres transmitted through various electronic media. Accordingly, the term multimodal genre has been used quite often in recent multimodal studies (e.g., Bateman et al 2007, Lemke 2009), and, "work on multimodal gcnrcs is an important focus of innovativc discoursc analysis" (Martin & Rose 2008: 232).

In multimodality research following SFL traditions (e.g., Kress & van Leeuwen 2006; Martin & Rose 2008; Bateman 2011; Bateman et al. 2017; Martin & Zappavignia 2018), semiotic modes are conceptualized as socially-shaped resources or potentials for making and exchanging meaning. An SFL multimodal approach to genre focuses on the meaningful combinations of written language, illustrations, photographs, diagrams, maps, layout and other modes of expression in any multimodal discourses.

However, previous studies have not differentiated the different degrees of abstraction of features or properties identified in multimodal artifacts. For instance, many studies spotlight the interplay between genre and medium, and identify new genres by the overall medium features (e.g., Askehave & Nielsen 2005; Bateman 2008, 2014, 2017; Bateman et al. 2017). McLuhan (1962) contended early in the 1960s, "the medium is the message". It can be seen that medium is one important part of genres transmitted on the website, but it's not all. From the perspective of viewers, it is more important to see what meanings it conveys or affords to convey and reveal how it realizes or assists in the realizations of meanings at different strata. For instance, the layout of data news as a homepage functions to introduce the user or viewer to the content and guide their reading of the content. This is a navigational function, the "gateway" to or the medium of the content which is more abstract. It is not the ultimate communicative goal of a piece of data news, but it contributes to the achievement of the ultimate communicative goal. This poses two questions to the study of multimodal genre: What role does medium play in genre identification? How do the meaning patterns of each semiotic mode in a multimodal discourse relate to genre? To answer these questions, let's first see what insights scholars get from linguistic and visual studies on multimodal genres.

3. 2. 1 Moving to Multimodal Genre from Linguistic Approaches

We have seen in the previous section that SFL attributes genres with a very particular social significance. If verbal and non-verbal artefacts are social practices which can be indicative of social relations, then genre must also be a useful category to apply regardless of semiotic modes (Bateman et al 2007).

There have been various attempts to apply the SFL studies of genre to multimodal texts. Kress and van Leeuwen (1998) applied functional grammar to developing an analytical framework for the analysis of newspaper genre. They regard all the elements on the front page, such as headlines, photographs and text blocks, as meaningful entities. The major contribution of their study is revealing the systems that realize the layout of front page. Bateman et al (2007) mapped the multimodal genres of traditional and electronic newspapers and aimed to capture the spatial information implicit in the visual design of traditional and electronic newspaper front pages. Their study also contributes to identifying and interpreting the layout structures in newspaper front pages. They also note that genres are changing with new forms of media and technology: "News genres are now forming very rapidly as new forms of expression are attempted with electronic documents. Old genres are changing under the influence of these news genres, while new genres also revise existing forms." (p. 148) Bateman (2008) extended the linguistic notion of genre to multimodality and takes it as the foundation of his comparative studies of multimodal documents. Knox (2007) discussed how digital, discursive and ideological convergences are contributing to the development of a grammar of visual design in the English-language online newspapers, which leads to the emergence of *Newsbite*, a new sub-genre of online news reports resembling "single-sentence news stories" in print newspapers. His study can be seen as an initial contribution to a critical description of the developments of online newspapers, the evolution of verbal news genres and the development of conventions of visual design. Caple and Bednareck (2010) identified the image-nuclear news story as a sub-genre of multmodal news stories and anzalyzed the image-text interaction in this genre.

The extension of linguistic genre to treat multimodal texts has revealed certain regularities in multimodal texts. It has also found genres of websites (Roberts 1998), genres of technical manuals (Hartley 1994), genre of non-linear hypertexts (Shepherd & Watters 1998), of e-mail messages (Gruber 2000), and of print and online newspapers (Bateman et al 2007), etc. It has also identified new sub-genres within these genres, for instance, image-nuclear news stories of print newspaper genre and newsbite within online newspaper genre. However, despite this " fashionability of multimodal analysis" (Bateman 2008: 201), a clear definition of multimodal genre and an overall framework for explanatory analyses of the differences and similarities of different genres of multimodal texts are still lacking.

3.2.2 Moving to Multimodal Genre from Studies on Visual Genre

The move to multimodal genre from linguistic approaches does not bring into full play the spatial arrangements of elements in a multimodal text. However, studies on visual genre offer more insights into the layout and spatial interplay of those elements. Visual studies of genre have not been concerned primarily with texts, but have included "notions of document types from design, of particular classes of document based on visual organizational features, as well as results that have been obtained in automating document class recognition in the document analysis community" (Bateman 2008: 196). The approaches to classifying types of multimodality by the visual composition (form) of documents (or texts) "do not typically begin by asking what purpose the document is serving, going on to investigate what texts and text-accompanying features may be observable, but instead go directly to the visual resources deployed" (Bateman 2008: 201). These approaches, however, often include treatments of document pages and layout and so contribute directly to the identification of layout in multimodal genre.

Bateman (2008) gave a systematized review of these approaches. According to him, classifications of visual forms can be made based on the interaction between visual form and design or between visual form and automatic document analysis.

The possibilities for visual form can be explored through the visual structure of documents. Twyman (1979) proposed a schema that classifies pages according to 28 categories of visual composition. These categories can be seen as set of candidates for visual genres. Walker (1982) offers a detailed classification of the typographical attributes of documents that goes beyond narrow typographical concerns of font or type face to include *spatial* characteristics (word spacing, line increment, margins, etc.), *graphic* characteristics (underlying, capitalization patterns, etc.), and *physical* attributes (produced with a typewriter, the paper used, and so on). These all can serve as a basis for exploring the generic features of a variety of genres. As we will see in Chapter 4, visual attributes of this kind are also within our stratified mode for multimodal texts.

The research from automatic analysis has made significant progress in "clustering visually related documents together into families of similar documents" and "such families consist of documents exhibiting similarities of 'style', both linguistically and visually". (Bateman 2008: 206). With respect to visual families, "members of the same class are considered to be visually similar; members of distinct classes are visually dissimilar" (ibid). Doermann et al (1997) argued that web documents can be classified according to their basic intended function. Distinction of genres of web texts can be made according to "use" and to "type". Eglin and Bres (2004) formulated a model of functional document analysis for assigning functional labels automatically. In this account, documents are first decomposed into textual and non-textual elements using filters of various kinds. A range of features are extracted from the visual properties of these elements, including salience, framing, and position with respect to other elements. This information is taken as the basis for functional labeling. They have applied the framework to a range of documents, including newspapers.

The extension of genre to treat multimodal artefacts has evidently been found quite natural in almost all research traditions that work explicitly with a notion of genre (Bateman 2008). The present study works mainly within the systemic functional framework on the study of genre, but also draws notions from studies on visual genres. To be specific, the study aims to describe the changes in news genres with the changing technology and social needs, to identify the features in each layer as described in the preset model, and to reveal how the communicative purposes of news stories and opinions are realized by the combination of language and images.

Bateman et al. (2007) argued that multimodal genres exhibit just as high a degree of regularity in their relationships with each other and with context as do traditional genres. Indeed, multimodal genres "show how a collection of semiotic resources pattern together in order to fulfill recurrent, recognizable social goals" (ibid: 158). Co-genericity in multimodal texts "arises out of all the modalities present in a text and assumes intertextual interpretation to apply equally across documents that are richly multimodal" (ibid). Therefore, the notion of multimodal genre offers a good foundation for a comparative study of distinct multimodal texts, which can reveal the patterns of similarity and difference between each single text. "Whenever we analyze a multimodal document, we need to consider the sets of documents that it resembles and the sets of documents with which it stands in contrast." (Bateman 2008: 177)

The generic study on multimodal news texts can also enhance the mutual predictability between genre and text. Knowing the genre to which a text belongs leads to particular predications concerning the form, function and contents of the text (Bateman 2008: 196). When we interpret a text belonging to one genre other than another, we discover certain "interpretative frames and expectations" (Bateman 2008: 178) or "certain sorts of semantic patterning" (Lemke 1998). Such frames and expectation or semantic patterning establishes constraints on text design and interpretation, which are helpful for identifying features in texts. Comparison of distinct texts can also reveal different sorts of semantic patterning, and such differences are the basis for identifying genres.

3. 2. 3 Defining Multimodal Genre

The term multimodal genre has been used quite often in recent multimodal studies, and studies on linguistic genres and visual genres have offered insights in the study of multimodal genres. Then what is a multimodal genre? It's necessary to offer a working definition for the present study.

Bateman et al. (2007) extended the functional linguistic notion of genre to map the multimodal genres of traditional and electronic newspapers. They defined the multimodal genre as "regularly occurring selections of features that may be linked with particular social practices: linguistic, layout, rhetorical, content, navigation, canvas (virtual artifact), production, and consumption" (Bateman et al 2007: 158). The definition embraces not only the inherent features of multimodal texts (linguistic, layout, rhetorical and content features), but also features from outside, (canvas, production, and consumption technologies). In their article, they distinguish print newspaper genre and website newspaper genre. The generic differences between print newspaper genre and website newspaper genre lie more in the canvas (one is printed paper, one is screen), and the way of production and consumption, but not in their inherent textual features. In other words, website newspapers announce their genre membership as newspapers for they share the similar textual structures with traditional print newspaper genre. Bateman (2008) pointed out the importance of generic structures for multimodal discourses presented through different media. He said, "Characterizing both generic structures and the particular constraints holding one element is certain to become increasingly important for all kinds of genre recognition—both of traditional print documents and in new media." (p. 208) Bateman et al. (2017) applied genre as "a theoretical construct covering very different kinds of communicative artefacts and situations" (p. 131). Bateman and his co-authors saw genres as bundles of strategies for achieving particular communicative purposes in particular ways. They held the view that genres define communicative purposes and it is then the discourse semantics of the modes provided by targeted media that must attempt to achieve those purposes. This echoes with Martin's definition of genres in language.

From Bateman et al.'s mapping of multimodal genre, we find multimodal genre can be defined according to the linguistic traditions of genre, concerned more with the inherent features of the multimodal text, such as multimodal news stories, multimodal news opinions, multimodal dramas, etc. In this sense, "a genre might be defined in terms of the social communicative purposes it allows to achieve, the meaning that it can carry" (Bateman et al. 2007: 152). Genre taxonomy is particularly applicable to the study of multimodal texts produced with the same canvas. For instance, the multimodal newspapers texts have the same canvas, and therefore, and the genre memberships of these texts should be made according to the inherent features each text presents. The inherent features include choices of typography, graphical elements, grammar that glue words and graphical elements into larger units, discourse relations and generic patterns realized by semiotic patterns.

Combing both Martin's genre model for language and Bateman's conceptualization of multimodal genre, we define **multimodal genres as configurations of meaning** which map culture and are realized by more than one semiotic modes. They determine the communicative purposes which are achieved step by step in multimodal discourses. In this way we have tried to open the door to multimodal realizations of genres, including various modalities of communication (Martin & Rose 2008: 232).

3. 3 Theoretical Foundations

Over the last several decades, SFL has developed a comprehensive theoretical architecture which aims at a social study of meaning (Hao 2015: 10-11). It takes language and other semiotic modes as meaning-making resources which organize themselves in principled ways and have evolved systems of meanings. The notions of denotative and connotative semiotics, the typological and topological perspectives to genre, the dimensions of metafunction, realization, stratification, discourse semantics and lexico-grammar, and the idea of coupling and commitment provide complementary perspectives for the present exploration of the data news genre.

3. 3. 1 Denotative and Connotative Semiotics

Context is interpreted as a connotative kind of semiotic system, within which multiple denotative semiotic systems operate (see Martin 1992; Martin & Rose 2008). The distinction of connotative and denotative semiotics was first made by Hjelmslev, who defined connotative semiotics as "semiotic systems which have another semiotic system as their expression plane" (Martin & Rose 2008: 16). Denotative semiotics have their own expression plane. In these terms, language, image, sound and other semiotic modes are denotative semiotics realizing context, the connotative semiotics. When different semiotic systems, such as language and "body language", language and image, or language and music, operate together in the creation of meaning in a multisemiotic system, they operate within one and the same context, and they are coordinated within this context. Functionally these different semiotic systems are integrated within the context they operate in so that they can create meaning seamlessly and synergistically. Context is the semiotic environment, the environment of meaning, in which all semiotic systems operate. Since one key "architectural" feature of all semiotic systems is that they are stratified into two planes, the content plane and the expression plane (each of which may be internally stratified into further levels of organization), context can be interpreted as the highest stratum within this hierarchy of stratification (see Halliday 1978; Martin 1992; Ghadessy 1999); it is the stratum above the content planes of all denotative semiotic systems. At the other end of the hierarchy of stratification, the expression plane, multisemiotic systems are, however, not integrated but they are instead diversified: they are realized through different expression systems, such as those of spoken language (vocalization), body language and music. Multimodality is a feature of the expression planes of semiotic systems in the first instance (Matthiessen 2009: 12).

Socio-semiotic systems give "meaning" to matter (cf. Halliday 2005): social systems impose social order ("value") on the world of matter, and semiotic systems impose semiotic order (meaning in its narrower sense of valeur and signification; cf. Hasan, 1985) on this social world. At the pole of minimal integration, two or more semiotic systems are completely separate as (denotative) semiotic systems—that is, separate in terms of both their content systems and their expression systems (Matthiessen 2009: 15); these systems can be integrated and coordinated at the highest level of semiotic organization, that is, within the (connotative) semiotic system of context.

3.3.2 Typology and Topology

We will combine the typological and topological perspectives to analyze the elemental genres in the sample text.

Typology is to classify genres, and it is "fundamentally a taxonomic exercise" (Martin & Rose 2008: 130), which means that it "establishes systems with two or more features that are categorically differentiated from one another" (Martin 2013: 120). In Martin's genre model, typology is located within a stratum of genre which is immediately above the stratum of register. One meaning pattern (e.g., a generic stage) will be privileged over another as more or less critical for categorization of genres. Systems or system networks formalize typological relations. Genre typology is supplemented by genre topology.

Topology, "proximating likeness, allows us to relate genres as more or less like one another, from as many angles as we wish" (Martin & Rose 2008: 131). It was introduced by Lemke (see Martin & Matthiessen 1991) as a perspective on genre agnation complementing that of typology. A topology "uses two or more axes representing clines to define a space in which categories can be positioned gradiently in relation to another" (Martin 2013: 120). It also functions as a "representation of agnation—of relatedness in paradigmatic organization" (Matthiessen et al. 2010: 130). Topological analysis is a useful tool for modeling relations among genres because "now and again we'll come across texts which are difficult to categorize as one genre or another (i.e., texts that 'blend' genres)" (Martin & Rose 2008: 133). In such cases, typological analysis which creates categorical distinctions is insufficient, a topological perspective, namely "thinking about things as ranged along a cline" (Martin & Rose 2008: 130), may prove to be more productive.

Painter et al. (2012) also pointed out that one weakness of describing meaning in terms of categorical "oppositions"—such as [positive] versus [negative], [interrogative] versus [declarative]—is that the description sets up very distinct "typological" either/or categories. It has been argued that even for describing language, this typological approach may need a complementary "topological" one that allows for fuzzy boundaries and points on a continuum rather than either/or extremes (Martin & Matthiessen,

1991). And it may well be the case that non-linguistic forms of semiosis, such as images, have even more fluid categories than does language.

In short, as modes of agnation, typology and topology work complementarily to help researchers think about the categorical differences among genres (namely their paradigmatic relations) and about their relations along a cline of likeness. So, we will adopt these two complementary perspectives in the preset study.

3.3.3 System and Structure

System and structure are two complementary perspectives in SFL's theorization of language. Halliday and many SFL scholars (e.g., Halliday 1994, 2008; Martin 2013) have expounded the two terms. Halliday (2008: 22) offered a simple yet clear explanation: "Structure is the syntagmatic ordering in language: patterns, or regularities, in what goes together with what. System, by contrast, is ordering on the other axis: patterns in what could go instead of what. This is the paradigmatic ordering." In other words, paradigmatic relations are represented as oppositions of meanings in a system and syntagmatic ones are represented as structure, the unfolding of meanings in a text. The notions of structure and system represent the basic mechanism by which signs have meaning: in combination with other signs and by substitution for other signs. A structure can be regarded as "the outward form taken by systemic choices" (Halliday 2008: 23); "each system—each moment of choice—contributes to the formation of the structure" (ibid: 24), while "a system is the central category representing paradigmatic organization at any stratum—phonological, grammatical, or semantic" (Matthiessen & Halliday 2009: 97).

A system is composed of any set of two or more alternatives or options, which together with its condition of entry, constitute a system. An option in a system is termed as "feature". Features are "the names for classes of semiotic phenomena" (Martin 2013: 14). An entry condition is the point of origin which allows access to a particular system (ibid: 15). A feature in a system can be the entry condition for its subsystem and this captures the characteristic that the choices in systems to the right are more specific; this scale relating more general systems to more specific ones is termed as delicacy. In language, it is common that two or more systems share an entry condition. In this case, features in these systems are in "both-and" relations and the systems are called simultaneous systems. In language, it is also possible that systems have "a complex condition—i. e., an entry condition consisting of more than a single feature" (Martin 2013: 17). Compared with formal approaches to language, SFL focuses more on the systemic or paradigmatic perspective while it describes structures. Halliday and other SFL scholars emphasized that "a language is a resource for making meaning, and meaning resides in systemic patterns of choices" (ibid: 23). Indeed, the paradigmatic or systemic focus of SFL has profoundly shaped its theoretical architecture (Martin 2012/2008).

A number of notational conventions have been developed in SFL to present systems and system networks. The conventions that are key for drawing SFL systems and systems networks include: system names are written in small caps; features are written in lower case font and are positioned at the end points of a right-facing square bracket; the square bracket indicates an "either-or" relation; and a right facing brace is used to present a simultaneous system. The conventions for system representation of language were summed up in Matthiessen and Halliday (2009: 98). But as some SFL scholars (e. g. Martin & Matthiessen 1991; Hood 2001) have noticed, there can be fuzzy boundaries and points on a continuum rather than either/or extremes, and non-linguistic forms of semiosis, such as images, have even more fluid categories than does language (Painter et al.

2013). To capture such features, Hood (2011) adopted the method of tilting the square brackets of any system that is a continuum or "cline" rather than a categorical opposition. In this book, we will follow this convention.

Table 3-1 Conventions in System Drawings

(Based on Matthiessen & Halliday 2009: 98)

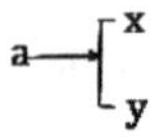	system: if "a", then "x" or "y"—abbreviated as "a: x/y"
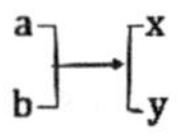	disjunction in entry condition: if "a/b", then "x/y"
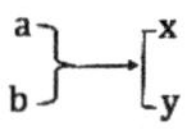	conjunction in entry condition: if "a" and "b" (abbreviated as "a & b")
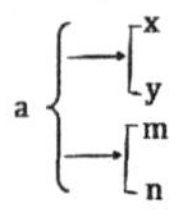	simultaneity: if "a", then simultaneously "x/y" and "m/n"
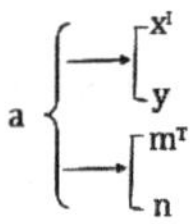	conditional marking①: If "x", then also "m"
	tilting bracket: representing a system that is a continuum or "cline" rather than a categorical opposition

① In Matthiessen and Halliday's summary, the symbols " * →" was used to indicate "if" condition and "→ * " to indicate "then". But in the systems of MOOD by Martin (2013), the letters "I" and "T" were used. We follow this convention.

SFL scholars supplement the description of meaning systems with the description along the lines of structure. At the stratum of lexicogrammar, a structure is made up of a configuration of grammatical functions, each of which may be realized by either a set of grammatical features or a set of lexical features (Matthiessen & Halliday 2009: 97). Both function and class labels are used for syntagmatic structure. Class is the systemic term for the term category in formal grammar. It generalizes the traditional notion of word classes and thus applies to morphemes, groups, phrases and clauses as well as words (ibid: 93). An arrangement of classes is called a syntagm in SFL. Function at the lexicogrammatical stratum is, more accurately, the micro-function, which contrasts with macro-function (language use in early child-language, before use and metafunction have become differentiated) and metafunction (generalized functional principle of linguistic organization). Function here refers to "functionally defined constituents", like Actor, Process, and Circumstance. In SFL, it's a convention to capitalize the first letter of a function label.

System and structure are two complementary perspectives in SLF's theorization of language. This complementary relationship between system and structure is called axis (Matthiessen & Halliday 2009; Martin 2013). Systems and system networks describe meaning potentials along the axis of choice; this highlights the systemic aspect. Structure captures the syntagmatic relations of the elements selected from systems; this is the axis of chain and highlights the functional aspect. Choices from a system are realized through structure along the axis of chain. The relationship between system and structure has been diagrammatically presented by Hao (2015) (see Figure 3-3).

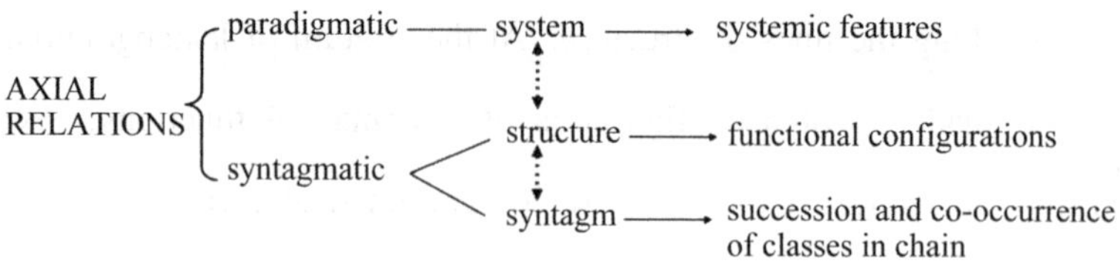

Figure 3-3 System and Structure, Paradigmatic and Syntagmatic Axis (Hao 2015: 20)

Multimodal discourse analysis can be approached from these two complementary perspectives as well. Following the SFL tradition, we will describe both the structural patterns and the systemic choices, but with the axis of choice as the focus. Figure 3-4 is an instantiated system network of ENTITY in news photos.

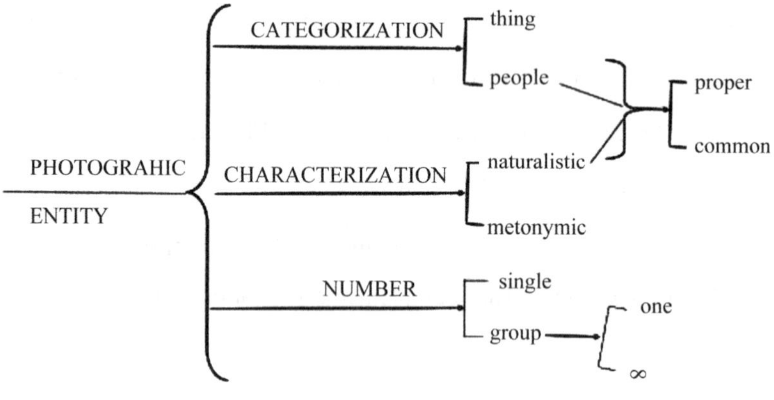

Figure 3-4 An Instantiated System Network of Entities in News Photos

"PHOTOGRAPHIC ENTITY" is the name of the system network and also the entry condition of three simultaneous systems, named "CATEGORIZATION", "CHRACTERIZATION" and "NUMBER" respectively. The three systems each have two features or options. It means that an instantiated news photo can depict people or things in a naturalistic or metonymic way and the depicted entity can be just one individual or thing, or more than one in number. If we choose [people] from the system of CATEGORAIZTION and [naturalistic] from CHARACTERIZATION, then we can also have a subsystem with two features, namely [proper] which is realized by photographs of famous people recognizable to viewers and [common] which depicts common or ordinary people who are difficult or unable to be identified just by their visual image.

3. 3. 4 Metafunction, Stratification, and Instantiation

The dimensions of metafunction, realization, and stratification provide complementary dimensions for our understanding of how genre and language relate to each other bi-directionally, of how systems or meaning potentials and instances relate to each other, and of how ranks within language relate to each other.

According to SFL, language is socially functional. Then what are the basic functions of language, in relation to our ecological and social environment and to the language itself? Halliday (1994, 2014) suggested three **metafuntions**: making sense of human experience, acting out human social relationships and organizing the above two into unified texts. The function that language construes human experience, naming things, construing them into categories, and construing categories into taxonomies is called ideational metafunction, which is further distinguished into two components, the experiential and the logical. While construing, language is always also enacting: enacting the personal and social relationships between people. Such a function is called interpersonal metafunction. The third function that relates to the construction of text is called textual metafunction. It is an enabling or facilitating function, since both the other two metafunctions depend on it to build up sequences of discourse, organize the discursive flow and create unity and continuity as discourse moves along (see Halliday 2014: 30-31). So, metafunctions are "the different bundles of meaning systems that are oriented to different social functions" (Hao 2015: 15). The idea of metafunctions has also been applied to analyze the systems and meaning potentials in semiotic modes other than language①, for instance images (Kress & van Leeuwen 1996, 2006), picture books (Painter et al. 2013), news photos (Caple 2009a, 2013, 2022), displayed arts (O'Toole, 1994, 1995), sound (van Leeuwen 1999; Caldwell 2022), movement (Martinec 2000, 2001), three-dimensional space (Ravelli 2000; Stenglin 2004, 2008), film (O'Halloran 2004; Bateman 2007, 2009), mathematics (O'Halloran 2008b; Doran 2022), and paralanguage (Martin & Zappavigna 2018; Logi & Zappavigna 2022).

SFL conceptualizes the relationship between language (now also including other semiotic modes) and context as natural and bi-directional—language symbolizes context, and context is symbolized by language. Genre and register constitute the two strata of context, while phonology/graphology, lexicogrammar and discourse semantics constitute the three strata of language. Genre and register, the highly abstract strata which have content but no form in Hjelmslev's terms, are connotative semiotics which have another semiotic system as their expression plane (Martin & Rose 2008: 16). Language is denotative semiotics which has both the content and expression planes. Discourse semantics and lexicogrammar are the content of language while phonology/graphology is its expression. **Stratification** relates these different orders of reality or meanings on a cline of abstraction (Hao 2015: 11), and metafunction organizes systems on a given stratum of language or semiotics.

The natural relationship between context and language (also other semiotic modes) is possible since three register variables (field, tenor, and

① For more details, please refer to section 2.3 of Chapter 2.

mode) correspond to the metafunctional organization of language. Following Halliday (e.g., 1978, 1985), field, concerned with what is going on in a social activity, is construed by ideational meanings of language; tenor, concerned with relationship between interactants, is enacted by interpersonal meanings; and mode, concerned with the role language or other semiotic mode plays in a text, is composed by textual meanings.

Instantiation explores the relationship between the reservoir of systems at each language or semiotic stratum and their manifestation in text. It is described as a cline, where we may observe a text from the point of view of the system at one end of the cline or from the standpoint of the text as an instance at the other. By system we mean the overall generalized meaning potential of language, and by instance, we mean the affording instance, the actual text as it is manifested in a particular context at a particular time. Their relation is like that between climate and everyday "weather" (Halliday 1992). The instance is the weather that we can observe, and the potential is the climate we can postulate as a generalization based on representative samples of weather. In the case of language, the instance pole of the cline is what speakers mean on a given occasion, their acts of meaning (Halliday 1993), and the potential pole is what speakers can mean. In other words, the entire pattern or meaning potential of a semiotic mode is made available in the generation of an instantiated text, just like we take water resource from a reservoir. Meanwhile, the choices made are constrained by the meaning potential or the whole reservoir. Every stratum on the stratification hierarchy instantiates.

Please note that there are two views on the specific stratum of genre and language. In terms of genre, (as has been reviewed above in section 3. 1. 2), Martin takes a stratified view of language, register and genre, while Halliday and Hasan do not differentiate the two. Martin sees genre realized by the configurations of the three register variables, which is different from Halliday who associates genre with relation to mode, and also from Hasan who associates genre with field. For the specific strata within language, Halliday (2014) proposed a model of four strata (see Figure 3-5), while Martin and his co-authors (e.g., Martin 1999, 2004/1992; Martin & Rose 2008) stuck to the idea of three strata (see Figure 3-6). Halliday and Matthiessen's strata for language are phonetics, phonology, orthography (or graphology), lexicogrammar and semantics. The strata of lexicogrammar and semantics belong to the "content" plane, which is "what allows the meaning potential of a language to expand, more or less indefinitely" (Halliday 2008: 24). Phonology or graphology, and phonetics belong to expression plane. The authors stratified the expression plane to separate "the organizing function from the function of interfacing

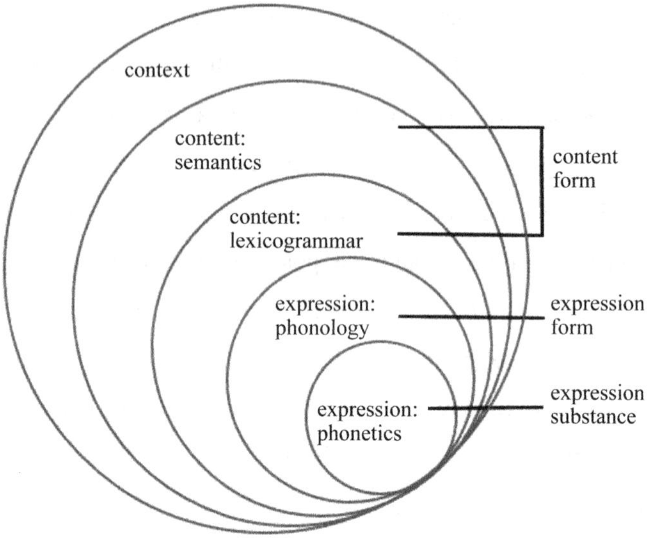

Figure 3-5 Halliday's Stratification of Context and Language

(Based on Halliday & Matthiessen 2013: 25)

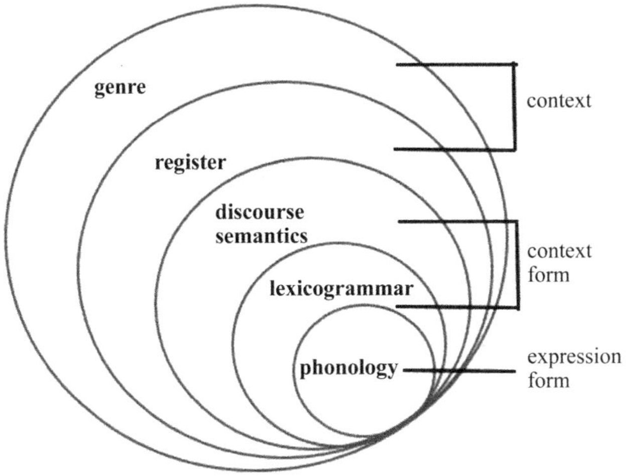

Figure 3-6 Martin's Stratification of Context and Language

(Based on Martin 1999, 2004/1992; Martin & Rose 2008)

with the environment" (ibid: 25). The environment here is the human body. Martin held the same view of stratifying the content plane into semantics and lexicogrammar, but he used the term "discourse semantics" instead of "semantics" because he aimed to reveal the meaning patterns of discourse not just of clauses. He did not stratify the expression plane, because in his view, phonetics which interfaces with the human body, is the substance in Hjelmslev's term. We agree with Martin's stratification of language and will apply his model to analyzing other semiotic modes.

In summary, the cline of instantiation, the spectrum of metafunction and the hierarchy of stratification are the global dimensions in the organization of language in context. The hierarchy of stratification is an ordering of levels of patterning in terms of abstraction (the different strata), the spectrum of metafunction is a sorting of patterns into different modes of meaning, and the cline of instantiation is a continuum of patterns in terms of generalization (Matthiessen et al. 2010). These global dimensions of organization all emerge gradually in ontogenesis, as a young child learns how to express/understand meaning (ibid). The cline of instantiation emerges when instances of potentially symbolic behavior become systemic—that is, when they occur again as instances of systemic contrasts; and every stratum on the stratification hierarchy instantiates. Besides, stratification and instantiation look at how language is organized or functions within a particular context and thus allow users and analysts to maintain two perspectives at once: language as system and as text (Halliday 2008; Martin 2010). In discourse analysis, we can interpret semiotic phenomena in terms of one semiotic dimension at a time, viewing them from the standpoint of one or more of the locations defined by a given dimension. We can also interpret semiotic phenomena in terms of two or more of the semiotic at a time. In the present study, we tend to interpret date news from all the three dimensions. Figure 3-7 is a diagrammatic representation of the interaction of the three dimensions.

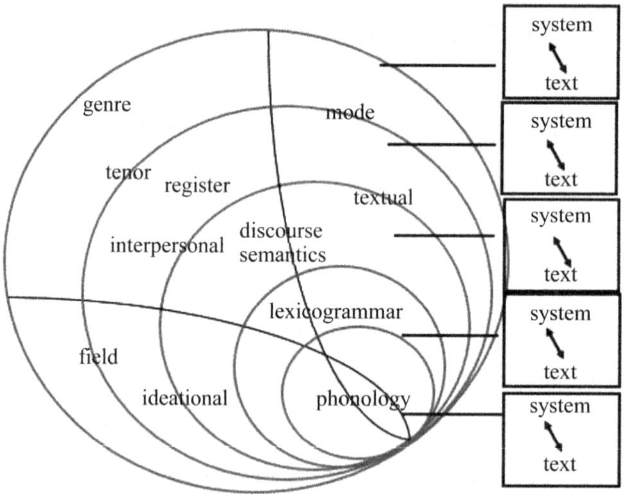

Figure 3-7 Stratification, Instantiation and Metafunctions in SFL

(Based on Martin 2010: 16, 22)

3. 3. 5 Realization

Realization is a key term in SFL. It is used in two senses. First, it refers to the symbolic inter-stratal relationship between the content and expression planes, and between the strata that make up these planes—between (discourse) semantics and lexicogrammar, between lexicogrammar and phonology (e.g., Halliday 2008; Matthiesen et al. 2010; Martin 2013). To be more specific, the relationship between each stratum along the hierarchy of stratification is realization: each stratum realizes the stratum at the higher level and is at the same time realized by the one at the lower level. It needs to be noted that the realizations along the cline are "not a chain of one-to-one relationships, but a non-linear way of relating patterns of meaning at one stratum to another" (Hao 2015: 13). In Lemke's (1984) term, such realizations are relationships of "metaredundancy", which means that meanings at a higher order stratum are patterns of meaning at the next lower order one. In other words, patterns or configurations of meaning at the strata of genre and register are realized in patterns or configurations of meaning of language and other semiotic modes.

Second, realization has been used to capture intra-stratal relationship: 1) the inter-rank relationship between a higher rank and the next lower rank on the rank scale of a given stratum, and 2) the inter-axial relationship between the paradigmatic axis and the syntagmatic axis of a given rank (Matthiessen et al. 2010: 172).

The realization relation is usually represented by a realization statement that specifies a structure fragment, such as the presence of a function or its ordering in relation to another function. In a system, it can be stated as a re-expression of a systemic feature or a combination of features. An arrow ↘ is used to symbolize the realization relation in a system. System networks represent implicate order in language, and terms in these networks are manifested through realization statements as explicate order in the form of structures. From the vantage point of realization statements, the system is like a "metarule" (Matthiessen et al. 2010: 212). This paradigmatic orientation of SFL's realization hierarchy has been a great strength as far as mapping the meaning potential of cultures has been concerned (Martin 2010).

3. 3. 6 Coupling and Commitment

Coupling and commitment are crucial concepts in multimodal discourse analysis, where synergies between modalities of communication are concerned (Martin 2010: 20).

The concept of coupling was first used to describe linguistic meaning combinations in the process of instantiation. In his article "Beyond exchange: appraisal systems in English", Martin (2012/2000) first introduced the notion of coupling to capture the linguistic fact that "what counts as appraisal depends on the field of discourse" (p. 222), that "ideational meanings that do not use evaluative lexis can be used to evoke appreciation, as with affect and judgment" (ibid). He called the alignment between appraisal and ideational meaning as "coupling of ideational meaning and appraisal". He argued that humor and sarcasm can be further explained "as involving discordant couplings—either between appraisal selections and what is being appraised, or among the appraisal variables themselves" (p. 225). He also pointed out that "every institution is loaded with couplings of this kind, and socialisation into a discipline involves both an alignment with the institutional practices involved and an affinity with the attitudes one is expected to have towards those practices" (ibid: 222). In this article, coupling was defined as "the combinationof ideational meanings and appraisal "at a particular point in the unfolding of a text, for the social subjects involved, at some moment in the evolution of the relevant institution" (ibid: 225).

This definition was extended in the article "Tenderness: realization and instantiation in a Botswanan town" (Martin 2012/2008). Martin defined coupling as "the ways in which meanings combine, as pairs, triplets, quadruplets or any number of coordinated choices from system networks" (ibid: 491). It is the binding of two meanings at any point along the cline of instantiation. In instantiated texts, an option does not occur alone; instead, options from different systems are combined and tend to show certain patterns in the texts. Martin stated clearly the mechanism of coupling: "What realization freely combines, instantiation specifically couples; the logic of the system networks allows us to state the relevant coupling at any point in delicacy." (ibid: 492) In the article, he identified the interpersonal coupling of judgment and amplification (coupling across simultaneous systems within the interpersonal metafiction) and the coupling of judgment with ideational meaning (coupling between two metafunctions). He also pointed out that a focus on coupling enables us to describe the frequency of selected expressions, to compare their patterns in combining these selected expressions, and to find out how they are combined. He highlighted the view that "it is interacting meanings that configure texts, text types, registers and genres" (ibid: 496).

The above studies focus on couplings within appraisal systems and between appraisal systems and other systems in language. Analyses and diagrammatic representations of couplings in language have been found in Zappavigna et al. (2010), Knight (2010), Hood (2010) as well as Szenes (2017).

The idea of coupling has also been extended to the analysis of multimodal discourses. The more theoretical conceptualization of intermodal coupling can be found in Martin (2010). In this article, Martin extended the notion of coupling to cover the combinations across semiotic modes and defined coupling as "the way in which meanings combine—across strata, metafunctions, ranks, and simultaneous systems and across modalities" (Martin 2010: 19). He took coupling and commitment as tools for exploring multimodality in relation to functional variation among texts. Coupling occurs in the cline of instantiation and instantiation can be seen as "a hierarchy of couplings" (Martin 2010: 26).

A wide range of studies have also focused more on the coupling patterns in different types of multimodal discourses. In the article co-authored by Zappavigna, Dwyer and Martin (2012/2008), the authors explored patterned couplings in Youth Justice conferencing dialogues. They elaborated on how meanings are coupled along the cline of instantiation and are involved in larger textual patterns. They adopted the idea of systemic probability to determine whether particular meanings are related and to measure the strength of association. They pointed out that "coupling is both syntagmatic, since items that are coupled are likely to occur very near each other logogenetically, and paradigmatic, since patterns of the same type of coupling are likely to re-occur across a text" (ibid: 63). They proposed to determine and measure the likelihood of particular couplings and model the tendencies in coupling from the perspective of systemic probability—"something is strongly coupled if it frequently co-occurs and loosely coupled if the logogenetic patterning is sparse" (ibid: 66). They also argued that "meaning potential does not bind directly into simple coupling but is instantiated through a process that involves interaction with co-text and context" (ibid: 63). Zappavigna et al. (2010) applied coupling to uncover the multimodal interactions of gesture and phonology in spoken discourse and explored how the meanings construed by the coupling of gesture and speech function in the particular context of situation in which they are deployed.

In *Reading Visual Narratives* (Painter et al. 2012), coupling was further developed as a perspective to analyze the binding patterns of two or more meanings in two or more semiotic modes. In this foundational manuscript on intermodal interaction in picture books from a SFL perspective, coupling was clearly defined and also more systematically elaborated. The authors defined coupling as the "repeated co-patterning within a text of realizations from two or more systems" (ibid: 143). They argued that, in principle, coupling can be within or across metafunctions, as "the realization hierarchy radically underspecifies the ways in which systems from different strata, metafunctions and ranks combine with one another; it is the responsibility of instantiation to account for the way in which cultures enact patterns of interacting meaning" (ibid). In addition, coupling can happen within one semiotic mode or across semiotic modes. For instance, intramodally there can be a consistent coupling of linguistic choices from two interpersonal systems such as graduation: force and attitude: affect/negative; multimodally, there might be a consistent co-patterning of particular ambience choices in the visual with complementary choices of positive attitude in the verbal (ibid). Be it convergent or divergent, coupling can make each semiotic amplify one another and thus multiply corresponding kinds of meaning. Converging ideational couplings create concurrence, converging interpersonal couplings create resonance, and converging textual couplings create synchrony across all or part of the text. More recently, Martin (2017) emphasized that couplings draw on meanings from different ranks, strata, metafuntions or different modalities and occur along the cline of instantiation as being complementary to analysis alongside the realization hierarchy. He argued that along the hierarchy of instantiation, it is important to show how choices from systems integrate in an apparently seamless unfolding text.

Commitment, a term used along with coupling, refers to "the amount of meaning potential activated in a particular process of instantiation"

(Martin 2012/2008: 497). It has to do with the degree to which meanings in optional systems are taken up and within systems, the degree of delicacy selected (ibid). It is of particular value to study the intermodal interaction or coupling across semiotic modes. For instance, in picture books, the verbal text and the image on a page may contribute the same amount of ideational meaning, i. e., equally committed ideationally, but they may be unequally committed interpersonally with the image realizing more interpersonal meaning by, say, the choices from the AMBIENCE system.

In short, coupling has to do with combining meanings at relevant levels of generality and commitment has to do with the amount of meaning manifested in instances of monomodal or multimodal discourses. They are two ways in which instantiation can be explored and so can relate with the dimensions of stratification, realization and metafunction.

3.4 Building up a Genre Framework for Data News Analysis

3.4.1 Strata for Data Stories

A systematic description of the lexiogrammatical and discourse semantic patterns can serve as the basis for capturing the generic features (Martin & Rose 2008). When analyzing English genres, we rely on Halliday (1994) as well as Halliday and Matthiessen (2004) for lexicogramar, on Kress and van Leeuwen (2006) as well as Caple (2013) for visual grammar, and on Martin (2004/1992), Martin and Rose (2007/2003), Painter et al. (2012) as well as Bednarek and Caple (2012) for discourse semantics. We will start with and focus more on the stratum of discourse semantics since this is the stratum which interfaces most directly with register and genre (Martin & Rose 2008: 30). We will identify generic stages and elemental genres in the sample text by describing the field-tenor-mode interaction as realized in the discourse semantic patterns.

3. 4. 1. 1 Discourse Semantics

(1) Martin's Discourse Semantic Systems in Language

SFL conceptualizes the relationship between language and context as natural and bi-directional—language realizes context, and context is realized through language. The highly abstract strata of genre and register are connotative semiotics which have another semiotic system as their expression plane (Martin & Rose 2008: 16). We will start with and focus more on the stratum of discourse semantics since this is stratum which interfaces most directly with register and genre (Martin & Rose 2008: 30).

Discourse semantics aims to explore the meaning beyond the clause. The term discourse semantics indicates that discourse is treated more than words in clause and a pure analysis of meaning patterns at the clause level is insufficient to reveal the interaction between language and context or social activity. It also suggests that discourse is "more than an incidental manifestation of social activity" (Martin & Rose 2014/2007: 1); rather, social activity is constructed through discourses. Discourse semantics, by looking at the meaning patterns at the stratum of discourse rather than grammar, offers a path to connect grammar, discourse and social activity: grammarians are invited to "reconsider meaning in the clause from the perspective of meaning in texts", and social theorists "to reconsider social activity as meaning we negotiate in discourse" (Martin & Rose 2007: 1). In other words, "discourse nestles within social activity and grammar nestles within discourse, suggesting three complementary perspectives on a single complex phenomenon" (ibid: 4). The mediating role of discourse semantics makes it a perfect toolkit for genre analysis.

Discourse semantics was first described systematically in the book

English Text: *System and Structure* (Martin 1992). In that monograph, four systems were introduced. They are NEGOTIATION, IDENTIFICATION, CONJUNCTION, and IDEATION. Later, in the two versions of *Working with Discourse* (Martin & Rose 2007/2003, 2014/2007), two more systems were included—the systems of APPRAISAL and PERIODICITY.

Resources for making meaning as text are organized into six sets or systems which realize meaning patterns at the stratum of register and are themselves realized by meaning patterns at the stratum of clause. **Appraisal**① is concerned with evaluation—the kinds of attitudes that are negotiated (the subsystem of ATTITUE), the strength of the attitudes involved (the subsystem of GRADUATION) and the space open for negotiation (the subsystem of ENGAGEMENT). Appraisals realize interpersonal metafunction or meaning which realizes variation in the tenor or social interactions enacted in discourses. **Negotiation**, which also realizes interpersonal meanings, is concerned with "interaction as an exchange between speakers—how they adopt roles and assign them to each other in dialogue and how moves are organized in relation to one another" (Martin & Rose 2014/2007: 17). Two sub-systems are developed for analyzing dialogues. The system of SPEECH FUNCTION captures the relationship between moves and their realization in grammar (their MOOD at clause level) and the system of NEGOTIATION describe the sequence of moves around the choices of knowledge or action, primary or secondary knower initiation, secondary knower follow up or no follow up. **Ideation** and **conjunction** realize ideational meanings which realize variation in field. **Ideation** is concerned with how our experience is construed in discourse. It "focuses on sequences of activities, the people and things involved in them,

① The book *The Language of Evaluation*: *Appraisal in English* (Martin & White 2005) has a more in-depth and comprehensive description of the APPRAISAL system.

and the associated places and qualities, and on how these elements are built up and related to each other as a text unfolds" (ibid: 73). It describes three types of relations—taxonomic relations between participants in a discourse, nuclear relations between processes, people, things, places and qualities within a clause, and activity sequences between activities. Taxonomic relations can be realized by semantic relations of repetition, synonymy, antonymy, hyponymy and meronymy. In Martin's analysis of nuclear relations, four degrees of nuclearity are recognized: center (Process/ Range: process), nucleus (Medium; Range: entity, quality or possession), margin (Agent; Beneficiary), and periphery (Circumstance). Activity sequences are series of events that are expected by a field and are analyzed in relation to the phases of a text. Ideational grammatical metaphor is also a concern for analyzing ideational meaning. **Conjunction**, later renamed as **connexion** (Hao 2015) as an exclusive term for the stratum of discourse semantics, looks at the logical meanings in discourses, namely the "inter-connections between activities" (ibid). Addition, comparison, time and consequence are the main logic relations that link activities and messages in a discourse. Identification and periodicity realize textual meanings which realize variation in mode. Identification is concerned with tracking participants—with introducing people, places and things into a discourse and keeping track of them. It describes resources for identifying people—presenting reference that introduces people and things whose identities are unknown, presuming reference tracking and recovering the identities of people or things who have been introduced, and comparative reference about how people and things are connected by comparative resources. Periodicity considers the rhythm of discourse and is concerned with organizing discourse as pulses of information (Martin & Rose 2007: 17). It extends the Theme/Rheme structure to capture the information flow between paragraphs and longer texts. Information in a paragraph or for several paragraphs can be predicted by hyperTheme (like a topic sentence) and summarized as hyperNew. In longer texts, there can be macroTheme and macroNew. This constitutes Martin's concept of a hierarchy of periodicity. Figure 3-8 below is a diagrammatic representation of the six systems and their realization relation with the three metafunctions.

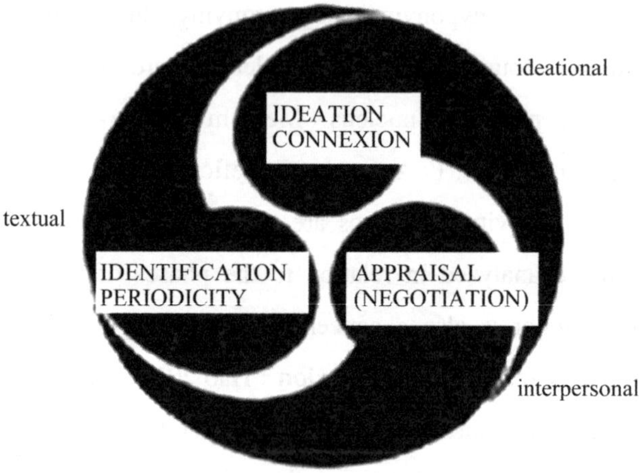

Figure 3-8 Discourse Semantic Systems (Based on Martin & Rose 2014/2007)

Bateman et al. (2017) also argued that all semiotic modes are taken to include discourse semantics. The authors took discourse semantics within any semiotic mode as "*relating particular deployments of 'semiotically charged' material to the contextualized communicative purposes they can take up*" (p. 116, original emphasis). They further pointed out that the discourse semantics of a semiotic mode provides the "*interpretive mechanisms* necessary (i) for relating any particular forms distinguished in a semiotic mode to their context of use and (ii) for demarcating the *intended range* of interpretations of those forms" (ibid: 116-116, original emphasis). Bateman and his co-authors stated that the genres define communicative purposes and the discourse semantics of semiotic modes provided must attempt to achieve those purposes. They also argued that discourse semantics do add significantly more to the power of semiotic modes—that is, we can do more with a semiotic mode because of the presence of its discourse semantics. Bateman's conceptualization is somewhat different from Martin's, yet their studies all point to the interpretive significance of discourse semantics in analyzing multimodal discourses and the relationships between context and multimodal discourses.

Therefore, the six discourse semantic systems proposed by Martin and his colleagues work as the starting point and the basic tools for capturing the generic features in the present study because it relates directly both to the strata of register and genre and also to the stratum of grammar below. The approach to discourse semantics is a trinocular one—looking from "above" in relation to the strata of register and genre, from below in relation to the stratum of lexicogrammar and around in terms of its relationship to the other semantic systems within the stratum of discourse semantics.

(2) Discourse Semantics in Picture Books and News Photos

The discourse semantic systems are also applicable to multimodal discourse analysis. As has been reviewed in Chapter 2, Painter et al (2012) analyzed picture books with a sequence of images. They built on Kress and van Leeuwen's visual grammar for analyzing the "grammar" of single images, but more importantly, they also move to the discourse level by looking at the character relations and action relations construing ideational meaning, affectual and ambient dimensions of interpersonal meaning, and framing and pictorial focus composing textual meanings. Apart from the discourse semantic systems in picture books, Badnareck and Caple (2012) described the resources for evaluation, conjunction, and reference in news photos, though their focus was news values in images. Other scholars (e.g., Martin 2012/2000; Economou 2006, 2008; Caple 2009a, 2013) have also conducted analysis of news discourses from the perspective of discourse semantics. These studies① offer insights into the analysis of meanings of news photos and text-image relations. They also prove the applicability of Martin's discourse semantics to describing meanings in other semiotic modes.

In the present study, we will take Martin's discourse semantic systems as the main frame, but will also refer to these studies when analyzing meaning patterns in the various types of images in data news.

3.4.1.2 Grammar

(1) Halliday's Lexicogrammar of Language

SFL treats grammar as a meaning-making resource and insists on the complementarity of system (paradigmatic relations) and structure (syntagmatic relations). Halliday's lexicogrammar (e.g., Halliday 1994; Halliday 2008) deals with the structure of the clause from the perspective of the metafunctional choices that give rise to it. The clause, like any other grammatical unit, is a multifunctional construct consisting of three metafunctional lines of meanings (Halliday 2008: 168). The metafunctional organization of the clause is also reflected in the different bundles of systems. Ideational metafunction or meaning has two subcategories: experiential and logical. Experiential metafunction is concerned with construing human experience and is realized by the system of TRANSITIVITY which is categorized according to process types—material, behavioral, mental, verbal, relational and existential. Structurally, the clause is represented as "a figure, or configuration of a process, participants involved in it and any attendant circumstances" (ibid: 169). Experiential metafunction can also be approached from the ergative

① See section 2.3.2 "Meanings in Images" for a more detailed description and interpretation of these studies.

perspective that focuses more on the agency or source of the process and is thus complementary to transitivity analysis of the clause. Logical meaning is concerned with sequencing the activities construing human experience and so actually it deals with relations between clauses in clause complexes. It is realized through logical semantic relation of expansion or projection. Interpersonal metafunction is realized through the systems of MOOD, POLARITY and MODALITY. The MOOD system looks at the clause from the interpersonal perspective of how the speaker negotiates meanings with the listener. The choices from the MOOD system can result in different mood structures consisting of Finite, Subject, Predicator, Complement and Adjunct. In English, the elements of Finite and Subject constitute the Mood, while Predicator, Complement and Adjunct are the Residue. The POLARITY system is about the positive/negative opposition in association with the clause as proposition or proposal. To put it simply, polarity is a choice between yes and no. But these two "are not the only possibilities; there are intermediate degrees, various kinds of indeterminacy that fall in between. These intermediate degrees between the positive and negative poles are known collectively as MODALITY" (ibid: 146-147). In a proposition, the resources realizing modality can demonstrate different degrees of probability and usuality, which are labeled as modalization choices. In a proposal, the resources can realize different degrees of obligation and inclination and they are termed as modulation choices. The resources realizing modality have different values: high, median or low, and they can explicitly or implicitly state the source of the conviction. Textual metafunction is concerned with the clause as a message. It is about how the clause contributes to the flow of discourse. It is realized by the Theme/Rheme structure and Given/New structure. The two structures relate to what comes at the beginning of the clause and what comes at the end.

The meaning patterns of clauses realize discourse semantic patterns, and are themselves realized by meaning patterns at the stratum of phonology or graphology. It should be emphasized that the realizations along the hierarchy of stratification are not a chain of one-to-one relationships, but a non-linear way of relating patterns of meaning at one stratum to another.

(2) Visual Grammar and Grammar of News Photographs

As has been reviewed in Chapter 2, there have been studies on the grammar patterns of single images that are organized around three metafunctions (e.g., Kress & van Leeuwen 2006; Caple 2013)①. We will make use of their frameworks in our description of meaning patterns in various images in the data.

As has been illustrated, the meaning patterns of clauses realize discourse semantic patterns and are themselves realized by meaning patterns at the stratum of expression form. However, discourse semantics is the stratum that relates directly with register and genre and so serves as the starting point and focus of the present analysis of data news genres. We will take a trinocular approach, which means that we will also describe the meaning patterns at this stratum of clause so as to demonstrate the interplay of meaning patterns within a semiotic mode and the way these meaning patterns realize configuration of meanings at the higher strata of discourse semantics, register, and genre.

3.4.1.3 Expression Form: Graphology and Graphic Choices

Both the verbal and visual modes of communication, within the boundaries of a single text, complement each other in the ways they project

① See section 2.3.2 "Meanings in Images" for more details.

meaning, but they are represented through different physical means or expression forms peculiar to the respective modes. Both of them are abstract system networks until they are materialized or expressed through their respective realizing systems (Lim 2004). In other words, the two modes have different "material stuff" (Kress 2010: 80) to realize metafuncitonal meanings on the expression plane. As has been reviewed in Chapter 2, writing (verbal text in data stories in the present study) has graphological systems to make meanings, while an image has graphical elements—color, shape, line, angle, distance, etc. —to make meanings. They are the more concrete realizations of meanings at the stratum of grammar.

As has been mentioned repeatedly, discourse semantics is the stratum that relates directly with register and genre and so serves as the starting point and focus of the present analysis of data news genres, but we will come to the meaning patterns at this stratum of expression form when necessary.

3.4.1.4 Register

As has been explained above, we follow Martin's stratification model of context into genre and register. Register, like genre, is a connotative semiotics which does not have an expression plane. In other words, it is realized through language and other semiotic modes. In the present study, register is regarded as a contextual category comprising field, tenor, and mode (Martin 2012/1984). The three register variables agentively determines choices of language as something outside of language. Register has a relationship of "metaredundancy" with genre and semiotic modes, which means that patterns or configurations of meaning at the stratum of register realize meaning patterns at the more abstract stratum of genre and are realized in patterns or configurations of meaning of language and other semiotic modes.

In the present study, a given field is defined as "a set of activity sequences oriented to some global institutional purpose, alongside the participant taxonomies and nuclear relations involved in these sequences" (Martin 1999: 33); tenor is concerned with the nature of social relations among interlocutors, with the dimensions of status and solidarity (Martin & Rose 2008: 12); and mode "deals with the channeling of communication, and thus with the texture of information flow as we move from one modality of communication to another" (ibid: 14). They are realized by the semiotic patterns. Field, tenor, and mode are resources for generalizing across genres, from the differentiated perspectives of ideational, interpersonal and textual meanings. This makes it easier for us to model relations among genres without being stuck in any one of tenor, field, or mode (Martin & Rose 2008: 16-17). Field, tenor, and mode values may shift from one stage of a genre to the next, as part of the accomplishment of a social process. This helps to identify phases and stages of a genre.

3.4.1.5 Genre

As has been reviewed above, genre and register are connotative semiotics which do not have an expression plane and take semiotic modes as their expression form. Genre is realized by configurations of register, which is realized by configurations of meaning in language. Genre and register serve as part of the semiotic environment for understanding semiotic systems, and the use of semiotic modes is constrained by context. Applying the theorization to the study of multimodal data news, we get the stratified model of context and semiotic modes shown in Figure 3-9.

Genres are related and distinguished by recurrent global patterns, such as sequences in time, complicating events, explaining processes, describing things, or arguing for a point of view. They are also distinguished by recurrent local patterns, such as the narrative stages Orientation ^ Complication ^ Resolution, or the phases within a stage like "setting",

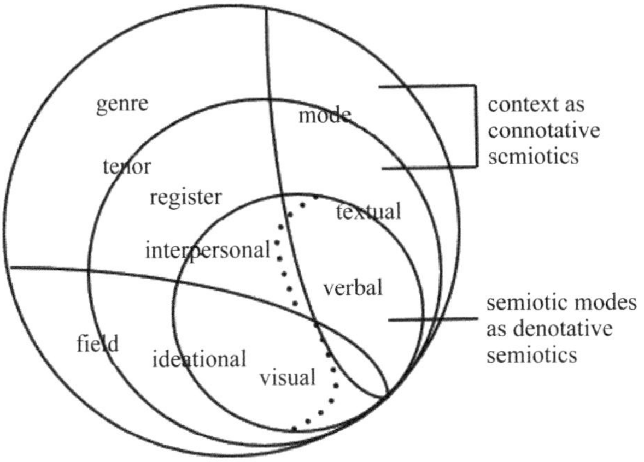

Figure 3-9 A Stratified Model of Context and Semiotic Modes from the Connotative and Denotative Perspective

"description", "events", "reaction", "problem" and "solution" in stories. In current SFL research, stages are steps that move to achieve the communicative goal(s) and phases are defined as smaller units of meaning within each stage, "that are more variable, and sensitive to register variations such as a text's field" (Rose 2006: 185). From a segmental perspective, phases consist of one or more messages, and one or more phases constitute a generic stage (Martin & Rose 2008: 79). In other words, phases are "the intermediate units between genre stages at the level of genre and messages at the level of lexicogrammar" (Rose 2006: 187). Phases within each stage are much more variable, and may be unique to the particular text. Stages unfold in highly predictable sequences, but phases may or may not occur within any stage, and in variable sequences. The relations between stage, phase and message are represented in Rose's discourse semantic rank scale (see Table 3-2). In the present study, we will identify stages and phases so as to capture the generic patterns of data news.

Table 3-2 The Discourse Semantic Rank Scale (Rose 2006: 187)

genre	minimal unit of text-in series in macrogenres such as textbooks, novels or conversation
stage	highly predictable segments in each genre
phase	more variable segments within each stage, carrying pulses of field and tenor
message	non-dependent, non-projected clause, together with associated dependent and projected clauses

3. 4. 2 Intermodal Interaction: A Coupling Perspective

Data news and data visualizations have introduced a new area for semiotic analysis. Full descriptions of the meaning patterns demonstrated in instances of data news and data visualizations should be conducted before we come to see their full meaning potential. Besides, data news as well as data visualizations are generally composed of verbal texts, images, and sometimes also of videos, which may be of equal or different commitment or semantic weight in the instances. As has been reviewed and explained in sections 2. 3. 3 and 3. 3. 6, coupling occurs along the cline of instantiation and can be identified at each stratum along the hierarchy of realization, and the coupling perspective on intermodal interaction offers a path for modelling multimodal genre. It is very appropriate for capturing the meaning patterns instantiated in data news.

3. 4. 3 A Multimodal Genre Model for Data News Analysis

Based on the above-mentioned reasoning and theoretical foundations, we can come to the genre model for data news analysis (see Figure 3-10).

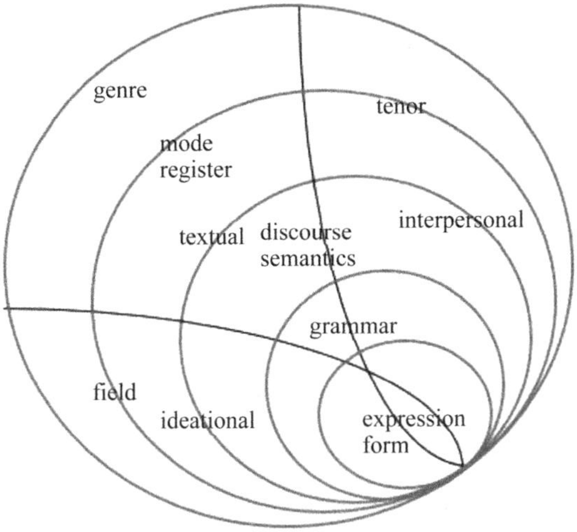

Figure 3-10 A Multimodal Genre Model for Data News Analysis

In the model, analysis can be conducted from the dimensions of metafunction, stratification and instantiation. In terms of stratification, genre is a pattern of register patterns, register is a pattern of discourse semantic patterns, and discourse semantics a pattern of grammatical patterns which are in turn a pattern of patterns of expression form. Discourse semantics relates directly with register, and so when analyzing the data, we start from this stratum and describe the meaning patterns or configurations at the strata of register and genre based on the meaning configurations at the stratum of discourse semantics. But by following the trinocular tradition in SFL studies, we will also analyze the corresponding meaning patterns at the strata of grammar and expression when necessary. Table 3-3 shows the semiotic systems which are realizations of register and their relations with register variables in our multimodal genre model for data news.

The intermodal interaction in the data is analyzed from the perspective of coupling along the process of instantiation, which can capture the inter-stratal, inter-metafunction, inter-system and intra-system interactions. Thus, the intermodal interaction mechanism can be integrated into the multimodal genre model.

In terms of metafunction, the axes of choice (system) and chain (structure) are also considered when we describe the meaning patterns at each stratum, though we may focus more on presenting the possible choices in systems.

Table 3-3 Relations Between Register, Discourse Semantics and Grammar

Register variable	Types of meanings	(Semiotics) Discourse semantic patterns	Grammatical patterns
Field	Ideational	IDEATION and CONNEXION (language); CHARACATER MANIFESTATION, CHARACTER APPEARANCE, INTER-EVENT and INTER-CIRCUMSTANCE (image)	TRANSITIVITY (language); NARRATIVE STRUCTURE and ANALYTICAL STRUCTURE (image)
Tenor	Interpersonal	APPRAISAL (language); ORIENTATION FOCALIZATION, AFFECT, AMBIENCE, GRADUATION (image)	MOOD and MODALITY (language); CONTACT, SOCIAL DISTANCE, ATTITUDE and MODALITY (image)
Mode	Textual	IDENTIFICATION and PERIODICITY (language); COMPLEMENTARITY, INTEGRATION, FRAMING, FOCUS (image)	Theme/Rheme and Given/New (language); Information value, Salience, and Framing (image)

3. 5 Research Design

3. 5. 1 Research Questions

Under the theoretical framework described above, we intend to answer the following questions:

1) What meaning patterns or configurations can be found in each semiotic mode in our data?

2) What patterns of intermodal interaction can be identified in the data?

3) How do the meaning patterns identified relate to register and what generic configurations can be revealed by the register patterns and discourse semantic configurations?

4) What are the relations between the elemental genres in the data and how are they modeled as genre complexes or macrogenres?

Chapter 4 will answer questions 1 and 2 as this is the basis and starting point for the following three questions. Chapter 5 will summarize the generical features based on the findings by relating the findings for questions 1 and 2 to questions 3 and 4.

3. 5. 2 Research Data

The data for the present research are 15 data works which are Data Journalism Awards winners from the year 2016 to 2019. These works or projects represent the "gold-standard of DDJ" (Loosen et al. 2017: 2). A study on the multimodal meaning-making processes in the projects can reflect the discursive features of data news.

As has been mentioned in section 1. 3. 1, the Data Journalism Awards were started in 2012 by the Global Editors Network (GEN) and stopped after 2019 due to lack of funding. It is the first international award recognizing outstanding work in data journalism. While the categories evolved somewhat over the years, those from 2016 to 2019 were almost identical. Besides, as all the projects were presented online, some projects were not accessible after the end of Data Journalism Awards in 2019. So, we focus on the winners' projects from 2016 to 2019.

Some of the categories in the Awards do not fit into the scope of data news as a multimodal discourse. For instance, the category of "Open data award" highlights the freedom of data use and the technological innovations in processing and presenting data and the categories of "Best individual portfolio", "Best team portfolio" and "Student and young journalist of the year" were awarded to individuals or teams, not to a single data journalism project. So, the data in the present study cover the following four categories: Investigation of the Year, Data Visualization of the Year, Website of the Year, Best Use of Data in a Breaking News Story, within first 36 hours. To reflect the diversity of nationalities, we also include the project of "Those Places High-Speed Rail Could Take You To" created by Caixin VisLab from Shanghai, China. Though it was not a winning project, it received three nominations, including Best Data Journalism Team, Data Visualization of the Year and the Microsoft Award for Public Choice, and Caixin VisLab received the Best Large Data Journalism Team Award. The project can also represent the "gold-standard of DJJ". The 2017 Website of the Year award was presented to Rutas del Conflicto of Columbia. The language used in the project was Spanish, which the present author does not understand, so it is not included in the data. There wasn't the category of best use of data in a breaking news story in 2016, so in all we get 15 projects.

Table 3-4 lists the 15 data works that are to be analyzed in the present study.

Table 3-4 Data Journalism Projects for the Present Study

No.	Award	Title	Link
1	2016 data visualization of the year	Spies in the Sky (BuzzFeed News, US)	See Maps Showing Where FBI Planes Are Watching From Above (buzzfeednews.com)
2	2016 Investigation of the year (small newsroom)	Medicmentalia	Medicamentalia
3	2016 Website of the year	FiveThirtyEight	What Would It Take To Flip States In The 2016 Election? | FiveThirtyEight
4	2017 Data visualization of the year	The Rhymes Behind Hamilton, *The Wall Street Journal*	How does 'Hamilton,' the non stop, hip-hop Broadway sensation tap rap's master rhymes to blur musical lines? - WSJ.com
5	2017 Investigation of the year	Unfounded, *The Globe and Mail*, Canada	Will police believe you? Find your region's unfounded sex assault rate—The Globe and Mail
6	2017 Best use of data in a breaking news story, within fist 36 hours	Fact Check and Full Transcript of the Fist 2016 PresidentialDebate, NPR	https://www.npr.org/2016/09/26/495115346/fact-check-first-presidential-debate
7	2018 Visualization of the year	Life in the Camps (Reuters)	Life in the camps (thomsonreuters.com)
8	2018 Investigation of the year	Easy Money (*The Globe and Mail*)	Investigation: White-collar thieves are repeatedly stealing millions from the unsuspecting, without fear of reprisal—The Globe and Mail

Continued

No.	Award	Title	Link
9	2018 Best use of data in a breaking news story, within first 36 hours	The Search Operation of the Submarine Ara San Juan (La Nacion)	The search operation of the submarine Ara San Juan—Proyectos / Projects (lanacion. com. ar)
10	2018 Website of the year	#SaferRoadsPH	https://www. rappler. com/moveph/169149-road-safety-awareness/ IN CHARTS: How deadly are Metro Manila roads? (rappler. com)
11	2018 Best large data journalism team	Caixin VisLab, China (Those Places High-speed Rail Could Take You to)	高铁3~6小时能到的地方，你想去哪个？(caixin. com)
12	2019 Visualization of the year	The Race to Save the River Ganges	https://www.reuters.com/graphics/INDIA-RIVER/010081TW39P/index.html
13	2019 Investigation of the year	Hurricane Maria's Dead	https: //hurricanemariasdead. com/index. html
14	2019 Best use of data in a breaking news story, within first 36 hours	Indonesia Plane Crash (Reuters)	https://www.reuters.com/graphics/INDONESIA-CRASH/0100810F1X2/index.html
15	2019 Website of the year	The Pudding (Colorism in High Fashion)	https: //pudding. cool/2019/04/vogue/

3.5.3 Methodology and Descriptive Principle

Overall, the present study is a qualitative research based on detailed descriptions of each project which is seen as an instance of multimodal discourse. The descriptions include the major types of images and data visualizations in the data; the discourse semantic patterns of these major types and their realizations at the strata of grammar and expression form; the intermodal interaction patterns of each project; and finally, the meaning configurations at the stratum of register and then at the stratum of genre. Analysis is done in Excel, which can visualize the findings.

When analyzing the meaning patterns in the data, we will follow the trinocular descriptive principle in SFL. SFL conceptualizes the relationship between language and context as natural and bi-directional—language realizes context, and context is realized through language and other semiotic modes. The highly abstract strata of genre and register are connotative semiotics which have another semiotic system as their expression plane (Martin & Rose 2008: 16). Therefore, a systematic description of the meaning patterns at the strata within each semiotic mode can serve as the basis for capturing the generic features (Martin & Rose 2008). The SFL description of meaning patterns in language is characterized from a trinocular perspective—looking "from above", "from below" and "from around" ①. This means that a meaning pattern at a certain stratum is described and interpreted by relating to the patterns from a stratum above, its realizations from a stratum below and other patterns at the same stratum. We rely on Halliday (1994), Halliday (2008) as well as Kress and van Leeuwen (2006) for describing meaning patterns at the stratum of grammar in both visuals and verbal texts, on Martin (2004/1992), Martin and Rose (2007/2003), Painter et al. (2012) as well as Bednarek and Caple (2012) for discourse semantic patterns in visuals and verbal texts. We will start with and focus more on the stratum of discourse semantics since this is stratum

① Matthiessen et al. (2010) used the wording "from roundabout".

which interfaces most directly with register and genre (Martin & Rose 2008: 30).

As has been introduced in section 3.3, SLF highlights the paradigmatic axis of organization, though it also describes the syntagmatic axis of organization. The paradigmatic relations are presented in systems and system networks (the axis of choice highlighting the systemic aspect) while the syntagmatic relations are described in structure (the axis of chain highlighting the functional aspect). The two pairs of notions of syntagmatic and paradigmatic, and structure and system represent the basic mechanism by which signs have meaning: in combination with other signs and by substitution for other signs. As in linguistic analysis, multimodal discourse analysis also needs to be based on structures, i.e., combinations of elements, and systems, i.e., sets of options that are available.

Following the SFL tradition, we will try to present in systems all the meaning patterns or choices identified in the data. However, as the choices are just generalized from instances of data news we collect, the systems are what Matthiessen referred to as "instantiated system" (Matthiessen et al 2010), for they are close to the "text" or "instance" end of instantiation cline rather the "system" end. Realization statements are also sometimes included in the system networks. These show the typical or congruent realizations of the feature in question.

3.6 Summary

Firstly, we introduced the SFL approach to genre and relevant theoretical concepts to lay the foundation for building a multimodal genre analytical framework for data news. The main theoretical concepts reviewed include connotative semiotics and denotative semiotics, system and structure, stratification, realization, discourse semantics, coupling and commitment. Then we moved to the multimodal genre model for data news (see Figure 3-10). Discourse semantics is a toolkit for genre analysis, and so when analyzing the data, we start from this stratum and describe the meaning patterns or configurations at the strata of register and genre based on the meaning configurations at the stratum of discourse semantics. But by following the trinocular tradition in SFL studies, we will also analyze the corresponding meaning patterns at the strata of grammar and expression. The intermodal interaction in the data is analyzed from the perspective of coupling, which can capture the inter-stratal, inter-metafunction, inter-system and intra-system interactions. Thus, the intermodal interaction mechanism can be integrated into the multimodal genre model.

Chapter 4 Meaning Patterns in Data News

A systematic description of lexiogrammatical and discourse semantic patterns can serve as the basis for capturing generic features. In this chapter we will answer the first two research questions raised in Chapter 3: 1) What meaning patterns or configurations can be found in each semiotic mode in our data? 2) What patterns of intermodal interaction can be identified in the data? To answer the first question, we start with and focus more on the stratum of discourse semantics, since this is the stratum which interfaces most directly with register and genre; but as we follow the trinocular descriptive principle in SFL, we will relate to the grammatical patterns when necessary. Based on the analysis of meaning patterns in each semiotic mode, we will then move to the intermodal interaction in the data from the coupling perspective. Coupling can occur at each stratum of semiotic modes in the process of instantiation and can capture the inter-stratal, inter-metafunction, inter-system and intra-system interactions. Thus, the intermodal interaction can be integrated into multimodal genre analysis. From a metafunctional perspective, many of the meanings are realized multimodally; in these cases, coupling patterns are analyzed together with the analysis of metafunctions and their realizations. Because each semiotic mode has rich affordances in meaning making and our ultimate goal is genre analysis, we do not and cannot describe all the meanings instantiated in the semiotic modes selected in our data; we focus on the patterns which contribute to the genre analysis.

4. 1 Semiotic Modes and Mode Families in the Data

Scholars (e.g., Kress et al. 2000; Kress 2003; Bateman et al. 2017) have noticed that the definition and scope of a semiotic mode may be specific to communities of users. Kress and his co-authors stated, "... the question of whether X is a mode or not is a question specific to a particular community. As laypersons we may regard visual image to be a mode, while a professional photographer will say that photography has rules and practices, elements and materiality quite different from that of painting and that the two are distinct modes" (Kress et al. 2000: 43). According to Bateman et al. (2017), modes "have a material dimension, relating back to the sensory channels that are used to perceive them" (p. 113), but they also "exhibit a semiotic dimension, i. e., the material used is given some kind of significance by its users" (ibid). In multimodal discourse analysis, it is the semiotic side that determines which kinds of distinctions in that material are actually "meaningful" in and for that mode. From the two dimensions we can say that news photographs, drawings and data visualizations have different semiotic affordances and even different materiality and so are different semiotic modes, at least in the eyes of journalists.

However, photographs, drawings, infographics, and data visualizations are also regarded as categories of images, because they are seen to operate in terms of associations to a far greater extent than representations such as those of language, and our visual processing system is able to recognize similarities in them with extreme speed and flexibility (Bateman et al. 2017). They are also organized by the logic of space and simultaneity rather than the logic of time and sequence as for both written and spoken language (Kress 2003). In other words, they have "a considerable amount of 'semiotic capabilities' in common" and make use of "semiotic organizations that appear to be at least partially 'shared'" (Bateman et al. 2017: 122). Semiotic modes of this kind can be regarded as "**mode families**" (ibid). Combing these points of view, we consider news photographs, drawings and data visualizations as members of the image mode family. One more instance is that written and spoken language can be regarded as members of semiotic mode family of "verbal language" (ibid).

As the data shows, the semiotic modes involved in the data news include image mode family, verbal texts and videos. More specifically, news photographs, drawings, infographics and data visualizations are the frequently selected members of the image mode family. Data visualizations can be presented in maps and various forms of diagrams, such as bar charts, histograms, waffle charts, and infographics. They can be static, dynamic and interactive. New forms of data visualizations are also emerging with the innovation of digital technologies and through novel ways of combining different semiotic modes. As our data shows, videos can be a new form of data visualization. The videos demonstrating the results of data analysis are usually generated by computers and are different from the more naturalistic videos shot by cameras. Based on the analysis, we differentiate two types of videos, data-driven computer-generated videos and camera-shot natural videos. The data-driven type is regarded as one creative form of data visualization and so will be discussed in the section on the meaning patterns of data visualizations, while the natural type will be discussed separately. Figure 4-1 summarizes the semiotic modes instantiated in our data.

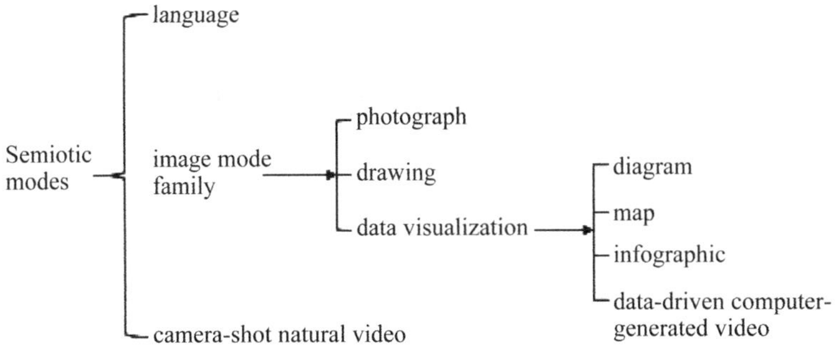

Figure 4-1 Semiotic Modes Instantiated in the Data

The instances of these semiotic modes in data news can be identified according to their different representations—language identified by their typographical realizations, image by their graphical realizations, and video by a "synchronized *integration* of modalities" (ibid: 340). They are generally separated by space or frames and easily identified as different parts of a piece of data news. In our data, image and language are the two main modes selected, so our analysis focuses on these two semiotic modes. For the videos, we will describe their discourse semantic patterns, grammatical patterns, and intermodal interaction patterns, but our description may lack the delicacy and systematicity of those for image and language. A systematic description of the meaning patterns is beyond the scope and manageability of the present study for two reasons: 1) videos, as multimodal discourses, are less explored from a discourse semantic perspective than image and language and 2) videos are highly complex multimodal discourses because "*everything* that is seen *and* heard on screen may have been planned and designed" (ibid: 327, original emphasis). We start with the meaning patterns of language, namely purely verbal texts, as language system has been better studied and can serve as a reference point for the meaning patterns of other semiotic modes.

4.2 Meaning Patterns in Verbal Texts

4.2.1 Ideation and Connexion Patterns

As has been introduced in Chapter 3, the systems of IDEATION and CONNEXION realize ideational metafunction and construe the register variable field, so their patterns are described and discussed in the same section. As our focus is genre analysis, we focus on the patterns which can differentiate genre or reveal genre relations.

Ideation focuses on "sequences of activities, the people and things involved in them, and their associated places and qualities, and on how these elements are built up and related to each other as a text unfolds" (Martin & Rose 2014/2007: 73). As a text unfolds, the people and things involved may build up taxonomic relations, which include classification, composition, repetition, synonym and contrast. The relations between an activity, the people or things involved, and the associated places and qualities can be described with nuclear relations. Nuclear relations can help to "inform analyses of taxonomic relations between things and qualities" (ibid: 99), for "including nuclear relations with the taxonomic relations analysis allow us to consistently track the relations of qualities and locations to each element in the lexical strings, despite their structural dispersal across various grammatical categories" (ibid). In the present analysis, we will relate the nuclear relations to their realizations at the lexicogrammatical stratum because this is more manageable and can reveal the patterns more directly. Martin and Rose (2014/2007) pointed out that a field of human experience is composed of recurrent sequences of activities. In other words, such recurrent sequences, together with taxonomic patterns and nuclear patterns, reveal consistent field patterns, and a shift in the patterns may indicate a new stage or phase.

Connexion looks at interconnections which realize activities, namely the logical meanings that link activities and messages in sequences (Martin & Rose 2014/2007; Hao 2015). Basically, there are four types of logical meanings: addition, comparison, sequence, and consequence. Options for addition including adding, subtracting and alternating; the basic options for comparison are similarity or difference, options for time sequence include successive or simultaneous; and options for explaining the cause-effect logic relation include cause, means, purpose and condition. There are various explicit resources realizing these logical meanings, such as furthermore and moreover for addition, similarly and by contrast for comparison, first, second and meanwhile for sequence, and thus and but for consequence. However, there are cases when no explicit resources are used yet logical meanings are created. For instance, sequence in time can be so consistently expected by story genres that there is no need to use any conjunctive resources (Martin & Rose 2014/2007). Be they explicit or implicit, the resources and patterns of logical meanings help to manage what we as readers expect to happen in a text.

When analyzing the data, we identify and analyze the patterns of the entities, patterns of the activities, the relations between entities and activities in the same Figure and the relations between activities throughout the whole data news text.

The first pattern we identify is that there are entities about the news events and entities describing the data journalism project (see Figure 4-2).

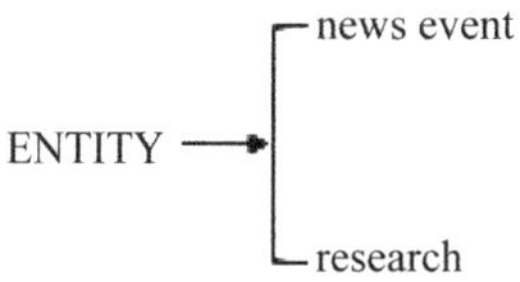

Figure 4-2 Entity Types in the Data

For instance, in the project Spies in the Skies by BuzzFeed News in the US, there are entities like planes, surveillance flight time, FBI, DHS, human entities at which the FBI and DHS aerial surveillance target, and high-tech equipment on the surveillance flights, etc. The planes and "surveillance flight time" are major entities in the news event and are repeated either by synonyms or exact repetition. FBI and DHS, as major entities or participants in the news event, are also repeated. Moreover, they are related as co-classes, and in this text they enter into relational antonymic relations with the human entities as targets of their surveillance, while the different types of high-tech equipment are co-classes and are related by classification. Some of the entities are illustrated in example 4-1, and Figure 4-3 is an instantiated system of the taxonomic relations we have identified. All these entities contribute to construing the news event field and we can term these as event entities.

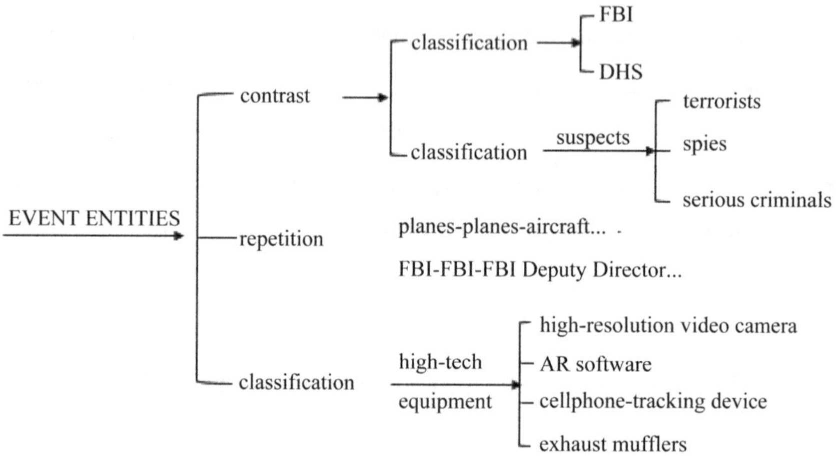

Figure 4-3 An Instantiated Taxonomic Relations of New Event Entities

Example 4-1 The FBI said that its planes are only used to target suspects in specific investigations of serious crimes...

"It should come as no surprise that the FBI uses planes to follow terrorists, spies, and serious criminals," said FBI Deputy Director Mark Giuliano, in that statement...

... the planes are fitted with high-resolution video camera, often working with "augmented reality" software ... At least a few planes have carried devices that can track the cell phone of people below. Most of the aircraft are small... and many use exhaust mufflers to mute their engine... (From "Spies in the Skies" by BuzzFeed News)

There is also the selection of entities "analysis, investigation, data and data source". In our view, these entities describe the journalists' or new agencies' investigation and establish a research field, which construes data reporting as a professional or even scientific activity that presents the findings (see the underlined parts in examples 4-2 and 4-3) or illustrates the expertise and/or professionalism in coming to the findings (see the underlined parts in examples 4-4 and 4-5). Examples 4-2 and 4-3 are presenting the findings of the investigation and examples 4-4 and 4-5 describing the process of carrying out the investigation. The type of entities can be referred to as research entities and are connected to each other mainly through repetition in our data.

Example 4-2 The BuzzFeed News analysis **found** that surveillance flight time dropped more than 70% on Saturdays, Sundays and federal holidays.

...

The BuzzFeed News analysis also **revealed** how the government responded to the mass shooting last December in San Bernardino, California. (From "Spies in the Skies" by BuzzFeed News)

Example 4-3 The Globe **found** one repeat offender with 17 regulatory orders on his file, spanning six provinces. Another has been hit with six orders in the same province.

The investigation found numerous examples of offenders who, unknown to regulators at the time, were conducting new financial crimes even as they sat in hearings to answer for past offences. (From "Easy Money" by *The Globe and Mail*)

Example 4-4 The Globe **sent** nearly 250 freedom of information requests to 178 police services to **obtain** confidential unfounded data from 1, 119 police jurisdictions across the country. We **received** responses from 873 jurisdictions, which represent 92 percent of the Canadian population. (From "Unfounded" by *The Globe and Mail*)

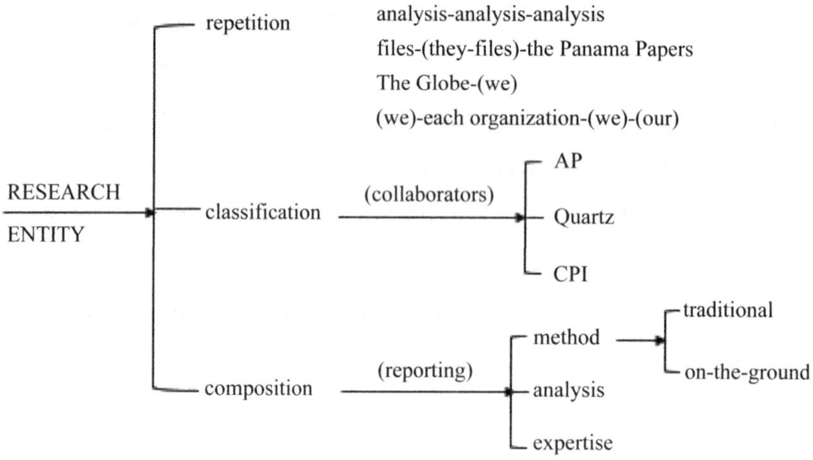

Figure 4-4 An Instantiated Taxonomic Relations of Research Entities in "Hurricane Maria's Dead"

Example 4-5 It was clear early on that it would be impossible to get at the scale of the death toll through traditional reporting methods alone. So we decided to **partner up**. Each organization **brought** unique strengths to the process without which the scale and depth of the project would have been impossible to achieve. By **working** together, we **enhanced** our individual expertise in key areas of our project, such as on-the-ground reporting and analysis, and **were able to cover** more ground... (From "Hurricane Maria's Dead" by AP, Quartz and CPI)

Besides, the entities about the findings couple with activities realized by projecting verbs like "find, reveal, show, indicate, suggest, and expose" or by verbal groups like "provide details of, contain new details, and reveal a pattern of...". These lexicogrammatical realizations realize activities construing relations between entities and also establish addition connection among the activities in a sequence. See examples 4-3 and 4-4: the bold parts are the processes realizing activities. When the investigation process is described, the more frequent selection is material process (see the bold parts in examples 4-5 and 4-6) and the Actor is generally the news agency or "we" (or nominal group with "our"), which may refer to the news agency or the writers. Example 4-5 also evaluates the significance of the collaboration of the three news organizations and the achievements of the collaborative investigation, so it is no wonder that relational processes are selected. These coupling patterns contribute to the identification of generic stages and phases.

In some projects, there can be no choices of research entities like "analysis, investigation, data and data source", but activities construing relations between entities are commonly selected and realized by relational processes when the writer(s) write(s) about the findings or results of their data analysis (see examples 4-7 and 4-8), or when the writer(s) describes the quality of something, particularly the data analysis tools (see example 4-9).

Example 4-6 Let's start with the first verse of the musical's opening number. Our algorithm **breaks** words into their component sounds and then **groups** similar-sounding syllable into rhyme families, which are color-coded. (From "The Rhymes Behind Hamilton" by *The Wall Street Journal*)

Example 4-7 It's a question no securities regulator has been able to get him to answer [Carrier +Process +Attribute]. And cases such as his are far from unique [Carrier +Process +Attribute]. (From "Easy Money" by *The Globe and Mail*)

Example 4-8 More than 86 percent of water samples tested positive [Carrier +Process +Attribute] for E. coli, an indicator for faecal contamination.

Sanitary latrines and the safe disposal of waste are urgent priorities [Carrier +Process +Attribute] ... (From "Life in the Camps" by Reuters)

Example 4-9 The algorithm was not infallible [Carrier +Process + Attribute] ... But as an initial screen for candidate spy planes, it proved very effective [Carrier +Process + Attribute]. (From "Spies in the Sky" by BuzzFeed News)

There are also activities about doing or happening. These doing or happening activities appear more often in the open part of the whole story when the writer(s) use(s) a personal story to introduce the topic or issue to be investigated (see example 4-10), or in the section where the writer(s) narrate(s) the news events (see example 4-11) or in the part where the writer(s) describe how they carry out their analysis or investigation (see examples 4-5, 4-6 and 4-12).

Example 4-10 More than 800,000 Rohingya Muslims live [happening: Actor + Process] in two official camps and several extension sites around Cox's Bazar on the southern tip of Bangladesh ... The speed and scale of the exodus has created the world's most densely-populated settlement of refugees [doing: Actor+ Process+ Goal] and tested governments and the international community [doing: Actor+ Process+ Goal]. (From "Life in the Camps" by Reuters)

Example 4-11 An Argentine submarine disappeared [doing: Actor + Process] and a rescue operation was deployed [doing: Goal+ Process]. (From "The Search Operation of the Submarine" *Ara San Juan* by *La Nacion*)

Example 4-12 First we made a series of calculations [doing: Actor + Process + Goal] to describe the flight characteristics of almost 20,000 planes ... Then we turned to an algorithm [doing: Actor + Process + Goal] called the "random forest", training it [doing: (Actor +) Process + Goal] to distinguish between the characteristics of two groups of planes... (From "Spies in the Sky" by BuzzFeed News)

We find that in the data news projects, two main types of activities can be identified—those of "doing" or "happening" which narrate the news events or describe the analytical process of the project and those construing relations between entities and realized by relational process. It can be argued that the "doing" or "happening" activities which narrate the news events construe news event fields while those describing the analytical process of the project and those construe realizing between entities construe research fields. Such meaning configurations contribute to the identification of stages and phases at the stratum of genre.

4. 2. 2 Appraisal Patterns

The systems of APPRAISAL and NEGOTIATION at the stratum of discourse semantics enact social metafunction and realize the register variable tenor. Negotiation deals with interaction between speakers in dialogue: how they adopt and assign roles to each other and how moves are organized in relation to one another. As the data in the present study involves no dialogues, negotiation patterns are not so salient and so we focus on appraisal patterns.

Appraisal is concerned with "the kinds of attitudes that are negotiated in a text, the strength of the feelings involved and the ways in which values are sourced and readers aligned" (Martin & Rose 2014/2007). For the comprehensive system of APPRAISAL, readers can refer to the highly cited book *The Language of Evaluation* by James R. Martin and Peter White (2005).

In the present study, we manually identify the evaluative resources that are conducive to genre analysis and analyze their meanings as shown in the following examples. Then we summarize the patterns shown in all the data.

Example 4-13 Behind the sensational [graduation: force: intensifying: upscaling + invoked appreciation: positive] success [inscribed appreciation: positive] of "Hamilton" are some of the most [graduation: upscaling] densely packed, complex [inscribed appreciation: positive] rhyming lyrics in the history of musicals. (From the first paragraph of "The Rhymes Behind Hamilton" by *The Wall Street Journal*)

Example 4-14 Our investigation has shown that sexual-assault cases are nearly twice [graduation: upscaling] as likely as physical assault to be designated unfounded. The number is also significantly [graduation: upscaling] higher [invoked appreciation: negative] than the false-reporting rate, which studies have shown to be somewhere between 2 and 8 percent.

…

Experts say [engagement: attribution: acknowledgement] these high [graduation: upscaling + attitude: invoked appreciation: negative] figures and large variations [graduation: upscaling+ invoked appreciation: negative] are evidence of a broken [attitude: inscribed appreciation: negative] system. (From the second section of "Unfounded" by *The Globe and Mail*)

Example 4-15 That's progress [attitude: inscribed appreciation: positive], but it doesn't change the fact that Lupita is the only [graduation: force: quantification] dark-skinned professional model on the cover of Vogue in the past nineteen years. Vogue (and the entire industry) can do better [attitude: invoked judgement: negative]. (From the CONCLUSION section of "Colorism in High Fashion" by the Pudding)

Example 4-16 Without better methods [attitude: inscribed appreciation: negative] of recording deaths during an emergency, local and federal authorities run the risk of responding ineffectively [inscribed judgement: negative] to future disasters, says Mario Marazzi [engagement: attribution: acknowledgement], the Statistics Institute director. (From the paragraph of "Hurricane Maria's Dead" by Quartz, AP and CPI)

Example 4-17 Of the 80 [graduation: force: quantification upscaling, intensifying the inscribed negative appreciation] worst-offender [graduation: force: intensification + attitude inscribed appreciation: negative] cases examined in depth by The Globe, at least 20 [coupling of graduation: force: intensification and force: quantification] showed [engagement: contraction: endorsement] clear signs of being serial offenders. (From "Easy Money" by *The Globe and Mail*)

Based on our manual analysis of each project, five patterns can be identified:

1) Quantification graduation resources are frequently selected and can intensify or invoke appreciation or judgement as examples 4-13 and 4-14 illustrate. Such resources realize values and increase the intensity of certain attitudes as evaluated prosodies are set up across the text. There are associated effects with respect to alignment and solidarity.

2) Attitudinal resources tend to couple with attribution resources. Negative attitude towards the entities involved in the data news tend to couple with attribution choices, as illustrated in example 4-14 which quoted experts' negative evaluation of Canada's broken system of reporting sexual assault, and 4-16 which quoted an expert's negative judgment of the Puerto Rico local government and the US federal government. The most frequent reporting verb realizing attribution is "say" in our data. The attribution allows space for other opinions, thus opening up the dialogic space for alternative views or opinions. The option of attributing evaluations to other voices offers the writer the potential to manage the persuasive impact of the discourse (Hood 2008). In our data, as the authors overtly reference other voices, mostly authoritative voices, the proposition or viewpoint is presented as "true" or "valid" and appears to be impersonalized, at least when compared with opinions conveyed by "I think" and "I believe". Interpersonal meanings are prosodic, which means that evaluation permeates the whole text. The texts in our data globally support the value positions of these sources. In this way, the reader is covertly positioned to regard the attributed views as highly credible and warrantable. It is also important to see the multi-voiced or heteroglossic (Martin & White 2005, after Bahktin) nature of the data news discourses.

3) Contraction resources of endorsement, illustrated in example 4-17, tend to appear in the section of findings of the data analysis. Unlike expansion resources, these resources fend off or restrict the scope of

dialogical space. They are usually realized by projecting verbs like "show, demonstrate, reveal, and make it clear that" which have been widely discussed in the literature in the context of the notion of "factivity" (e.g., Kiparsky & Kiparsky 1970; Martin & White 2005). They are dialogically contractive and by dint of this contractiveness they clearly align the reader into the value position being advanced in the text.

4) Attitudinal resources tend to appear in the sections or parts describing the findings or in the conclusion part, as can be seen in the above examples. This contributes to the identification of generic stages.

5) Appraisal meanings are more frequently instantiated in categories of investigation of the year and data visualization of the year than website of the year and best use of data in a breaking news story.

These meaning patterns do contribute to the identification of generic stages and phases and to the differentiation of genres of data news. As our main purpose is genre analysis, our analysis deals mainly with the more global patterns which are conducive to genre analysis, while those that do not demonstrate salient patterns are not presented.

4.2.3 Periodicity and Identification Patterns

The systems of PERIODICITY and IDENTIFICATION realize textual metafunction and organize the idea, so their patterns are described and discussed in the same section.

Periodicity deals with information flow, "with the way in which meanings are packaged to make it easier for us to take them in" (2007/2003: 175). Discourse has a beat or regular patterns to organize information as a flow, and the information flow is like the patterns of waves (Pike 1959; Halliday 1994; Halliday 2014; Martin & Rose 2007/2003; 2014/2007). In other words, textual metafunction is realized by periodic structures and a discourse organizes waves of information as peaks of prominence. At the clause level, there are two complimentary peaks of information: Theme at the beginning of the clause and Rheme at the end that usually matches a major pitch movement (see Halliday 1994, 2008, 2014). The Theme/Rheme structure creates little waves at the clause level. At the discourse level, information can be organized as bigger waves or higher-level Theme or Rheme which reflect "larger scale patterning of phases of discourse" (Martin & Rose 2007/2003: 181). A hyperTheme, usually a topic sentence for the events or contents which follow, is one kind of higher-level theme. It gives readers an orientation to what is to come in a phase. It is also predictive, for it can establish expectations about how the text will unfold. Whereas hyperThemes predict each phase of discourse, hyperNews accumulate each phase. Beyond a hyperTheme, there can be larger waves of information which are termed as macroThemes. Typical macroThemes include topic sentences in the beginning of a text or in the beginning of a stage of the text predicting the hyperThemes. Summarizing sentences at the end of a text or a stage of the text accumulating the hyperNews are macroNews.

Identification is concerned with "tracking participants—with introducing people and things into a discourse and keeping track of them once there" (Martin & Rose 2014/2007: 155), so the resources are closely related to participants or entities realizing ideational meanings. The resources for introducing entities who are unknown to the readers are presenting reference and those for tracking entities already introduced are presuming reference. Presenting reference is strongly associated with first mention and presuming reference categorically associated with second and later mention (Martin 2004/1992). Choices of presenting reference include anaphora, cataphora, esphora, homophora, endophora and exophora. These resources have been widely discussed as phoricity in many other studies (e.g., Givon 1985; Levinson 1983). Participants can also be introduced and tracked by comparative reference, which refers to the identity of related participants. There is also the third system of [generic/specific] that cross-classifies [presenting/presuming] and [comparison/-]. Martin (2004/1992) pointed out that generic reference is selected when the whole of some experiential class of participants is at issue rather than a specific manifestation or member of that class; this type of reference is typical of scientific report writing.

In the present study, we manually identify the periodicity and identification resources that are conducive to genre analysis and then summarize the patterns shown in all the data.

Data news texts in our data, though often divided into different sections, are organized with clear periodic structures, with the headline (sometimes with a strapline) as a superTheme, subheads or titles of each section as macroThemes, and topic sentences of each stage or phase as hyperThemes. *Headline* is the title of a news text. It performs two functions in the multimodal text. First, it draws the attention of reader to the news report and so is often specially designed and presented with salience through, say, larger fonts than the body part. Second, it usually summarizes the main point of the text and conveys the significance and meaning behind the text (Hodgson 1993; Ganesh 2006). It can therefore predict the main content to be presented in the body part and function as a macroTheme. A *strapline* is a subsidiary or introductory headline which comes first or after the main headline. It is usually a smaller line of heading containing a separate statement (Hodgson 1993: 90). It works together with the Headline to give readers an orientation to what is to come in the whole report. For instance, in the Colorism in High Fashion project, the headline together with the strapline below it functions as the superTheme of the whole data news text (see Figure 4-5). In our data, 6 of the 15 projects have a multimodal headline (see Figure 4-5), with a verbal headline and/or a strapline, and a photograph as the background (see section 4. 3. 1 for more analysis) and 1 project has a verbal headline, a strapline and a drawing (see section 4. 3. 2 for more information).

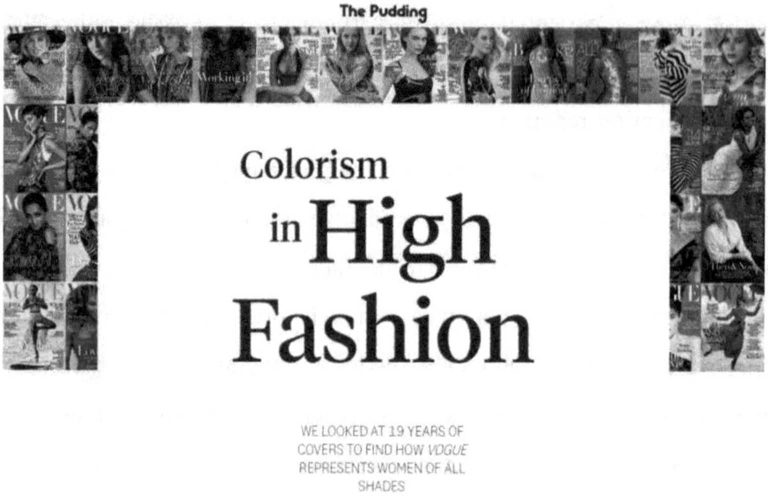

Figure 4-5 An Example of Multimodal Headline Functioning as SuperTheme (From "Colorism in High Fashion" by the Pudding)

Subhead is a small headline placed within the text of a news report, used to break up sections of long pieces. In our data, a subhead, presented in larger fonts than the verbal texts in the body part, is often the title of a separate section and covers the content of that particular section. Therefore, it can function as a higher-level theme. For instance, the titles or subheads in the Colorism in High Fashion project predict what can be expected in the particular section (see Figure 4-6): "THE CALCULATIONS" orients readers to the methods, tools and procedure of the data analysis, the "SKIN TONES" to the findings related to skin tones of the women models represented in *Vogue* and the "TOKENISM" to the findings related to skin color preference, the "REPEAT MODEL" to models who appear more than once on *Vogue*'s cover. If each section is regarded as a genre, smaller phases can be identified within the section. Therefore, these subheads also function as macroTheme, but one layer below the headline macroTheme. The layers of Theme in our data are presented diagrammatically in Figure 4-6.

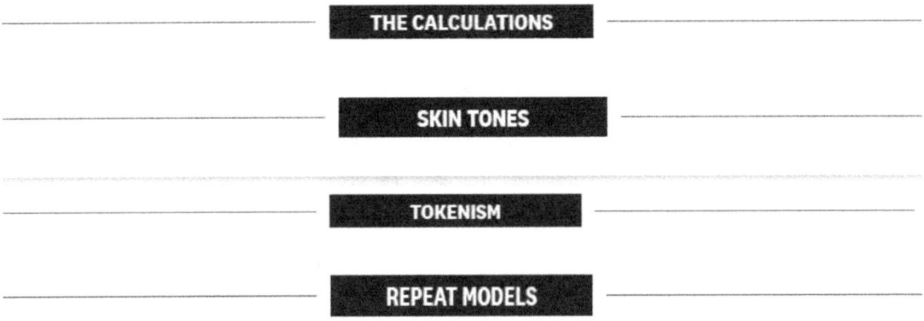

Figure 4-6 Titles of Each Section Functioning as MacroTheme
(From "Colorism in High Fashion" by the Pudding)

Within each section with a subhead, there can be a topic sentence for each phase (sometimes instantiated in one paragraph and sometime in several paragraphs). In our data, a stage or phase, like the headline we discussed above, can also be realized multimodally by verbal texts and images (photographs, drawings, videos or data visualizations), or by verbal texts and videos. For instance, within the "SKIN TONES" section in the Colorism in High Fashion project, the verbal clause complex "Let's look at where these women fall on the lightness spectrum" predicts what is going to be displayed and revealed by the subsequent data visualization after the face skin color of each model is compared—preference for lighter color. This is the first finding presented multimodally and so the phase of "Finding 1 (Synchronic comparison)". Then another verbal clause "Let's look at another dimension: time" predicts the second finding from the dimension of time—skin color diversity before and after the year 2005, and this is phase 2 "Finding 2 (Diachronic comparison)" (see Figure 4-7). This phase is also realized by data visualizations and dynamic verbal texts and so is multimodally realized. The topic sentences like these two examples can be regarded as hyperTheme.

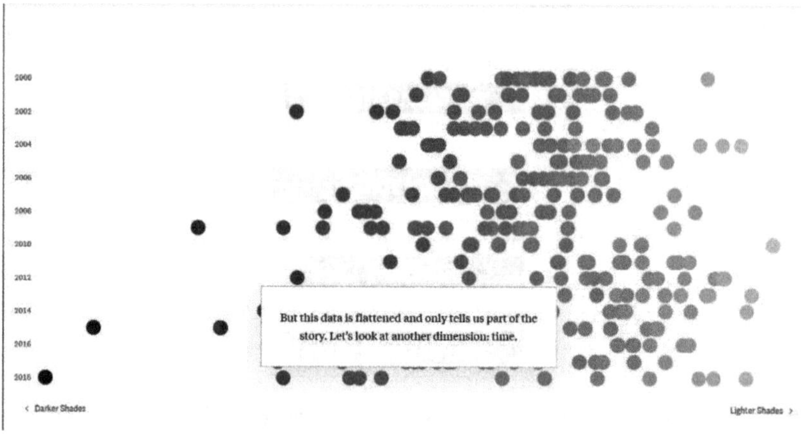

Figure 4-7 An Example of Verbal Clause as HyperTheme for a Multimodally Realized Phase (From "Colorism in High Fashion" by the Pudding)

There can also be a section entitled "CONCLUSION". That section presents the major findings of the whole project and distills the new information. It can be regarded as a superNew. It is interesting to notice that hyperNew or macroNew for each section is rarely found in our data.

Based on our analysis of each project, we summarize the instantiated periodic structures in Figure 4-8.

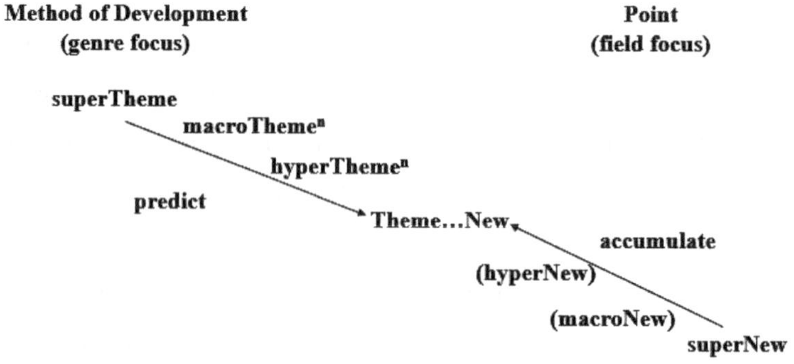

Figure 4-8 Periodicity in the Data ("n" means that the choice can be repeated)

In terms of identification resources, generic reference indicates generic entities which are less dependent on context in the way specific entities are, unless their realization involves demonstrative pronouns which have to be recovered from the context. Uncountable and plural nouns lacking an indefinite article (e.g., grass, frogs) provide referents for other nominal groups three times less than when an indefinite article was present (e.g., some grass, some frogs) (Martin 2004/1992: 107). Choosing among the presuming resources depends in part on how much experiential meaning needs to be made explicit to identify the participants in question. In our data, various identification resources are selected to introduce and track participants in the texts. Identification resources can also be used to connect verbal texts and data visualizations. It is hard to generalize a single pattern, but the choices of identification resources, together with the taxonomic relations realizing ideational meanings, contribute to the identification of stages or phases in a genre. Following is an example from the project "The Race to Save the River Ganges".

Example 4-18

Open drains

Between them, homes and factories pump incredible amounts of waste water into the river every day. The most detailed report on how sewage from residential drains and industry pollutes the Ganges was published by India's CPCB in 2013. The data from that report is visualised in the diagram below.

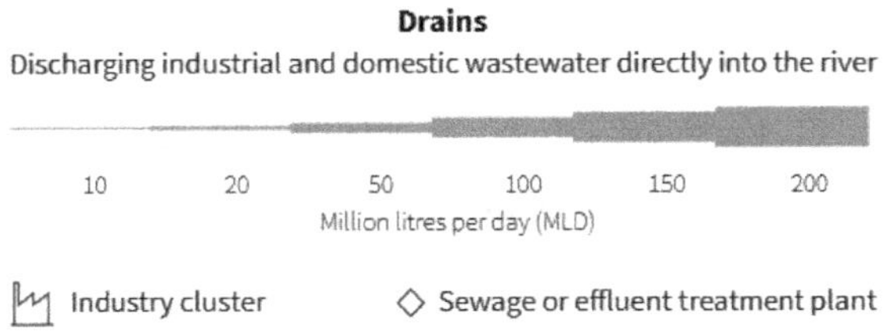

In this example, both pronominal and nominal presuming resources are selected. "them" is an anaphoric pronoun referring to the open drains, and the nomical group complex "residential drains and industry" relates to "open drains" by presuming the identity of the group of participants to which it belongs to, because "residential drains" and "industry (drains)" are members of the open drain class. "The data from that report" relates to "the most" also by presuming the identity of the group of participants to which it belongs to. The nominal group "the diagram" cataphorically refers to the visualization below. These resources indicate that these parts, including the data visualization, centre on the same finding found from the report—sewage levels in the open drains. The co-referencing relation between the verbal text and the data visualization is an instance of intermodal coupling realizing the same metafunction and offers rationale for us to theorize data visualzations as being an embedded genre in some data news texts.

The periodicity and identification patterns not only contribute to genre analysis but also demonstrate that the whole data news text should be regarded as a coherent multimodal text.

4.3 Meaning Configurations in Image Mode Family

As has been mentioned in the first section of this chapter, news photographs, drawings and data visualizations are frequently selected. We regard them as members of the image mode family, because they are seen to operate in terms of associations to a far greater extent than representations such as those of language, and our visual processing system is able to recognize similarities in them with extreme speed and flexibility (Bateman et al. 2017), and because they are organized by the logic of space and simultaneity rather than the logic of time and sequence as for both written and spoken language (Kress 2003). They have "a considerable amount of 'semiotic capabilities' in common" and make use of "semiotic organizations that appear to be at least partially 'shared'" (Bateman et al. 2017: 122). In this section, we will first describe separately their meaning patterns and then try to summarize some of the "'semiotic capabilities' in common" and the semiotic organizations that appear to be shared or at least partially shared. Meaning configurations in each semiotic mode in our data are described at the strata of discourse semantics and grammar and organized around the three metafunctions.

4.3.1 Meaning Configurations in Photographs

In our data, news photographs represent both human and non-human entities that appear singularly or form a photo series with other photos, as illustrated in Figure 4-9, Figure 4-10 and Figure 4-11 respectively.

All the photos have captions, with the photos being more salient. Figures 4-9 and 4-10 are two examples. These may have been edited, but readers cannot perceive that, so they belong to the natural image type. We call these photos natural image-privileged photographs. There are also news photos that can be perceived to be edited, as illustrated in Figure 4-11. The edited photograph(s) tend(s) to appear in the headline and the verbal text is more committed to the meanings, but the photo(s) still realize(s) meanings which are not realized in the verbal texts. This type is called edited text-privileged photograph.

Before we further our analysis, it is important to acknowledge the difficulties in providing consistent image analysis. Bednarek and Caple (2012) held the same view and listed some of the difficulties. For example, it is not easy to decode the poses, gestures, and facial expressions of image participants or whether a close-up, long shot, or wide angle carries the same meaning every time an image makes use of these compositional tools. Considering the difficulties, we focus on the patterns of discourse semantics and their grammatical realizations that are conducive to genre analysis.

Figure 4-9 An Example of Single Human Entity and Natural Image-Privileged Photograph (From "Race to Save the Ganges" by Reuters)①

Figure 4-10 An Example of Group Non-human Entities and Natural Image-privileged Photograph (From "Spies in the Skies" by BuzzFeed News)

---

① The caption reads "A Hindu devotee prepares to take a dip in a polluted canal flowing into the Ganges River during a religious procession in Kolkata, India". REUTERS/ Danish Siddiqui.

Figure 4-11 An Example of Group Entities and Edited Text-privileged Photograph (From "Colorism in High Fashion" by the Pudding)

As O'Halloran (1999: 322) pointed out, "with multi-semiotic texts, the most important stage is a step-by-step analysis of the text through the reading path determined by the choices within different semiotic modes". Kress (2003) and Guo (2004) further explained the relation between reading path and the analysis of multimodal discourses. According to Kress (2003), very often the intersemiotic aspect of the reading path is that the reader first conducts a brief "modal scanning" (p. 159) of the page, or quickly peruses the visually salient elements, usually images, then moves to the verbal text, then to the non-linguistic resources and then to the verbal text again. Guo (2004) held a similar view. He said, "Initially the visual image on the page exerts a strong impact upon the reader through choices such as Color and Framing. After the initial visual impact subsides, however, he or she normally begins to study the verbal text in greater detail." (p. 203)

Photographs are instances of multimodal discourses themselves and part of the more complex multimodal data news. Their textual or compositional features draw the reader's attention and guide their reading path. The textual features also guide our analysis path: we begin with a quick scanning of the overall intermodal layout, then move to the meaning patterns of each semiotic mode, to the intermodal interaction in greater detail and finally to the generic patterns of the whole multimodal data news. In other words, the layout features serve as the starting point for our analysis of patterns of ideational meanings, interpersonal meaning patterns and intermodal interaction. As a result, the textual patterns, including the intermodal layout, are analyzed first.

4.3.1.1 Textual Patterns

The photos appearing singularly in our data are presented in demarcated parts and placed side by side with the longer verbal texts or vertically between the verbal texts. If there is a series or group of photos, they are placed between the verbal texts. In other words, the photographs and the verbal texts show a complementary horizontal or descending layout. Whatever their positions are, the photographs are visually salient because of their size and color and thus are termed image-privileged photographs. In terms of the intermodal layout, the choices are [complementary: descending + adjacent] or [complementary: horizontal+ adjacent].

There are also news photos where the image and verbiage come together so that the words feature within the image, rather than being placed in demarcated parts. As shown in Figure 4-11, the verbiage and image are integrated to form a visual unity, and the verbiage is overlaid onto the image so that it most clearly becomes part of the image itself. This is the option of [integrated: expanded: subsumed]. In this type of intermodal integrating layout, the image serves as the background and the verbiage is thus highlighted. In our data, such a layout is used to create a multimodal headline. To be more specific, the verbal text is the verbal headline and usually draws more attention because of its foreground position. The photo realizes meanings which are not realized in the verbal headline, but due to its background position, it does not play a role equal to the verbal headline in meaning commitment. This type of photographs is labelled as text-privileged photographs and the realization of the intermodal layout is [integrated: subsumed]. The layout features serve as the starting point for our analysis of patterns of ideational meanings, interpersonal meaning patterns and intermodal interaction.

According to Painter et al. (2012), verbiage and image in picture books can be integrated to form a visual unity in two distinct ways: either by utilizing the choice of [projected] or that of [expanded]. In our data, no instances of [projected] integration have been found. This type of integration is used to project the thoughts or locutions of a participant by means of bubbles. It is common in genres like picture books and comics which involve thoughts and dialogues of characters. The absence of this type of layout in the photographs indicates that photographs do not represent thoughts or locutions of the participants.

4.3.1.2 Ideational Patterns

Now, let's turn to the ideational meaning patterns. We are first concerned with the identity and attributes of the participants—both in a single photo and in photo series. In our data, news photographs represent both human and non-human participants that appear singularly or form a photo series with other photos, as illustrated in Figure 4-9, Figure 4-10 and

Figure 4-11 respectively. The human participants can be ordinary people or elite persons like experts and officials. When ordinary people are photographed, the caption usually does not tell their names or identities and generic reference is preferred to introduce them. The relation between the caption and the represented participant(s) is analogous to an attributive relational clause. For instance, in Figure 4-9, the participant in the photo is introduced by "a Hindu devotee". Translated into verbiage, it is like "The woman is a Hindu devotee". This is in contrast with the nominal group identifying an elite participant who is often identified by a proper noun which is usually followed by a nominal group elaborating the participant's profession or social role. In other words, the experiential meaning of participants is expanded by elaborating elements (Xing & Zhu 2018). For instance, in the project "Medicamentalia", there is a photo of an elite person, and the caption reads "Kwasi Poku Boateng, director of Cepat, in his office". The caption identifies the represented participant in the photo and the elaborating nominal group "director of Cepat" specifies his identity. Photographs offer relatively iconic representations of an entity or activity.

The choice of a proper noun in the caption to identify represented participants shows a coupling pattern with the interpersonal meanings of the verbal texts. Proper nouns are selected when the relevant verbal text quotes from an expert or elite figure as acknowledge or distance resources. Acknowledge and distance are two sub-categories of the sub-system of attribution which is a feature in the system of ENGAGEMENT. Attribution represents a proposition as grounded in the subjectivity of an external voice. With attribution, the textual or authorial voice represents the proposition as but one of a range of possible positions—it thereby entertains or invokes these dialogic alternatives (Martin & White 2005). "Acknowledge" is usually indicated by reporting verbs such as say, report, declare, announce, and think. In locutions of this type, there is no overt indication, at least via the choice of framer, as to where the authorial voice stands with respect to the proposition. In locutions of the "distance" type, there is an explicit distancing of the authorial voice from the attributed material. The verb "claim" is a common realization of distance attribution. Acknowledging and distancing formulations are dialogistically expansive. They explicitly ground the proposition in an individualised, contingent subjectivity, that of some external source. They are dialogic in that they associate the proposition being advanced with voices and/or positions which are external to that of the text itself and present the authorial voice as engaging interactively with those voices. This coupling pattern provides rationale for us to analyze photos as an embedded genre in the whole text. Following Szenes (2017), we visualize the coupling pattern in Figure 4-12.

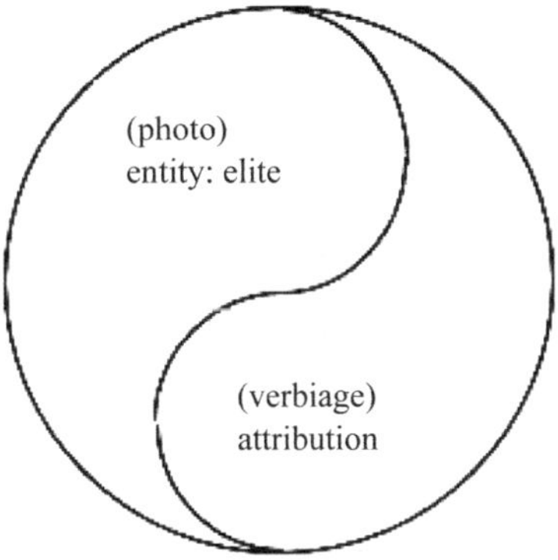

Figure 4-12 Inter-metafunctional and Inter-semiotic Coupling: Entity and Attribution

In photo series, the represented participants can be non-humans, ordinary people and elite people. When ordinary people are photographed, the caption usually does not tell their names or identities and generic reference is preferred to introduce them, while for photographs of elites, the represented participant is identified by a proper noun and a nominal group which elaborates his or her identity or social role. In photo series, the represented participants, be they humans or things, can establish classificational taxonomic relations. For instance, the four airplanes in Figure 4-10 are all members of the aircraft class. The instantiated classificational taxonomy is presented in Figure 4-13.

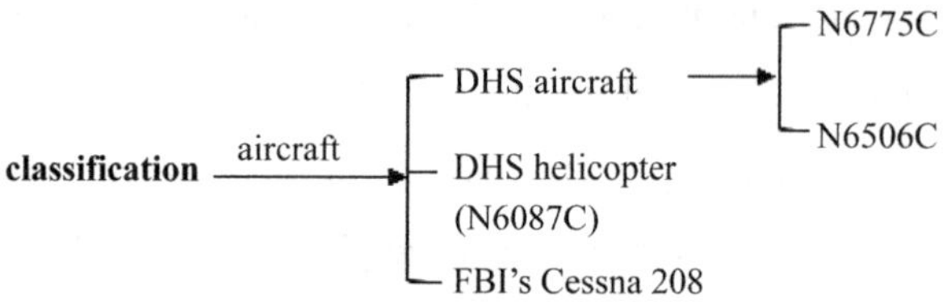

Figure 4-13 An Instantiated Classificational Taxonomy in Photo Series

When human participants are represented, their activities can be realized through transactional and non-transactional processes and their attributes by analytical processes. In Figure 4-9, the female devotee's stirring the water is a transactional process, with the devotee as the Actor, her two arms as the vector and the water as the Goal. The devotee as a whole is also a Carrier, with her dress, her hairstyle and her skin color as the Attributes which as a whole reveal her identify. When non-human participants are presented, the focus is their attributes realized through attributive processes, as was illustrated in Figure 4-10.

The setting of a process is recognizable because of the foreground/ background contrast and contrasts in color saturation and overall darkness or lightness between foreground and background. The photographs offer a visual image of the participants, their activities and/or attributes, many of which are also depicted through language.

4. 3. 1. 3 Interpersonal Patterns

There are some interpersonal meaning patterns. A pattern is that when human participants are presented, there can be no eye contact between the represented participant and the viewer, as illustrated in Figure 4-9. This choice of [offer], rather than [demand], often couples with the choice of [long shot] that realizes Impersonal social distance or the choice of [oblique] angle that realizes Detachment, which has the effect of distancing the producer and the viewer from the represented world. The coupling pattern is visualized in Figure 4-14. It is perhaps because of these interpersonal patterns that news photos are associated with notions such as record of reality, objective truth or evidence of having been there (Bednarek & Caple 2012; Caple 2020). However, evaluations can be invoked through ideational meanings. For instance, in the photo in Figure 4-9, piles of rubbish as the Circumstance evoke negative appreciation of the Ganges.

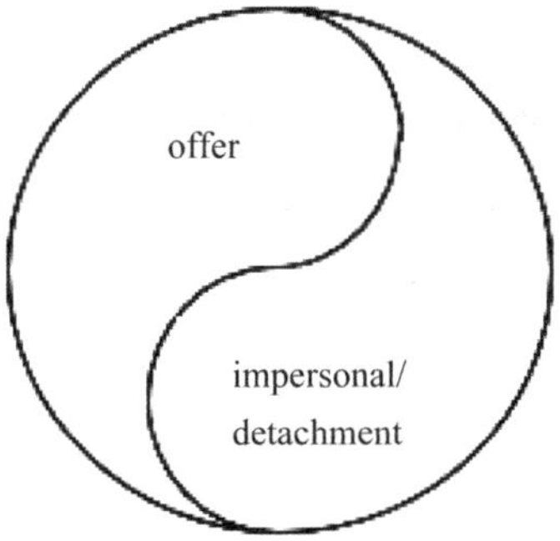

Figure 4-14 Intra-metafunctional and Intra-modal Coupling: Offer and Impersonal/Detachment

Another pattern is that in photographs of non-human entities, no inscribed attitudinal resources have been identified, but attitudes may be invoked by ideational meanings. For instance, in the photo presented in Figure 4-15, the verbal text commits more—there are inscribed and invoked negative appreciation of Indian's sewage and an inscribed negative appreciation of its northern plains, while in the photo, no inscribed evaluative meanings and realizations have been found, but perhaps a negative appreciation can be invoked by the image of "sewage water into the river" and the verbal text. It seems that the interpersonal relationship enacted in the photograph is relatively detached and observing, rather than involved and participating, with the scene offered as a physical existence just being there. This is in line with the journalists' goal of achieving "objectivity" in reporting.

4.3.1.4 Intermodal Interaction

(1) Macro-level Interaction

A noticeable and more global pattern is that the image-privileged photographs tend to just interact locally with only part of the verbal text, while the text-privileged photographs tend to form a multimodal news headline which functions as the superTheme for the whole data news (See section 4.2.3 for more detailed description and explanation of superTheme, macroTheme, and hyperTheme). In this type of interaction, the photo and the verbal texts complement each other to form a multimodal headline. This multimodal realization of periodicity contributes a lot to the identification of stages and phases in the genre analysis, so it is conceptualized as macro-level interaction.

Let's illustrate the intermodal interaction between the longer verbal text and the image-privileged photograph with an example from the project "The Race to Save the River Ganges" which won the Data Visualization of the Year Award in 2019. The example is presented in Figure 4-15.

Sewage

In many places, India's antiquated sewage system is unable to handle the huge amounts of waste produced along the river. A 2016 report by the Centre for Science and Environment found that 78% of sewage in India remains untreated.

Untreated sewage from a residential area flows into the Ganges river in Mirzapur, India. REUTERS/Danish Siddiqui

Over three-quarters of the sewage generated in the towns and cities of India's crowded northern plains flows untreated into the Ganges, according to a National Mission for Clean Ganga (NMCG) presentation seen by Reuters in 2017, which has not been made public.

Figure 4-15 An Example of [Complementary: Descending] Photo-text Layout (from "The Race to Save the Ganges")

The photograph is placed vertically between two paragraphs of the verbal text. By analyzing the salient ideational and interpersonal meanings in the two semiotic modes, we can see that meanings are realized multimodally, and so coupling patterns are analyzed as well. In terms of ideational meanings, the verbal text and the photo generally have an equal role in meaning commitment—the major participants, the major process and the circumstance are realized multimodally (or restated). Some participants are realized multimodally, but the image offers more details. In this case, the coupling pattern is complementing. Some participants are represented in just one semiotic mode. For instance, the human participants are just represented in the photo. In this case, the coupling is termed as adding. In terms of interpersonal meaning, as has been analyzed above, the verbal text commits more—there are inscribed and invoked negative appreciations of Indian's sewage and inscribed negative appreciations of its northern plains, while in the photo, no inscribed evaluative meanings and realizations have been found and perhaps negative appreciation can be invoked by the image of "sewage water into the river" and the verbal text. The coupling pattern is adding.

Generally speaking, choices made within the two semiotics will always amplify one another, multiplying corresponding kinds of meaning by means of "convergent" coupling. The coupling can be instantiated as restating the same meaning, complementing each other on the same meaning, or with one mode adding meaning to the other.

Table 4-1 lists the multimodal realizations of major ideational and interpersonal meanings, the meaning commitment and coupling patterns.

Another global pattern is the multimodal headlines that has been analyzed in section 4. 2. 3 when we analyze the periodicity pattern. In our data, 6 of the 15 projects select a headline photograph to form a multimodal news headline (see Table 4-2). It is also interesting to see that such a pattern appears most frequently in projects winning Data Visualization of the Year Award and it does not appear in the Breaking News category.

Table 4-1 Analysis of Photo-text Interaction

metafunctions		verbal realization	photographic realization	coupling and commitment
ideational	Participant	sewage (system) waste; river	drainage water river	convergence: restating equal commitment
		places	houses, plants, rocks, etc.	convergence: complementing equal commitment
			humans; geographic features	convergence: adding photo more committed
		towns and cities; northern plains, etc		convergence: adding verbiage more committed
	Process	flow (material)	running (non-transactional)	convergence: restating
		generated		convergence: adding verbiage more committed
	Circumstance	in many places (location)	locational	convergence: restating
interpersonal	inscribed appreciation	antiquated; crowded		verbiage more committed; convergence: adding
	invoked appreciation	unable to handle... untreated, etc.	sewage water into the river invoked by the verbal text	verbiage more committed; convergence: restating
	intensification	over		verbiage more committed

Table 4-2 Projects with Text-privileged Headline Photograph

Projects	Category
Spies in the Sky (2016)	Data Visualization of the Year
The Rhymes Behind Hamilton (2017)	Data Visualization of the Year
Medicmentalia (2016)	Investigation of the Year
Life in the Camps (2018)	Data Visualization of the Year
The Race to Save the Ganges (2019)	Data Visualization of the Year
Colorism in Fashion (2019)	Website of the Year

The multimodal headline functions as the superTheme for the whole data news. The verbal text, namely the news title, is more committed to the meanings, but the photo(s) still realize(s) meanings which are not realized in the verbal texts. These headline photographs and their interaction is a case of complementing convergent coupling because they work together to function as the superTheme of the whole news text. Here is another

Figure 4-16 An Example of Multimodal Supertheme Headline Realized by a Photo and Verbal Texts

example, the headline of the project is "Life in the Camps".

(2) Micro-level Interaction

The relation between a photo and its caption is another type of intermodal interaction. As this interaction occurs at a more local level, not affecting much the genre analysis, we see it as a case of micro image-text coupling (see section 4.5.1 for a summary discussion). Literature on this type can be found in studies like Caple (2009a, 2013) and Bednareck and Caple (2012).

As was discussed previously, the caption of a photo usually identifies the represented participant. The represented participant is identified by a proper noun. For representing human participants, the proper noun can also be followed by a nominal group that elaborates his or her identity or social role. The caption-photo interaction is analogous to an identifying clause in language. But when ordinary people are photographed, the caption usually does not tell their names or identities and generic reference is preferred to introduce them. The relation between the caption and the represented participant(s) is analogous to an attributive relational clause.

The meaning patterns of the news photos in our data are generalized and presented in Table 4-3.

Table 4-3 Metafunctional Meanings and Meaning Patterns in Photographs

stratum / metafunction	discourse semantics	grammar
textual	layout (intermodal): [complementary: descending + image privileged+ adjacent] integrated: text privileged +text-central+ subsumed	space+ salience (size) +framing

Continued

stratum / metafunction	discourse semantics	grammar
ideational	taxonomy: classification activity: attributes narrative	classificational processes analytical and symbolic processes non-transactional process
interpersonal	affect: no affect focalization: observe and unmediated proximity: impersonal and detached invoked attitude	no facial expressions offer: no contact social distance: long shots and oblique angle processes and circumstances
intermodal interaction	image-privileged photo	micro: caption-photo coupling: convergence-identifying macro: photo-text coupling: convergence-restating (realizing a stage or phase)
	text-privileged photo	macro: text-photo interaction: coupling-convergence complementing (multimodal super-Theme)

4.3.2 Meaning Configurations in Drawings

Drawings also offer iconic representations of an entity. Though less frequently selected compared with data visualizations (see Table 4-5 for more information) and photographs, they do contribute to the meanings in some data news projects. They share some meaning patterns with photographs while also having their unique ones.

4. 3. 2. 1 Textual Patterns

Same as the photos, the drawings in our data can appear singularly or as a group. Different from the photos, when they are presented in demarcated parts, they are placed vertically between the verbal texts; no one is placed side by side with the longer verbal texts. In other words, the drawings and the verbal texts show a complementary descending layout. They are visually salient because of their size and color and are called image-privileged drawings. In terms of layout, the choices are [complementary: descending + adjacent].

Like the [integrated: subsumed] headline photograph, there is also a case of a headline drawing where the drawing and verbiage come together so that the words feature within the image, rather than being placed in demarcated parts. As shown in Figure 4-17, the verbiage and image are

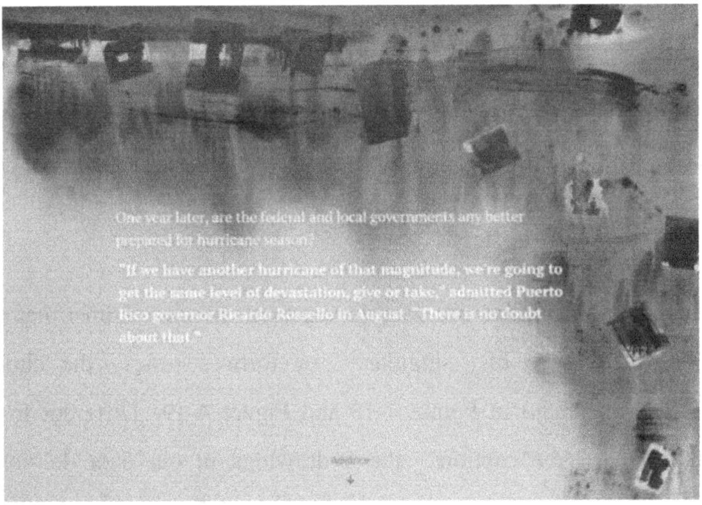

Figure 4-17 An Example of [Integrated: Subsumed] Multimodal Headline
(From "Hurricane Maria's Dead")

integrated to form a visual unity, and the verbiage is overlaid onto the image so that it most clearly becomes part of the image itself. This is the option of [integrated: subsumed]. In this type of intermodal integrating layout, the image serves as the background and the verbiage is thus highlighted. In our data, such a layout is used to create a multimodal headline. To be more specific, the verbal text is the verbal headline and usually draws more attention because of its foregrounded position. The drawing realizes meanings which are not realized in the verbal headline, particularly ambience meaning created by the circumstances. Due to its backgrounded position, it does not play a role equal to the verbal headline in meaning commitment. This type of drawings is labelled as text-privileged drawing. The realization of the intermodal layout is [integrated: subsumed].

In short, the text-privileged drawings, like text-privileged photographs, are selected as the headlines and function as the superTheme of the whole multimodal data news texts. On the contrary, the image-privileged may appear at the beginning or the end, or in the middle of the text and they tend to relate to part of the verbal texts and thus part of a stage or phase.

As with photographs, no instances of [projected] integration have been found. The absence of this type of layout indicates that drawings do not represent thoughts or locutions of the participants.

4.3.2.2 Ideational Patterns

In our data, drawings are used to represent human entities that appear singularly, the choice of [singular], or form a series, the choice of [group], as illustrated in Figure 4-18 and Figure 4-19. Different from the photographs that have captions, the 5 drawings in our data do not have legends and are from four projects (see Table 4-5 for more details). In terms of frequency, they may not be as representative as other image types, but they have salient unique features in meaning-making and in realizing the generic purpose.

Figure 4-18　An Example of [Affectless: Singular] Human Entity

(From "Unfounded" by *The Globe and Mail*)

Figure 4-19　An Example of [Affectless: Group] Human Entities

(From "Unfounded" by *The Globe and Mail*)

The human entities are not represented with so much detail as the photographs or as the advertisements analyzed by Kress and van Leeuwen (2006). They are all sketches without any facial features, and no transactional or reactional processes are salient. In the drawing series about human beings, the represented participants can establish classificational taxonomic relations, the five sketchy images in Figure 4-19 being female. The five sketchy female images can be interpreted as representing females of different races, skin color, appearances, etc. Attributes like skin color and hairstyle can be identified, but without much detail. No other ideational patterns can be observed. Finally, no circumstances or only defused ambience can be identified. In the drawing with circumstance, it's also just black strokes which may have symbolic meanings.

These features mean that their commitment to ideational meaning is quite low, compared with the photographs we analyzed. The implications and generic features of these choices are to be discussed with interpersonal patterns as the interpersonal meaning patterns seem to be more salient in these drawings.

4.3.2.3 Interpersonal Patterns

The most salient pattern in the two drawings about human entities is the drawing style, namely, the degree of detail and realism of the human entities. In the data, we have found that human entities can be presented without any facial features or affect, as shown in Figure 4-18 and Figure 4-19.

Kress and van Leeuwen (2006) regarded the realism of a depiction as an expression of modality (and thus relating to the truth value of the image) in their visual grammar. Painter et al. (2012) interpreted the style of character drawing in picture books "as realizing a system of reader alignment, or pathos, and as affording particular ways of presenting a character's emotions or affect" (p. 231). On the basis of the degree of detail and realism of the drawing, they categorized the entities in picture books into three broad styles: "minimalist", "generic" and "naturalistic". The minimalist style for a human character is one that uses circles or ovals for people's heads, with dots or small circles for eyes, has restricted variation in head angles (perhaps only front on and side views), does not need to maintain accurate facial or body proportions and—in its extreme form—has minimal depth (Tian 2012). In terms of affect, the minimalist style in picture books is "more iconic and stylized, focusing on un/happiness" (Painter et al. 2012: 32). It realizes minimal affect. In our data, these pictorial realizations of human entities without any facial features are interpreted as conveying no affect or emotion, so we need to add a new choice of [affectless]. These [affectless] choices tend to present the entities as a generic class rather than specific individuals. Specific individuals are mostly presented in photographs as we discussed in the meaning patterns of news photographs.

The combination of entity realizing ideational meaning and affect realizing interpersonal meaning is a case of inter-metafuncational coupling, in which case choices from two metafunctional systems complement to the meaning-making in the drawing. Based on this coupling realization, we can

Figure 4-20 Inter-metafunctional and Intra-modal Coupling: Entity and Affect

conclude that the human entities, like the non-human, are not presented as an individual that can have affect or emotion, but as an objectified entity or group.

In terms of choices of ambience, the two image-privileged drawings are without much circumstantial elements, and thus non-ambient. In the text-privileged drawings, black and white are a more frequent combination in the data news samples of the present research, which is different from their choices in picture books (Painter et al. 2012). In picture books, this type of combination is atypical. But in the projects "Hurricane Maria's Dead" (see Figure 4-17) and "Unfounded" (see Figure 4-18), the color of black creates a dark and solemn ambience, which is consistent with the grave and somewhat negative topics of the two projects.

The affectless entity or entity group and the choices of non-ambience or downplaying ambience objectify the drawings and are consistent with the objectivity goal to be achieved in journalism.

4. 3. 2. 4 Macro-level Interaction

As the drawings in our data do not have legends, the interaction occurs at the macro level, namely the intermodal interaction between the drawings and the headline or the title of a subsection.

A global pattern is the subsumed multimodal headline that has been analyzed in section 4. 2. 3 when we analyze the periodicity pattern and in section 4. 3. 1 when we analyze the meaning patterns of photographs. Though there is only one case, it shows that a headline for a piece of data news can be instantiated multimodally, with a verbal headline, a verbal strapline and a text-privileged drawing, or with a verbal headline (often with a verbal strapline) and a photograph as analyzed in the previous section. The multimodal headline with a verbal headline and a drawing is presented in Figure 4-17. The multimodal headline functions as the superTheme for the whole data news.

Of the two image-privileged drawings, one interacts with the verbal headline and becomes part of the multimodal headline functioning as the superTheme of the whole news, while the other with the title of the section it is in and forms a multimodal macroTheme. Let's illustrate the interaction with the drawing interacting with the verbal text in the project Unfounded. The multimodal headline is presented in Figure 4-17.

In terms of textual meaning, the drawing is placed below the headline as a demarcated part and the layout choices are [complementary: descending + adjacent]. In terms of ideational interaction, the pronoun "You" in the verbal headline refers to any of the females that are represented by the five sketchy female images. As was analyzed above, the five images represent females as a generic class rather than specific individuals. The female participants are realized multimodally, but the image offers more details. In this case, the coupling pattern is complementing. By contrast, the entity "the police" is merely represented in verbiage. This belongs to the convergence pattern of adding. In terms of interpersonal meaning, it seems that the two modes have contrastive meanings—the interrogative mood requires an answer from the readers and is engaging, while the affectless feature makes the drawing detached and observing, rather than involved and participating. This is a case of intermodal divergence. As a whole, choices made within the two semiotics will always amplify one another, multiplying corresponding kinds of meaning by means of convergent coupling. In this drawing, a case of interpersonal divergence is also identified. This shows that the report tries to be objective in doing analysis and reporting, but also to engage the female readers and win their empathy.

Table 4-4 summarizes the meaning patterns of the drawings analyzed in this section.

Table 4-4 Metafunctional Meanings and Meaning Patterns in Drawings

stratum / metafunction	discourse semantics	grammar
textual	framing layout (intermodal interaction): complementary: descending + image privileged+ adjacent integrated: text privileged +text-central+ subsumed	space position salience
ideational	human entity: classification no activity	classificational processes no process
interpersonal	attitude:: no affect ambience: non-ambient or defused	no facial expressions hyper-real body parts or silhouette no setting contrast of white and black
intermodal interaction	image-privileged drawing	macro: convergence: complementing
	text-privileged drawing	macro: coupling-interpersonal divergence, ideational convergence: complementing (multimodal super-Theme)

4. 3. 3 Meaning Patterns in Data Visualizations

Data visualizations are multimodal in nature. As a first step in our social semiotic approach, we must "begin by inventorizing the semiotic resources that are typical of data visualization across media and contexts" (Aiello 2020: 54). We must identify and catalogue resources that are representative of data visualization as a whole. This is a particularly challenging task, both because uses of data visualization cut across a vast range of social spheres, and because the existing empirical base to systematically describe key data visualization resources is still thin.

The data visualization forms in our data include infographics, charts, maps, and computer-generated videos. All these forms can be static, dynamic or interactive and appear singly or form a series with some others. Computer-generated videos are selected exclusively in the Project Rhymes Behind Hamilton that explores the rhyme patterns of the music play. Table 4-5 presents the times each form is selected and the number of projects that include the form.

These forms of data visualizations share some affordances, but they also have their own unique mechanisms to make meaning. Therefore, we analyze the meanings patterns of each form before we summarize the shared affordances.

Table 4-5 Choices of Semiotic Modes in the Data

type	photo	drawing	data visualization				camera-shot video
			infographic	chart	map	generated video	
total times	14	5	4	**34**	**19**	15	9
projects	8	4	3	**15**	**8**	1	2

4. 3. 3. 1 Infographics

Infographics in the present study refers to diagrams that present qualitative data. Figure 4-21 is a typical example of infographics.

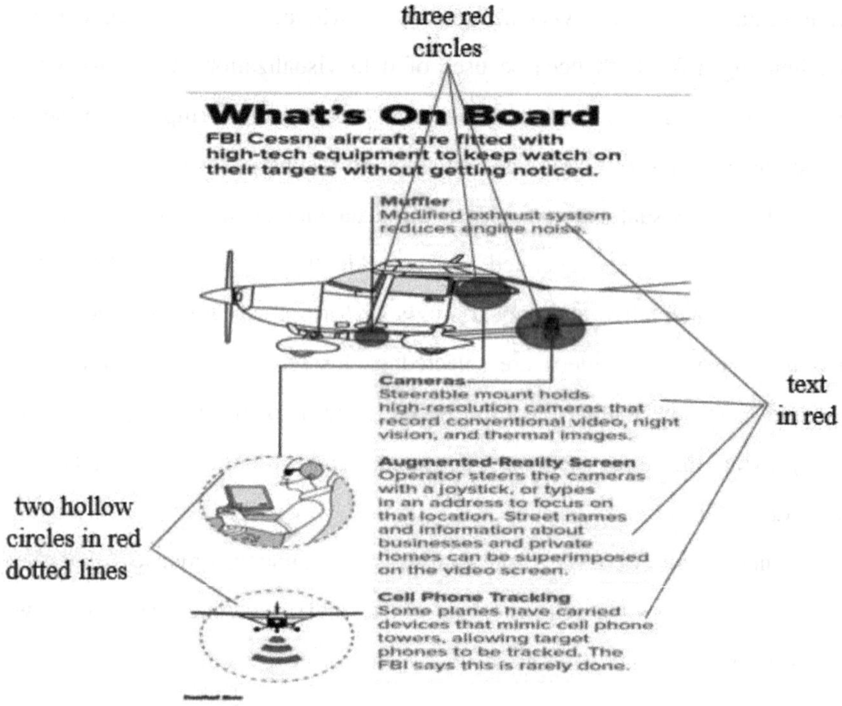

Figure 4-21 An Example of Infographics

(From "Spies in the Skies" by BuzzFeed News)

(1) Textual Patterns

First is the layout pattern. Unlike the layouts of the photos and the drawings that can also be instantiated as [complementary: descending + adjacent], the infographics in our data present just one pattern in layout, namely [integrated]. Another difference lies in the choices within the system of [integrated]. In the photos and the drawings, the choice is [integrated: expanded: subsumed], which means that the verbiage is overlaid onto the image so that it most clearly becomes part of the image itself. In infographics, as is illustrated in Figures 4-21 and 4-22, the verbiage and the images are placed side by side in demarcated places. In picture books, there are similar layout choices, with the verbiage and the image sharing white space background. Painter et al. (2012) called this choice [co-located]. In short, the most frequent layout choice in infographics is [integrated: expanded: co-located]. This may imply that in infographics, the verbiage and the image share equal commitments to meaning making. But like photographs and drawings, no instances of [projected] integration have been found. The absence of this type of layout indicates that infographics do not represent thoughts or locutions of the participants.

Another pattern is the combination of multiple semiotic modes in the infographics. For instance, in Figure 4-21, 6 verbal texts, two schematic drawings, a planform, three red circles, two hollow circles and three connecting lines can be identified. The silhouette and the sign representing wireless signals on the bottom left is a planform, a type of technical drawings "commonly used to portray the shape of an object" (Bateman et al. 2017: 291). In addition, the black and red colors perform textual function: different colors separate the elements on the same canvass into different sections, while the same color connects elements to achieve cohesion and coherence. They also construe ideational meanings: the red color conveys meanings related with each type of high-tech equipment. Color in this infographic can also be regarded as a semiotic mode (see Kress & van Leeuwen 2002 for more details of color as a semiotic mode). This infographic has a periodic structure, with the verbal text "What's On Board" functioning as the hyperTheme. Typographical resources like font size and boldness also play a role in demarcating and grouping the elements on the page.

In Figure 4-22, instances of three semiotic modes can be identified: two cubes (instances of geometrical shapes), a drawing of the Statue of Liberty, and 6 blocks of verbal texts. This is in line with Bateman et al. 's observation that infographics tightly integrate different means of expressions

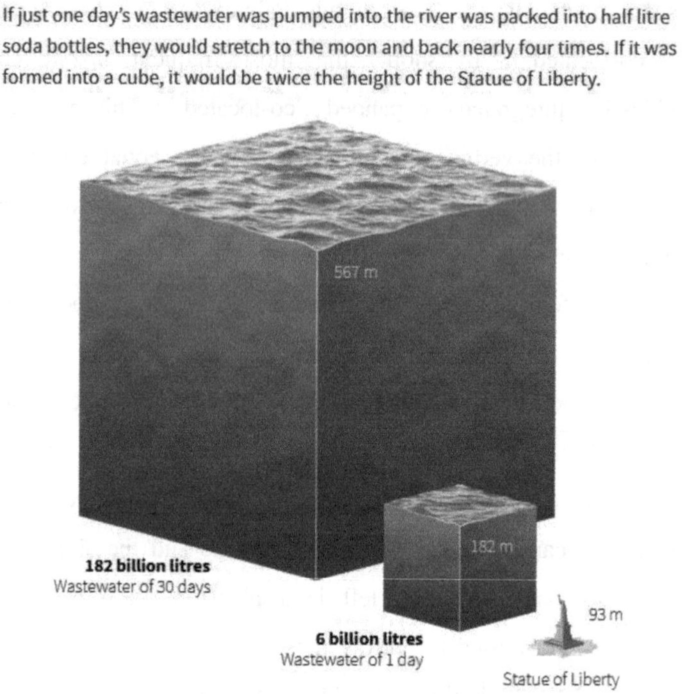

Figure 4-22 One More Example of Infographics

(From the "Race to Save the River Ganges")

from different semiotic modes, which enables infographics to be composite units and a member of the "diagrammatic mode" (Bateman et al. 2017; Aiello 2020). It is because of the features of the diagrammatic mode presented in this image that we take it as an infographic rather than a drawing. In this instance, the sizes of the cubes highlight their prominence.

Such a layout pattern indicates that the ideational and interpersonal meanings in infographics are realized multimodally and that the image and the verbiage are inseparable and commit equally to the meanings. Without either of them, the meanings would be incomplete. Meaning multiplication is achieved by combinations of different semiotic modes.

(2) Ideational Patterns

The most salient ideational pattern we have identified is that infographics are employed to explain relations between entities. This is different from drawings, which focus more on individual entities, their activities and/or attributes. Let's illustrate with two examples. One is from the project "Spies in the Skies" by BuzzFeed News shown in Figure 4-21, and the other from "The Race to Save the River Ganges", presented in Figure 4-22.

In Figure 4-21, classificational, compositional and spatial taxonomic relations are salient. As summarized in Figure 4-23, the four high-tech gadgets visualized through the combination of circles, connecting lines, a drawing of an FBI Cessna aircraft, and four blocks of verbal texts in red are members of the high-tech equipment, thus establishing a classificational taxonomy. This combination of multiple semiotic resources also visualizes the locations of the four mentioned devices. The drawing also gives a visual representation of the compositional structure of the plane, thus establishing a

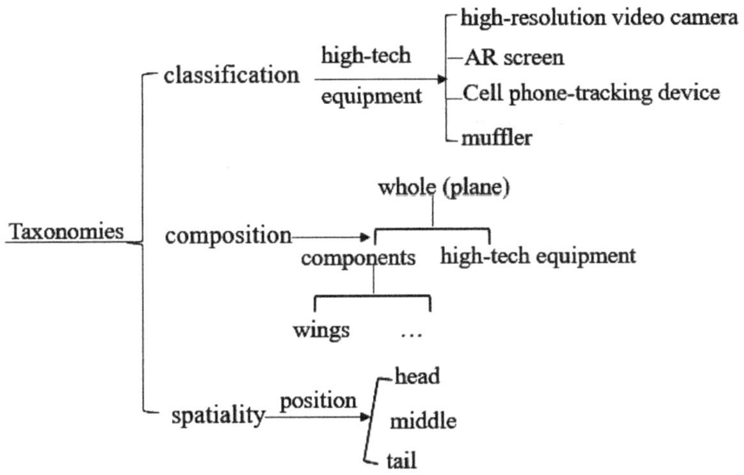

Figure 4-23 An Instantiated System of Taxonomic Relations in the Infographics①

① Tilting the square bracket means that the system is a continuum or "cline" rather than a categorical opposition. See section 3. 3. 3 for more details.

compositional taxonomy. Then we go into detailed analysis of the verbal texts. We can find that the functions or features of the four gadgets and the general function of fitting high-tech equipment are described.

In the infographic presented in Figure 4-22, a contrastive taxonomy is construed: the heights of the three entities—the cube representing the wastewater of 30 days, the one representing the wastewater of 1 day and the drawing of the Statue of Liberty—form a series from small to large. They are in opposition in terms of scales. Contrasts are important resources in many genres for constructing classifying taxonomies or for constructing arguments and interpretations (Martin & Rose 2014/2007: 87). In this example, the contrast is employed to offer visual and verbal interpretations and explanations of the wastewater dumped into the Ganges. Then, the heights of the three entities are also realized in numbers, which establishes a repetition taxonomy with the two cubes and the drawing. The taxonomic relations are realized multimodally. In terms of intermodal interaction, it is a coupling pattern of convergence.

There are other ideational meanings, like the activity of a man operating the AR screen in Figure 4-21 and the attributes of the cubes and the Statue of the Liberty in Figure 4-22. These meanings are more local, so they are not included.

(3) Interpersonal Patterns

One pattern is that no inscribed attitudinal resources have been found in the infographics. The lack of inscribed attitudes gives infographics a sense of objectivity through "inferences of transparency and facticity" (Kennedy et al. 2016: 20), enabling them to do persuasive work, and "to become valued as explanations of our complex social world" (ibid: 10). But attitudes can be invoked through ideational meanings. For instance, in Figure 4-22, the comparison between the heights of the cubes formed by wastewater of 30 days and of 1 day and the height of the Statue of Liberty can invoke negative appreciation towards the pollution of the Ganges and negative judgment towards the government's capability (failure to treat the wastewater and to reduce the water pollution in the river). In Figure 4-21, the coupling between the participant "high-tech equipment" and the material process "keep watch on their targets without getting noticed" can trigger negative judgment of FBI for the activity of surveillance is often associated with intruding the target's privacy. Infographics do realize evaluative meanings, but they are conveyed more implicitly.

Another pattern is the different ways to engage the readers. As has been reviewed in Chapter 1, data journalism practitioners and scholars have grouped data visualizations into two broad categories—static or interactive visualizations. The distinction is made based on the interactivity with viewers or readers, rather than the number of variables involved (e.g., Weber & Rall 2012; Touriño 2017). In our understanding, such a categorization captures the way data visualizations, including infographics, can enact relationships between the reader and the visualization or its producer(s). They realize interpersonal meanings.

Engebretsen and Weber (2017: 280) identified four sets of categories or possibilities that data visualizations can enact interpersonal meanings: static vs. dynamic, interactive vs. non-interactive, explorative vs. illustrative, and pictorial vs non-pictorial. They also argued that the categories are not mutually exclusive or in either-or oppositions. Rather, they should be conceptualized as extremes on a scale. In our understanding, the first three sets are capturing the interaction between the reader and the visualization and are engagement resources realizing interpersonal meanings of infographics and other types of data visualizations. The fourth set is about the representational forms and so more closely related to textual meanings. In our data, there are static and dynamic infographics.

Based on Engebretsen and Weber's analysis, we argue that static infographics display entities or relations that cannot move or change, while dynamic ones display those that move and change. Historically, infographics have been static according to the affordances of print media, but the digital technologies and media have enriched their affordances, making them dynamic. The categories of interactive and non-interactive refer to the degree and the way the reader can influence what is displayed in the infographics. In our data, the static visualizations just offer information and are the least interactive; some dynamic visualizations require the reader to scroll the mouse to read on and are more interactive. The categories of explorative and illustrative capture the degree infographics open for individual exploration and the degree it is displayed to illustrate a narrative, explanative or argumentative statement. In our data, all infographics lean more to the illustrative end. Different degrees of interactivity are visual resources to enable "dialogues" between the infographics and the reader. In other words, they are engagement resources. Figure 4-24 outlines the system of interactivity as engagement resources in infographics.

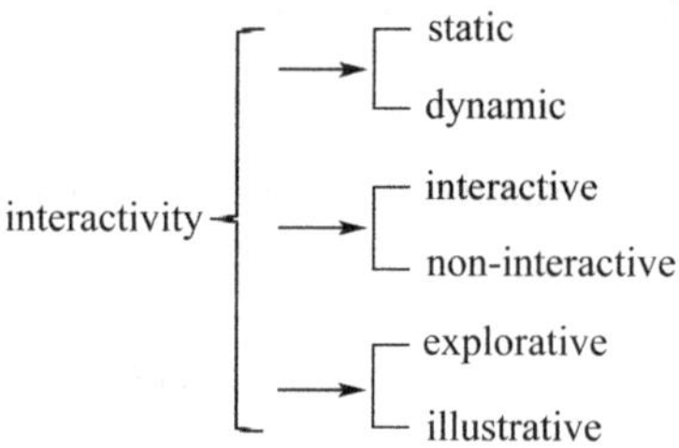

Figure 4-24 Interactivity as Engagement Resources

In other studies, the concept of engagement can refer to the actual interaction with a data visualization, being engaged with it, or to emotional and practical responses, getting engaged by it (Kennedy & Engebretsen 2020: 24). Kennedy and Hill (2017) also argued that data visualizations awaken a wide range of feelings in people who engage with them, activated either by the textual content of the visualizations, contextual factors like users' earlier experiences (with visualizations, their subject matter, or other relevant phenomena), or by the physical and psycho-social situation of use. Their ideas are similar to our "dialogic" view of the relationship between the reader and the infographics.

(4) Intermodal Interaction

① Macro-level Interaction

A noticeable and more global pattern is that the infographics interact locally with part of the longer verbal texts. Let's illustrate the intermodal interaction between the longer verbal texts and the whole infographics with the example shown in Figure 4-22.

The infographic is placed vertically below the paragraph of the verbal texts. In terms of layout, it is instantiated as [complementary: descending: adjacent]. In terms of ideational meanings, the verbal text and the infographic restate some meanings while both convey meanings that are not present in the counterpart. The comparison between the wastewater of 1 day and the drawing of the Statue of Liberty is realized both in the verbal text and the infographics. This is a case of restating coupling. But the wastewater of 30 days and its comparison with the Statue of Liberty are only represented in the infographics, while the verbal text explains the amount of the wastewater of 1 day by comparing it with the distance to the moon. In this case, the coupling is termed as adding.

In terms of interpersonal meaning, attitudes in the verbal text and the infographic are invoked through ideational meanings. As was analyzed previously, the comparison between the heights of the cubes formed by wastewater of 30 days and of 1 day and the height of the Statue of Liberty in the infographic can invoke negative appreciation towards the pollution of the Ganges and negative judgment towards the government's capability.

Similarly, in the verbal text, the process "stretch to the moon and back nearly four times" and "be twice the height of the Statue of Liberty" can also invoke negative appreciation. This is a case of restating coupling.

From the above analysis, we can see that both the verbal text and the infographic aim at offering interpretations and explanations of the wastewater dumped into the Ganges. In the genre analysis, they work together to realize a phase in the whole data news.

② Micro-level Interaction

As was discussed previously, the taxonomic relations can be realized multimodally. As illustrated in Figure 4-22, the nominal groups "wastewater of 30 days" "wastewater of 1 day" and "Statue of Liberty" identify the entities realized in the cubes and the drawing. The nominal groups with Numerative identify the meanings realized by the sizes of the cubes and the drawing. In terms of intermodal interaction, it is a coupling pattern of restating convergence.

Table 4-6 summarizes the meaning patterns in the infographics. Taking into consideration of all these patterns, we can decide on the generic purpose of an infographic, to describe, explain or narrate.

Table 4-6 Metafunctional Meanings and Meaning Patterns in Infographics

stratum / metafunction	discourse semantics	grammar
textual	layout (intermodal): integrated; expanded: co-located	space, shape, connecting lines
ideational	taxonomy: classification, composition, spatiality, comparison (activity and attributes are less important)	connecting lines; nominal groups

Continued

stratum / metafunction	discourse semantics	grammar
interpersonal	invoked attitude engagement	ideational meanings degrees of interactivity
intermodal interaction	micro layer: coupling within the infographic: convergence-identifying/ restating macro layer: infographic-text coupling: convergence-restating/ adding (realizing a stage or phase)	

4.3.3.2 Quantitative Data Visualizations

Data visualizations presenting quantitative data are discussed in the same section. In our data, diagrams and maps are the most frequent choices.

(1) Textual Patterns

First is the layout pattern. Like the infographics, quantitative data visualizations in our data also present just one pattern in layout, namely [integrated: expanded]. But different from the only [co-located] choice in the infographics, they can have the option of [integrated: expanded: subsumed], which means that the verbiage is overlaid onto the image, as illustrated in Figure 4-25. This option appears more frequently in dynamic data visualizations than in the static and interactive ones. In some cases, the subsumed verbiage appears after the mouse is scrolled. There are also instances of [integrated: expanded: co-located] layout, in which the verbiage and the images are placed horizontally or vertically side by side in demarcated places. Figure 4-26 is an example. Also, no instances of [projected] integration have been found. The absence of this type of layout indicates that charts and maps (like infographics) do not represent thoughts or locutions of the participants

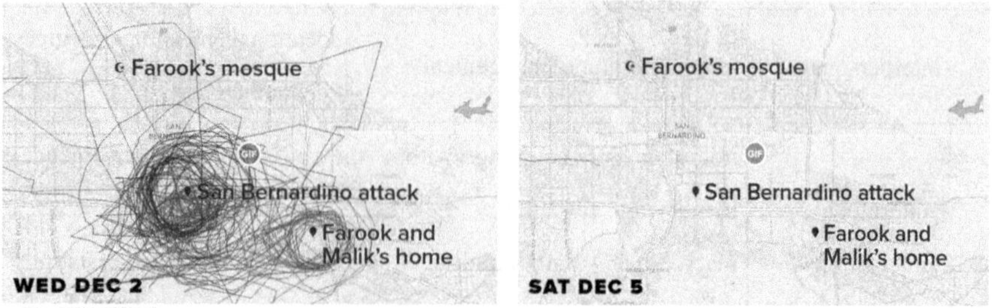

Figure 4-25 Two Screenshots of a Dynamic Map (From "Spies in Skies" by BuzzFeed News)

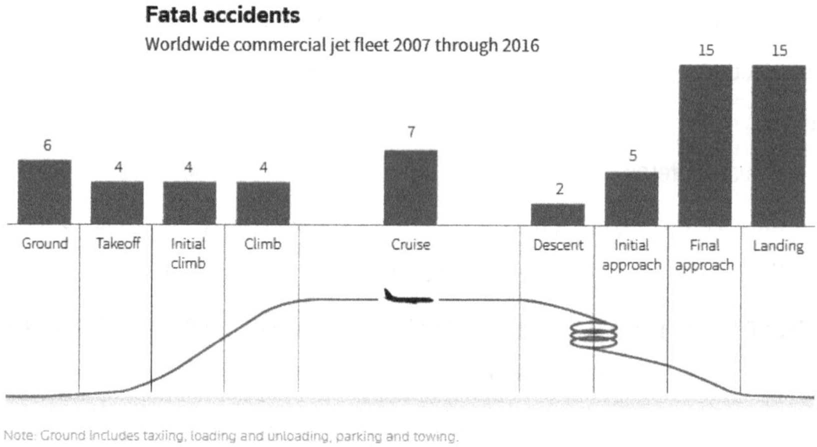

Figure 4-26 An Example of Static Charts(From "Indonesia Plane Crash" by Reuters)

Another pattern is the combination of multiple semiotic modes in the quantitative data visualizations. They are typical of the diagrammatic mode, which may be readily combined with many other semiotic modes. For instance, in Figure 4-26, geometric shapes (rectangles, curve lines and straight lines), a drawing of an airplane, and verbiage are integrated to make meanings. But in terms of compositional value, there are cases of charts in which image and language are equally important, as shown in Figures 4-25 and 4-26, or cases of language-dominated data visualizations as exemplified in Figure 4-27. In data visualizations like Figure s 4-25 and 4-26, the graph and verbal text(s) commit equally to present the quantitative messages, and without either of the two modes, the messages would be incomplete. Though lacking numbers or figures, cases like shown in Figure 4-27 are still data visualizations, because the meanings, particularly the interactive engagement of the viewer, are supported with an invisible big database. These are termed as language-dominated visualizations as verbal language has more meaning commitments.

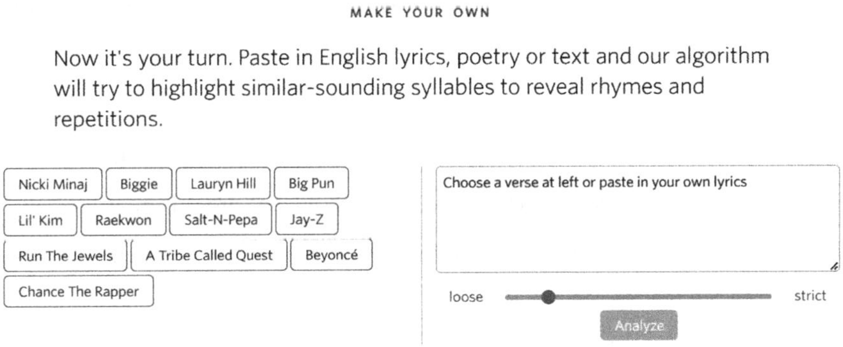

Figure 4-27 An Example of Language-dominated Interactive Data Visualization (From "The Rhymes Behind Hamilton" by *The Wall Street Journal*)

There is also a case of a subsumed multimodal title. It shows that a title for a piece of data news can be instantiated multimodally with a verbal headline, a strapline, and a data visualization. The multimodal headline with a verbal headline and a drawing is presented in Figure 4-28. The multimodal title functions as the macroTheme for the whole section.

Figure 4-28 A MacroTheme Realized by a Data Visualization and Verbal Texts (From "Medicamentalia" by Civio)

It should be pointed that in the project "The Race to Save the River Ganges", the most important data visualization is presented innovatively in the form of a "tree", with a trunk and many branches. The trunk gets bigger as more and more drainage water is dumped and accumulated from the first city on the river to the last one. The branches are different in sizes, which represents the amount of drainage water each city dumps into the river. Besides the branches, there are blocks of verbal texts which specify the names of the cities and the amount of drainage water dumped. This innovative data visualization also follows the [integrated: expanded: co-located] layout, but the tree layout reveals that technologies enrich the layout choices and the meaning potentials of data visualizations, and that no single research can cover all the features of the diverse forms of data visualizations.

(2) Interpersonal Patterns

The most unique pattern is the degrees of interactivity between the reader and the data visualization. In the previous section, we discussed the interactivity of the infographics and found that different choices of interactivity are engagement resources. From the semiotic perspective, the potentials of charts and maps to realize interpersonal meanings can be more complex than infographics. Based on Engebretsen and Weber's categorization (2017), we found that in our data, static visualizations offer information and are the least interactive, some dynamic visualizations require the reader to scroll the mouse to read on and are more interactive, and some others need the reader to type in certain "orders" to read the desired information or message, "support manipulation or navigation" (ibid) by the reader and so are the most interactive. In the scrolling type of interactivity, the scrolling movement can be combined with zooming effects. The categories of explorative and illustrative capture the degree the data visualization opens for individual exploration and the degree it is displayed to illustrate a narrative, explanative or argumentative statement. Different from the infographics which are more to the illustrative end, the dynamic data visualizations that support manipulation or navigation from the reader are explorative. Figure 4-24 in the previous section outlines the system of interactivity as engagement resources in quantitative and qualitative data visualizations.

Then, there are a few cases of inscribed appreciation resources in verbiage of the data visualizations in the project Medicamentlia, but attitudes in the images are invoked by ideational meanings. Let's illustrate this with the interactive dot chart from the Prices section of the project Medicamentalia (a screenshot is presented in Figure 4-29). In the legend offering explanation of the diagrammatic information, the adjective phrases "the most expensive" and "the least affordable" are inscribed instances of negative appreciation towards Simvastatin, a cholesterol-lowering medication. The superlative expressions "the most" and "the least" are also upscaling graduation resources. In the subsumed block of verbiage, the nominal group with Numerative "45. 45 days of work" can invoke negative appreciation of the high price of Simvastatin in Sao Tome and Principe. It also resonates with "the most expensive" and "the least affordable". In the image, the position of each small dot can invoke appreciation towards the prices of Simvastatin in different countries: the higher the position, the more negative. Negative appreciation is inscribed or invoked in the image and verbal texts. In terms of intermodal interaction, it is a coupling pattern of [convergence: restating].

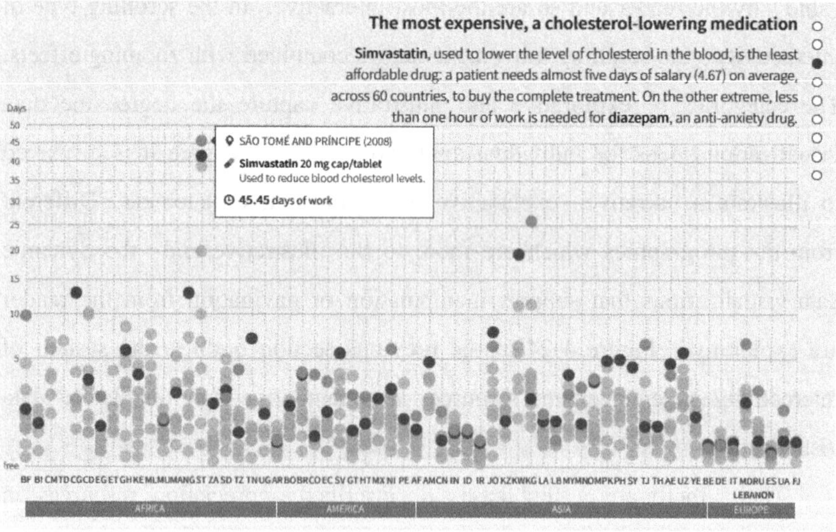

Figure 4-29 A Screenshot of the Interactive Chart in the Project "Medicamentalia"

According to Kress and van Leeuwen (2006), scientific and technical images, such as diagrams, maps and charts, usually encode an objective attitude. This tendency or goal to achieve objectivity may be a reason that no affect or judgment has been identified, and that even appreciation is realized implicitly in quantitative data visualizations.

Finally, in some projects, the data sources are offered and the dataset is downloadable. For data journalists and their collaborators, these practices are ways of representing data accurately and of providing evidence that the analysis has been done seriously and the findings can be verified (Kennedy et al. 2016). Semiotically, these practices are resources to establish credibility in argument and lend more authority to the analysis and the findings.

It should be emphasized that attitudinal meanings are realized in data visualizations, though in more implicit ways. In addition, Economou (2008) suggested that visual evaluative meanings are expanded through layout features (size, framing) and modality (color, light, contrast). Kennedy and Engebretsen (2020) also argued that colors and layout of data visualizations trigger our senses in particular ways and therefore enacts interpersonal meanings as well. We are sorry that considering our ultimate goal and due to time and space constraints, we are unable to reveal and present how colors and layout features can enact interpersonal meanings. We will reserve the exploration of the meaning potential of colors and layout for our future research.

(3) Ideational Patterns

The most salient ideational pattern we have identified is that quantitative data visualizations are employed to explain relations between entities. This is similar to the infographics and different from drawings and photographs, which focus more on individual entities, their activities and/or attributes.

Multiple taxonomic relations can be construed in one data visualization. For instance, in Figure 4-29, classificational and contrastive taxonomic relations are construed simultaneously. The dots in different colors that represent different medicines form classificational relations, each dot being one member in the class of medicine. The positions of the dots, together with the country variable presented in the horizontal axis, establish comparisons between the prices of the medicines in different countries.

Dynamic and interactive visualizations in our data often include several charts which appear one by one when the reader scrolls the mouse. In other words, there is a series of charts in one dynamic or interactive visualization. For instance, the image shown in Figure 4-29 is just one dot chart in an interactive visualization which includes 10 charts. Taxonomic relations can be formed across the charts. For instance, Kyrgyzatan in the first chart, Ghana in the second, Sao Tome and Principe in the third and fourth, Morocco in the fifth, Kuwait in the sixth, Sudan in the seventh, Brazil in the eights and Ethiopia in the nineth form classificational relations. So do the medicines like Ciprofloxacin, Amoxicillin, and Diclofenac. Logical relations are also construed between the images within one dynamic or interactive visualization. The contrastive taxonomic relations are sustained in all the charts in the series, but each time with new entities. In this case, additive logical relation is formed. Contrastive logical relation is also identified across several charts. For instance, chart 1 visualizes the prices of Sakbutamol; chart 2 visualizes the prices of Captopril. The different prices of different medicines in different countries are visualized in a series. There are no conjunctions to connect the events depicted, but the consistence in the choice of visual elements, color and nominal groups can be regarded as visual realizations of logical relations at the stratum of grammar.

In maps, spatial structure of the depicted entities can be realized. Maps can depict the movement of an entity in space and implicitly in time (Weber 2020). In interactive diagrams and maps, sequentiality can also be realized. One option is to use the (parallax) scrolling technique (Weber 2020). Here, the effect is twofold: stepping from one event to the next while scrolling down the mouse, thus causing a transformation of the visualization (ibid). The dynamic map in the project "Life in the Camp" is a typical example. The two screenshot images (shown in Figure 4-30) depict the

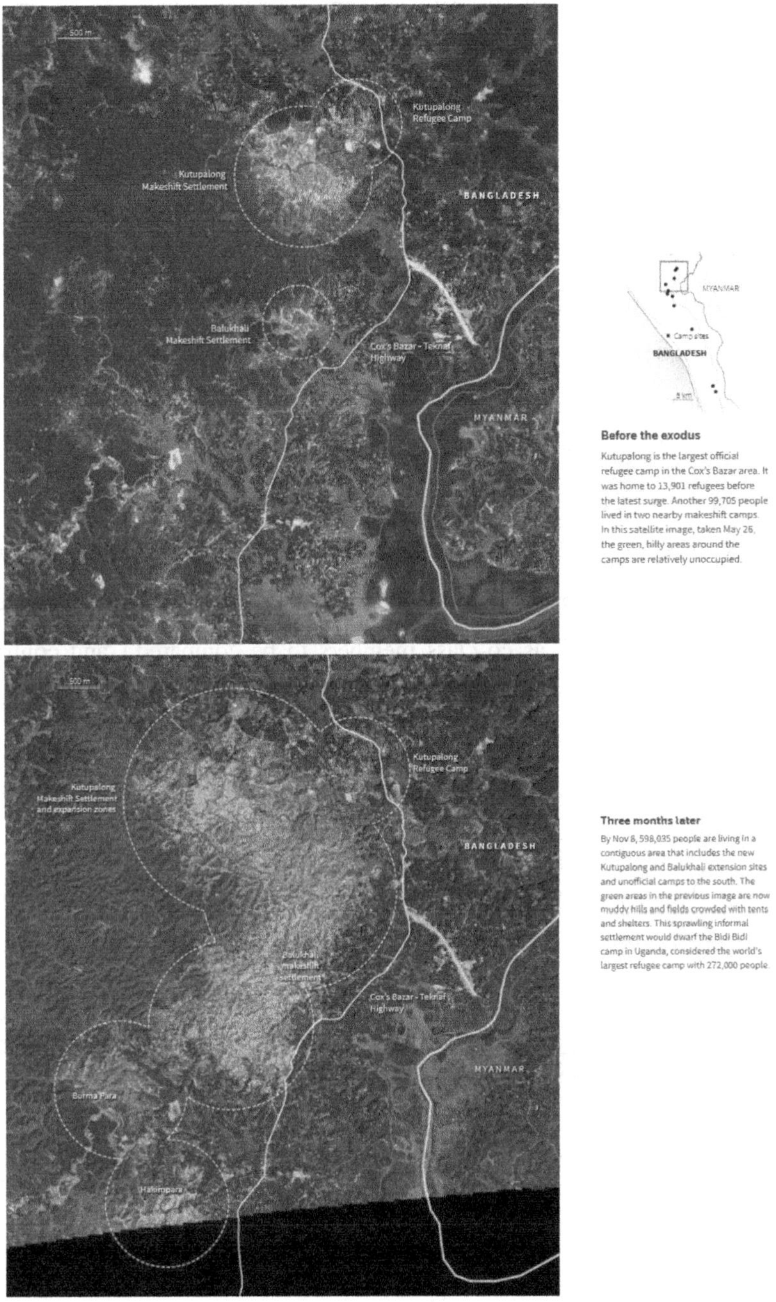

Figure 4-30 Two Screenshots of the Interactive Map Realizing Sequentiality

changes of the density of the refugee camps around Cox's Bazar on the southern tip of Bangladesh. The refugee camps were inhabited by Rohingya Muslims who fled a military crackdown in Myanmmar's Rakhine State in 2017. The two images appear one after another as the reader scrolls down the webpage and present the situations before the exodus and three months later. In addition to locational information of the place and the contrastive relations realized by the different sizes of the circles, sequentiality or temporal sequence is realized through the scrolling technique and the sequence in which the charts appear. With the verbal legends on the right, the sequence is made even clearer.

Data visualizations can construe correlational relations rather causal relations. The chart in Figure 4-31 is an example. Like other visualizations, this chart also construes multiple taxonomies—classification (different phases during the flight as co-class members to be compared) and contrast (represented by the heights of the bars and the figures above the bars). Besides this, a correlation can be found between the fatal accidents and the phases during the flight. The red line together with an iconic drawing of a

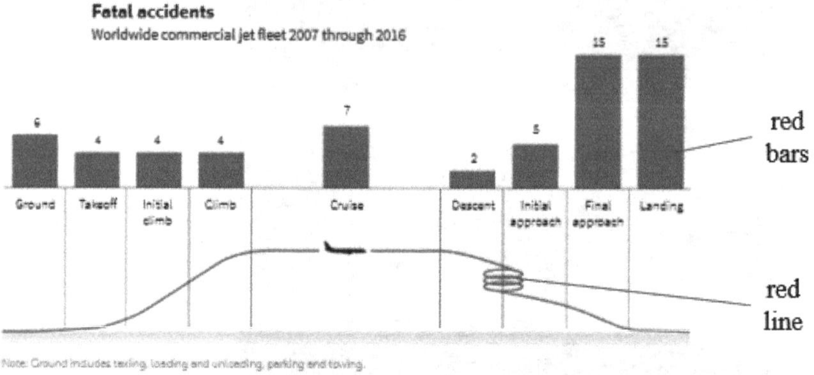

Figure 4-31 Diagrams Realizing Correlation

(From "Indonesia Plane Crash" by Reuters)

plane and its changes along presents the fatal accidents at each phase. From its simple and clear layout, the reader can see that accidents have some correlation with the phases of the fight—they are most common during the final approach and landing and least common during the climb and descent.

As we analyze the data visualizations in our data, we are increasingly awed and sometimes frustrated by their diversity and complexity in making meaning. Each type and subtype of data visualizations has rich affordances and construes ideational meaning in different ways. For instance, maps have the analytical structure: there is a Carrier and they may provide quite distinct analyses of what seems to be the same Carrier (Kress & van Leeuwen 2006: 88). Some maps focus on geographical features such as waterways, altitude, etc., while others concentrate on social and political boundaries. Analysis always involves selection. Some attributes or characteristics of the Carrier are singled out as criteria in the given context or generally, while others are ignored or treated as non-essential and irrelevant. But as our focus is on the global patterns that contribute to the genre analysis of data news, we do not and are also unable to offer a full description of all the ideational meanings.

(4) Intermodal Interaction

① Macro-level Interaction

Like infographics, quantitative data visualizations interact locally with part of the longer verbal texts. Let's illustrate the intermodal interaction between the longer verbal texts and the whole infographics with the example shown in Figure 4-29.

The visualization is placed vertically below two paragraphs of the verbal texts (They are screenshot and presented in Figure 4-32). Textually, the layout is [complementary: descending: adjacent].

Because price is one of the main barriers to access to medicines—**although not the**

only one, —as it drains governments' budgets and excludes the poorest people from treatment. According to the WHO, **one third of the world's population** has trouble accessing the medicines they need while, at the same time, 15% of the population consumes 90% of the global spending on pharmaceutical products.

This interactive chart shows the data that we have collected from HAI and from several official sources in Argentina, Italy, Spain and Germany. The final dataset can be downloaded here. If you want to include information about your country to the project, learn more about our methodology and the reasons why we have used these particular datasets, you can stop by here.

Figure 4-32 Verbal Texts Adjacent to the Data Visualization in Figure 4-29

Ideationally, the interactive chart interacts with both paragraphs, but in different ways and realizes different communicative purposes. In the first paragraph, price is construed as a factor affecting the accessibility of medicines and it also describes the accessibility disparity in the world. It is like a topic sentence in a verbal paragraph. The interactive chart offers more detailed information: the accessibility in different countries in relation to the different prices of the 14 medicines. As analyzed previously, the different prices of different medicines in different countries are visualized in a series. In the series, multiple taxonomic relations and contrastive logical relations are construed. The interactive chart adds meanings to the verbal text, thus the coupling of [convergence: adding]. Meanwhile, the chart and the verbal text complement each other in periodicity, with the verbal text as the hyperTheme. This can be seen a coupling of [convergence: complementing].

In terms of interpersonal meaning, attitudinal meanings are often invoked in the verbal text and the data visualization through ideational meanings, though there are a few cases of inscribed appreciation. For instance, in the project "Medicamentalia" we analyzed previously, negative appreciation is inscribed in the legend, and is invoked in the verbiage in the block and the chart. In terms of intermodal interaction, it is a coupling pattern of [convergence: restating].

From the above analysis, we can see that the first paragraph and the interactive chart aim at offering comparisons of prices of 14 medicines in different countries. They work together to present the findings and so realize a stage in the whole discourse. By contrast, the second paragraph shifts gears (See Chapter 5 for more details) in several aspects: new research entities like "data, official sources, dataset" and "you" which addresses and interacts directly with the reader, and two hyperlinks. Because of these shifts, the second paragraph belongs to another stage.

As analyzed previously, there is also a case of subsumed multimodal title realized by verbal texts and a data visualization (illustrated in Figure 4-28). The verbal title, strapline and the visualization as the setting together predict the main contents in the text. The intermodal interaction is [convergence: complementing].

② Micro-level Interaction

The coupling patterns of identifying, adding and complementing have been identified at the micro-level interaction, namely the interaction between the realizations of the semiotic modes within the data visualizations. As illustrated in Figure 4-31, the nominal groups identify the entities realized in the bars and the figures identify the numbers of fatal accidents visualized by the height of the bar. In terms of intermodal interaction, it is a coupling pattern of identifying. The red line with the drawing of a plane symbolizes altitude changes during a flight. This is not expressed in the verbal texts. Similarly, the ideational meaning realized in the nominal group "Worldwide commercial jet fleet 2007 and through 2017" adds more information about the amount of data, which is not expressed in the chart. These are cases of adding. The chart offers details to the verbal title "Fatal accidents" and the verbiage in the Note offers a more detailed categorization with the phase

"Ground". These are cases of complementing.

The major meaning patterns are summarized in Table 4-7.

Table 4-7 Metafunctional Meanings and Meaning Patterns in Quantitative Data Visualizations

stratum / metafunction	discourse semantics	grammar
textual	layout (with the whole discourse): integrated: expanded: co-located layout (within DV): integrated: expanded: subsumed/ co-located	space, shape, connecting lines, color
ideational	taxonomy: classification, contrast, spatiality connexion: addition, contrast, correlation, time/sequentiality	connecting lines; nominal groups; color consistence in the use of visual elements, nominal groups, scrolling, sequence of appearance
interpersonal	invoked attitude engagement	ideational meanings degrees of interactivity
intermodal interaction	micro: convergence-identifying/ adding/complementing macro: convergence-restating/adding/complementing (realizing a stage or phase; multimodal macroTheme)	

4.3.3.3 Computer-generated Data-driven Videos

Most readers are familiar with data visualizations presented as graphs, yet in our data there are 15 cases of computer-generated data-driven videos in the project "The Rhymes Behind Hamilton". These videos commit fully to the meaning in the project and are a key mode in the project. They are not produced by photographers with cameras, instead they are generated by data journalist Joel Eastwood and developer Erik Hinton with computers. They do not present human entities and activities or naturalistic scenes, instead they present the rhyming patterns in the lyrics of the musical play, which are actually the result of the two authors' data analysis. They are regarded by the authors as "a new data visualization type that could capture the lyrical complexity of rhyming verse"①. Indeed, this is new and creative—data visualizations can be represented in the form of video as well. These videos, though without figures or graphs demonstrating the results of data analysis, are data-driven, so they are termed as computer-generated data-driven videos to distinguish from the natural videos shot by photographers with cameras. From the social semiotic perspective, these videos blend together choices from audio and visual semiotic modes and are multimodal in nature.

A basic unit for analyzing natural camera-shot videos is shot, which is defined as a single continuous take from starting to stopping the camera (Bateman et al. 2017: 329). One criterion for identifying shots is to see whether there is an obvious shift of screen, especially the background of screen (He 2020). But the standard "technical details" in relation to shots in natural videos, including shot scales, camera angles, camera movements and shot transitions are not applicable in these videos and there is no obvious shift of screen, especially the background of screen. If we borrow the term shot, then each of these videos is just a single shot. In the present analysis, we take each video as a unit for analysis. Our analysis from the social

① The two authors have explained the methods and procedure of their data analysis and visualization in an online article entitled "The Hamilton Algorithm". See https://source.opennews.org/articles/hamilton-algorithm/.

semiotic perspective also provides rationale for distinguishing these computer-generated videos from camera-shot videos and for theorizing them as one type of data visualizations.

Like the infographics, diagrams and maps we have analyzed, these videos are also composite units. They involve music, lyrics, color blocks representing different syllables and interacting with colored syllables, the name and source of the rap song, and a black-white photograph of the singer. As the project aims at revealing and visualizing the rhyming patterns in Hamilton, the music, the color blocks and the lyrics are the major modes. The meanings and meaning patterns are described from the coupling perspective.

Textually, the integrated layout is a key realization for their textual meanings. The instantiated semiotic resources are integrated as visual elements into composite units. The visual elements are placed in demarcated parts and so form a co-located integrated layout. Then the colors play a vital role in connecting the two important semiotic modes in the squares and the lyrics: a same color is used to visualize the square and the lyrics that represent a same rhyme.

The visualizations also have the features of videos—they can be played and paused and so demonstrating the linear and sequential quality of videos. The color blocks and colored syllables appear in a row when the video is being played. The syllables disappear when the next one appears while the color blocks remain there after their appearance (see Figure 4-33). When the video ends, the rhyming syllables in the lyrics become color-coded as well (see Figure 4-33). A color is selected for each group of rhyming syllables and the same color is selected for the block, the singled-out rhyming syllables accompanying the color blocks and the syllables in the lyrics.

Figure 4-33 Two Screenshots from the First Video in "The Rhymes Behind Hamilton"

Ideationally, the color blocks, together with colored syllables, show the rhymes in the songs of the musical play. Music, more like language, is organized by the logic of time and sequence rather than the logic of space and simultaneity of images. It is "arguably the purest 'time-based' form of expression" (Bateman et al. 2017: 28).

Interpersonally, no inscribed attitudinal resources have been identified. The bright colors and the music melody can invoke positive responses from the reader.

Integrating the patterns, we can find that the videos serve to explain and illustrate the rhyming patterns in the musical play and function as stages from the perspective of genre.

4. 3. 3. 4 Commonalities of Data Visualizations

"[D]ata visualizations have innovative semiotic forms and result in novel types of communication and interactivity" and "their meaning potentials for meaning making, for evoking emotions, democratic participation, and other forms of engagement is also in a state of transformation" (Kennedy & Engebretsen 2020: 20). Our data also shows that data visualizations have innovative ways to combine semiotic modes and their realizations, that these ways result in novel and diverse forms of data visualizations, and that their potential for meaning making is multiplied. Whatever innovative ways and transformations may be involved, the various forms of data visualizations share commonalities in the meaning-making process.

Textually, a noticeable and more global pattern is the intermodal layout. When the data visualizations interact with part of the longer verbal texts, they are usually placed vertically between two paragraphs of verbal texts. Unlike photographs, they have not found to be placed horizontally by the side of the longer verbal texts. In other words, the layout is instantiated as [complementary: descending: adjacent]. Within the data visualizations, no instances of [projected] integration have been found. Then, in most data visualizations, the image and the verbiage are inseparable and commit equally to the meanings. Without either of them, the meanings would be incomplete. Meaning multiplication is achieved by combinations of different semiotic modes.

Ideationally, data visualizations are graphical representations of qualitative and quantitative formation. They construe relations between or among different entities. The entities can be persons, places, prices, relations, to mention just a few. Data visualizations of qualitative data can visualize classificational, compositional and spatial structures of certain entities (e.g., Figure 4-21). They can also visualize contrastive relation between entities (like Figure 4-22). Those of quantitative data, besides visualizing classificational, compositional and spatial structures of certain entities, can present logical relations of sequentiality, comparison and contrast, and correlation. In our data, no causal relation or implication has been realized in data visualizations; it is realized in verbal texts. Data visualizations can be field-specific. Certain meanings are consistently associated with particular types of visualizations.

Interpersonally, data visualizations realize different degrees of interactivity. As has been analyzed, data visualizations can engage the reader through different ways of interactivity. Then, the lack of inscribed attitudes gives data visualizations a sense of objectivity (Kress & van Leeuwen 2006; Kennedy et al. 2016), enabling them to do persuasive, rhetorical work, and "to become valued as explanations of our complex social world" (ibid: 10). This may explain why most scholars and practitioners (e.g., Ledin & Machin 2018; Nœrland 2020; Ricker et al. 2020) argue for the significance of data visualizations as a public discourse. But it does not mean that data visualizations do not realize evaluative meanings. Rather, the evaluative meanings are conveyed more implicitly. This may explain, at least partially, why some scholars (e.g., Cairo 2020) question the objectivity of data visualizations at large. Anyway, just as Kenney and Engebretsen (2020) pointed out, data visualizations can convey facts quickly and visualize patterns effectively, thus offering insights into societal patterns otherwise invisible and unnoticed.

Our data also demonstrate that a data visualization can be a multimodal discourse independently and combines with other semiotic modes to form a more complex discourse. In terms of generic purposes, the diverse forms of data visualizations can be used to narrate events or stories, to present and explain facts, and to persuade. This resonates with Aiello's comment that "data visualization has emerged rapidly as what Engebretsen and Weber (2017) have defined as a 'super-genre' that is used to accomplish a wide variety of communicative tasks across an increasing number of professional and institutional communities of users" (p. 49). Yet, the patterns identified in our data also indicate that the data visualizations can be employed to realize a stage or a phase as an embedded genre.

4.3.4 Outlining Semiotic Capabilities of the Image Family Members

Textually, no instances of [projected] integration have been found. The absence of this type of layout indicates that the images in our data do not represent thoughts or locutions of the participants.

Ideationally, just as Rose (2012) pointed out, various types of images in our data show two sets of features or capabilities. First, images such as photographs or realistic drawings may be relatively iconic representations of an entity or activity, data visualizations may be symbolic representations, and in between there are indexical images like outline drawings that indicate some recognizable features of the represented entity or activity. Second, the images can classify (classification) or de/compose entities (composition) and represent a single activity (simple) or a sequence (complex). Entities within an image may be explicitly labelled, or implicit for the reader to infer—from the accompanying verbal text or assumed knowledge of field.

Interpersonally, the news photographs, drawings and data visualizations in our data not only convey facts but also enact profound emotional interactions between the news and the reader, but there are some differences. Drawings and data visualizations can work to argue a viewpoint in a detached objective way (e.g., informing readers what happened or explaining what may result, to supporting viewpoints), while news photos with affect can engage readers emotionally to the contents.

4. 4 Meaning Patterns in Camera-shot Natural Videos

As has been mentioned, the videos in our data range from natural representations of reality by cameras to computer generated artefacts which mix artificially generated scenes and blend together choices from audio and visual semiotic modes. Whatever the production methods, the videos create coherent, perceptually continuous units. Computer generated videos are data-driven, so their meaning patterns have been discussed in section 4. 3. 3.

Camera-shot natural videos, like films, pose a great challenge for semiotic scholars for the "extreme degree of orchestration and integration of very diverse forms of expression in order to achieve a coherent audiovisual artefact" (Bateman et al. 2017: 328). A "shot" (Bateman et al. 2017) is usually taken as the basic unit on the expression plane to unpack the meaning patterns of camera-shot natural videos. He (2020) proposed a method to identify different shots in videos—looking at whether there is an obvious shift of screen, especially the background of screen. Considering the complexity of meanings in videos and the focus of our analysis, we do not analyze the videos shot by shot. Instead, we take each video as a whole and analyze the salient patterns that contribute to our genre analysis.

The first pattern is that the videos can center on human entities and their verbiage. In videos of this types, the choice of a proper noun in the caption to identify represented participants shows a coupling pattern with the interpersonal meanings of the verbal texts. Proper nouns are selected when the relevant verbal text quotes from an expert or elite figure as attribution resources. There is an inter-metafuctional coupling of human entity and attribution.

The videos can also center on non-human entities, like the Makola

Market illustrated in Figure 4-34. Videos of this type aims to describe the situations and features of the entities or the typical activities occurring in a locational entity like the Makola Market.

Makola market in Accra. | Video: Elio Stamm and Miguel Á. Gavilanes

Figure 4-34 A Screenshot of the Video Introducing a Medicine Market (From "Medicamentalia")

Another pattern is that all the videos are placed horizontally beside the longer verbal text and tend to just interact locally with part of the verbal text. Like the photographs, choices made within the two semiotics will always amplify one another, multiplying corresponding kinds of meaning by means of "convergent" coupling. The coupling can be instantiated as restating the same meaning, complementing each other on the same meaning, or with one mode adding meaning to the other. This pattern indicates that the videos tend to realize a stage or a phase as an embedded genre.

4. 5 Intermodal Coupling Patterns

Image (including news photos, drawings, data visualizations), language, and videos form data news as multimodal communicative artefacts and work together to realize the communicative goal(s). It is also important to describe and discover the possibility of specifying what happens when semiotic modes combine to create meaningful discourses. Based on our previous analysis, two layers of intermodal interaction can be identified from the data. One is the image-text interaction within a news photo, a drawing, a data visualization, and image-text-sound interaction within a video, and the other is the interaction between a news photo, a data visualization, a video as a whole and the verbal text of the whole data news. We refer to the first category as micro image-text coupling and the latter as macro image-text coupling.

4. 5. 1 Micro Image-text Coupling

As has been explained in section 4. 1, the major types of images in the data include news photos, drawings and data visualizations and they are multimodal in nature, and intermodal interaction occurs first at the micro level. To be more specific, in a news photograph, couplings can occur between the photograph and the caption; in a drawing or a data visualization, couplings can occur between the image and the verbal text; and in a video, coupling can occur between/among the image, the speech, the caption and the music.

The coupling pattens have been analyzed in terms of textual, ideational and interpersonal meanings. All the couplings are convergent at the micro-level interaction in the photographs, videos and data visualizations. The coupling patterns of identifying, adding and complementing have been identified. In other words, choices made within these semiotic modes always multiply corresponding kinds of meaning by means of 'convergent' coupling. In the photographs and videos, the caption identifies the entities realized in the images. In data visualizations, usually, the verbal nominal groups integrated into the image or in the legends identify the entities realized in the images. This is the identifying coupling. In the photographs and the videos, the proper noun in the caption is always followed by a nominal group that elaborates the profession or social role of the human entities, or adds locations, features, or qualities of non-human entities. In data visualizations, the visual image usually offers more details to the verbal texts, particularly the verbal titles functioning as the hyperTheme. Though meanings are expanded through elaborating or offering more details, the two modes complement each on the same meaning (s). This is the complementing type of coupling. Some meanings are just realized in the visual image or in the caption/legend. The coupling is adding because meanings are added. As the drawings in the data have no captions or legends, there are no micro-level couplings.

Based on our analysis in Sections 4. 3 and 4. 4, we summarize the micro-level coupling patterns in Figure 4-35.

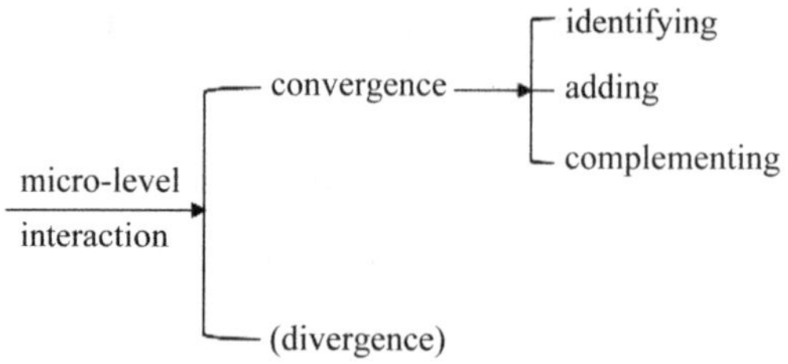

Figure 4-35 Micro-level Coupling Patterns

4. 5. 2 Macro Image-text Coupling

Intermodal interaction also exists between a news photo, a drawing, a data visualization, or a video as a whole and part of the verbal text of the whole data news, as has been illustrated and analyzed in sections 4. 3 and 4. 4. The coupling pattens have been analyzed in terms of textual, ideational and interpersonal meanings as well.

At the macro level, a photo, a drawing, a data visualization or a video can interact locally with part of the longer verbal texts, and a photo, a drawing, or a data visualization can form a multimodal headline with verbal texts.

In the former case, most couplings are convergent and can be instantiated as restating the same meaning, complementing each other on the same meaning, or with one mode adding meaning to the other. When a same meaning is realized in the semiotic modes instantiated, it is a restating coupling. When the same meaning is realized but one semiotic mode offers more details, it is a complementing coupling. For instance, some participants are realized both in the verbal text and the photo, but the photo offers more details. In this case, the coupling pattern is complementing. When a meaning is realized only in one semiotic mode, the coupling is termed as adding. There is only one case of interpersonal divergence in the project "Unfounded" (See section 4. 3. 2). The divergence occurs in the instantiation of interpersonal meaning. The two modes have contrastive meanings—the interrogative mood requires an answer from the readers and is engaging, while the affectless feature highlights the genericity of the cases and makes the drawing representative and detached. The choice can reflect that data news texts attempt to achieve objectivity and facticity and to win the readers' alignment.

In the latter case, namely the multimodal headlines which function as the superTheme for the whole data news, the photo, drawing or data visualization and the verbal texts complement each other to form a multimodal headline. The coupling pattern is [complementing].

The coupling patterns are presented diagrammatically in Figure 4-36.

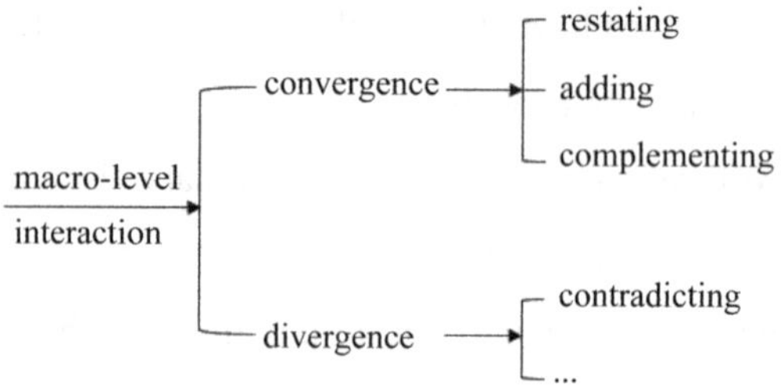

Figure 4-36 Macro-level Coupling Patterns

4.6 Summary

In this chapter, we analyzed the meaning patterns or configurations in each semiotic mode and the patterns of intermodal interaction in our data. We started with and focused more on the stratum of discourse semantics since this is the stratum which interfaces most directly with register and genre; but as we follow the trinocular descriptive principle in SFL, we related to the lexicogrammatical patterns when necessary. From a metafunctional perspective, many of the meanings are realized multimodally; in these cases, coupling patterns are analyzed together with the analysis of metafunctions and their realizations. We identified two layers of intermodal interaction, namely the micro-level interaction within an image or a video, and the macro-level between an image as a whole or a video and the verbal texts. As our focus is genre analysis, we give priority to patterns which can differentiate genre or reveal genre relations over the more local patterns, so the affordances of videos and members of the image mode family have not been fully described.

Chapter 5 Register and Genre Analyses of Data News

In this chapter, we will answer the latter two research questions raised in Chapter 3: How do the meaning patterns identified relate to register and what generic configurations can be revealed by the register patterns and discourse semantic configurations? And what are the relations between the elemental genres in the sample news projects and how are they modeled as genre complexes or macrogenres?

5.1 Register Analysis

Following Martin's genre model (See Chapter 3 for more details), genre is well positioned in our model as a resource for coordinating communication across modalities in multimodal texts as our understandings of inter-modality unfold (Martin & Rose 2008: 232). We conceptualize the relationship between context and semiotic modes as natural and bi-directional—semiotic modes realize context, and context constrains the meaning-making processes of each semiotic mode. We hold the view that a systematic description of the lexiogrammatical and discourse semantic patterns can serve as the basis for capturing the generic features, yet we start with and focus more on the stratum of discourse semantics since this is the stratum which interfaces most directly with register and genre. The mediating role of discourse semantics makes it a perfect toolkit for genre analysis. In the analysis process, we adopt the SFL trinocular perspective—looking "from above", "from below" and "from around". This means that a meaning pattern at a certain stratum is described and interpreted by relating to the patterns from a stratum above, its realizations from a stratum below and other patterns at the same stratum. In the present analysis, we look at both the meaning patterns or configurations at the strata of discourse semantics and grammar when we identify register and genre patterns.

As has been expounded in Chapter 3, we follow Martin's view on genre and see it realized by the configurations of the three register variables of field, tenor, and mode, which are in turn realized by discourse semantic patterns. Intermodal interaction between images and verbal texts is described from the perspective of coupling that can occur at all the three strata of denotative semiotics. So, before we move to meaning patterns at the stratum of genre, we will discuss the meaning configurations at the stratum of register by relating to the discourse semantic patterns of each semiotic mode and the intermodal coupling. We see field, mode and tenor working together to generalize knowledge, multimodality and social relations across genres. But we apologize that we have not done enough to analyze genre as a configuration of field, tenor, and mode variables for lack of quantitative statistics.

5. 1. 1 Meaning Patterns of Mode

In data news which is usually presented on online and mobile media, the semiotic modes for communication are expanded to include language, photographs, drawings, data visualizations, videos, etc. Apart from the meaning potentials of each of these modes, another key issue is how these individual modes can combine with one another to create a unified and coherent but also complex multimodal discourse. As Martin and Rose (2008) pointed out, while SFL work on the grammars and meaning patterns of various non-linguistic modalities has developed rapidly since 1990s, work towards a theory of multimodality started later and is therefore relatively underdeveloped. By relating the discourse semantic meaning patterns to the variable mode, we can have some insights into the multimodality in data news.

5.1.1.1 Multimodal Layout

Mode, as a variable of register, deals with the channeling of communication (Halliday & Hasan 1985; Martin & Rose 2008). In multimodal discourses, mode can be regarded as "the contextual variable that would have been developed to coordinate the meaning across modalities" (Martin & Rose 2008: 15) and it deals with the texture of information flow as we move from one modality of communication to another (Martin & Rose 2008: 14). Multimodal layout plays a most important role in organizing the different elements of data news into a coherent whole while also keeping their individual properties.

Our analysis in Chapter 4 shows that there are two types of intermodal layout—integration and complementarity. First, instantiated options from different semiotic modes can be presented as demarcated parts and placed vertically or horizontally side by side. This is an intermodally complementary layout. This type of layout is more often seen when a photograph, a drawing, a data visualization, or a video as whole interacts with the longer verbal texts. Then, within a data visualization, the verbiage is often integrated into the image to make the data visualizations a unified whole.

Our analysis in Chapter 4 also shows that multimodal realizations of periodicity are a pattern realizing textual metafunction in our data. Data news texts in our data are organized with clear periodic structures, with the headline (sometimes with a strapline) as a superTheme, subheads or titles of each section as macroThemes, and the topic sentence of each stage as hyperThemes.

In these ways, the multimodal layout enriches the textual resources to coordinate ideational and interpersonal meanings.

5. 1. 1. 2 Constituting Field

One important variable to characterize meaning patterns at the stratum of register is the amount of work language is doing in relation to what is going on (Martin & Rose 2008). This variation of the roles of language and other semiotic modes is characterized by Martin and Rose as a cline from language in action to language as reflection. In our data, data news can be instantiated as data visualizations, as is illustrated by Caixin VisLab's project "Those Places High-speed Rail Could Take You To". Data visualizations are themselves multimodal discourses with graphs, language, color and music. But as has been shown previously, data news is more often instantiated as complex composite multimodal discourses with language, photographs, drawings, data visualizations and videos. In other words, data visualizations can be instances of data news and be part of more complex multimodal data news. In either case, language and data visualizations play a big role as they reflect what is going on. They constitute the field they realize. This means that in our genre analysis, the contribution of each semiotic mode should be taken into consideration, but the focus is more on language and data visualizations.

5. 1. 2 Meaning Patterns of Field

The kind of knowledge or experience involved in genre is a matter for field, where professional, disciplinary, recreational and domestic activity would be described. As our analysis in Chapter 4 has shown, two fields are construed by the discourse semantic patterns. The "doing" or "happening" activities which narrate the news events construe news event field, while those describing the analytical process of the project and those construing relations between entities construe research field. The research field renders

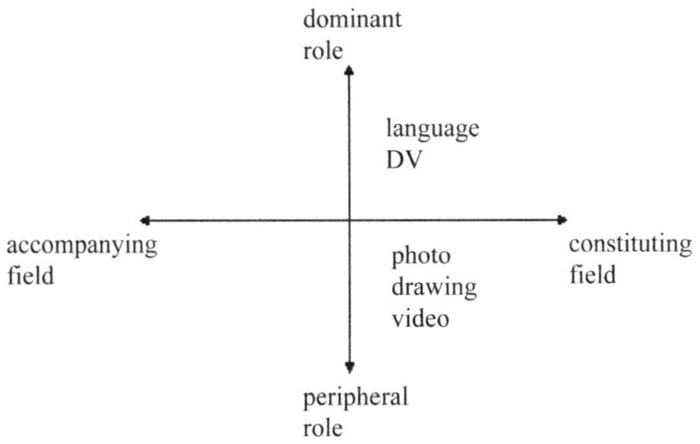

Figure 5-1 The Roles of Semiotic Modes in the Data

data reporting as a professional or even scientific activity that presents the findings or illustrates the expertise and/or professionalism in coming to the findings. In the news event field, there are also field-specific technical terms. For instance, in Civio's Medicamentalia which investigated into access to medicines around the world, there is a profusion of medicine names: omeprazole, simvastatin, diazepram, Sovaldi, asthma inhaler (salbutamol), ciprofloxacin, etc. Though they are technical terms, they are related with the topic of the news events.

Data visualizations can be field-specific. For the Hamilton project, music and sound patterns are presented audially, rather than visually as news photos or diagrams. The choices are related to the topic or field of the project—the project analyzes the rhyming pattens in the opera.

5. 1. 3 Meaning Patterns of Tenor

Two types of interpersonal relations are enacted in the data news texts—relationship between professionals and relationship between news producers and news consumers. The professionals may include journalists, data analysts and researchers in journalism, etc. The necessary link between semiotic modes and communities of users also plays an important role here. Just as power and knowledge are distributed within society, so is the ability to deploy particular semiotic modes. Thus, expert users of a semiotic resource (such as a professional photographer) might use those resources in a way that composes distinct material effects to create meanings that are simply not available to the novice (Bateman et al. 2017: 115). This may affect the ways to engage the readers into the text, namely whether to engage them as participants or observers. In the stages presenting findings, static and dynamic data visualizations tend to engage the readers as observer, while the interactive ones tend to engage the readers as participants.

5.2 Genre Analysis

Genre is well positioned in our model as a resource for co-ordinating communication across modalities in multimodal texts as our understandings of inter-modality unfold (Martin & Rose 2008: 232). It is considered as configurations of meaning which realize the generic goal(s) step by step. The steps are referred to as stages which are set up by phases. Therefore, our first concern is what generic stages can be identified in each elemental genre.

In Chapter 3 when we introduced the theoretical foundations for the multimodal genre model in the present study, we explained Martin's conceptualization of genre rank. He proposed the concepts of macrogenre or genre complex and embedded genre to theorize the ways elemental genres are combined. By applying Halliday's logicosemantic relations, Martin modelled macrogenres as serial structures, i.e., the combination of several elemental genres into a univariate serial structure (Szenes 2017). Macrogenre is like a clause complex, and so it is also called genre complex.

He also proposed the term of embedded genre to describe the situation in which an elemental genre is made to function as one stage in another genre (Martin 2012/1994: 102). In other words, apart from combining genres into a serial univariate structure, longer and more complex texts can also grow bigger through embedded genres (Martin & Rose 2008; Szenes 2017). To differentiate the two ways of genre combination, we use the term **macrogenre** exclusively to describe texts with embedded genres and the term **genre complex** to describe the situation when several elemental genres are combined into a univariate serial structure. In a text instantiated as a genre complex, there can be embedded genres as well. The ideas of elemental genre, embedded genre, macrogenre, and genre complex are important for us to capture the genre relations in data news which are often instantiated as complex multimodal discourses.

5.2.1 Process of Genre Analysis

The process of genre analysis begins with close analytical attention to patterns of meaning in texts including patterns of ideational, interpersonal, and textual meanings. And as was explained in Chapter 3, genres in SFL are conceptualized as being enacted in unfolding stages of meanings and it is these stages that distinguish one genre from another. The consistency of certain meaning patterns helps analyzers to identify a stage. But texts may shift gears, from one configuration of meaning to another (Martin & Rose 2008: 239). In other words, texts, be they monomodal or multimodal, may shift gears in the meaning patterns. For this reason, close attention is paid both to the discourse semantic patterns shared and also to those in which the unfolding text signals its shifts in meaning, as the consistency and the shift are of great help to the identification of stages and phases. The consistent choices of ideational, interpersonal and textual meanings in a text can be identified within a same stage, while the shifts can usher in a new stage or phase. For detailed explanations and illustrations of this process in the analysis and discussion of diverse kinds of texts, please refer to Martin and Rose's (2008) canonic monograph *Genre Relations: Mapping Culture*. In the following section, we just illustrate the process with a few examples.

Following this process of genre analysis, we provide brief illustrations of analyses of elemental genre, macrogenre and genre complex in the subsequent sections.

5. 2. 2 Data Visualization as Elemental Genre

As has been pointed out above, data visualizations in our data can be instances of data news, though the only case in our data is Caixin VisLab's project "Those Places High-speed Rail Could Take You To".

The project is visualized as an interactive data visualization, with a map of China, lines in different colors, shinning dots, and 4 blocks of verbal texts (those in the red boxes shown in Figure 5-2). The map is in dark color, on which are overlaid lines in four colors, numerous tiny shining dots, and tiny blue triangles. The legend in the right corner explains what these geometrical shapes mean. The dots stand for stations or stops for high-speed rails; the triangles for national scenic spots; and the four colors for the different time taken from one city to other cities: yellow for 3 hours, orange 4, pink 5 and purple 6. The hours are also represented dynamically in the verbal title (highlighted in the orange box in Figure 5-2). The hours in the title rotate quickly from 3, to 4, then to 5 and 6. The verbal text below the title provides two ways for readers to select what they want to read: by clicking the shinning dots on the map or by selecting a place in the white rectangle, the readers can select any city as the departure city and then see its distances to other cities. The city of departure is highlighted with a map annotation symbol. All the places high-speed rails could take you to are visualized in just one single data visualization. Other information includes the logo of Caixin Vislab in the left top corner and the names of the journalist and the designer at the end of the legend.

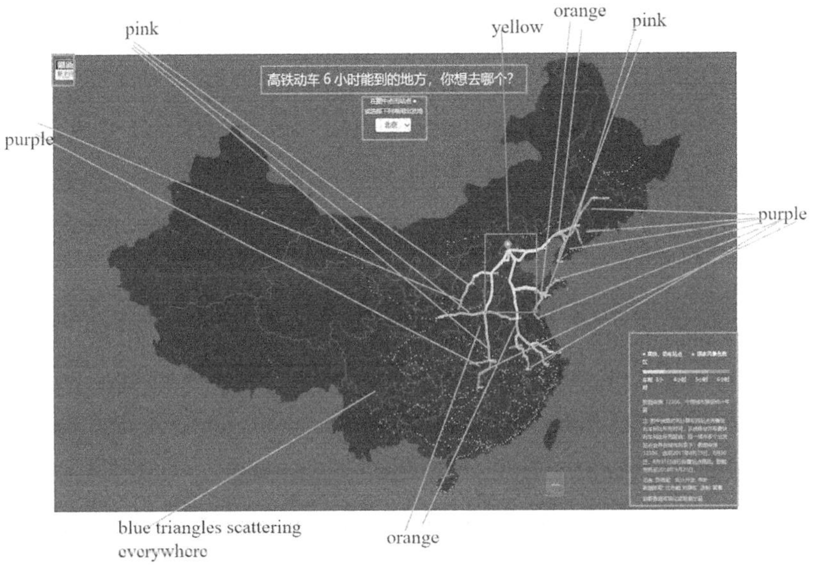

Figure 5-2 A Screenshot of the Project "Those Places High-Speed Rail Could Take You To"

Textually, both the [integrated: co-located] and [integrated-subsumed] layout choices are present. The visualization is integrated as a unified whole with different parts contributing to the meaning making. The title "高铁(3~6)小时能到的地方，你想去哪个?(Those Places High-Speed Rail Could Take You To)" is presented in larger fonts and in the top middle. The map is placed in the center, which indicates that the information presented there is the key one.

Ideationally, the major entities or participants are high-speed rails, the departure city, destination cities, and the stations or stops. Then the map does not present unfolding actions and events which are of narrative structure

(Kress & van Leeuwen 2006). Rather, it has a conceptual structure (ibid), showing the multiple interconnections between the major entities. To be more specific, the participants are represented more in terms of "their more generalized and more or less stable and timeless essence" (ibid: 79), and the activities construed multimodally on the map are mainly spatial and relational—the cities high-speed rails can travel to, the high speed of trains, and the distances between cites. For instance, in 3 hours' time, high-speed rails can travel from Beijing to many cities: Tianjin and Qinhuangdao to the northeast, Shijiazhuang, Taiyuan, and Zhengzhou to the southwest, and Jinan and Xuzhou to the South. The high speed of the rails is visualized on the map through the spatial relation among the cities and the lines that connect the cities. The lines together with the map visualize the distance between a departure city and the destination cities, and the train direction as well.

In terms of interpersonal meaning, the pronoun "you" invites the readers to participate and get the information they need or are interested in. This is consistent with the interactive nature of the visualization. Then, no inscribed attitudinal resources have been identified. "High-speed" in the title functions as a Classifier which means that high-speed rails are one of the types of the rails① in China. This strengthens the facticity and objectivity of the visualization. The great number of the dots is a quantification resources which can invoke a positive appreciation of the high-speed trains. The numerous stations or stops also mean high-speed trains are accessible in most cities in China. The high speed and the easy accessibility rails can invoke positive appreciation of China's rails. An implicit message can be conveyed: It is really convenient to travel in China

① High-speed rails are also called bullet rails/trains. The other type is non-bullet or regular trains. G, D, and C trains are high-speed trains. Z, T, K, and four-digit number trains are non-bullet trains, or regular trains.

by high-speed rails.

From the above analysis, we can see that the visualization mainly depicts the features of high-speed rails multimodally: high speed, easy accessibility and directions. Its generic purpose is to describe the characteristics of a Phenomenon, so it is a description. The analysis is summarized in Table 5-1.

Table 5-1 Genre Analysis of the Project "Those Places High-Speed Rail Could Take You To"

Generic purpose	Stage	Meaning patterns and realizations
	Phenomenon/Object	Entity: high-speed rails (verbal: nominal phrase)
To describe	Description speed	departure city (verbal text +map), destination cities (verbal text +map), stations (dots) Spatiality: 3-hour, 4-hour, 5-hour, 6-hour (verbal texts+ lines)
	easy accessibility directions	geographical locations (dots+ legend) Quantification + Entity: numerous dots lines in four colors, map

5. 2. 3 Macrogenre and Embedded Genre

Let's take the project *Spies in the Skies* as an example. First, the consistent choices of entities in a text can be identified within a same stage while the shifts can usher in a new stage or phase.

Example 5-1

Each weekday, dozens of US government aircraft take to the skies

> (Actor + Process + Circumstance) and slowly circle over American cities (Actor + Process +Circumstance). Piloted by agents of the FBI and the Department of Homeland Security (DHS), the planes are fitted (Goal +Process) with high-resolution video cameras... At least a few planes have carried devices that can track the cell phones of people below (Actor + Process +Goal)... and many use exhaust mufflers (Actor + Process+Goal) to mute their engines...
>
> The government's **airborne surveillance** has received (Carrier + Process) little public scrutiny—until now. (**Topic/Phenomenon**). ***BuzzFeed News*** has assembled an unprecedented picture of the operation's scale and sweep (Actor + Process + Goal) by analyzing aircraft location data (Actor + Process+ Goal) collected by the flight-trafficking website Flightradar 24 from mid-August to the end of December last year, identifying about 200 federal aircraft (Actor + Process+ Goal). (**Methodology**) Day after day, dozens of these planes **circled** above cities across the nation (Actor + Process; past tense). (**Findings: weekday**)
>
> ...
>
> The BuzzFeed analysis **also** revealed how the government responded to the mass shooting last December in San Bernardino, California. (Sayer + Process; past tense; connexion: addition) (**Findings: weekend**)

The first paragraph centers on "the planes" and the entities form a taxonomic relation of [repetition]. The clauses in the part feature the choice of material process. The nominalized entity "the government's airborne surveillance" summarizes the contents in the previous paragraph. The consistency in the choice of entity help to identify these clauses as realizing the same stage. Yet, in the clause complex "***BuzzFeed News*** has assembled... by analyzing... identifying...", there is an obvious shift in the choice of entity. Taking into account the processes, we identify this clause complex realizing a new stage and label it [Methodology]. The next clause shifts to the planes again and the tense selected is past simple. Integrating these meaning patterns, we identify this new stage as [Findings].

The textual layout also helps the identification of the two phases of [Findings]—The finding of weekday surveillance and that of weekend surveillance are restated and highlighted in large bold font beside the other verbal texts (See the parts in the red boxes in Figure 5-3).

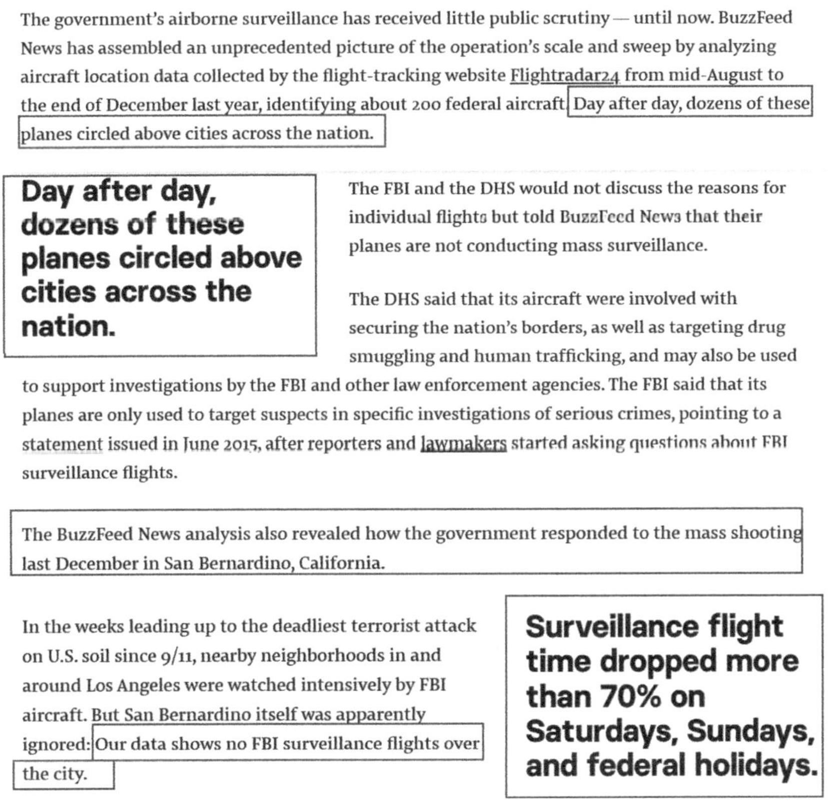

The government's airborne surveillance has received little public scrutiny — until now. BuzzFeed News has assembled an unprecedented picture of the operation's scale and sweep by analyzing aircraft location data collected by the flight-tracking website Flightradar24 from mid-August to the end of December last year, identifying about 200 federal aircraft. Day after day, dozens of these planes circled above cities across the nation.

Day after day, dozens of these planes circled above cities across the nation.

The FBI and the DHS would not discuss the reasons for individual flights but told BuzzFeed News that their planes are not conducting mass surveillance.

The DHS said that its aircraft were involved with securing the nation's borders, as well as targeting drug smuggling and human trafficking, and may also be used to support investigations by the FBI and other law enforcement agencies. The FBI said that its planes are only used to target suspects in specific investigations of serious crimes, pointing to a statement issued in June 2015, after reporters and lawmakers started asking questions about FBI surveillance flights.

The BuzzFeed News analysis also revealed how the government responded to the mass shooting last December in San Bernardino, California.

In the weeks leading up to the deadliest terrorist attack on U.S. soil since 9/11, nearby neighborhoods in and around Los Angeles were watched intensively by FBI aircraft. But San Bernardino itself was apparently ignored: Our data shows no FBI surveillance flights over the city.

Surveillance flight time dropped more than 70% on Saturdays, Sundays, and federal holidays.

Figure 5-3 A Layout Restating and Highlighting the Two Findings

Then, the two findings are visualized in the dynamic map which summarizes and elaborates the findings with location and comparison. The map covers the surveillance time from December 2nd to 8th. December 5th and 6th are instances of weekends and the other days as instances of weekdays. The red lines represent the routes of panes piloted by FBI agents while the blue ones represent those piloted by DHS agents. In this case, the

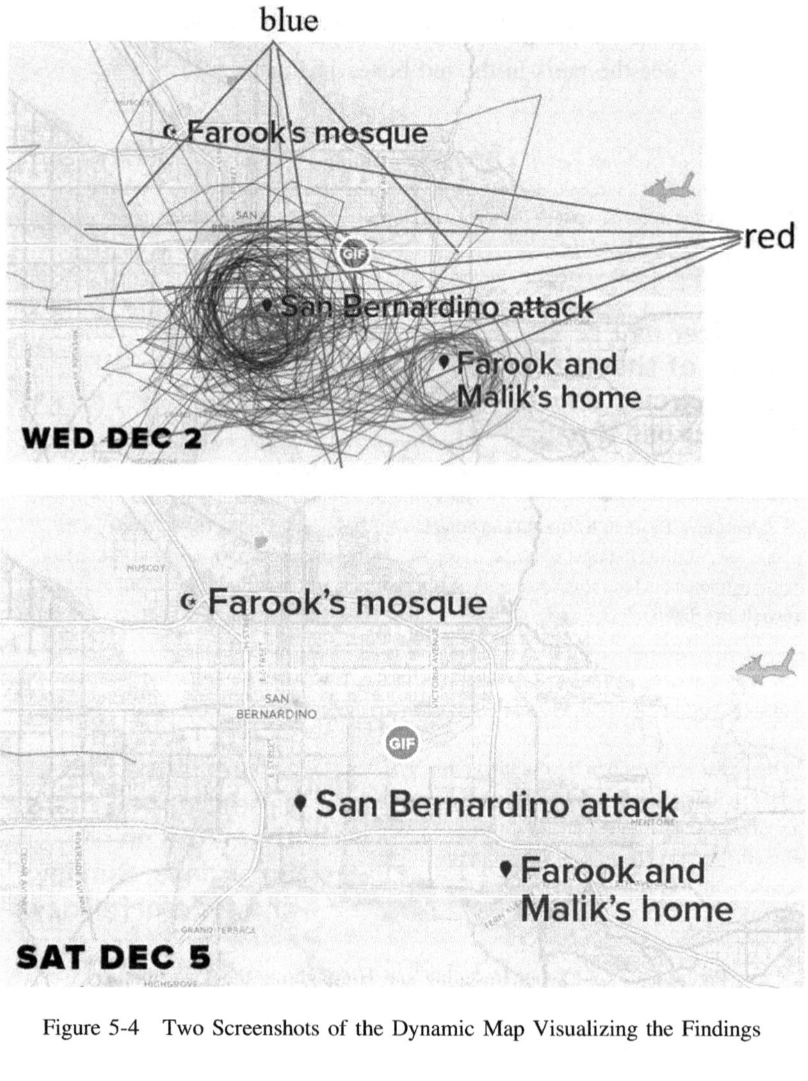

Figure 5-4 Two Screenshots of the Dynamic Map Visualizing the Findings

dynamic map is analyzed as a third phase [**Findings: summary**]. Here, the dynamic map does not function as an independent genre; instead, it is **rankshifted** to function as a phase in a more complex instance of multimodal data news. In this case, it is called **an embedded genre**.

After these two findings of the general patterns, there are more specific findings which are analyzed as phases of the [Finding] stage. They are identified with realizations like "**The BuzzFeed News analysis** almost certainly underestimates the scope of surveillance by federal aircraft" [**Findings: scope**] and "In some cases, **the BuzzFeed News analysis** showed that FBI aircraft indeed seemed to be following a vehicle from place to place..." [**Findings: route**].

Then, the way the data was collected and analyzed is described with more details in verbiage after presenting and analyzing the findings. The shift to the entity Buzzfeed News as well as the consistent choices of the pronoun "we" and material processes facilitate the identification of the stage [**Methodology**]. See Example 5-2.

Example 5-2

Buzzfeed News extended the list of FBI front companies (Actor + Process+ Goal), drawing from other resources that have investigated that agency's airborne operations. ***We*** then looked for planes (Actor + Process+ Goal) registered to these front companies in data provided by Flightradar24...

We detected nearly 100 FBI fixed-wing planes (Actor + Process+ Goal), mostly small Cessnas, plus about a dozen helicopters...

We also tracked more than 90 aircraft (Actor + Process+ Goal), about two-thirds of them helicopters, that were registered to the DHS, which is responsible for border protection, customs, and immigration... (**Methodology**) (From Spies in the Skies by BuzzFeed News)

The final stage is [**Description**], which focuses on describing the high-tech equipment in the FBI and the DHS airplanes. The classificational taxonomic relation among the entities, the choice of synonymic taxonomy among entities like "paperwork" "official records" and "documents", and the choice of repetitions to track entities like the FBI and the DHS help us to identify the stage and phases within the stage. Figure 5-5 presents the classification taxonomy of the high-tech devices. The four categories are also visualized in the infographic, which restates the entities and elaborates them with locational meanings. See Section 4.3.3 for more detailed description of the meaning patterns in infographics.

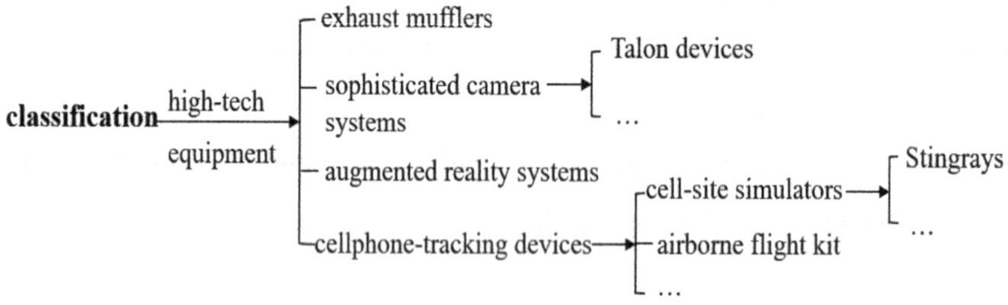

Figure 5-5 Classification Taxonomy in the [Description] Stage of "Spies in the Skies"

We summarize in Table 5-2 the generic purpose(s) and the meanings patterns that contribute to the genre analysis in the project "Spies in the Skies". In this project, the dynamic data visualization, the static infographics and the camera-shot video are **rankshifted** from an independent genre to function as a phase in the whole multimodal data news. They are called **embedded genres** and the whole multimodal discourse is a **macorgenre** because all the stages work to achieve the global generic purpose—to describe and inform readers of the surveillance in the United States.

Table 5-2 Genre Analysis of "Spies in the Skies"

Generic purpose	Stages	Phases	Meaning patterns
To inform and describe	Phenomenon		Ideational: classificational taxonomy; material and relational processes
	Methodology	(general)	Ideational: repetition; material processes
	Findings	weekday^ weekend^ summary (DV)^ scope^ route	Ideational: repetition; past event; restatement Connexion: addition Textual: prominence Intermodal: restatement; elaboration
	Methodology	(more detailed)	Ideational: repetition; material processes
	Description	equipment (text + infographics) ^ function (text +video)	Ideational: classificational taxonomy material process Interpersonal: no inscribed appraisal resources Textual: repetition as tracking resource Intermodal: restating

5.2.4 Genre Complex

Let's illustrate the identification of generic patterns in genre complexes with the project of Medicamentalia by Civio News. The project reports on the issues behind access to medicine in African countries. It consists of five parts or discourses, each having a title and a strapline and being placed on the access page with the same color and equal size (See Figure 5-6).

The five parts are separated while also constituting a composite by being framed with white spaces. Clicking each title, the reader can access the contents of each componential part through a separate window. The five parts are linked with each other not only by being placed as a list on the same access page, but also through hyperlinks within the first four parts. At the end of these parts there is a hyperlink "NEXT STORY" navigating the reader to the next part. The list of the five parts is followed by 6 key findings, which are presented on a bluish green canvas. The findings distill the key messages from the four parts, excluding the part of "Methodology". The first two findings are from Part One "Prices", the third from Part Two "Counterfeits", the fourth and fifth from Part Three "Patents" and the sixth from Part Four "Compulsory Licenses". A click on each of the findings navigates the reader to the corresponding part.

The discourses produced are long and complex. If put in print, the whole project would be more than 100 pages long. The first part is titled "Prices" with two straplines—"11 days' wages to buy an asthma inhaler" (highlighted with a larger font) and "14 medicines, 61 countries. Compare and analyze the differences between them". This part is mainly about comparisons of the prices of 14 drugs and their accessibility in different countries, highlighting particularly the exorbitant prices of these drugs in African countries. The headline is instantiated multimodally with a dot chart as the background and the verbal title with more prominence. As we analyzed in Chapter 4, the multimodal headline together with the strapline works together with the Headline to give readers an orientation to what is to come in the whole report and functions as the macroTheme of the whole data news text. The body part is instantiated with 5 paragraphs of verbal texts and a series of 9 dynamic dot charts and an interactive dot chart which summarizes and presents all the variables and readers can manipulate the findings displayed by choosing different variables. The variables are value (price and days of work), sanitary system (public vs. private), countries (ordered by zone or GDP), and filter (by region or by drug). This interactive chart alone conveys multiple and complex meanings, but as we focus on genre patterns, we just analyze the global patterns that can reveal generic patterns.

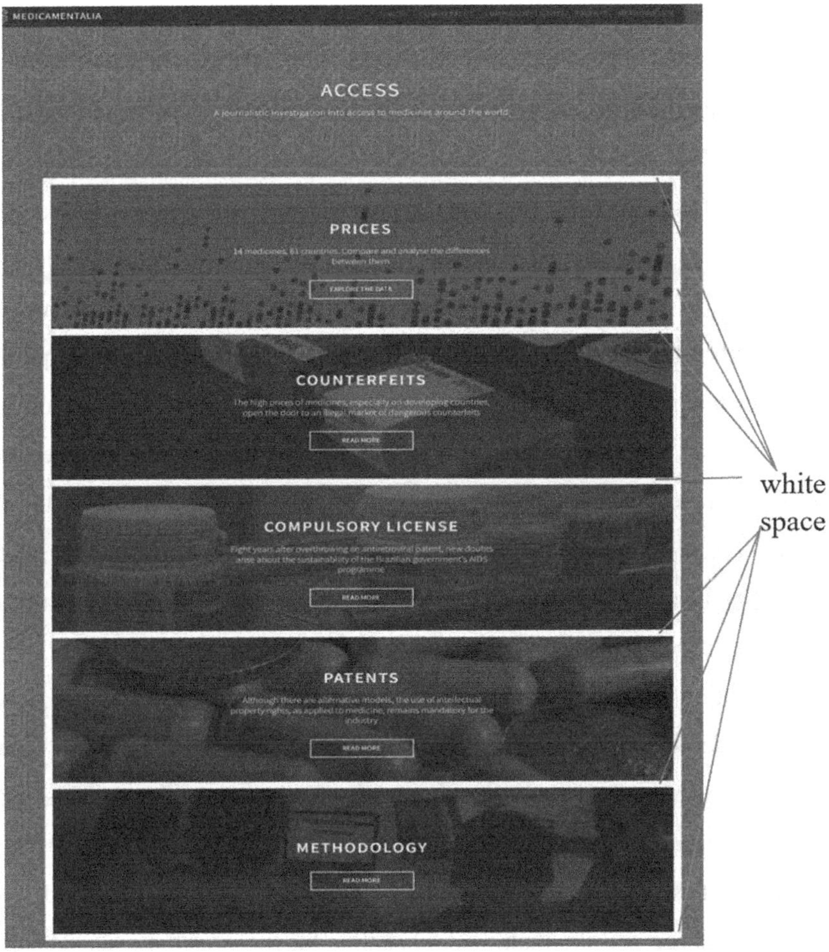

Figure 5-6 A Screenshot of the Access Page of "Medicamentalia"

The second part is titled "Counterfeits" with the straplines "False friends in the fight against malaria" (highlighted with a larger font) and "The high prices of medicines, especially on developing countries, open the door to an illegal market of dangerous counterfeits". As the first part "Prices", the headline of this part is instantiated multimodally with the verbal title of more prominence and the multimodal headline functions as the macroTheme of the whole part. The only difference is that the background is a photo of boxes of medicine. The body part is made up of three sections. Section 1, titled "Ditches" is instantiated with 20 paragraphs of verbal texts, 1 natural camera-shot video, and 4 single photos (3 of humans and 1 of pills). The second section is titled "Low tech/ High tech" with a strapline "How to distinguish the genuine from the fake". It mainly introduces the technologies adopted by mPedigree and POM to detect counterfeits in African countries. It is instantiated with 23 paragraphs of verbal texts, 1 natural camera-shot video, 1 dynamic interactive map, 2 photos of humans and a series of four photos of pills. The third section is titled "Porous borders" with a strapline "How to stop the counterfeit medicines trade". The body part contains 16 paragraphs of verbal texts, 1 natural camera-shot video, and two single photos (1 about a place and 1 of a single human entity). The title and the strapline of each section functions as the hyperTheme of the section.

The third part is "Compulsory Licenses" with the straplines "A sovereign act to bypass a patent" (highlighted with a larger font) and "Eight years after overwhelming an antiretroviral patent, new doubts are about the sustainability of the Brazilian government's AIDS program". The headline of this part is also instantiated multimodally with the verbal title of more prominence and the multimodal headline functions as the macroTheme of the whole part. It consists of six sections. Section one "What is it" defines what compulsory licensing is. It is instantiated with 3 paragraphs of verbal texts and a natural camera-shot video. Section two "The previous path" explains the way Brazil came to approve compulsory licensing of efavirenz, a drug used with other HIV medications to help control HIV infection. It has 6 paragraphs of verbal texts and 1 camera-shot video. Section three, titled "The decision", describes the decision made by the Brazilian government to approve compulsory licensing of efavirenz and the responses to the decision. It contains 5 paragraphs and 1 camera-shot video. Section four "The effects" explains the direct consequences of the decision. It is instantiated with 8 paragraphs, 1 camera-shot video and 1 static bar chart. Section five "Brazil today", with 4 paragraphs and 1 camera-shot video, describes the health situation in the country. The final section is titled "Once, and never again". It relates the compulsory licensing of efavirenz to that of other drugs and explains why the use of compulsory licensing hasn't been repeated in Brazil. The section begins with a camera-shot video and is then followed by 5 paragraphs of verbal texts.

The fourth part is "Patents" with the straplines "A toll on health" (highlighted with a larger font) and "Although there are alternative methods, the use of intellectual property rights, as applied to medicine, remains mandatory for the industry". The headline of this part is also instantiated multimodally with the verbal title of more prominence and the multimodal headline functions as the macroTheme of the whole part. It consists of 4 sections. Section one, without a title and realized only with verbal texts, introduces the topic of patent system by describing the unaffordability problem of sofosbuvir brought by enacting the patent system. Section two "The patent system" introduces the international agreement TRIPS and highlights that there are 161 ways of applying it. It contains 3 paragraphs and a series of 6 dynamic infographics explaining how patents work. Section three "The cost of developing a new drug" presents the controversy over the drug companies' investment in research and the opposing views on the role of patents in promoting innovation and medicine accessibility. This section begins with a camera-shot video and then proceeds with 9 paragraphs of verbal texts. Section four is titled "Alternatives", with a strapline "Working around the traditional intellectual property", introduces other ways to protect intellectual property and describes the problem of "market failures" (no companies innovate the treatments for 17 neglected diseases).

The fifth part "Methodology" introduces the methodology and the team of journalists and data analysts. It ends with a call for help in data collection and donation.

The five complex componential parts are regarded by the creators as five "stories", but our analyses show that they have different meaning configurations at the strata of discourse semantics and grammar and achieve different generic purposes. From an SFL genre perspective, they do not merely belong to the story genre. We analyze the meaning patterns that help to identify stages and phases and the generic purpose(s) of each part before we describe and explain their genre relations. Let's illustrate the analysis with Part One "Prices" and Part Two "Counterfeits".

The first meaning pattern identified in the first part "Prices" is the inscribed and invoked appreciation resources in the first paragraph, like "more striking" and "remarkable" as negative appreciation of price differences, "essential to develop evidence-based policies and to provide data and arguments to governments and organizations for their negotiations with pharmaceutical companies" as positive appreciation of the project's research on the price difference of drugs. This paragraph is presenting the significance of the project. According to Martin (2000: 147), "[A] ppreciation 'institutionalizes feelings as propositions (about things)'. In other words, expressions of appreciation shift feelings or emotions from a personal to an institutional framework. This avoidance of a personal orientation in favor of an institutional one in the expression of attitude is frequently evident in academic writing". In this sense, this part is like an academic discourse.

Then paragraph 2 shifts to describe the methodology of the research, with research entities like "we, methodology, calculations". By clarifying their analysis methods, the writers aim to demonstrate the reliability of their research. These resources help us to identify this paragraph as the second stage and show that this part has the discursive features of academic writing.

The expression "The first conclusion" in paragraph 3 clearly indicates that this paragraph presents the findings of the research. "The first" is also a conjunctive resource, which indicates that other conclusions will follow. Another conjunctive realization is "also" in the legend of the 7th chart. Then, in paragraphs 3, 4 and 5, and the following interactive chart, the major entities like countries, price and medicines are related by classification (e.g., Captopril and Simvastatin are categories of medicine), or contrast (e.g., developing countries and developed countries are relational antonyms). In addition, the entities are mostly generic, namely referring to a group or a class, rather than to specific individuals. Here are some examples: a citizen, a treatment, an asthma inhaler, and medicines like Captopril and Simvastatin. Finally, the logical relations of addition and contrast are realized in the verbal texts and the visualization. Therefore, these sections realize a stage—Findings of the research. Within the stage, by the conjunctive resources "the first" and "also", and by the shift of entities, we identify four phases—three specific findings and a visualized summary of the findings. The analysis of quantitative data visualization in Section 4. 3. 3 offered a more detailed analysis of the meanings realized in the interactive data visualization.

The paragraph below the interactive data visualization shifts to research entities, like "we, data, official sources, dataset, methodology". The readers are also addressed as "you" so as to invite them to explore the dataset and methodology used in the project. These meaning patterns help to identify this part as a new stage.

By combining the meaning patterns (shown in Table 5-3), we identify 4 different stages and the phases within them.

In the "Counterfeits" part, there are some other meaning patterns. First, the choices of Wh-questions as subtitles for each of the three questions: "Why does counterfeit medicine exist?" "How to distinguish the genuine from the fake?" "How to stop the counterfeit medicine trade?". These subtitles together with the titles are the hyperThemes of the three sections and indicate that the communicative purpose is to explain the causes of counterfeit medicine, to describe and explain the methods or techniques to distinguish the genuine from the fake, and to discuss the solutions to stop the counterfeit medicine trade. Second, choices like "leading causes and because" realize the implication relation, particularly in the first section "Ditches". Third, imperative mood and future tense are used in the final section. Taking into consideration other patterns showing consistency or shifts in entities, events and logical connections (summarized in Table 5-3), we identified the stages and phases of the part (shown in Table 5-3). Due to space and layout considerations, we do not present the genre analysis for the other three parts.

The five parts are instantiated with different resources in realizing ideational and interpersonal meanings, but they share certain patterns in composing textual meanings. The most salient one is the selection of periodicity. First, a multimodal headline with a strapline function as the macroTheme of each part. Then, if within a part, the verbal title of each section along with a strapline function as the hyperTheme of that section. In terms of the overall structure, Part One "Prices" functions like the Lead of a piece of traditional news which presents the most important information

Table 5-3 Genre Analysis of the First Two Parts of "Medicamentalia"

Parts	Generic purpose(s)	Stages	Phases	Meaning patterns	
				Exclusive	Shared
Prices	**To argue and engage**	Significance		inscribed appreciation: more striking, remarkable, essential, etc.	Periodicity: bimodal head-line with straplines as macro-Theme; title of each section as hyper-Theme;
		Methodology	data^ variables	research entity: we; methodology; calculations, etc.	
		Findings	finding 1 (**text** + **DV**①) ^ finding 2 (**DV**) ^ finding 3 (**DV**) ^ summary (**DV**)	generic news event entity: a citizen; a treatment; an asthma inhaler, etc. taxonomy: classification (developing countries: Kyrgyzstan, Ghana, Congo, etc); contrast (developing vs. developed countries) connexion: addition (the first; another) comparison and contrast (colors and positions of dots)	

① DV stands for data visualization.

Continued

Parts	Generic purpose(s)	Stages	Phases	Meaning patterns	
				Exclusive	Shared
		Data Description	source^ access^ more access	research entity: interactive chart; official sources, etc. research entity: final dataset; hyperlink "here" research entity: project, methodology, reason, dataset engagement: "you" "your"	Taxonomy: classfication; repetition
Counter-feits	("Ditches" section) **To explain** (**why**)	Pheneme-non	ditches with waste and mosquitos (**text +video**)①	**connexion: implication**	subtitle: wh-question

① The arrow symbolizes cause-effect or implication relation. The photographs and videos do not convey implication relations. The implication relations are realized in the verbal texts. See Chapter 4 for more details.

Continued

Parts	Generic purpose(s)	Stages	Phases	Meaning patterns	
				Exclusive	Shared
		Explanation	diseases: malaria in Ghana	periodicity: hyperTheme (why does counterfeit medicine exist)	
			children mortality	specific news event entity: Accra, the whole town, Kwame Agyekum, the local pharmacists, etc.	
			prevention problem	generic: mosquitos, children, malaria deaths, etc.	
			high drug price and low income		
			counterfeits	taxonomy: classification (disease-choloera-malaria) synonymy (drugs-medicines-anti-malaria drugs)	

Continued

Parts	Generic purpose(s)	Stages	Phases	Meaning patterns	
				Exclusive	Shared
	(" Low/High tech section) **To explain** (**how**)	Case 1 mPedigree: Introduction^ Description ^ Comparison (authentic vs. fake Co-artem) ^ Analysis	location ^ background purpose ^ method ^ company profile package ^ composition (counterfeits) consequence^ **origin** ^ **route** (**text + DV**)	Ideation: specific news event entity; locational entity; classification Connexion: comparison; implication; spatiality (interactive map) DV-text interaction: adding	
		Case 2 PQM: Purpose ^ Step ^	weight ^ content (tech: HPLC; CD-3) (**text + photo**)	Ideation: specific news event entity; terms; classification; composition Connexion: time; addition Photo-text interaction: restating + co-referencing (entity)	

Continued

Parts	Generic purpose(s)	Stages	Phases	Meaning patterns	
				Exclusive	Shared
	(“Porous border” section) **To describe, explain and discuss (solutions)**	Prediction Problem 1 ^ Solution (Ghana) Problem 2 ^ Solution	future situation ^ proposal (counterfeits) **Agency (text + photo)** ^ hi-tech measure ^ traditional measure ^ **effects (text + photo)** (porous borders for drug trafficking) measure 1^ measure 2 ^ measure 3 ^ a case (text +video)	Interpersonal: imperative mood; future tense Ideation: specific news event entity; terms; classification; Connexion: addition; Photo-text interaction: co-referencing (entity)	

and other parts offer more details. It can be argued that the whole project follows the inverted pyramid structure.

Another pattern is the similar or identical layout choices. The five parts are separated while also constituting a composite by being framed with white spaces. With a click on each title the reader can access the contents of each componential part through a separate window. The five parts are linked with each other not only by being placed on the same access page, but also by a hyperlink at the end of each part other than the final one.

Based on the above analysis, we can see that the whole project achieves multiple generic purposes—to describe, to explain, to argue for a view and to call for action. Therefore, it is an instance of genre complex.

One more thing to be noted: In this exemplar analysis of complex genre, we also see that news photos and data visualizations are rankshifted from an independent genre to function as a stage or a phase in the whole text. In other words, an embedded genre constitutes a macrogenre, which can be part of a genre complex.

5.3 Summary: Relations Among Genres in the Data

Longer texts such as websites, novels or textbooks have complex social purposes, within an overall goal that takes multiple genres to accomplish (Rose & Martin 2012: 289). Data news is one of such longer texts. This means that we have also thought about the question of genre relations -one genre to another as a piece of multimodal data news unfolds.

The data news projects in our data can be instantiated as a data visualization which just describes a phenomenon (Caixin's project "Those Places High-Speed Rails Could Take You To"), but more often the projects are realized with verbal texts, photographs, drawings, data visualizations and/or videos. More than that, they usually include different parts. In other words, they are mixed texts or discourses. Our analysis shows that like histories and scientific writings, data news can realize various generic purposes: narrate an event, describe a situation, explain causes or correlations, argue for a view, and/or call for action. Semiotically, it is inaccurate to regard data news as being just one genre. Our analysis also reveals that data visualizations can be an independent elemental genre, or an embedded genre that functions as a stage or phase in a macrogenre, or just be part of a long and complex text with multiple generic purposes.

In our data, 12 out of the 15 projects of data news are instantiated as macrogenres with data visualizations as an embedded stage, 2 instantiated as genre complexes, and 1 case of data visualization as an elemental genre. There is a clear tendency of genre hybridity or hybridization (Varghese & Sunita 2004; Chandler & Munday 2011; Mäntynen & Shore 2014), or genre colony (Bhatia 2004), or discursive hybridity (Fairclough 2003) in data news.

Table 5-4 is a summary of the genre relations identified in our data.

Table 5-4 Genre and Genre Relations in the Projects

Genre or genre relations	Generic purpose(s)	Number of cases
Elemental genre: data visualization	Describe a phenomenon	1
Macrogenre (12 cases)	Present a news event	3 (breaking news category)
	Argue for a view: with explanations of causes or correlations + describe methodologies	9
Genre complex	Multiple purposes	2

Postscript

In his accessible and usable introduction to social semiotics, van Leeuwen (2005) pointed out three things that semioticians do. They first "collect, document and systematically catalogue semiotic resources—including their history" (p. 3). Second, they "investigate how these resources are used in specific historical, cultural and institutional contexts, and how people talk about them in these contexts—plan them, teach them, justify them, critique them, etc." (ibid). Finally, they "contribute to the discovery and development of new semiotic resources and new uses of existing semiotic resources" (ibid). The present study on data news, which is a typical instance of multimodal discourses, focuses on how meanings are shaped, realized and negotiated in data news and has tried to do these three things.

We have collected samples of data news that are representative cases that stand out due to their quality and innovation and catalogued some resources that are representative of their componential semiotic modes, namely verbal texts, data visualizations, drawings, photographs, and videos. After analyzing various forms of data visualizations, we have demonstrated the complexity of the "diagrammatic mode" (Ledin & Machin 2016a) which can manifest itself both independently but also in combination with other semiotic modes (Aiello 2020). Our data and analysis show that there are fewer standalone visualizations and much more convergence of semiotic modes to produce data news, combining texts, videos, photographs, drawings, and data visualizations. The more dominant trend is what journalists and media scholars call "integrated storytelling". In this sense, in addition to the meaning potentials of each semiotic mode, the ways that semiotic modes interact to achieve the generic purpose(s) and to realize the meaning configurations at the stratum of genre are a key concern for multimodal discourse analysis.

To address the above concerns, we proposed the multimodal genre model (See section 3.4 in Chapter 3) in which all the meaning patterns at different levels of abstraction in different semiotic modes can be covered, the intermodal interaction between different semiotic modes can be described, and the multimodal data news can be interpreted as a unified and coherent whole. We have identified some patterns of intermodal combinations and the ways in which semiotic choices and their combinations are mobilized for specific generic purposes. Integrating all the features we have identified at the strata of discourse semantics and grammar, we found that data visualizations can be an independent elemental genre or function as embedded genres and as a stage or phase, and that the data news projects in our data can just describe relations, but more often the projects argue a viewpoint in a detached objective way based on data analysis. Semiotically, it is inaccurate to regard data news as being just one genre; instead, like histories and scientific writings, data news can narrate an event, describe a situation, explain causes or correlations, argue for a view, and/or call for action. There is a clear tendency of genre hybridity or discursive hybridity in data news.

In explaining the meaning-making processes of data news, we also help to make data accessible and understandable to the general public, rather than just being "a useful resource for experts and decision makers" (Kennedy & Engebretsen 2020: 20). We also find that the new "language" of data news as well as data visualizations is not only grounded in principles of image or verbal text, but also in visual design (e.g., web and graphic design) (Aiello 2020). This can have pedagogic implications for multiliteracy development.

"Describing the modalities, their combinations, their histories of uptake in other media and the affordances of those combinations then offers much of value for explaining the take-up and spread of particular media practices at particular socio-historical points in time. The ability to tease apart the distinct communicative 'modes' that are involved becomes increasingly important the more capable the medium is of carrying distinct modes." (Bateman et al. 2017: 70-71) The present study has demonstrated once again that two areas are important in multimodal discourse analysis—the affordances of each semiotic mode, and what's more important, the affordances and meaning potentials expanded by limitless ways of combining different semiotic modes (see also Martin & Rose 2008; Bateman et al. 2017, etc.). The affordances and potentials can become unimaginably vast, which opens a vast area for future semiotic studies. Topics include yet are not restricted to semiotic resources and semiotic combinations that technology makes available, and "a systematic mapping of semiotic resources together with an empirical investigation of how such resources came to be the way they are, how they are used or understood by a variety of individuals and groups of people, and how they are shaped by dominant practices and regulated by given institutions" (Aiello 2020: 50).

The present research has its limitations. First, the meaning patterns and meaning-making process of data news represent some "broader shifts in discursive practices (which) are often aimed at changing the ways in which given situations—e.g., news media, universities, and governments—and public think and act in relation to particular issues" (Aiello 2020: 58), but the present research focuses more on the internal structures and properties of data news as a multimodal discourse and does not explore the broader shifts in depth. Such shifts can be an important area for future research. Second, in this book we do not cover all the meanings patterns, particularly those of data visualizations, in which semiotic modes are combined creatively and meanings are multiplied. Data visualizations and natural camera-shot videos, as complex multimodal discourses, are insufficiently explored from a discourse semantic perspective because we have chosen to neglect the more detailed and local patterns of these semiotic modes so as to focus on the more global meaning patterns of data news as a whole. The meaning patterns of data visualizations will be the topic for our next project. Finally, our treatment of semiotic realizations has been necessarily sketchy and exemplary, as we have noted in the Introduction. More corpus-based empirical studies are welcomed. This has also been noticed by other scholars. For instance, Hiippala (2020) and Bateman et al. (2017) pointed out that the widespread use of data visualizations makes their multimodal analysis challenging, requiring extensive empirical research to cover the whole range of phenomena from production to consumption. In future studies, it is also of great importance to investigate the relationship between semiotic technologies and semiotic practices.

The literature on data journalism from the production side has grown exponentially in the past decade and become one of the preferred tendencies in current research on journalism and communication (Ausserhofer et al. 2020; Larrondo-Ureta & Ferrera-Rodriguez 2021), but the meaning-making mechanisms of data news and data visualizations as multimodal discourses have been underexplored. We hope that the present research can spur more in-depth, systematic, and valuable research from the semiotic perspective in the future.

References

Aiello, G, Inventorizing, Situating, Transforming: Social Semiotics and Data Visualization[C]. Kennedy, H. & Engebretsen, M. (eds.) *Data Visualization in Society*. Amsterdam: Amsterdam University Press, 2020.

Allan, S. *Online News: Journalism and the Internet*[M]. Maidenhead: Open University Press, 2006.

Amit-Danhi, E. R. & Shifman, L. Digital Political Infographics: A Rhetorical Palette of an Emergent Genre[J]. *New Media &Society*, 2018, 20(10): 3540-3559.

Anderson, C. W., Bell, E. & Shirky, C. *Post-Industrial Journalism: Adapting to the Present*[C]. New York: Tow Center for Digital Journalism, Columbia Journalism School, 2012.

Appelgren, E. 2004. Convergence and Divergence in Media: Different Perspectives[C]. *Elpub 2004—8th International Conference on Electronic Publishing*. Brasilia (Brazil), 2004: 237-248.

Appelgren, E. & Nygren, G. Data Journalism in Sweden: Introducing New Methods and Genres of Journalism into 'Old' Organizations[J]. *Digital Journalism*, 2015, 2(3): 394-405.

Arceneaux, N. Radio Facsimile Newspapers of the 1930s and 40s: Electronic Publishing in the Pre-digital Era[J]. *Journal of Broadcasting & Electronic Media*, 2011, 55: 344-359.

Archer, A. 2016. Multimodal Academic Argument: Ways of Organizing

Knowledge Across Writing and Image[C]//Archer, A. & Breuer, E. (eds.) *Multimodality in Higher Education*. Leiden: Brill, 2016.

Askehave, I. & Nielsen, A. E. Digital Genres: A Challenge to Traditional Genre Theory [J]. *Information Technology and People*, 2005, 18 (2): 120-141.

Ausserhofer, J., Futounig, R., Oppermann, M., Matiasek, S. & Goldgruber, E. The Datafication of Data Journalism Scholarship: Focal Points, Methods, and Research Propositions for the Investigation of Data-intensive Newswork[J]. *Journalism*, 2017, 21(7): 950-973.

Bardoel, J. & Deuze, M. Network Journalism: Converging Competences of Media Professionals and Professionalism[J]. *Australian Journalism Review*, 2001, 23 (2): 91-103.

Barnett, St. *The Rise and Fall of Television Journalism* [M]. London: Bloomsbury Academic, 2011.

Barthes, R. *Image-Music-Text*[M]. London: Fontana, 1977.

Barthes, R. The Photographic Message[C]//Translated by Stephen Heath. V. Goldberg (ed.) *Photography in Print: Writings from 1816 to the Present*. Albuquerque: University of New Mexico Press, 1988.

Bateman, J. A. *Multimodality and Genre: A Foundation for the Systemic Analysis of Multimodal Documents* [M]. New York: Palgrave Macmillan, 2008.

Bateman, J. A. Genre in the Age of Multimodality: Some Conceptual Refinements for Practical Analysis[C]//Allori, P. E., Bateman, J. A. & Bhatia, V. K. (eds.) *Evolution in Genres: Emergence, Variation, Multimodality* (*Linguistic Insights*). Frankfurt: Peter Lang, 2014.

Bateman, J. A. Multimodality and Genre: Issues for Information Design [C]//Black, A., Luna, P., Lund, O. & Walker, S. (eds.) *Information Design: Research and Practice*. London: Routledge, 2017.

Bateman, J. A. The Decomposability of Semiotic Modes [C]//

O'Halloran, K. L. & Smith, B. A. (eds.) *Multimodal Studies: Multiple Approaches and Domains: Routledge Studies in Multimodality*. London: Routledge, 2011.

Bateman, J. A., Delin, J. L. & Henschel, R. Mapping the Multimodal Genres of Traditional and Electronic Newspapers[C]//Royce, T. D. & Bowcher, W. L. (eds.) *New Directions in the Analysis of Multimodal Discourse*. Mahwah, New Jersey: Lawrence Erlbaum Associates, 2007.

Bateman, J. A. & Schmidt, K. H. *Multimodal Film Analysis*[M]. London: Routledge, 2012.

Bateman, J., Wildfeuer, J. & Hiippala, T. *Multimodality: Foundations, Research and Analysis—A Problem-Oriented Introduction*[M]. Berlin: De Gruyter Mouton, 2017.

Bednarek, M. *Evaluation in Media Discourse: Analysis of a Newspaper Corpus*[M]. New York and London: Continuum, 2006.

Bednarek, M. Evaluation in the News: A Methodological Framework for Analyzing Evaluative Language in Journalism[J]. *Australian Journal of Communication*, 2010, 37 (2): 15-50.

Bednarek, M. & Caple, H. *News Discourse*[M]. London/New York: Continuum, 2012.

Beer, D. & Burrows, R. Popular Culture, Digital Archives and the New Social Life of Data[J]. *Theory, Culture and Society*, 2013, 30(4): 47-71.

Bell, A. *The Language of News Media*[M]. Oxford: Blackwell, 1991.

Beniger, J. R., & Robyn, D. L. Quantitative Graphics in Statistics: A Brief History[J]. *The American Statistician*, 1978, 32(1): 1-11.

Bezemer, J. & Kress, G. Visualizing English: A Social Semiotic History of a School Subject[J]. *Visual Communication*, 2009, 8(3): 247-262.

Bhatia, V. *Analyzing Genre: Language Use in Professional Settings*[M].

New York: Longman, 1993.

Bounegru, L. Data Journalism in Perspective[EB/OL]. [2018-09-02]. DataJournalism. com.

Bounegru, L. & Forceville, C. Metaphors in Editorial Cartoons Representing the Global Financial Crisis[J]. *Visual Communication*, 2011, 10 (2): 209-229.

Boyles, J. L. & Meyer, P. Letting the Data Speak: Role Perceptions of Data Journalists in Fostering Democratic Conversation[J]. *Digital Journalism*, 2016, 4(7): 944-954.

Bradshaw, P. What Is Data Journalism? [EB/OL]. [2018-09-02]. DataJournalism. com.

Britannica.[2018-09-02].www.britannica.com/biography/Lee-de-Forest.

Cairo, A. *The Functional Art: An Introduction to Information Graphics and Visualization*[M]. Berkley: New Riders, 2013.

Cairo, A. *The Truthful Art: Data, Charts, and Maps for Communication* [M]. Berkley: New Riders, 2016.

Cairo, A. Foreword: The Dawn of a Philosophy of Visualization[C]// Kennedy H. & Engebretsen, M. (eds.) *Data Visualization in Society*. Amsterdam: Amsterdam University Press, 2020.

Caldwell, D. A Hip-hop battle: Describing Sound in the Contested Academy[C]//Caldwell D., Knox J. & Martin J. R. (eds.) *Appliable Linguistics and Social Semiotics: Developing Theory from Practice*. London: Bloomsbury, 2022.

Caple, H. Intermodal Relations in Image-nuclear News Stories[C]//L. Unsworth (ed.) *Multimodal Semiotics: Functional Analysis in Contexts of Education*. London: Continuum, 2008a.

Caple, H. Reconciling the Co-articulation of Meaning Between Words and Pictures: Exploring Instantiation and Commitment in Image-nuclear News Stories[C]//Mahboob, A. & Knight, N. (eds.) *Questioning*

Linguistics. Newcastle: Cambridge Scholars Press, 2008b.

Caple, H. Multisemiotic Communication in an Australian Broadsheet: A New News Story Genre[C]//Bazerman, C., Bonini, A. & Figueiredo, D. (eds.) *Genre in a Changing World: Perspectives on Writing*. Fort Collins: The WAC Clearinghouse and Parlor Press, 2009a.

Caple, H. 2009b. Playing with Words and Pictures: Intersemiosis in a New Genre of News Reportage[D]. Department of Linguistics, University of Sydney.

Caple, H. 2010. Doubling-up: Allusion and Bonding in Multi-semiotic News Stories[C]//Bednarek, M. & Martin, J. R. (eds.) *New Discourse on Language: Functional Perspectives on Multimodality, Identity, and Affiliation*. London/New York: Continuum.

Caple, H. (Co-authored with Bednareck, M.) *Photojournalism: A Social Semiotic Approach*[M]. London: Palgrave MacMillan, 2013.

Caple, H. A Balancing Act: Theorizing Compositional Choices in Photographs[C]//Caldwell, D., Knox, J. & Martin J. R. (eds.) *Appliable Linguistics and Social Semiotics: Developing Theory from Practice*. London: Bloomsbury, 2022.

Caple, H. & Bednarek, M. Double-take: Unpacking the Play in the Image-nuclear News Story[J]. *Visual Communication*, 2010, 9 (2): 211-229.

Caple, H., Huan, C. & Bednarek, M. *Multimodal News Analysis Across Cultures*[M]. Cambridge: Cambridge University Press, 2020.

Caple, H. & Knox, J. Online News Galleries, Photojournalism and the Photo Essay[J]. *Visual Communication*, 2012, 11 (2): 207-236.

Carlson, M. The Robotic Reporter: Automated Journalism and the Redefinition of Labor, Compositional Forms and Journalistic Authority[J]. *Digital Journalism*, 2014, 3(3): 426-431.

Chandler, D. & Munday, R. *A Dictionary of Media and Communication*

[Z]. Oxford: Oxford University Press, 2011.

Chang, J. & Yang, Q. (常江，杨奇光). Data Journalism: Concepts, Methods and Influence(数据新闻：理念、方法与影响力)[J]. *Journal of Journalism and Communication* (新闻界), 2014, 12: 10-18.

Christie, F. *Classroom Discourse Analysis: A Functional Perspective*[M]. London: Continuum, 2002.

Christie, F. (ed.) *Pedagogy and the Shaping of Consciousness: Linguistic and Social Processes*[C]. London: Cassell, 1999.

Coddington, M. Clarifying Journalism's Quantitative Turn: A Typology for Evaluating Data Journalism, Computational Journalism, and Computer-assisted Reporting[J]. *Digital Journalism*, 2015, (3): 331-348.

Coffin, C. Reconstrual of the Past—Settlement or Invasion? The Role of Judgement Analysis[C]. Martin J. R. & Wodak, R. (eds.) *Re/reading the Past: Critical and Functional Perspectives on Time and Value*. Amsterdam: Benjamins, 2003.

Conway, M. Before the Bloggers: The Upstart News Technology of Television at the 1948 Political Conventions[J]. *American Journalism*, 2007, 24(1): 33-58.

Convoy, M. *Journalism: A Critical History*[M]. London/California/New Delhi: Sage, 2004.

Cotter, C. & Perrin, D. *The Routledge Handbook of Language and Media*[M]. Oxon/New York: Routledge, 2018.

Couldry, N. A Necessary Disenchantment: Myth, Agency and Injustice in a Digital World[J]. *The Sociological Review*, 2014, 62 (4): 880-897.

Crisell, A. *An Introductory History of British Broadcasting*[M]. London: Routledge, 1997.

Crook, T. *International Radio Journalism: History, Theory and Practice*

[M]. London and New York: Routledge, 1998.

Czitrom, D. J. *Media and the American Mind: From Morse to McLuhan* [M]. Chapel Hill: The University of North Carolina Press, 1982.

Delin, J., Bateman J. A. & Allen P. A Model of Genre in Document Layout[J]. *Information Design Journal*, 2003(1): 54-66.

Dennis, E. E. Television's Convergence Conundrum[J]. *Television Quarterly*, 2006, 37 (1): 22-27.

De Maeyer, J. & Libert, M. Waiting for Data Journalism: A Qualitative Assessment of the Anecdotal Take-up of Data Journalism in French-speaking Belgium[J]. *Digital Journalism*, 2015, 3(3): 432-446.

De Sola Pool, T. *Technologies of Freedom*[M]. Cambridge: The Belnap Press of Harvard University Press, 1984.

Deuze, M. Online Journalism: Modelling the First Generation of News Media on the World Wide Web[J]. *First Monday*, 2001, 6 (10).

Deuze, M. What is Journalism? Professional Identity and Ideology of Journalists Reconsidered[J]. *Journalism*, 2004, 6 (4): 442-464.

Díaz Noci, J. A History of Journalism on the Internet: A State of the Art and Some Methodological Trends[J]. *Revista Internacional de Historia de la Comunicación*, 2013, 1(1): 253-272.

Dick, M. *A History of Data Graphics in News and Communications*[M]. Massachusetts: The MIT Press, 2015.

Dimitrova, D. V. & Neznanski, M. Online Journalism and the War in Cyberspace: A Comparison Between US and International Newspapers [J]. *Journal of Computer-mediated Communication*, 2006, 12 (1): 248-263.

Doermann, D., Rosenfeld, A. & Rivlin, E. The Function of Documents [C]. P*roceedings of the* 4th *International Conference on Document Analysis and Recognition*, Vol. 2. Ulm, Germany, 1997.

Doherty, S. Hypertext and Journalism: Paths for Future Research [J].

Digital Journalism, 2014, 2(2): 124-139.

Domingo, D. Inventing Online Journalism: Development of the Internet as a News Medium in Four Catalan Online Newsrooms[D]. Barcelona: Universitat Autonoma de Barcelona, 2006.

Doran, Y. J. Semiotic Description: Grappling with Mathematics[C]// Caldwell, D., Knox, J. & Martin J. R. (eds.) *Appliable Linguistics and Social Semiotics: Developing Theory from Practice*. London: Bloomsbury, 2022.

Dörr, K. Mapping the Field of Algorithmic Journalism[J]. *Digital Journalism*, 2016, 4(6): 700-722.

Dwyer, T. *Media Convergence* [M]. New York: Open University Press, 2010.

Economou, D. The Big Picture: The Role of the Lead Image in Print Feature Stories[C]//Lassen, I., Strunck, J. & Vestergaard, T. (eds.) *Mediating Ideology in Text and Image: Ten Critical Studies*. Amsterdam: John Benjamins, 2006.

Economou, D. Pulling Readers in: News Photos in Greek and Australian Broadsheets[C]//White, P. R. R. and Thomson, E. A. (eds.) *Communicating Conflict: Multilingual Case Studies of the News Media*. London: Continuum, 2008.

Eggins, S. *An Introduction to Systemic Functional Linguistics*[M]. London: Pinter, 1994.

Eggins, S. & Martin, J. R. Genres and registers of discourse[C]//Wang, Z. (ed.) *Genre Studies, Vol. 3 in the Collected Works of J. R. Martin*. Shanghai: Shanghai Jiao Tong University Press, 2012/1997.

Eglin, V. & Bres, S. Analysis and Interpretation of Visual Saliency for Document Functional Labelling[J]. International Journal on Document Analysis and Recognition, 2004, 7: 28-43.

El Refaie, E. Understanding Visual Metaphor: The Example of Newspaper

Cartoons[J]. *Visual Communication*, 2003, 2 (1): 75-95.

Engebretsen, M. & Weber, W. Graphic Modes: The Visual Representation of Data [C]//Cotter, C. & Perrin, D. (eds.) *The Routledge Handbook of Language and Media*. London & New York: Routledge, 2017.

Facsimile and Multiplex Transmission Test by RCA Communications Approved[R]. 1934.

Fairclough, N. *Discourse and Social Change* [M]. Cambridge: Polity, 1992.

Fairclough, N. *Critical Discourse Analysis* [M]. Harlow: Longman, 1995.

Fairclough, N. Technologization of discourse [C]//C. R. Caldas-Coulthard & M. Coulthard (eds.). *Texts and Practices: Readings in Critical Discourse Analysis*. London: Routledge, 1996.

Fairclough, N. *Analyzing Discourse: Textual Analysis for Social Research* [M]. London: Routledge, 2003.

Fang, J. & Yan, D. (方洁, 颜冬). Data Journalism: Theory and Practice (全球视野下的“数据新闻”: 理念与实践)[J]. *Chinese Journal of Journalism & Communication* (国际新闻界), 2013, (6): 73-83.

Fend, D. Identifying the Participants: Reference in the Television News [J]. *Visual Communication*, 2015, 15(2): 167-198.

Feng, D. (冯德正). New Development of Visual Grammar: A Framework for Visual Narrative Analysis (视觉语法的新发展: 基于图画书的视觉叙事分析框架)[J]. *Foreign Language Education* (外语教学), 2015, 36(3): 23-27.

Fink, K. & Anderson, C. W. Data Journalism in the United States: Beyond the ‘Usual Suspects’ [J]. *Journalism Studies*, 2014, 6(4): 467-481.

Finnemann, N. The Internet and the Public Space [J]. *Nordic Media*

Trends, 2006, 9 (1): 11-28.

Forceville, C. *Pictorial Metaphor in Advertising* [M]. London and New York: Routledge, 1996.

Forceville, C. & Urios-Aparisi E. (eds.) *Multimodal Metaphor* [C]//Berlin: Mouton de Gruyter, 2009.

Friendly, M. The Golden Age of Statistical Graphics [J]. *Statistical Science*, 2008a, 23(4): 502-535.

Friendly, M. A Brief History of Data Visualization [C]//Chen, C., Härdle, W. K. & Friendly, M. (eds.) *Handbook of Data Visualization*. Berlin: Springer, 2008b.

Freedman, A. & Medway, P. (eds.). *Genre and the New Rhetoric* [C]. London: Taylor & Francis, 1994a.

Freedman, A. & Medway, P. Introduction: New Views of Genre and Their Implications for Education [C]// Freedman, A. & Medway, P. (eds.) *Learning and Teaching Genre*. Portsmouth, NH: Boynton/Cook, 1994b.

Freund, G. *Photographie et Societe* [M]. Translated by John Tittensor. Paris: Le Seuil, 1974.

Ganesh, T. K. *News Reporting and Editing in Digital Age* [M]. Delhi: Virgo Press, 2006.

Gee, J. P. *An Introduction to Discourse Analysis: Theory and Method* [M]. Beijing: Foreign Language Teaching and Research Press, 2000.

Ghadessy, M. (ed). *Text and Context in Functional Linguistics* [C]. Amsterdam: John Benjamins Publishing Company, 1999.

Gidal, T. *Modern Photojournalism: Origin and Evolution, 1910-1913* [M]. New York: Collier Books, 1973.

Giles, V. & Hodgson, F. W. *Creative Newspaper Design* [M]. Oxford: Heinemann Professional Publishing Ltd., 1990.

Gómez-Jiménez, E. An Introduction to Graphology: Definition, Theoretical

Background and Levels of Analysis [J]. *Miscelánea: A Journal of English and American Studies*, 2015 (51): 71-85.

Gondwe, G. & White R. A. Data Journalism Practice in Sub-Saharan African Media Systems: A Cross-national Survey of Journalists' Perceptions in Zambia and Tanzania[J]. *African Journalism Studies*, 2021.

Gordon, R. The Meanings and Implications of Convergence [C]// Kawamoto K. (ed.) *Digital Journalism: Emerging Media and the Changing Horizons of Journalism*. Lanham: Rowman and Littlefield Publishers, 2003.

Graefe, A. Guide to Automated Journalism. [EB/OL]. [2019-05-07]. https://www.cjr.org/tow_center_reports/guide_to_automated_journalism.php.

Graphic News. [2019-05-07]. http://www.graphicnews.com/base/info.php? q=179&s=GN.

Gray, J. & Bounegru, L. (eds). *The Data Journalism Handbook* 2: *Towards a Critical Data Practice* [C]. [2019-05-07]. https://datajournalism.com/read/handbook/two.

Gray, J., Bounegru, L. & Chambers, L. (eds.) *The Data Journalism Handbook* 1 [C]. [2019-05-07]. http://datajournalismhandbook.org/1.0/en/index.html.

Gruber, H. Scholarly Email Discussion List Postings: A Single New Genre of Academic Communication? [C]// Pemberton, L. & Shurrille, S. (eds.) *Words on the Web: Computer-Mediated Communication*. Exeter: Intellect Ltd., 2000.

Grunig, J. E. Organizations and Public Relations: Testing a Communication Theory[J]. *Journalism Monograph*, 1976. https://www.researchgate.net/publication/247083659.

Guo, L. Multimodality in a Biology Textbook[C]//O'Halloran, K. (ed.) *Multimodal Discourse Analysis: Systemic Functional Perspectives*.

London/New York: Continuum, 2004.

Ha, L. & James, L. Interactivity Reexamined: A Baseline Analysis of Early Business Websites[J]. *Journal of Broadcasting & Electronic Media*, 1998, 42(4): 457-474.

Halliday, M. A. K. *A Course in Spoken English: Intonation*[M]. London: Edward Arnold, 1970.

Halliday, M. A. K. *An Introduction to Functional Grammar* (2nd edition) [M]. London: Arnold, 1994.

Halliday, M. A. K. (Revised by Matthiessen, C. M. I. M) *An Introduction to Functional Grammar* (4th Edition) [M]. Oxon and New York: Routledge, 2014.

Halliday, M. A. K. *Language as Social Semiotic: The Social Interpretation of Language and Meaning* [M]. London: Edward Arnold, 1978.

Halliday, M. A. K. Language as System and Language as Instance: The Corpus as a Theoretical Concept[C]// Svartivik, J. (ed.) *Directions in Corpus Linguistics: Proceedings of Nobel Symposium* 82. Berlin and New York: Mouton de Gruyter, 1992.

Halliday, M. A. K. The Act of Meaning[C]// Alatis, J. E. (ed.) *Georgetown University Round Table on Languages and Linguistics* 1992: *Language, Communication and Social Meaning*. Washington, D. C.: Georgetown University Press, 1993.

Halliday, M. A. K. The Notion of "Context" in Language Education [C]//Ghadessy, M. (ed.) T*ext and Context in Functional Linguistics*. Amsterdam: Benjamins, 1999.

Halliday, M. A. K. (Revised by Matthiessen, C.) *An Introduction to Functional Grammar* (3rd edition)[M]. Beijing: Foreign Language Teaching and Research Press, 2008.

Halliday, M. A. K. & Hasan, R. *Language, Context and Text: Aspects of Language in a Social-Semiotic Perspective*[M]. Geelong: Deakin

University Press, 1985.

Halliday, M. A. K. & Martin, J. R. *Writing Science: Literacy as Discursive Power*[M]. London: Falmer, 1993.

Halliday, M. A. K., Mcintosh, A. & Strevens, P. D. *The Linguistic Sciences and Language Teaching* [M]. London: Longman, 1964.

Hammond, P. From Computer-assisted to Data-driven: Journalism and Big Data[J]. *Journalism*, 2015, 18(4): 408-424.

Hannaford, L. Computational Journalism in the UK Newsroom: Hybrids or Specialists? [J]. *Journalism Education*, 2015, 4(1): 6-21.

Hannaford, L. The Discourse of Data Journalism[J]. *Journalism*, 2022 (0): 1-21.

Hao, J. Construing Biology: An Ideational Perspective[D]. Sydney: University of Sydney, 2015.

Harris, R. *Information Graphics: A Comprehensive Illustrated Reference* [M]. New York: Oxford University Press, 1999.

Hartley, J. *Designing Instructional Text* (3rd edition) [M]. New Jersey: Nicholas, East Bruswick, 1994.

Hartley, J. *Understanding News*[M]. London: Metbuen Co. Ltd., 1982.

Hasan, R. Text in the Systemic-functional Model [C]// Wolfgang, D. (ed.) *Current Trends in Text Linguistics*. Berlin: de Gruyter, 1978.

Hasan, R. Meaning, Context and Text: Fifty Years After Malinowski [C]// Benson, J. D. & Greaves, W. S. (eds). *Systemic Perspectives on Discourse*. Norwood: Ablex, 1985.

Hasan, R. The Place of Context in a Systemic Functional Model[C]//Halliday, M. A. K. & Webster, J. (eds.) *Continuum Companion to Systemic Functional Linguistics*. London and New York: Continuum, 2009.

Hasan, R. Towards a Paradigmatic Description of Context: Systems, Metafunctions, and Semantics[J]. *Functional Linguistics*, 2014, 2

(9): 1-54.

He, Y. Animation as a Semiotic Mode: Construing Knowledge in Science Animated Videos[D]. Sydney: University of Sydney, 2020.

Heravi, B. Teaching Data Journalism[C]//Mair, J., Keeble, R., Lucero, M. & Moore, M. (eds.) *Data Journalism: Past, Present and Future*. Suffolk: Abramis Academic Publishing, 2017.

Heravi, B. 3WS of Data Journalism Education: What, Where and Who? [J]. *Journalism Practice*, 2019, 13(3): 349-366.

Heravi, B., Cassidy, K., Davis, E. & Harrower N. Preserving Data Journalism: A Systematic Literature Review[J]. *Journalism Practice*, 2021.

Heravi, B. & Lorenz. M. Data Journalism Practices Globally: Skills, Education, Opportunities and Values[J]. *Journalism and Media*, 2020, 1(1): 26-40.

Hermida, A. & Young, M. L. From Peripheral to Integral? A Digital-born Journalism Not for Profit in Times of Crises[J]. *Media and Communication*, 2019, 7(4): 92-102.

Hiippala, T. The Localization of Advertising Print Media as a Multimodal Process[C]//Bowcher, W. L. (ed.) *Multimodal Texts from Around the World: Linguistic and Cultural Insights*. London: Palgrave, 2012.

Hiippala, T. A Multimodal Perspective on Data Visualization[C]//Kennedy, H. & Engebretsen, M. (eds.) *Data Visualization in Society*. Amsterdam: Amsterdam University Press, 2020.

Hintz, A., Dencik L. & Wahl-Jorgensen K. *Digital Citizenship in a Datafied Society*[M]. Cambridge: Polity Press, 2019.

Hodgson, F. W. *Subediting: A Handbook of Modern Newspaper Editing and Production*[M]. Massachusetts: Focal Press, 1993.

Hood, S. Summary Writing in Academic Contexts: Implicating Meaning in

Processes of Change[J]. *Linguistics and Education*, 2008, 19: 351-365.

Hood, S. *Appraising Research: Evaluation in Academic Writing*[M]. New York: Palgrave, 2010.

Hopkins, A. & Dudley-Evans, T. A Genre-based Investigation of the Discussion Sections in Articles and Dissertations[J]. *English for Specific Purposes*, 1988, 7(2): 113-122.

Horton, B. (Associated Press) *Guide to Photojournalism* (2nd edition) [M]. New York: McGraw-Hill, 2001.

Houston, B. *Computer-assisted Reporting: A Practical Guide*[M]. New York: St. Martin's, 1996.

Hu, M. &Li, Z. (胡明霞，李战子). Multimodal Genre: Concept Clarification and Research Prospects(多模态语类：概念辨析与研究前景)[J]. *Journal of PLA University of Foreign Languages* (解放军外国语学院学报), 2018, 41(3): 10-18.

Huan, C. Journalistic Engagement Patterns and Power Relations: Corpus Evidence from Chinese and Australian Hard News Reporting[J]. *Discourse & Communication*, 2016, 10(2): 137-156.

Huang, Y. & Qiu, Y. (黄雅兰、仇筠茜). Informing or Engaging: A Comparative Analysis of the Practice of Visualization on Four Data News Columns (信息告知还是视觉吸引？对中外四个数据新闻栏目可视化现状的比较研究)[J]. *Journalism Research* (新闻大学), 2018 (1): 1-8, 34.

Hudson, G. & Rowlands, S. *The Broadcast Journalism Handbook*[M]. Essex: Pearson Education Limited, 2007.

Hyon, S. Genre in Three Traditions[J]. *TESOL Quarterly*, 1996, 30, (4): 693-722.

IBM. Big Data Analytics. [2022-12-20]. https://www.ibm.com/analytics/big-data-analytics.

Infotendencias Group. Media Convergence[C]//Siapera, E. & Veglis, A. (eds.) *The Handbook of Global Online Journalism*. West Sussex: Wiley-Blackwell, 2012.

Jenkins, H. *Convergence Culture: Where Old and New Media Collide* [M]. New York: New York University Press, 2006.

Jewitt, C. Multimodal Approaches [C]//Norris, S. & Meier, C. D. (eds.) *Interactions, Images and Texts: A Reader in Multimodality*. Berlin: Mouton De Gruyter, 2014.

Jianjie, P. E. et al. Development and Thoughts of Digital Sound Broadcasting[J]. *Radio & TV Broadcasting Engineering*, 2016(12): 25.

Joeng, S. Visual Metaphor in Advertising[J]. *Journal of Marketing Communication*, 2008, 14 (1): 59-73.

Jonsson, A. M & Ornebring, H. User-generated Content and the News[J]. *Journalism Practice*, 2011, 5(2): 127-144.

Kalogeras, S. *Transmedia Storytelling and the New Era of Media Convergence in Higher Education* [M]. New York: Palgrave Macmillan, 2014.

Karlsen, J. & Stavelin, E. Computational Journalism in Norwegian Newsrooms[J]. *Journalism Practice*, 2014, 8 (1): 34-48.

Kayser-Bril, N., Anderton-Yang, D., Kayser-Bril, N., Howard, A., Teixeira, C. V., Slobin, S., Vermanen & Slobin. J. S. Why Is Data Journalism Important? [EB/OL]. [2019-05-09]. DataJournalism.com.

Kennedy, H. & Engebretsen, M. (eds.) *Data Visualization in Society*[C]. Amsterdam: Amsterdam University Press, 2020.

Kennedy, H. & Hill. R. L. The Feeling of Numbers: Emotion in Everyday Engagement with Dat and Their Visualizations[J]. *Sociology*, 2017, 52 (4): 830-848.

Kennedy, H., Hill, R. L., Aiello, G. & Allen, W. The Work That Visualization Conventions Do [J]. *Information, Communication and Society*, 2016, 19(6): 715-735.

Kirk, A. *Data Visualization: A Handbook for Data Driven Design* [M]. London: Sage, 2016.

Knight, N. K. Wrinkling Complexity: Concepts of Identity and Affiliation in Humor [C]//Bednareck, M. & Martin, J. R. (eds.) *New Discourse on Language: Functional Perspectives on Multimodality, Identity, and Affiliation*. London/ New York: Continuum, 2010.

Knox, J. S. Visual/Verbal Communication on Online Newspaper Home Pages [J]. *Visual Communication*, 2007, 6 (1): 19-53.

Knox, J. S. Punctuating the Home Page: Image as Language in an Online Newspaper [J] *Discourse and Communication*, 2009, 3 (2): 145-172.

Knox, J. S. Online Newspapers: Evolving Genres and Evolving Theory [C]//Coffin, C., Lillis, T. & O'Halloran, K. (eds.) *Applied Linguistics Methods: A Reader*. London/New York: Routledge, 2010.

Kong, K. A Taxonomy of the Discourse Relations Between Words and Visual [J]. *Information Design Journal*, 2006, 14(3): 207-230.

Kotenidis, E. & Veglis, A. Algorithmic Journalism: Current Applications and Future Perspectives [J]. *Journal Media*, 2021, 2(2): 244-257.

Indah, S. N. & Hasanah, K. Infographic Data Visualization as an Alternative Form of News [J]. *The Indonesian Journal of Communication Studies*, 2022, 15 (1): 30-45.

Kress, G. Texture and Meaning [C]//Andrews, R. (ed.) *Narrative and Argument*. Milton Keynes: Open University Press, 1989.

Kress, G. *Literacy in the New Media Age* [M]. London: Routledge, 2003.

Kress, G. *Multimodality: A Social Semiotic Approach to Contemporary Communication* [M]. London & New York: Routledge, 2010.

Kress, G., & van Leeuwen, T. *Multimodal Discourse: The Modes and Media of Contemporary Communication*[M]. London: Arnold, 2001.

Kress, G. & van Leeuwen, T. Color as a Semiotic Mode: Notes for a Grammar of Color[J]. *Visual Communication*, 2002, 1(3): 343-368.

Kress, G, & van Leeuwen, T. *Reading Images: The Grammar of Visual Design* (2nd ed.)[M]. London: Routledge, 2006.

Kuyucu, M. Digital Convergence of Radio: Effects of Digitalization on Radio Media[D]. Conference Paper at the 6th International Communication Days Digital Transformation Symposium, 2019. https://www.researchgate.net/publication/348135497.

Larrondo-Ureta, A. & Ferrera-Rodriguez, E. The Potential of Investigative Data Journalism to Reshape Profession Culture and Values[J]. *Communication &Society*, 2021, 34 (1): 41-56.

Lassila-Merisalo, M. Story First: Publishing Narrative Long-form Journalism in Digital Environments[J]. *Journal of Magazine & New Media Research*, 2014, 15(2): 1-15.

Ledin, P. & Machin, D. Strategic Diagrams and the Technologization of Culture[J]. *Journal of Language and Politics*, 2016a, 15(3): 322-336.

Ledin, P. & Machin, D. The Evolution of Performance Management Discourse in Corporate Strategy Diagrams for Public Institutions[J]. *Discourse, Context &Media*, 2016b, 13: 122-131.

Ledin, P. &Machin, D. *Doing Visual Analysis: From Theory to Practice*[M]. London: Sage, 2018.

Lemke, J. Multimodal Genres and Transmedia Traversals: Social Semiotics and the Political Economy of the Sign[J]. *Semiotica*, 2009, 173(1): 283-297.

Lemke, J. Multiplying Meaning: Visual and Verbal Semiotics in Scientific

Text[C]// Martin, J. R. & Veel R. (eds.) *Reading Science: Critical and Functional Perspectives on Discourse of Science*. London: Routledge, 1998.

Lemke, J. *Semiotics and Education* [M]. Toronto: Victoria University, 1984.

Levinson, S. *Pragmatics* [M]. Cambridge: Cambridge University Press, 1983.

Lexico. Infographic. [2019-07-07]. http://www.oxforddictionaries.com/definition/english/infographic.

Logi, L. & Zappavigna, M. Affiliation: An Appliable Framework for Exploring Community and Identity in Disourse[C]. Caldwell, D., Knox, J. & Martin J. R. (eds.) *Appliable Linguistics and Social Semiotics: Developing Theory from Practice*. London: Bloomsbury, 2022.

Li, B. (李彬). *A History of Global News and Communication* (全球新闻传播史)[M]. Beijing: Tsinghua University Press (北京：清华大学出版社), 2009.

Li, J. (李京). Application of Visual Framing in Data Journalism (视觉框架在数据新闻中的修辞实践)[J]. *Journalism and Mass Communication* (新闻界), 2017(5): 9-15.

Li, L. & Zhong, Y. (李良荣, 钟怡). *The Internet and New Media* (互联网新闻制作)[M]. Shanghai: Fudan University Press (上海：复旦大学出版社), 2020.

Li, X. (黎信). *A Practical Guide for International News Reporting in English* (英语对外新闻报道指南)[M]. Beijing: Foreign Languages Press (北京：外文出版社), 2009.

Light, J. S. Facsimile: A Forgotten "New Medium" from the 20th Century[J]. *New Media & Society*, 2006, 8(3): 355-378.

Lim, F. V. Developing an Integrative Multi-semiotic Model [C]// O'Halloran Kay (ed.) *Multimodal Discourse Analysis: Systemic-Func-*

tional Perspectives. London: Continuum, 2004.

Liu, T. (刘涛). China in Western Data Journalism: Searching for an Analytic Framework of Visual Frame Based on Visual Rhetoric (西方数据新闻中的中国：一个视觉修辞分析框架) [J]. *Journalism & Communication* (新闻与传播研究), 2016, 23 (2): 5-28, 126.

Loosen, W. Four Forms of Datafied Journalism: Journalism's Response to the Datafiction of Society [D]. Communicative Figurations Working Paper No. 18, 2018. www. kofi. uni-bremen. de/fileadmin/user _ upload/Abreitspapiere/CoFi_EWP_No-18_Loosen.pdf.

Loosen, W. Data-driving Gold-standards: What the Field Values as Award-worthy Data Journalism and How Journalism Co-evolves with the Datafication of Society [C]//Bournegru, L. & Gray J. (eds.) *The Data Journalism Handbook 2: Towards a Critical Data Practice*. 2021. www. degruyter. com/document/doi/10. 1515/9789048542079/html#contents.

Loosen, W., Reimer, J. & De Silva-Schmidt, F. Data-driven Reporting: An On-going (R) evolution? An Analysis of Projects Nominated for the Data Journalism Awards 2013-2016 [J]. *Journalism*, 2017, 21 (9): 1-18.

Ludwig, M. D. & Gilemore, G. *Modern News Editing* (5th Edition) [M]. Iowa: Blackwell Publishing, 2005.

Machin, D. *Introduction to Multimodal Analysis* [M]. London: Bloomsbury, 2007.

Mäntynen, A. & Shore, S. What is Meant by Hybridity? An Investigation of Hybridity and Related Terms in Genre Studies [J]. *Text & Talk*, 2014, 34 (6). https: //doi. org/10. 1515/text-2014-0022.

Marconi F. & Siegman, A. *The Future of Augmented Journalism: A Guide for Newsrooms in the Age of Smart Machines* [D]. About AP Insights, 2017. https://insights. ap. org/uploads/ images/the-future-of-augmented-journalism_ap-report.pdf.

Mari, W. Technology in the Newsroom: Adoption of the Telephone and the Radio Car from 1920 to 1960[J]. *Journalism Studies*, 2017. http://dx.doi.org/10.1080/1461670X.2016.1272432.

Martin, J. R. A Context for Genre: Modelling Social Processes in Functional Linguistics[C]// Devilliers, J. & Stainton R. (eds.) *Communication in Linguistics: Papers in Honor of Michael Gregory.* Toronto: GREF (Theoria Series 10), 2001.

Martin, J. R. Beyond Exchange: Appraisal System in English [C]// Wang, Z. (ed.) *Discourse Semantics, Vol.* 2 *in the Collected Works of J. R. Martin.* Shanghai: Shanghai Jiao Tong University Press, 2012/2000.

Martin, J. R. *English Text: System and Structure*[M]. Beijing: Peking University Press, 2004/1992.

Martin, J. R. Fair Trade: Negotiating Meaning in Multimodal Texts [C]//Coppock, P. (ed.). *The Semiotics of Writing: Transdisciplinary Perspectives on the Technology of Writing.* Belgium: Brepols, 2000.

Martin, J. R. Language, Register and Genre[C]//Wang, Z. (ed.) *Register Studies, Vol. 4 in the Collected Works of J. R. Martin.* Shanghai: Shanghai Jiao Tong University Press, 2012/1984.

Martin, J. R. Genre and Field: Social Processes and Knowledge Structures in Systemic Functional Semiotics [C]//Wang, Z. (ed.) *Register Studies, Vol. 4 in the Collected Works of J. R. Martin.* Shanghai: Shanghai Jiao Tong University Press, 2012/2007.

Martin, J. R. Intermodal Reconciliation: Mates in Arms [C]//L. Unsworth (ed.). *New Literacies and the English Curriculum: Multimodal Perspective.* London: Continuum, 2008.

Martin, J. R. Macro-proposals: Meaning by Degree[C]// Mann, W. C. &

Thompson, S. (eds.) *Discourse Description: Diverse Analyses of a Fund-raising Text.* Amsterdam: Benjamins, 1992.

Martin, J. R. Macro-genres: The Ecology of the Page[C]// Wang, Z. (ed.) *Genre Studies, Vol. 2 in the Collected Works of J. R. Martin.* Shanghai: Shanghai Jiao Tong University Press, 2012/1994.

Martin, J. R. Modelling Context: The Crooked Path of Progress in Contextual Linguistics[C]// Ghadessy, M. (ed.) *Text and Context in Functional Linguistics.* Amsterdam: Benjamins (CILT Series IV), 1999.

Martin, J. R. Multimodal Semiotics: Theoretical Challenges[C]//Dreyfus, S., Hood, S. & Steglin, M. (eds.) *Semiotic Margins: Meaning in Multimodalities.* London: Continuum, 2011.

Martin, J. R. Negotiating Difference: Ideology and Reconciliation[C]// Pütz, M., van Aertselaer, J. N. & van Dijk, T. A. (eds.) *Communicating Ideologies: Language, Discourse and Social Practice.* Frankfurt: Peter Lang, 2004.

Martin, J. R. Process and Text: Two Aspects of Semiosis[C]//Benson, J. & Greaves, W. (eds.) *Systemic Perspective on Discourse, Vol. 1: Selected Theoretical Papers from the 9th International Systemic Workshop.* Norwood: Ablex, 1985.

Martin, J. R. Register and Genre: Modelling Social Context in Functional Linguistics — Narrative Genres[C]// Pedro, E. R. (ed.) *Discourse Analysis: Proceedings of First International Conference on Discourse Analysis.* Lisbon: Colibri/Portuguese Linguistics Association, 1997.

Martin, J. R. Revisiting Field: Specialized Knowledge in Secondary School Science and Humanities Discourse[J]. *Onomazein*, 2017: 111-148.

Martin, J. R. The Development of Register[C]//Wang, Z. (ed.) *Register Studies, Vol. 4 in the Collected Works of J. R. Martin.* Shanghai: Shanghai Jiao Tong University Press, 2012/1983.

Martin, J. R. Semantic Variation: Modelling Realization, Instantiation and Individuation in Social Semiosis[C]//Bednareck, M. & Martin, J. R. (eds.) *New Discourse on Language: Functional Perspectives on Multimodality, Identity, and Affiliation*. London/ New York: Continuum, 2010.

Martin, J. R. *Systemic Functional Grammar: A Next Step into the Theory—Axial Relations*(系统功能语法理论之再探——轴关系)[M]. (王品, 朱永生译). Beijing: Higher Education Press, 2013.

Martin, J. R. Tenderness: Realization and Instantiation in a Botswanan Town[C]//Wang, Z. (ed.) *SFL Theory, Vol. 1 in the Collected Works of J. R. Martin*. Shanghai: Shanghai Jiao Tong University Press, 2012/2008.

Martin, J. R., Maton, K. & Matruglio, E. Historical Cosmologies: Epistemology and Axiology in Australian Secondary School History[J]. *Revista Signos*, 2010, 43(74): 433-463.

Martin, J. R. & Matthissen, C. M. I. M. Systemic Typology and Topology[C]//F. Christie (ed.) *Literacy in Social Processes: Papers from the Inaugural Australian Systemic Functional Linguistics Conference*. Melbourne: Deakin University, 1991.

Martin, J. R. & Rose, D. *Working with Discourse: Meaning Beyond the Clause* (1st Edition)[M]. Beijing: Peking University Press, 2007/2003.

Martin, J. R. & Rose, D. *Working with Discourse: Meaning beyond the Clause* (2nd edition)[M]. Continuum/Peking University Press, 2014/2007.

Martin, J. R. & Rose D. *Genre Relations: Mapping Culture*[M]. London: Equinox, 2008.

Martin, J. R. & White, P. R. R. *The Language of Evaluation—Appraisal in English*[M]. New York: Palgrave, 2005.

Martin, J. R. & Zappavigna, M. (Translated by Wu, Q. & Wang, Z.) (詹姆斯·马丁、米歇尔·扎帕维尼娅著, 吴启竞、王振华译). Embodied Meaning: A Systemic Functional Perspective on Paralanguage (副语言意义研究——系统功能语言学视角)[J]. *Contemporary Rhetoric* (当代修辞学), 2018(1): 2-33.

Martin, J. R., Zappavigna, M. & Dwyer, P. Negotiating Evaluation: Story Structure and Appraisal in Youth Justice Conferencing[C]//A. Mahboob & N. Knight (eds.) *Appliable linguistics: Texts, Contexts, and Meanings*. London: Continuum, 2010.

Martin, J. R., Zappavigna, M. & Dwyer, P. Syndromes of Meaning: Exploring Patterned Coupling in a NSW Youth Justice Conference [C]//Wang, Z. (ed.) *Forensic Linguistics, Vol.* 8 *in the Collected Works of J. R. Martin*. Shanghai: Shanghai Jiao Tong University Press, 2012.

Martin, J. R., Zappavigna, M., Cleirigh, C. & Dwyer, P. The Coupling of Gesture and Phonology[C]//M. Bednarek & J. Martin (eds.) *New Discourse on Language: Functional Perspectives on Multimodality, Identity and Affiliation*. London: Continuum, 2010.

Martin, M. *Wireless Transmission of Photographs*[M]. London, UK: The Wireless Press, LTD., 1916.

Martinec, R. Interpersonal Resources in Action[J]. *Semiotica*, 2001, 135 (1/4): 117-145.

Martinec, R. Types of Process in Action[J]. *Semiotica*, 2000, 130 (3/4): 243-268.

Martinec, R. & Salway, A. A System for Image-text Relations in New (and Old) Media[J]. *Visual Communication*, 2005, 4 (3): 337-371.

Matheson, D. Weblogs and the Epistemology of the News: Some Trends in Online Journalism[J]. *New Media & Society*, 2004(6): 443-468.

Matthiessen, C. M. I. M. & Halliday, M. A. K. *Systemic Functional Grammar: A First Step into the Theory*(系统功能语法：理论之初探)[M].(黄国文、王瑞阳译). Beijing: Higher Education Press (高等教育出版社), 2009.

Matthiessen, C. M. I. M, Teruya, K. & Lam, M. *Key Terms in Systemic Functional Linguistics* [Z]. London/ New York: Continuum, 2010.

McChesney, R. W. Press-radio Relations and the Emergence of Network, Commercial Broadcasting in the United States, 1930-1935 [J]. *Historical Journal of Film, Radio and Television*, 1991, 11: 41-57.

McFarlane, M. D. A Historical Look at Facsimile[J]. *IEEE Transactions on Education*, 1980, 23: 151-156.

Mcintosh, A. Graphology and Meaning [J]. *Archivum Linguisticum*, 1961, 13: 107-120.

McLuhan, M. *The Gutenberg Galaxy: The Making of Typographic Man* [M]. London: Routledge & Kegan Paul Ltd., 1962.

Miller, C. R. Genre as Social Action[J]. *Quarterly Journal of Speech*, 1984, 70: 151-167.

Meyer, P. *Precision Journalism: A Reporter's Introduction to Social Science Methodology*[M]. Bloomington: Indiana University Press, 1973.

Mirkin, B. *Core Concepts in Data Analysis: Summarization, Correlation and Visualization*[M]. London: Springer, 2011.

Mutsvairo, B. Data Journalism: International Perspectives[D]. Accessed from the Oxford Research Encyclopedia, Communication, 2019. DOI: 10. 1093/acrefore/9780190228613. 013. 797.

Myatt, G. J. & Johnson, W. P. *Making Sense of Data II: A Practical Guide to Data Visualization, Advanced Data Mining Methods, and Applications*[M]. New Jersey: Wiley, 2009.

Nänny, M. Iconic Functions of Long and Short Lines[C]//Nänny, M. & Fisher, O. (eds.) *Form Miming Meaning: Iconicity in Language and*

Literature 2. Amsterdam: Benjamins, 2001.

Nœrland, T. U. The Political Significance of Data Visualization: Four Key Perspectives[C]//Kennedy, H. & Engebretsen, M. (eds.) *Data Visualization in Society*. Amsterdam: Amsterdam University Press, 2020.

Negrine, R. *Politics and the Mass Media in Britain*[M]. London: Routledge, 2001.

Newhall, B. *The History of Photography: From 1839 to the Present*[M]. New York: The Museum of Modern Art, 1949.

Newman, N. Journalism, Media, and Technology Trends and Predictions [R]. Oxford Reuters Institute for the Study of Journalism[EB/OL]. [2019-09-12]. Journalism, Media, and Technology Trends and Predictions 2017 (ox. ac. uk).

Nielson, K. P. & Kreutzfeldt, J. The Resonance 107. 3 FM Radio Art Collection: Towards an Archive Methodology of Radio as Resonance[J]. *Radio Journal: International Studies in Broadcast & Audio Media*, 2016, 14 (2): 159-175.

Nørgaard, N. The Semiotics of Typography in Literary Texts: A Multimodal Approach[J]. *Orbis Litterarum*, 2009, 63(2): 141-160.

Nørgaard, N. Teaching Multimodal Stylistics[C]//Leslie J. & McIntyre D. (eds.) *Teaching Stylistics*. London: Palgrave, 2010.

Norris, S. *Analyzing Multimodal Interaction: A Methodological Framework*[M]. New York: Routledge, 2004.

Norris, S. Developing Multimodal (Inter)action Analysis: A Personal Account[C]//Norris, S. & Maier, C. D. (eds). *Interactions, Images and Texts: A Reader in Multimodality*. Berlin and New York: Mouton de Gruyter, 2014.

Nwogu, K. N. Structure of Science Popularizations: A Genre Analysis Approach to the Schema of Popularized Medical Texts[J]. *English for*

Specific Purposes, 1991, 10 (2): 111-123.

O Dowling, D. Interactive Documentary and the Reinvention of Digital Journalism, 2015-2020[J]. *Convergence: The International Journal of Research into New Media Technologies*, 2022, 28 (3): 905-924.

O'Halloran, K. Interdependence, Interaction and Metaphor in Multisemiotic Texts[J]. *Social Semiotics*, 1999, 9(3): 317-354.

O'Halloran, K. L. Visual Semiosis in Film [C]//O'Halloran, K. L. (ed.) *Multimodal Discourse Analysis: Systemic Functional Perspectives*. London: Continuum, 2004.

O'Halloran, K. L. Systemic Functional-multimodal Discourse Analysis (SF-MDA): Constructing Ideational Meaning Using Language and Visual Imagery[J]. *Visual Communication*, 2008a, 7(4): 443-475.

O'Halloran, K. L. *Mathematical Discourse: Language, Symbolism and Visual Images*[M]. London: Bloomsbury, 2008b.

O'Halloran, K. L. & Tan, S. Big Data and Managing Multimodal Complexity[C]//Caldwell, D., Knox, J. & Martin J. R. (eds.) *Appliable Linguistics and Social Semiotics: Developing Theory from Practice*. London: Bloomsbury, 2022.

O'Reilly Media. *The Data Journalism Handbook: How Journalists Can Use Data to Improve the News* [C]. 2012. https://datajournalism.com/read/handbook/one.

O'Toole, M. *The Language of Displayed Art*[M]. London: Leicester, 1994.

Painter, C., Martin, J. R. & Unsworth, L. *Reading Visual Narratives* [M]. London: Clare, 2012.

Parasie, S. & Dagiral, E. Data-driven Journalism and the Public Good: "Computer-assisted-reporters" and "Programmer-journalists" in Chicago[J]. *New Media & Society*, 2012, 15(6): 853-871.

Paulussen, S. Innovation in the Newsroom[C]// Witschge T., Anderson

C. W., Domingo D. & Hermida A. (eds). *The Sage Handbook of Digital Journalism*. London: Sage, 2016.

Pavlik, J. *Disruption and Digital Journalism: Assessing News Media Innovation in a Time of Dramatic Change*[M]. London/New York: Routledge, 2021.

Pavlik, J. The Impact of Technology on Journalism[J]. *Journalism Studies*, 2000, 1(2): 229-237.

Perloff, R. M. *The Dynamics of News: Journalism in the* 21*st-Century Media Milieu* [M]. New York/Oxon: Routledge, 2020.

Pike, K. L. Language as Particle, Wave, and Field[J]. *The Texas Quarterly*, 19592 (2): 37-54. (Reprinted in Brend, R. (ed.) *Kenneth L. Pike: Selected Writings*[C]. The Hague: Mouton, 1972.)

Post, F. H., Nielson, G. M. & Bonneau, G. *Data Visualization: The State of the Art*[M]. New York: Springer Science+Business Media, 2003.

Postman, N. *Amusing Ourselves to Death: Public Discourse in the Age of Show Business*[M]. Penguin Books, 2005.

Rafaelin, S. Interactivity: From New Media to Communication [C]// Hawkings, R. P., Wiemann, J. M. & Pingree S. (eds.) *Advancing Communication Science: Merging Mass and Interpersonal Process*. California: Sage, 1988.

Richer, B., Kraak, M. & Engelhart, Y. The Power of Visualization Choice: Different Images of Patterns in Space[C]//Kennedy, H. & Engebretsen, M. (eds.) *Data Visualization in Soviety*. Amsterdam: Amsterdam University Press, 2020.

Roberts, G. The Home Page as Genre: A Narrative Approach[C]. *Proceedings of the* 31st *Annual Hawaii International Conference on System Science*, Vol. 2. Los Alamitos: IEEE Computer Society Press, 1998.

Rogers, S. *Facts are Sacred: The Power of Data*[M]. London: Faber & Faber, 2013.

Rogers, S. Introduction to Data Journalism[EB/OL]. [2018-06-08]. https:simongogers.net/2014/05/25/introduction-todata-jounalism/.

Rogers, S. From the Guardian to Google News Lab: A decade of working in data journalism[C]. Bournegru L. and Gray J. (eds.) *The Data Journalism Handbook: Towards a Critical Data Practice*, 2021. www. degruyter. com/document/doi/10. 1515/9789048542079/html # contents

Rooney, D. Thirty Years of Competition in the British Tabloid Press: The *Mirror* and the *Sun*[C]. Sparks, C. & Tulloch, J. (eds.) *Tabloid Tales*. Oxford: Rowman and Littlefield, 2000.

Rose, D. Genre in the Sydney School[C]// Wang, Z. (ed.) *Genre Studies, Vol. 2 in the Collected Works of J. R. Martin*. Shanghai: Shanghai Jiao Tong University Press, 2012.

Rose, D. Reading Genre: A New Wave of Analysis[J]. *Linguistics and the Human Sciences*, 2006, 2(2): 185-204.

Rose, D. & Martin, J. R. *Learning to Write, Reading to Learn: Genre, Knowledge and Pedagogy in the Sydney School*[M]. Bristol & Sheffield: Equinox, 2012.

Rosenbaum. M. Data Stories. 2012. [2018-06-08]. DataJournalism. com.

Rudin, R. & Ibbotson, T. *An Introduction to Journalism: Essential Techniques and Background Knowledge*[M]. Oxford: Focal Press, 2002.

Salager-Meyer, F. Discoursal Flaws in Medical English Abstracts: A Genre Analysis per Research- and Text-Type. *Text*, 1990, 10 (4): 365-384.

Salaverría, R. Digital Journalism: 25 Years of Research[J]. *El Profesional de la Información*, 2019, 28 (1), e280101.

Salaverria, R. & de-Lima-Santos, M. Towards Ubiquitous Journalism: Impacts IoT on News[C]//Vazquez-Herrero J., Direito-Rebollal S., Silva-Rodriguez, A. & Lopez-Gaicia X. (eds.) *Journalistic Metamorphosis: Media Transformation in the Digital Age*. Cham, Switzerland: Springer, 2020.

Shen, K. (沈括). *Dream Pool Essays*(梦溪笔谈)[M]. (Annotated by Xie Yuchen, 谢雨辰译注)[M]. Shanghai: China Publishing House (中华书局), 2020.

Shepherd, M. & Watters, C. The Evolution of Cybergenres[C]. *Proceedings of the 31st Annual Hawaii International Conference on System Science, Vol. 2*. Los Alamitos: IEEE Computer Society Press, 1998.

Shipley, C. & Fish, M. *How the World Wide Web Works*[M]. Emeryville, CA: Macmillan Computer Publishing, 1996.

Simmons, C. A Marriage of Friends or Foes? Radio, Newspaper, and the Facsimile in the 1930[J]. *Journal of Broadcasting & Electronic Media*, 2016, 60 (3): 410-424.

Singer, J. B. Journalism and Digital Technologies[C]//Lowrey, W. & Gade, P. J. (eds.) *Changing the News: The Forces Shaping Journalism in Uncertain Times*. New York & London: Routledge, 2011.

Sobrino, P. P. *Multimodal Metaphor and Metonymy in Advertising*[M]. Amsterdam/ Philadelphia: John Benjamins, 2017.

Stanford-Poynter. Stanford-Poynter Project-Eye Tracking Online News[R]. [2018-06-08]. www.poynter.org/eyetrack2000/.

Steensen, S. Online Journalism and the Promises of New Technology: A Critical Review and Look Ahead[J]. *Journalism Studies*, 2011, 12 (3): 311-327.

Steensen, S. & Westlund, O. *What Is Digital Journalism Studies?* [M]. London & New York: Routledge, 2021.

Stenglin, M. K. Binding: A Resource for Exploring Interpersonal Meaning in Three-dimensional Space[J]. *Social Semiotics*, 2008, 18(4): 425-447.

Stenglin, M. K. *Packaging Curiosities: Towards a Grammar of Three-dimensional Space*[D]. Sydney: The University of Sydney, 2004.

Stephens, Mitchell. *A History of News: From the Drum to the Satellite* [M]. New York: Viking, 1988.

Sundar, S. Jia, H., Bellur, S., Oh, J. & Kim, H. S. News Informatics: Engaging Individuals with Data-rich News Content Through Interactivity in Source, Media, and Message[C]. Proceedings of the 2022 CHI Conference on Human Factors in Computing Systems, 2022: 1-17.

Swales, J. Citation Analysis and Discourse Analysis[J]. *Applied Linguistics*, 1986 (7): 39-56.

Swales, J. *Genre Analysis: English in Academic and Research Settings* [M]. Cambridge: Cambridge University Press, 1990.

Szenes, E. *The Linguistic Construction of Business Reasoning: Towards a Language-Based Model of Decision-Making in Undergraduate Business* [D]. Sydney: The University of Sydney, 2017.

Tabary, C. Provost, A. M. & Trottier, A. Data Journalism's Actors, Practices and Skills: A Case Study from Quebec [J]. *Journalism: Theory, Practice, and Criticism*, 2016, 17(1): 66-84.

Tan, S. Modelling Engagement in a Web-based Advertising Campaign[J]. *Visual Communication*, 2009, 9(1): 91-115.

Tan, S. Facts, Opinions, and Media Spectacles: Exploring Representations of Business News on the Internet. *Discourse and Communications*, 2011(5): 169-194.

Tan, S. & Marissa, K. L. E. *Discourse, Modes, Media and Meaning in an Era of Pandemic: A Multimodal Discourse Analysis Approach* [C]. New York and London: Routledge, 2023.

Tandoc, E. C. & Oh, S. K. Small Departures, Big Continuities? Norms, Values, and Routines in the Guardian's Big Data Journalism[J]. *Journalism Studies*, 2017, 18(8): 997-1015.

Thompson, S. Frameworks and Contexts: A Genre-based Approach to Analyzing Lecture Introduction[J]. *English for Specific Purposes*, 1994,

13 (2): 171-186.

Thorsen, E., Allan, S., & Carter, C. Citizenship and Public Service: The Case of BBC News Online[C]// Tunney, S. & Monaghan, G. (eds.) *Web Journalism: A New Form of Journalism*? Sussex: Sussex Academic Press, 2010.

Tian, P. Co-articulating "Worry" in Children's Picture Books: Multi-modal Discourse Analysis on Children's Picture Books[C]// Dreyfus, S., Hood S. & Stenglin, M. K. (eds.) *Semiotic Margins: Reclaiming Meaning*. London: Continuum, 2012.

Tseng, C. Cohesion in Film and the Construction of Filmic Thematic Configuration: A Functional Perspective [D]. Bremen: University of Bremen, 2009.

Tseng, C. *Cohesion in Film: Tracking Film Elements*[M]. Basingstoke: Palgrave Macmillan, 2013.

Tseng, C. & Bateman, J. A. Multimodal Narrative Construction in Christopher Nolan's *Memonto*: A Description of Analytic Method [J]. *Visual Communication*, 2010, 11 (1): 91-119.

Tong, B. *Journalism and Communication in China and the West: A Study of History, Education and Regulation*[M]. Beijing: China Renmin University Press, and Singapore: Palgrave Macmillan, 2020.

Touriño, A. C. Nerd Journalism: How Data and Digital Technology Transformed News Graphics[D]. Barcelona: Universitat Oberta de Catalunya, 2017.

Tufte, E. R. *The Visual Display of Quantitative Information*[M]. Cheshire: Graphics Press, 1983.

Tufte, E. R. *Visual Explanations: Images and Quantities, Evidence and Narrative*[M]. Cheshire: Graphics Press, 1997.

Túñez-López, J. M., Toural-Bran, C. & Frazão-Nogueira, A. G.. From Data Journalism to Robotic Journalism: The Automation of News Processing[C]//Vazquez-Herrero J., Direito-Rebollal S., Silva-Rodriguez A. & Lopez-Gaicia X. (eds.) *Journalistic Metamorphosis: Media Transformation in the Digital Age.* Cham, Switzerland: Springer, 2020.

Twyman, M. A Schema for the Study of Graphic Language[C]. Kolers, P. A., Wrolstad, M. E. & Bouma, H. (eds.) *Processing of Visible Language*, Vol. 1. New York and London: Plenum, 1979.

Unwin, A. Good Graphics? [C] Chen, C., Härdle, W. & Unwin, A. (eds.). *Handbook of Data Visualization.* Berlin: Springer, 2008.

Unwin, A., Chen, C. & Härdle, W. K. Introduction[C]. Chen, C., Härdle, W. & Unwin, A. (eds.). *Handbook of Data Visualization.* Berlin: Springer, 2008.

Uskail, T. & Kuutti, H. Models and Streams of Data Journalism[J]. *The Journal of Media Innovations*, 2015, 2 (1): 77-88.

van Dijk, T. A. *News as Discourse*[M]. Hillsdale, N. J.: Lawrence Erlbaum Associate, 1988.

van Leeuwen, T. Conjunctive Structure in Documentary Film and Television[J]. *Continuum*, 1991, 5 (1): 76-114.

van Leeuwen, T. *Introducing Social Semiotics*[M]. London and New York: Routledge, 2005.

van Leeuwen, T. New Forms of Writing, New Visual Competencies[J]. *Visual Studies*, 2008, 23(2), 130-135.

van Leeuwen, T. *Speech, Music, Sound*[M]. London: Macmillan, 1999.

van Leeuwen, T. Towards a Semiotics of Typography[J]. *Information Design Journal+ Document Design*, 2006, 14(2): 139-155.

van Leeuwen, T. & Jewitt, C. *Handbook of Visual Analysis*[M]. London: Sage, 2001.

van Peer, W. Typographic Foregrounding[J]. *Language and Literature*,

1993, 2(1): 49-61.

Varghese, S. A. & Sunita A. Book-length Scholarly Essays as a Hybrid Genre in Science[J]. *Written Communication*, 2004, 21(2): 201-231.

Vάzquez-Herrero, J., López-García, X. & Irigaray, F. The technology-led narrative turn[C]//Vazquez-Herrero J., Direito-Rebollal S., Silva-Rodriguez A. & Lopez-Gaicia X. (eds.) *Journalistic Metamorphosis: Media Transformation in the Digital Age*. Cham, Switzerland: Springer, 2020.

Veglis, A. & Maniou, T. A. Chatbots on the Rise: A New Narrative in Journalism[J]. *Studies in Media and Communication*, 2019, 7(1): 1-6.

Velasco, S. Reclaiming the Word "Infographics," Once Again. [2018-07-12]. https://5wgraphicsblog.com/2015/02/26/reclaiming-the-word-infograph-ics-once-again/.

Ventola, E. The Dynamics of Genre[J]. *Nottingham Linguistics Circular*, 1984, 13 (Special Issue on Systemic Linguistics): 103-123.

Walker, S. Describing Graphic Language: Practicalities and Implications [J]. *Information Design Journal*, 1982, 3(2): 102-109.

Wang, H. & Wang, G. (王欢, 王国凤). Linguistic Context and the Interpretation of News: Strategies for Evaluating English Hard News Discourse (语言语境与新闻理解——英语硬新闻语篇评价策略解读)[J]. *Foreign Language Teaching and Research* (外语教学与研究), 2012, 44(5): 671-681.

Wang, X. The Impact of IoT on News Media in the Smart Age[J]. *Mobile Information Systems*, 2022. https://doi.org/10.1155/2022/2238233.

Wang, Z. (王振华). Attitudes in "Hard News"—Application of APPRAISAIL System ("硬新闻"的态度研究——"评价系统"应用研究之

二)[J]. *Foreign Language Education* (外语教学), 2004 (5): 31-36.

Weber, P. Discussions in the Comments Section: Factors Influencing Participation and Interactivity in Online Newspapers' Reader Comments [J]. *New Media & Society*, 2014, 16 (6): 941-957.

Weber, W. Exploring Narrativity in Data Visualization in Journalism[C]. Kennedy, H. & Engebretsen, M. (eds.) *Data Visualization in Society*. Amsterdam: Amsterdam University Press, 2020.

Weber, W. Interactive Information Graphics: A Framework for Classifying a Visual Genre [C]//Black A., Luna P., Lund O. & Walker S. (eds.) *Information Design: Research and Practice*. New York: Routledge, 2017.

Weber, W., Engerbresten, M. & Kennedy, H. Data Stories: Rethinking Journalistic Storytelling in the Context of Data Journalism[J]. *Studies in Communication Sciences*, 2018, 18 (1): 191-206.

Weber, W. & Rall, H. Data Visualization in Online Journalism and its Implications for the Production Process[C]. 16th International Conference on Information Visualization, 2012.

Wen, W. & Li, B. (文卫华, 李冰). (Data News Reporting in the Era of Big Data: A Case Study of Practices of *the Guardian* (大数据时代的数据新闻报道——以英国《卫报》为例)[J]. *Modern Communication* (*Journal of Communication University of China*)(现代传播(中国传媒大学学报)), 2013, 35(5): 139-142.

White, P. R. R. Death, Disruption and the Moral Order: The Narrative Impulse in Mass Media "Hard News" Reporting[C]//F. Christie and J. R. Martin (eds.) *Genres and Institutions: Social Processes in the Workplace and School*. London: Cassell, 1997.

White, P. H. The Language of News Media[D]. Sydney: The University of Sydney, 1998.

White, P. R. R. Media Objectivity and the Rhetoric of News Story Structure [C]//E. Ventola (ed.), *Discourse and Community: Doing Functional Linguistics* (Language Performance 21). Tübingen: Gunter Narr Verlag, 2000.

White, P. R. R. Subjectivity, Evaluation and Point of View in Media Discourse[C]//Coffin, C. (ed.) *Applying English Grammar: Functional and Corpus Approaches*. London: Arnold, 2004.

White, P. R. R. Evaluative Semantics and Ideological Positioning in Journalistic Discourse: A New Framework for Analysis[C]//I. Lassen, J. Strunck and T. Vestergaard (eds.) *Mediating Ideology in Text and Image: Ten Critical Studies*. Amsterdam: John Benjamins, 2006.

White, P. R. R. The Appraisal Framework and Analyses of Journalistic Discourse: Objectivity, Subjectivity and Attitudinal positioning[C]// Caldwell, D., Knox, J. & Martin J. R. (eds.) *Appliable Linguistics and Social Semiotics: Developing Theory from Practice*. London: Bloomsbury, 2022.

Wien, C. Defining Objectivity Within Journalism[J]. *Nordicom Review*, 2005, 26 (2). DOI: 10.1515/nor-2017-0255.

Wignell, P. *Making the Abstract Technical: On the Evolution of the Discourse of Social Science* [D]. Sydney: The University of Sydney, 1997.

Wu, B. (吴伯凡). *The Ecstasy of Solitariness: Social Interaction in the Digital Era* (孤独的狂欢——数字时代的交往) [M]. Beijing: China Renmin University Press (北京：中国人民大学出版社), 1998.

Wu, K. (吴坤). Data Journalism: Concepts, Theories and Dimensions (数据新闻：理论承递、概念适用与界定维度) [J]. *Journalism and Communication* (新闻与传播研究), 2017, 10: 120-126.

Xie, J. (谢金文). *A Brief History of Journalism in China and the World* (中外新闻史概要) [M]. Shanghai: Shanghai People's Publishing

House(上海：上海人民出版社)，2015.

Xing, J. (幸君珺). Towards a Genre-Based Analysis Model for Multimodal Newspaper Texts(基于语类的多模态报纸语篇分析模式)[D]. Shanghai: Fudan University (上海：复旦大学), 2012.

Xing, J. (幸君珺). A Case Study of Semantics of Participants in Data Journalistic Report America Under the Gun (语篇语义视角下数据新闻语篇参与者的语义性研究——以数据新闻 *America Under the Gun* 为例)[C]. Lai, L., Yan, M. & Wang, G. (eds.)(赖良涛、严明、王革编著). *Educational Linguistics Studies* (教育语言学研究)[M]. Shanghai: East China Normal University Press (上海：华东师范大学出版社), 2019.

Xing, J. & Zhu, Y. (幸君珺, 朱永生). A Study of Identification in News Reports from the Perspective of Discourse Semantics (语篇语义视角下新闻报道参与者的身份识别资源研究)[J]. 外语教学 (*Foreign Language Education*), 2018, 39(2): 14-18.

Yang, X. (杨学燕). A Stylistic Analysis of English Editorials (社论英语的文体研究)[J]. *Foreign Language Teaching and Research* (外语教学与研究), 2001, 33 (5): 367-373.

Yates, J., & Orlikowski, W. J. Genres of Organizational Communication: A Structurational Approach to Studying Communication and Media[J]. *Academy of Management Review*, 1992, 17: 299-326.

Young, M. L., Hermida, A. & Fulda, H. What Makes for Great Data Journalism[J]. *Journalism Practice*, 2017. DOI: 10. 1080/17512786. 2016. 1270171.

Zalizer, B. When Facts, Truth and Reality are God-terms: on Journalism's Uneasy Place in Cultural Studies[J]. *Communication and Critical/Cultural Studies*, 2004(1): 100-119.

Zappavigna, M., Dwyer, P. & Martin, J. Syndromes of Meaning: Exploring Patterned Coupling in a NSW Youth Justice Conference[C]//

Wang, Z. (ed.) *Forensic Linguistics, Vol. 8 in the Collected Works of J. R. Martin*. Shanghai: Shanghai Jiao Tong University Press, 2012/2008.

Zappavigna, M., Cleirigh, C., Dwyer, P. & Martin, J. R. The Coupling of Gesture and Phonology [C]//Bednareck, M. & Martin, J. R. (eds.) *New Discourse on Language: Functional Perspectives on Multimodality, Identity, and Affiliation*. London/ New York: Continuum, 2010. (Also collected in Wang, Z. (ed.) *Forensic Linguistics, Vol. 8 in the Collected Works of J. R. Martin*[C]. Shanghai: Shanghai Jiao Tong University Press, 2012.)

Zeng, Q., Lu, J. & Wu, X. (曾庆香, 陆佳怡, 吴晓红). Data Journalism: Concept Explication and Exploration (数据新闻: 一种社会科学研究的新闻论证)[J]. *Journalism and Communication* (新闻与传播研究), 2017, 12: 79-91.

Zhang, C. (张超). Four Dimensions of Complex Storytelling in Data Journalism (数据新闻复杂叙事的四个维度)[J]. *TV Research* (电视研究), 2018 (2): 38-40.

Zhang, D. & Wang, Z. (张德禄, 王正). A Theoretical Framework for Multimodal Interaction Analysis (多模态互动分析框架探索)[J]. *Foreign Languages in China* (中国外语), 2016, 13(2): 54-61.

Zhang, D. (张德禄). A Systemic-functional Synthetic Framework for Multimodal Discourse Analysis (系统功能理论视域下的多模态话语分析综合框架)[J]. *Modern Foreign Languages* (现代外语), 2018, 41(6): 731-743.

Zhao, X. (赵秀凤). Interactive Blending of Multimodal Irony and Conceptual Metaphor and Metonymy: Cases of Verbal-pictorial Irony (多模态反讽与概念隐/转喻的互动整合——以图文反讽为例)[J]. *Foreign Language Education* (外语教学), 2019, 40(5): 8-12.

Zhao, X. (赵秀凤). Ecological Discourse Analysis Based on Multimodal

Metaphor Scenarios: A Case of Bioenergy Political Cartoons (基于多模态隐喻场景的生态话语分析——以生物能源政治漫画为例)[J]. *Foreign Languages in China* (中国外语), 2022, 19 (6): 60-69.

Zheng, S. & Feng, J. A Step Forward: Exploring the Diffusion of Data Journalism as Journalistic Innovations in China[J]. *Journalism Studies*, (published online), 2018. DOI: 10. 1080/1461670X. 2018. 1513814.

Zhu, Y. (朱永生). Theory and Methodology of Multimodal Discourse Analysis (多模态话语分析的理论基础与研究方法)[J]. *Foreign Language Research* (外语学刊), 2007(5): 82-86.